Frommer's

W9-ANY-338

Nashville & Memphis
8th Edition

by Linda Romine

Here's what the critics say about Frommer's:

"Amazingly easy to use. Very portable, very complete."

—*Booklist*

"Detailed, accurate, and easy-to-read information for all price ranges."
—*Glamour Magazine*

"Hotel information is close to encyclopedic."

—*Des Moines Sunday Register*

"Frommer's Guides have a way of giving you a real feel for a place."
—*Knight Ridder Newspapers*

WILEY

Wiley Publishing, Inc.

About the Author

Linda Romine has been a professional writer for nearly two decades. With a background in music, she has worked on the editorial staffs of various newspapers and magazines as a reporter, music critic, travel editor, and restaurant reviewer.

Published by:

Wiley Publishing, Inc.

111 River St.
Hoboken, NJ 07030-5774

Copyright © 2008 Wiley Publishing, Inc., Hoboken, New Jersey. All rights reserved. No part of this publication may be reproduced, stored in a retrieval system or transmitted in any form or by any means, electronic, mechanical, photocopying, recording, scanning or otherwise, except as permitted under Sections 107 or 108 of the 1976 United States Copyright Act, without either the prior written permission of the Publisher, or authorization through payment of the appropriate per-copy fee to the Copyright Clearance Center, 222 Rosewood Drive, Danvers, MA 01923, 978/750-8400, fax 978/646-8600. Requests to the Publisher for permission should be addressed to the Legal Department, Wiley Publishing, Inc., 10475 Crosspoint Blvd., Indianapolis, IN 46256, 317/572-3447, fax 317/572-4355, or online at http://www.wiley.com/go/permissions.

Wiley and the Wiley Publishing logo are trademarks or registered trademarks of John Wiley & Sons, Inc. and/or its affiliates. Frommer's is a trademark or registered trademark of Arthur Frommer. Used under license. All other trademarks are the property of their respective owners. Wiley Publishing, Inc. is not associated with any product or vendor mentioned in this book.

ISBN: 978-0-470-18197-3
Editor: Elizabeth Fellows Heath
Production Editor: Lindsay Conner
Cartographer: Tim Lohnes
Photo Editor: Richard Fox
Production by Wiley Indianapolis Composition Services

Front cover photo: Nashville: Lower Broadway area, neon sign for Jack's Bar-B-Que
Back cover photo: Memphis, Graceland: Elvis Presley's Las Vegas costumes and gold records on display

For information on our other products and services or to obtain technical support, please contact our Customer Care Department within the U.S. at 800/762-2974, outside the U.S. at 317/572-3993 or fax 317/572-4002.

Wiley also publishes its books in a variety of electronic formats. Some content that appears in print may not be available in electronic formats.

Manufactured in the United States of America

5   4   3   2   1

Contents

List of Maps

An Invitation to the Reader

In researching this book, we discovered many wonderful places—hotels, restaurants, shops, and more. We're sure you'll find others. Please tell us about them, so we can share the information with your fellow travelers in upcoming editions. If you were disappointed with a recommendation, we'd love to know that, too. Please write to:

Frommer's Nashville & Memphis, 8th Edition
Wiley Publishing, Inc. • 111 River St. • Hoboken, NJ 07030-5774

An Additional Note

Please be advised that travel information is subject to change at any time—and this is especially true of prices. We therefore suggest that you write or call ahead for confirmation when making your travel plans. The authors, editors, and publisher cannot be held responsible for the experiences of readers while traveling. Your safety is important to us, however, so we encourage you to stay alert and be aware of your surroundings. Keep a close eye on cameras, purses, and wallets, all favorite targets of thieves and pickpockets.

Other Great Guides for Your Trip:

Frommer's Atlanta

Frommer's The Carolinas & Georgia

Frommer's National Parks with Kids

Frommer's Portable Savannah

Frommer's USA

Frommer's Virginia

Frommer's Star Ratings, Icons & Abbreviations

Every hotel, restaurant, and attraction listing in this guide has been ranked for quality, value, service, amenities, and special features using a **star-rating system.** In country, state, and regional guides, we also rate towns and regions to help you narrow down your choices and budget your time accordingly. Hotels and restaurants are rated on a scale of zero (recommended) to three stars (exceptional). Attractions, shopping, nightlife, towns, and regions are rated according to the following scale: zero stars (recommended), one star (highly recommended), two stars (very highly recommended), and three stars (must-see).

In addition to the star-rating system, we also use **seven feature icons** that point you to the great deals, in-the-know advice, and unique experiences that separate travelers from tourists. Throughout the book, look for:

Finds	Special finds—those places only insiders know about
Fun Fact	Fun facts—details that make travelers more informed and their trips more fun
Kids	Best bets for kids and advice for the whole family
Moments	Special moments—those experiences that memories are made of
Overrated	Places or experiences not worth your time or money
Tips	Insider tips—great ways to save time and money
Value	Great values—where to get the best deals

The following **abbreviations** are used for credit cards:

AE	American Express	DISC	Discover	V	Visa
DC	Diners Club	MC	MasterCard		

Frommers.com

Now that you have the guidebook to a great trip, visit our website at **www.frommers.com** for travel information on more than 3,600 destinations. With features updated regularly, we give you instant access to the most current trip-planning information available. At Frommers.com, you'll also find the best prices on airfares, accommodations, and car rentals—and you can even book travel online through our travel booking partners. At Frommers.com, you'll also find the following:

- Online updates to our most popular guidebooks
- Vacation sweepstakes and contest giveaways
- Newsletter highlighting the hottest travel trends
- Online travel message boards with featured travel discussions

What's New in Nashville & Memphis

If you haven't been to Nashville or Memphis in a few years, you're in for a pleasant surprise. Tennessee's two largest cities continue to evolve into reenergized metropolitan communities that manage to pay loving homage to their storied musical pasts while offering an increasing array of new cultural attractions, professional sports, and dining and lodging options to please travelers with varied tastes and interests.

NASHVILLE

Nashville is basking in a resurgence of popularity unmatched since the mid-1940s, when singer/songwriters such as Hank Williams first came to town and helped launch American country music. But Nashville is so much more than this. First-class cultural institutions, a thriving restaurant and club scene, and a vibrant and diverse community centered around the city's outstanding universities all contribute to Nashville's attractive quality of life and appeal to tourists.

WHERE TO STAY The number of new hotels is growing exponentially in Nashville, as the city experiences a development boom downtown, especially in the emerging Gulch district. Among the newest properties are the 154-room **Hampton Inn and Suites,** 310 Fourth Ave. S. ((C) 615/277-5000). Opened in summer 2007, it lies just a stone's throw from the Country Music Hall of Fame and Museum. Rooms average $189 to $359 per night.

WHERE TO DINE If you like to try out new restaurants while you travel, come to Nashville hungry. Excellent eateries, nightclubs, and coffee shops are popping up across the city.

In the trendy Gulch area, **Watermark,** 507 12th Ave. S. ((C) 615/254-2000), has been tantalizing tastebuds since its late 2005 launch. An upscale fine-dining restaurant with modern decor and polished service, it offers stunning views of the Nashville skyline.

Jason Brumm, chef-owner of **Radius 10,** an upscale restaurant in The Gulch, is branching out. While maintaining Radius 10, he plans to open **Dos Locos,** a casual Mexican eatery at 2015 Belmont Blvd. He promises a fun, margarita-fueled atmosphere and inexpensive menu, with all items costing $10 or less. Dos Locos will be open for lunch and dinner daily, with brunch offerings on Sundays.

A few blocks west of downtown, **Chappy's on Church,** 1721 Church St. ((C) 615/322-9932) has found a following. Long-time chef/restaurateur John Chapman fled to Nashville when his Gulf Coast eatery, Chappy's, was wiped out in Hurricane Katrina. He relocated here permanently, and has garnered acclaim for his traditional New Orleans and Creole cooking.

In the West End, **Cabana,** 1910 Belcourt Ave. ((C) 615/577-2262), has emerged as an energetic nightspot, where beautiful young people gather to party in a tree-rimmed patio. Fun, affordably

From Elvis Sights to Goo Goo Clusters: How Do Memphis & Nashville Compare?

Tennessee's two largest cities have much in common, but that doesn't necessarily mean they're the same. Here's an off-the-cuff primer on what's what:

• **Barbecue:** The cities tie in this category. The slow-cooked, pulled-pork sandwiches served up at Memphis-based barbecue landmark **Corky's Bar-B-Q**, 5259 Poplar Ave. (✆ **901/685-9744**), are just as good at the newer location in Nashville (100 Franklin Rd., Brentwood; ✆ **615/373-1020**). If you have an aversion to coleslaw sharing bun space with the pig meat, remember to order yours without the customary cabbage topping.

• **Brew Pubs:** The oven-roasted gourmet pizzas and specialty-brewed beers of **Boscos**, a Tennessee-based chain that originated in suburban Germantown (outside Memphis), are also great in either city. Both boast prime locations: In Memphis, there's a Boscos in Midtown's Overton Square, 2120 Madison Ave. (✆ **901/432-2222**); while Nashville's is not far from Vanderbilt University in the West End, 1805 21st Ave. S. (✆ **615/385-0050**).

• **Elvis:** If a home is a man's castle, **Graceland**, 3734 Elvis Presley Blvd. (✆ **800/238-2000**), was The King's. Memphis may have the best Elvis Presley sights, from the infamous Jungle Room at Graceland to the slick souvenir shops that enshrine the late entertainer. Nashville, however, offers a lesser-known and less-exploited facet of Elvis's career in the **RCA Studio B**, 30 Music Square W., a small, nondescript studio on Music Row where he recorded albums.

• **Football:** Yes, the **Tennessee Titans** (✆ **615/565-4200**; www.titansonline.com), the pride of Nashville and the city's first NFL team, have an embarrassing past. When the former Houston Oilers moved to Tennessee and awaited Nashville to build a new stadium, the future Superbowl competitors played their first season in Memphis. Snubbed at not landing the team, Memphians stayed away from the games in droves.

priced bar foods include chicken-wing lollipops, deep-fried fruit pies and root beer floats with oven-warm cookies.

In East Nashville, **Marche Artisan Foods**, 1000 Main St. (✆ 615/262-1111), is a humble slice of Parisian splendor right here in Music City. Chef-owner Margot McCormack (also of **Margot Café and Bar,** just around the corner), has created an inviting spot for brunch and dinner, with old wooden farm tables, fresh flowers, and sumptuous bistro fare, coffee, and pastries. The market also sells cheeses, breads, and imported olive oils and pastas.

Bethel Ethiopian Cuisine (1909 Division St.; ✆ 615/275-8217; www.bethelrestaurant.com) opened in late 2007, in the space formerly occupied by **Ken's Hibachi Grill.** That's good news for fans of Ethiopian-born owner Seble Sebsebie's exotic cuisine. She also operates Horn of Africa on Murfreesboro Pike. The new restaurant is open daily, offering a $7 lunch buffet during weekdays.

Whole Foods, which opened in the Green Hills area in November 2007, has launched a cooking school called **Salud.** Located on a second floor above the store, Salud offers cooking lessons, chef

- **Goo Goo Clusters:** You can buy Goo Goo Clusters in both cities, but they might taste gooier in Nashville, where the nutty, chocolate-covered marshmallow-crème candies rose to fame as a one-time sponsor of the *Grand Ole Opry.*
- **Music:** Sometimes stereotypes are true. While both cities offer more than one musical genre, when boiled down to basics, their musical personalities stack up like this: Memphis is lowdown, greasy **blues** played in smoky juke joints or along neon-studded Beale Street. Nashville is plaintive **bluegrass** performed in concert halls or rowdy, boot-scootin' **country** blaring away in barn-sized clubs.
- **Parks: Overton Park** in Memphis is a lush oasis in an urban setting. Ditto for **Centennial Park** in Nashville; however, Music City's green space is also home to an impressive replica of Greece's Parthenon.
- **Rivers:** Nashville has the **Cumberland,** a bucolic tributary that wends through one edge of town, while Memphis has become synonymous with **Old Man River,** the broad and muddy Mississippi River that slices between Tennessee and Arkansas.
- **Statues of Famous Sons:** Guitar slung over one shoulder, the bronze **Elvis** statue on Memphis's Beale Street is a favorite place for a photo op, as are the larger-than-life likenesses of the two kings—**Elvis and B.B. King**—at that city's Tennessee State Welcome Center. But Nashville, with all its august state capital buildings, has **Sergeant Alvin York,** a beloved Tennessee war hero and Quaker (immortalized in the movies by Gary Cooper). Trivia-loving shutterbugs take note that this stately statue bears a flaw: The rifle the World War I soldier is holding is from World War II.

demonstrations, and wine tastings. It's being run by Merijoy Rucker, formerly of Viking Culinary Center in Franklin. For more information, call © **615/ 440-5117;** www.wholefoodsmarket.com/ stores/nashville.

EXPLORING NASHVILLE A worthy cultural exhibition to look for when trip-planning is *Family Tradition: The Hank Williams Legacy.* Set to open in March 2008 at the **Country Music Hall of Fame and Museum,** the show will be on view through December 2009. The museum is located at 225 Fifth Ave. S. (© **800/852-6437** or 615/416-2001).

MEMPHIS

Downtown Memphis continues its revitalization, following a decade of solid growth and steady development. Although some might see the empty storefronts along some parts of Main Street as indications that progress has been slow here, those of us who have seen the neglect and blight that once plagued the area can appreciate the transformation that has occurred.

WHERE TO STAY Following the 2004 opening of the new **FedEx Forum** arena, home of the NBA's Memphis Grizzlies, the area around Beale Street has flourished with new commercial developments.

A prime example is Tennessee's first Westin Hotel property, the 203-room luxury **Westin-Memphis Beale Street,** 170 Lt. George W. Lee Ave. (© **901/ 334-5900**). Located at the front doorstep of the FedEx Forum and the foot of Beale Street, the swank hotel is reasonably priced at rates averaging about $199 per night for doubles.

WHERE TO DINE Like Nashville, Memphis has a slew of new restaurants and clubs that have opened within the past two years. The cream of the crop include chef-owner John Bragg's **Circa,** 119 S. Main St. (© **901/522-1488**), which offers a sophisticated dining experience and a mind-boggling wine list. Nearby, after two decades piloting the stoves at The Peabody's elegant **Chez Philippe,** chef de cuisine Jose Gutierrez set out on his own to open **Encore,** 150 Peabody Place (© **901/528-1415**). The minimalist decor and satisfying bistro fare have been very successful.

Finally, in downtown's historic South Main Street area, another well-known chef/restaurateur, Judd Grisanti, is drawing raves for **Spindini,** 383 S. Main St. (© **901/578-2767**). The signature wood-fired pizzas, as well as meats, fish, and poultry entrees, are served in plentiful portions and still sizzling from the ovens.

AFTER DARK Here again, the big news revolves around the Beale Street area downtown, as groundbreaking began in 2007 for the opening of a new nightspot. **Ground Zero Blues Club** will be the first outpost of the famed, Clarksdale, MS-based juke joint, which is known as much for its gritty atmosphere and live blues music as it is for one of its co-owners, Oscar-winning actor Morgan Freeman (who hails from this part of the country). The 5,800-square-foot club, next door to the Westin hotel and a stone's throw from the FedEx Forum, is expected to be open by May 1, 2008—just in time for the massive Beale Street Music Festival that kicks off the month-long Memphis in May International Festival.

Ground Zero is also expecting company in the neighborhood, along Lt. George W. Lee Avenue, just off of Beale Street. At press time, **Red Rooster Bar and Music Hall** announced plans to open a rock-and-blues bar and restaurant, just a few doors down from Ground Zero.

In addition, negotiations to open a jazz club in between the two blues bars were also in the works at the time of this book's deadline. Tentative opening date for the as-yet unnamed jazz venue is also late April or early May. If it flies, this would be a boon to local, long-suffering jazz fans, who have lacked a premier venue for this American musical art form.

Meanwhile, the **Gibson Lounge,** a performance venue next to the downtown guitar factory, has closed temporarily, but is still open for special events. The two Gibson music venues, in both Nashville and Memphis, have had sporadic on-again/off-again operating hours, so be sure to call in advance if you plan to head out to either club.

The Best of Nashville

Nashville may be the capital of Tennessee, but it's better known as Music City, the country music mecca. Yet it is so much more. Combining small-town warmth with an unexpected urban sophistication, Nashville is an increasingly popular tourist destination that boasts world-class museums and major-league sports teams; an eclectic dining and after-hours scene; and an eye-catching skyline ringed by a beautiful countryside of rolling hills, rivers and lakes, and wide-open green spaces.

Ultimately, though, Nashville is the heart and soul of country music, that uniquely American blend of humble gospel, blues, and mountain music that has evolved into a $2-billion-a-year industry. At its epicenter, Nashville is still the city where unknown musicians can become overnight sensations, where the major record deals are cut and music-publishing fortunes are made, and where the *Grand Ole Opry* still takes center stage.

Symbolic of Nashville's vitality is downtown, an exciting place that is finally breathing new life. Once-tired and abandoned warehouses now bustle in the entertainment area known as The District. This historic neighborhood teems with tourist-oriented nightclubs and restaurants, including B.B. King Blues Club & Grill, the ubiquitous Hard Rock Cafe that's become a staple of most large cities, and the one-and-only Wildhorse Saloon (the most famous boot-scootin' dance hall in the land). Luckily, The District isn't yet all glitz and tour-bus nightclubs. Along lower Broadway, there are still half a dozen or more dive bars where the air reeks of stale beer and cigarettes and live music plays day and night. In these bars, aspiring country bands lay down their riffs and sing their hearts out in hopes of becoming tomorrow's superstars. With so many clubs, restaurants, shops, and historic landmarks, The District is one of the South's most vibrant nightlife areas.

Folks looking for tamer entertainment head out to the Music Valley area, home to the *Grand Ole Opry*, the radio show that started the whole country music ball rolling back in 1925. Clustered in this land the locals sometimes refer to as "Nashvegas" are other music-related attractions, including the epic Opryland Hotel; the nostalgic *General Jackson* showboat; several modest souvenir shops posing as museums; and theaters featuring family entertainment, with the majority showcasing performers from the *Grand Ole Opry*. Dozens of other clubs and theaters around the city also feature live music of various genres.

Country isn't the only music you'll hear in this city. Mainstream rock stars are also being lured by the city's intangible vibe. (Kid Rock is one of the high-profile stars to have moved here recently.) They come here for inspiration, to record new material, or for crossover collaborations with local music pros. No matter the genre, the city seems to attract more musicians each year, which means there's enough live music here in Nashville to keep your toes tappin' even long after you hit the highway home.

1 Frommer's Most Unforgettable Travel Experiences

- **Catching a Show at the Ryman Auditorium:** Known as the "Mother Church of Country Music," the Ryman Auditorium, 116 Fifth Ave. N. (© 615/254-1445), was the home of the *Grand Ole Opry* for more than 30 years. Now restored, it once again has country music coming from its historic stage. And, yes, the old church pews are still there and just as uncomfortable as they always were. See p. 99.

- **Attending the *Grand Ole Opry:*** This live radio broadcast is an American institution and is as entertaining today as it was when it went on the air nearly 80 years ago. Luckily, the current Grand Ole Opry House, 2804 Opryland Dr. (© 800/SEE-OPRY), is quite a bit more comfortable than the old Ryman Auditorium

  where the *Opry* used to be held. See p. 126.

- **Checking Out Up-and-Comers at the Bluebird Cafe:** With its excellent acoustics and two shows a night, the Bluebird Cafe, 4104 Hillsboro Rd. (© 615/383-1461), is Nashville's most famous venue for country songwriters. Only the best make it here, and many of the people who play the Bluebird wind up getting "discovered." See p. 130.

- **Line Dancing at the Wildhorse Saloon:** What Gilley's once did for country music, the Wildhorse Saloon, 120 Second Ave. N. (© 615/251-1000), has done again. The country line dancing craze that swept the nation a few years ago reached its zenith in this massive saloon. The fun continues today. See p. 130.

2 The Best Splurge Hotels

- **The Hermitage,** 231 Sixth Ave. N. (© 888/888-9414 or 615/244-3121): Built in 1910 in the Beaux Arts style, the Hermitage boasts the most elegant lobby in the city. The marble columns, gilded plasterwork, and stained-glass ceiling recapture the luxuries of a bygone era. This is a classic grand hotel, conveniently located in the heart of downtown Nashville. See p. 56.

- **Loews Vanderbilt Plaza Hotel,** 2100 West End Ave. (© 800/23-LOEWS or 615/320-1700): If you want to be near the trendy West End area of town, treat yourself to a stay at this sophisticated luxury hotel. European tapestries and original works of art adorn the travertine-floored lobby. Service is gracious and attentive. See p. 61.

3 The Best Moderately Priced Hotel

- **Hampton Inn Vanderbilt,** 1919 West End Ave. (© 800/HAMPTON or 615/329-1144): This immaculate, efficiently run property is a good bet if you're traveling here on business.

  Scads of great restaurants surround the busy hotel, which is convenient to Vanderbilt University and just a few blocks from Music Row. See p. 63.

4 The Most Unforgettable Dining Experiences

- **Slurping a Chocolate Shake at the Elliston Place Soda Shop:** Sure, every city has its retro diner these days, but the Elliston Place Soda Shop, 2111 Elliston Place (© 615/327-1090), is the real thing. It's been in business since 1939 and makes the best chocolate shakes in Nashville. See p. 83.

- **Sopping up Red-Eye Gravy with Homemade Biscuits at the Loveless Cafe,** 8400 Tenn. 100 (© 615/646-9700): This perennially popular country cookin' outpost serves the best traditional Southern breakfasts in the entire area. But be prepared to wait for a table. See p. 86.

- **Sipping Wine while Perusing the Extensive Menu at Sunset Grill,** 2001 Belcourt Ave. (© 615/386-FOOD): The Sunset Grill abounds with fresh, flavorful fare such as salads with field greens, apples, blue cheese, and almonds, and interesting fusions of tastes and styles. For years now, this has been one of the trendiest restaurants in town—and consistently one of the best. See p. 82.

5 The Best Things to Do for Free (Or Almost)

- **Pretending You're a Star Shopping for New Clothes at Manuel's,** 1922 Broadway (© 615/321-5444): Manuel Exclusive Clothier sells work clothes—work clothes for country music stars, that is. You know, the rhinestone-cowboy sort of ensembles that look great under stage lights. Maybe these aren't the kind of duds your boss would approve of, but, hey, maybe one day you'll be able to quit your day job. See p. 124.

- **Getting That Old-Time Religion at Cowboy Church,** Texas Troubadour Theatre, 2416 Music Valley Dr. (© 615/859-1001): If you're looking for a down-home dose of gospel music ministry, make it to the Cowboy Church on time: The old-timey, nondenominational services kick off Sundays at 10am sharp. Come as you are or don your best Stetson and bolo tie. Either way, you'll fit right in with the eclectic, all-ages congregation of locals and tourists alike that packs the pews every week for a patriotic praise-and-worship service. See p. 126.

Planning Your Trip to Nashville & Memphis

1 Visitor Information & Maps

For information on the state of Tennessee, contact the **Tennessee Department of Tourism Development,** P.O. Box 23170, Nashville, TN 37202 (© **800/836-6200** or 615/741-2158). Before heading to Music City, you can get more information on the city by contacting the **Nashville Convention & Visitors Bureau,** 150 Fourth Ave. N. (© **800/657-6910** or 615/259-4700). You can also find information about Nashville at the following websites:

- Nashville Convention & Visitors Bureau: **www.visitmusiccity.com**
- The *Nashville Scene,* Nashville's main arts and entertainment weekly: **www.nashvillescene.com**

- The *Tennessean,* Nashville's morning daily newspaper: **www.tennessean. com**

For information on Memphis, contact the Memphis Convention & Visitors Bureau, 47 Union Ave., Memphis, TN 38103 (© **800/8-MEMPHIS** or 901/ 543-5300). You can also get information online at **www.memphistravel.com**.

- The *Memphis Flyer* is Memphis' main arts and entertainment weekly: **www.memphisflyer.com**.
- The *Commercial Appeal* is Memphis's morning daily newspaper: **www. commercialappeal.com**.

2 Entry Requirements

PASSPORTS

For an up-to-date, country-by-country listing of passport requirements around the world, go to the "Foreign Entry Requirement" Web page of the U.S. State Department at **http://travel.state.gov**. International visitors can obtain a visa application at the same website. *Note:* Children are required to present a passport when entering the United States at airports. More information on obtaining a passport for a minor can be found at http://travel.state.gov.

VISAS

For specifics on how to get a visa, go to http://travel.state.gov/visa.

The U.S. State Department has a **Visa Waiver Program (VWP)** allowing citizens of the following countries (at press time) to enter the United States without a visa for stays of up to 90 days: Andorra, Australia, Austria, Belgium, Brunei, Denmark, Finland, France, Germany, Iceland, Ireland, Italy, Japan, Liechtenstein, Luxembourg, Monaco, the Netherlands, New Zealand, Norway, Portugal, San Marino,

Nashville & Memphis

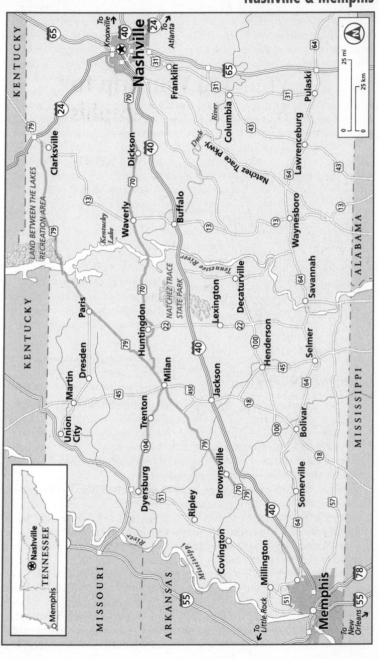

Singapore, Slovenia, Spain, Sweden, Switzerland, and the United Kingdom. Canadian citizens may enter the United States without visas; they will need to show passports and proof of residence, however. *Note:* Any passport issued on or after October 26, 2006, by a VWP country must be an **e-Passport** for VWP travelers to be eligible to enter the U.S. without a visa. Citizens of these nations also need to present a round-trip air or cruise ticket upon arrival. E-Passports contain computer chips capable of storing biometric information, such as the required digital photograph of the holder. (You can identify an e-Passport by the symbol on the bottom center cover of your passport.) If your passport doesn't have this feature, you can still travel without a visa if it is a valid passport issued before October 26, 2005, and includes a machine-readable zone, or between October 26, 2005, and October 25, 2006, and includes a digital photograph. For more information, go to **www.travel.state.gov/visa**.

Citizens of all other countries must have (1) a valid passport that expires at least 6 months later than the scheduled end of their visit to the United States, and (2) a tourist visa, which may be obtained without charge from any U.S. consulate.

As of 2004, many international visitors traveling on visas to the United States will be photographed and fingerprinted on arrival at Customs in airports and on cruise ships in a program created by the Department of Homeland Security called **US-VISIT.** Exempt from the extra scrutiny are visitors entering by land or those (mostly in Europe) that don't require a visa for short-term visits. For more information, go to the Homeland Security website at **www.dhs.gov/dhspublic**.

MEDICAL REQUIREMENTS

Unless you're arriving from an area known to be suffering from an epidemic (particularly cholera or yellow fever), inoculations or vaccinations are not

---

Pre-Departure Checklist

- Are there any **special requirements** for your destination? Vaccinations? Special visas, passports, or IDs? Detailed road maps? Bug repellents? Appropriate attire? If you're flying, are you carrying a current, government-issued ID, such as a driver's license or passport?
- Did you find out your daily ATM withdrawal limit?
- Do you have your credit card PIN numbers?
- To check in at a kiosk with an e-ticket, do you have the credit card you bought your ticket with or a frequent-flier card?
- If you purchased traveler's checks, have you recorded the check numbers, and stored the documentation separately from the checks?
- Did you bring ID cards that could entitle you to discounts, such as AAA and AARP cards, and student IDs?
- Did you leave a copy of your itinerary with someone at home?
- Do you need to book any theater, restaurant, or travel reservations in advance?
- Did you make sure your favorite attraction is open? Many mom-and-pop restaurants and lesser-known attractions in Tennessee have irregular hours, so always call ahead to make sure the place you plan to visit will be open.

U.S. Entry: Passport Required

New regulations issued by the Homeland Security Department now require virtually every air traveler entering the U.S. to show a passport—and future regulations will cover land and sea entry as well. As of January 23, 2007, all persons, including U.S. citizens, traveling by air between the United States and Canada, Mexico, Central and South America, the Caribbean, and Bermuda are required to present a valid passport. Similar regulations for those traveling by land or sea (including ferries) are expected as early as January 1, 2008.

required for entry into the United States. If you have a medical condition that requires **syringe-administered medications,** carry a valid signed prescription from your physician; syringes in carry-on baggage will be inspected. Insulin in any form should have the proper pharmaceutical documentation. If you have a disease that requires treatment with **narcotics,** you should also carry documented proof with you—smuggling narcotics aboard a plane carries severe penalties in the U.S.

For **HIV-positive visitors,** requirements for entering the United States are somewhat vague and change frequently. For up-to-the-minute information, contact **AIDSinfo** (© **800/448-0440** or 301/519-6616 outside the U.S.; www.aidsinfo.nih.gov) or the **Gay Men's Health Crisis** (© **212/367-1000;** www.gmhc.org).

CUSTOMS

For information on what you can bring into and take out of the United States, visit the U.S. Customs and Border Protection website at www.cbp.gov.

3 When to Go

CLIMATE

Summer is the peak tourist season in Nashville and Memphis. Unless you're specifically visiting Nashville for the Country Music Fan Fair in June, or going to Graceland for Elvis Week in August, you might want to avoid traveling during these times when hotels sell out and prices go through the roof.

Summer is also when both cities experience their worst weather. During July and August, and often in September, temperatures can hover around 100°F,

with humidity at close to 100%. (Can you say "muggy"?) Spring and fall, however, last for several months and are both quite pleasant. Days are often warm and nights cool, though during these two seasons the weather changes, so bring a variety of clothes. Heavy rains can hit any time of year, and if you spend more than 3 or 4 days in town, you can almost bet on seeing some rain. Winters can be cold, with daytime temperatures staying below freezing, and snow is not unknown.

Nashville's Average Monthly Temperatures & Rainfall

	Jan	Feb	Mar	Apr	May	June	July	Aug	Sept	Oct	Nov	Dec
Temp (°F)	37	41	49	59	68	76	80	79	72	60	48	40
Temp (°C)	3	5	9	15	20	25	27	26	22	15	9	4
Days of rain	11	11	12	11	11	9	10	9	8	7	10	11

Memphis's Average Monthly Temperatures & Rainfall

	Jan	Feb	Mar	Apr	May	June	July	Aug	Sept	Oct	Nov	Dec
Temp (°F)	40	44	52	63	71	79	82	81	74	63	51	43
Temp (°C)	4	7	11	17	22	26	28	27	23	17	11	6
Days of rain	10	11	10	9	9	9	8	7	6	9	10	10

CALENDAR OF EVENTS

For an exhaustive list of events beyond those listed here, check http://events.frommers.com, where you'll find a searchable, up-to-the-minute roster of what's happening in cities all over the world.

NASHVILLE CALENDAR OF EVENTS

April

Gospel Music Awards, downtown. Also known as the Dove Awards, this ceremony honors the best in gospel, praise and worship, and contemporary Christian music. Tickets are available to the public (© 615/242-0303). Early April.

Tin Pan South, various venues, sometimes including the Ryman Auditorium. Sponsored by the 4,000-member Nashville Songwriters Association, this five-day festival showcases some of the best new and established songwriters in the country (© 615/256-3354). Early to mid-April.

May

Tennessee Renaissance Festival, in Triune (20 miles south of downtown Nashville). Maidens, knights, gypsies, jugglers, jousters, games, and food—think whole turkey legs that you can eat like a barbarian—are some of the diversions you'll find at this medieval fair held on the grounds of the **Castle Gwynn** (© 615/395-9950). Weekends in May, including Memorial Day.

Tennessee Crafts Fair, Centennial Park. With the largest display of Tennessee crafts, this fair opens the summer season. Food, demonstrations, and children's craft activities (© 615/385-1904). Early May.

Running of the Iroquois Steeplechase, Percy Warner Park. This horse race has been a Nashville ritual for more than 50 years. A benefit for Vanderbilt Children's Hospital, the event is accompanied by tailgate picnics (© 615/322-7284 or 615/343-4231). Second Saturday in May.

Tennessee Jazz & Blues Society's Jazz on the Lawn, various locations. Every Sunday evening May through October, the society performs on lawns of historic homes such as Cheekwood Botanical Garden, the Hermitage, and Belle Meade Plantation (© 615/301-5121). Sundays May through October.

June

Bluegrass Nights at the Ryman, Ryman Auditorium. Thursday nights at the historic Ryman Auditorium play host to top-name bluegrass acts such as Alison Krauss and Ricky Skaggs (© 615/889-3060). Thursdays June through July.

Country Music Association (CMA) Music Festival (formerly Fan Fair), Coliseum. This is a chance for country artists and their fans to meet and greet each other in a weeklong music celebration. Glitzy stage shows and picture/autograph sessions with country music stars are all part of the action. A Texas barbecue and tickets for sightseeing are included in the price of a ticket, along with a bluegrass concert and the Grand Masters Fiddling Championship. This is the biggest country music event of the year in Nashville, so book your tickets far in advance. Contact the CMA Office (℃ **615/ 244-2840**) for ticket information. Mid-June.

American Artisan Festival, Centennial Park. Artisans from 35 states present a wide range of crafts from blown glass to leather and quilts. Children's art booth and music, too (℃ **615/298- 4691**). Mid-June.

July

Independence Day Celebration, Riverfront Park. This family-oriented, alcohol-free event attracts 100,000 people for entertainment, food, and fireworks (℃ **615/862-8400**). July 4.

August

Annual Tennessee Walking-Horse National Celebration, Celebration Grounds, Shelbyville (40 miles southeast of downtown Nashville). The World Grand Championship of the much-loved Tennessee walking horse, plus trade fairs and dog shows (℃ **931/ 684-5915**). Late August.

September

Music City J.A.M. (Jazz and More) Festival, Riverfront Park. The festival coincides with the John Merritt Classic football game (and battle of the marching bands) at Tennessee State University (℃ **800/791-8368** or 615/506-5114). Labor Day weekend.

Tennessee State Fair, Tennessee State Fairgrounds. Sprawling livestock and agriculture fair, with 4-H Club members and Future Farmers well represented—and a midway, of course (℃ **615/862-8980**). Early to mid-September.

Belle Meade Plantation Fall Fest, Belle Meade Plantation. Antiques, crafts, children's festival, garage treasures sale, and food from local restaurants (℃ **800/270-3991** or 615/356-0501). Mid-September.

African Street Festival, Tennessee State University, main campus. Featured entertainment includes gospel, R&B, jazz, reggae music, and children's storytelling (℃ **615/251-0007**). Mid-September.

TACA Fall Crafts Fair, Centennial Park. This upscale fine-crafts market features artisans from throughout Tennessee (℃ **615/385-1904**). Late September.

October

Oktoberfest, Historic Germantown, at the corner of Eighth Avenue North and Monroe Street. Tours of Germantown, polka dancing, accordion players, and lots of authentic German food (℃ **615/256-2729**). Early to mid-October.

Annual NAIA Pow Wow, place to be determined. Native Americans from the United States and Canada gather for this powwow sponsored by the Native American Indian Association (℃ **615/232-9179**). Mid-October.

Birthday of the *Grand Ole Opry,* Grand Ole Opry House. Three-day party with performances, autographs, and picture sessions with *Opry* stars. In recent years, the all-star lineup has run the gamut from Ralph Stanley to Alan Jackson (℃ **615/889-3060;** www.gaylordopryland.com). Mid-October.

November

Longhorn World Championship Rodeo, Tennessee Miller Coliseum, outside of Murfreesboro. Professional cowboys and cowgirls participate in this rodeo to win championship points (℃ **800/357-6336** or 615/ 876-1016; www.longhornrodeo.com). Third weekend in November.

Christmas at Belmont, Belmont Mansion, Belmont University Campus. The opulent antebellum mansion is decked out in Victorian Christmas finery, and the gift shop is a great place to shop for Christmassy Victorian reproductions (© **615/460-5459**). Late November to late December.

A Country Christmas, Opryland Hotel. More than two million Christmas lights are used to decorate the grounds of the hotel. A musical revue featuring the "Dancing Waters" fountain show, holiday dinner, and crafts fair round out the holiday activities here (© **877/456-OPRY**). November 1 to December 25.

MEMPHIS CALENDAR OF EVENTS

January

Elvis Presley's Birthday Tribute, Graceland. International gathering of Presley fans to celebrate the birthday of "The King" (© **800/238-2000**). Around January 8.

Martin Luther King, Jr.'s Birthday, citywide. Events to memorialize Dr. King take place on the nationally observed holiday (© **901/521-9699**). Mid-January.

February

Beale Street Zydeco Music Festival, along Beale Street. More than 20 acts perform during this two-day event (© **901/529-0999**). Mid-February.

Regions Morgan Keegan Tennis Championship, Racquet Club of Memphis. World-class players compete in this famous tour event (© **901/ 765-4400**). Mid- to late February.

April

Dr. Martin Luther King, Jr. Memorial March, downtown. This somber event remembers the assassination of the civil rights leader (© **901/525-2458**). April 4.

Memphis International Film Festival, midtown. Filmmakers and cinema lovers converge in Memphis (© **901/ 273-0014**). Second week in April.

Africa in April Cultural Awareness Festival, downtown. A several-day festival centering around African music, dance, theater, exhibits, arts, and crafts (© **901/947-2133**). Third week in April.

May

Memphis in May International Festival, citywide. A month-long celebration of a different country each year with musical, cultural, and artistic festivities; business, sports, and educational programs; and food unique to the country. More than a million people come to nearly 100 sanctioned events scheduled throughout the city. The most important happenings are the Memphis in May Beale Street Music Festival (first weekend in May), the World Championship Barbecue Cooking Contest (mid-May), and the Sunset Symphony (last weekend of May). Call Memphis in May (© **901/ 525-4611; www.memphisinmay.org**). Entire month of May.

Federal Express St. Jude Golf Classic, Tournament Players Club at Southwind. A benefit for St. Jude Children's Research Hospital, this is a PGA event (© **901/748-0534**). Late May to early June.

June

Carnival Memphis, citywide. Almost half a million people join in the exclusive activities of exhibits, music, crafts, and events (© **901/278-0243**). Early June.

Germantown Charity Horse Show, Germantown Horse Show Arena. Four-day competition for prizes (© **901/ 754-0009**). Second week in June.

July

Star-Spangled Celebration, Shelby Farms. Fourth of July entertainment and fireworks (℃ **901/726-0469**). July 4.

Blues on the Bluff, downtown. Listener-supported radio station WEVL-FM presents two concerts on the grounds of the National Ornamental Metal Museum, overlooking the Mississippi River (℃ **901/528-0560**). Late July and early August.

August

Elvis Tribute Week, Graceland and citywide. Festival commemorating the influences of Elvis (℃ **800/238-2000**). Second week in August.

September

Beale Street Labor Day Music Festival, Beale Street. Memphis musicians are featured Labor Day and night in restaurants and clubs throughout the Beale Street district (℃ **901/526-0110**). Labor Day weekend.

Memphis Music and Heritage Festival, Center for Southern Folklore. A celebration of the diversity of the South (℃ **901/525-3655**). Early September.

Cooper Young Festival, midtown. Neighborhood festival featuring food, arts, crafts, and family activities (℃ **901/276-7222**). Mid-September.

Mid-South Fair, Mid-South Fairgrounds. Ten days of fun-filled rides, food, games, shows, a midway, and a rodeo (℃ **901/274-8800**). Last week of September.

Southern Heritage Classic, midtown. Classic college football rivalry at the Liberty Bowl Stadium (℃ **901/398-6655**). September.

October

Pink Palace Crafts Fair, Audubon Park. Artists and performers in one of the largest crafts fairs in Tennessee (℃ **901/320-6320**). First weekend in October.

November

Freedom Awards, downtown. Human rights activists are honored by the National Civil Rights Museum (℃ **901/521-9699**) with public lectures and other ceremonies. Past recipients include Oprah Winfrey, Bono, Colin Powell, and Bill Clinton. Early November.

Mid-South Arts and Crafts Show, Memphis Cook Convention Center. Artists and craftspeople from more than 20 states sell their handiwork (℃ **423/430-3461**). Third week in November.

International Blues Competition. Blues musicians from around the country meet for performances at various venues, with the W. C. Handy Awards and post-show jam. For more information, call the Blues Foundation at ℃ **901/527-BLUE.** Throughout November.

December

Merry Christmas Memphis Parade, downtown. Christmas parade with floats and bands (℃ **901/575-0540**). Early December.

AutoZone Liberty Bowl Football Classic, Liberty Bowl Memorial Stadium. Intercollegiate game that's nationally televised (℃ **901/274-4600**). Late December.

Bury Your Blues Blowout on Beale, Beale Street. New Year's Eve celebration both inside the clubs and outside on Beale Street (℃ **901/526-0110**). December 31.

4 Getting There

BY PLANE

Nashville (airport code: BNA) is served by the following major airlines: **American Airlines** (© 800/433-7300); **Continental** (© 800/525-0280); **Delta** (© 800/221-1212); **Northwest-KLM** (© 800/225-2525); **Southwest** (© 800/435-9792); **United Airlines** (© 800/241-6522); and **US Airways** (© 800/428-4322).

Southwest is the city's largest carrier, with some 87 daily flights out of the city. Most Southwest flights will depart and arrive from the airport's Concourse C. Southwest Airlines also offers air/hotel packages. For details, visit **Southwest Airlines Vacations** online at **www.swavacations.com**, or call © **800/423-5683.**

Memphis is served by the following airlines: **American Airlines** (© 800/433-7300); **Delta** (© 800/221-1212); **KLM** (© 800/374-7747); **Northwest** (© 800/225-2525); **Southwest** (© 800/435-9792); **United Airlines** (© 800/241-6522); and **US Airways** (© 800/428-4322).

Northwest has a hub in Memphis and is the city's largest carrier. It's also your best bet for package deals. For details, visit **Northwest Airlines** online at **www.nwavacations.com**, or call © **800/225-2525.**

FLYING FOR LESS: TIPS FOR GETTING THE BEST AIRFARE

- Passengers who can book their ticket either **long in advance or at the last minute,** or who **fly midweek** or **at less-trafficked hours** may pay a fraction of the full fare. If your schedule is flexible, say so, and ask if you can secure a cheaper fare by changing your flight plans.
- Search **the Internet** for cheap fares. The most popular online travel agencies are **Travelocity.com** (www.travelocity.co.uk); **Expedia.com** (www.expedia.co.uk and www.expedia.ca); and **Orbitz.com.** In the U.K., go to **Travelsupermarket** (© **0845/345-5708;** www.travelsupermarket.com), a flight search engine that offers flight comparisons for the budget airlines whose seats often end up in bucket-shop sales. Other websites for booking airline tickets online include **Cheapflights.com, SmarterTravel.com, Priceline.com,** and **Opodo** (www.opodo.co.uk). Meta search sites (which find and then direct you to airline and hotel websites for booking) include **Sidestep.com** and **Kayak.com**—the latter includes fares for budget carriers like Jet Blue and Spirit as well as the major airlines. **Site59.com** is a great source for last-minute flights and getaways. In addition, most **airlines** offer online-only fares that even their phone agents know nothing about. British travelers should check **Flights International** (© **0800/0187050;**

Tips **Don't Stow It—Ship It**

Though pricey, it's sometimes worthwhile to travel luggage-free, particularly if you're toting sports equipment, meetings materials, or baby equipment. Specialists in door-to-door luggage delivery include **Virtual Bellhop** (www.virtualbellhop.com); **SkyCap International** (www.skycapinternational.com); **Luggage Express** (www.usxpluggageexpress.com); and **Sports Express** (www.sportsexpress.com).

Tips Getting Through the Airport

- Arrive at the airport at least 1 hour before a domestic flight and 2 hours before an international flight. You can check the average wait times at your airport by going to the TSA **Security Checkpoint Wait Times** site (waittime/tsa.dhs.gov).
- Know what you can carry on and what you can't. For the latest updates on items you are prohibited to bring in carry-on luggage, go to **www.tsa. gov/travelers/airtravel**.
- Beat the ticket-counter lines by using the self-service electronic ticket kiosks at the airport or even printing out your boarding pass at home from the airline website. Using curbside check-in is also a smart way to avoid lines.
- Bring a current, government-issued photo ID such as a driver's license or passport. Children under 18 do not need government-issued photo IDs for flights within the U.S., but they do need passports for international flights to most countries.
- Help speed up security before you're screened. Remove jackets, shoes, belt buckles, heavy jewelry, and watches and place them either in your carry-on luggage or the security bins provided. Place keys, coins, cellphones, and pagers in a security bin. If you have metallic body parts, carry a note from your doctor. When possible, pack liquids in checked baggage.
- Use a TSA-approved lock for your checked luggage. Look for Travel Sentry certified locks at luggage or travel shops and Brookstone stores (or online at www.brookstone.com).

www.flights-international.com) for deals on flights all over the world.

- Watch local newspapers for **promotional specials** or **fare wars,** when airlines lower prices on their most popular routes. Also keep an eye on price fluctuations and deals at websites such as **Airfarewatchdog.com** and **Farecast.com.**
- Try to book a ticket **in its country of origin.** If you're planning a one-way flight from Johannesburg to New York, a South Africa–based travel agent will probably have the lowest fares. For foreign travelers on multi-leg trips, book in the country of the first leg; for example, book New York–Chicago–Montréal–New York in the U.S.

- **Consolidators,** also known as bucket shops, are wholesale brokers in the airline-ticket game. Consolidators buy deeply discounted tickets ("distressed" inventories of unsold seats) from airlines and sell them to online ticket agencies, travel agents, tour operators, corporations, and, to a lesser degree, the general public. Consolidators advertise in Sunday newspaper travel sections (often in small ads with tiny type), both in the U.S. and the U.K. They can be great sources for cheap international tickets. On the down side, bucket shop tickets are often rigged with restrictions, such as stiff cancellation penalties (as high as 50% to 75% of the ticket price). And keep in mind that most of what you see advertised is of limited availability. Several reliable consolidators are worldwide and available online. **STA Travel** (www.statravel.com) has been the world's leading consolidator for students since purchasing Council Travel, but their fares are competitive for travelers of all ages. **Flights.com** (© 800/TRAV-800; www.flights.com) has excellent fares worldwide, particularly to Europe. They also have "local" websites in 12 countries. **FlyCheap** (© 800/FLY-CHEAP; www.1800flycheap.com) has especially good fares to sunny destinations. **Air Tickets Direct** (© 800/778-3447; www.airticketsdirect.com) is based in Montreal; they also book trips to places that U.S. travel agents won't touch, such as Cuba.

• Join **frequent-flier clubs.** Frequent-flier membership doesn't cost a cent, but it does entitle you to free tickets or upgrades when you amass the airline's required number of frequent-flier points. You don't even have to fly to earn points; **frequent-flier credit cards** can earn you thousands of miles for doing your everyday shopping. But keep in mind that award seats are limited, seats on popular routes are hard to snag, and more and more major airlines are cutting their expiration periods for mileage points—so check your airline's

Flying with Film & Video

Never pack film—exposed or unexposed—in checked bags, because the new, more powerful scanners in U.S. airports can fog film. The film you carry with you can be damaged by scanners as well. X-ray damage is cumulative; the faster the film, and the more times you put it through a scanner, the more likely the damage. Film under 800 ASA is usually safe for up to five scans. If you're taking your film through additional scans, U.S. regulations permit you to demand hand inspections. In international airports, you're at the mercy of airport officials. On international flights, store your film in transparent baggies, so you can remove it easily before you go through scanners. Keep in mind that airports are not the only places where your camera may be scanned: Highly trafficked attractions are X-raying visitors' bags with increasing frequency.

Most photo supply stores sell protective pouches designed to block damaging X-rays. The pouches fit both film and loaded cameras. They should protect your film in checked baggage, but they also may raise alarms and result in a hand inspection.

You'll have little to worry about if you are traveling with **digital cameras.** Unlike film, which is sensitive to light, the digital camera and storage cards are not affected by airport X-rays, according to Nikon.

Carry-on scanners will not damage **videotape** in video cameras, but the magnetic fields emitted by the walk-through security gateways and hand-held inspection wands will. Always place your loaded camcorder on the screening conveyor belt or have it hand-inspected. Be sure your batteries are charged, as you may be required to turn the device on to ensure that it's what it appears to be.

Tips Coping with Jet Lag

Jet lag is a pitfall of traveling across time zones. If you're flying north–south and you feel sluggish when you touch down, your symptoms will be the result of dehydration and the general stress of air travel. When you travel east–west or vice-versa, however, your body becomes thoroughly confused about what time it is, and everything from your digestive system to your brain is knocked for a loop. Traveling east, say from San Francisco to Boston, is more difficult on your internal clock than traveling west, say from Atlanta to Hawaii, because most peoples' bodies are more inclined to stay up late than fall asleep early.

Here are some tips for combating jet lag:

- **Reset your watch** to your destination time before you board the plane.
- **Drink lots of water** before, during, and after your flight. Avoid alcohol.
- **Exercise and sleep well** for a few days before your trip.
- If you have trouble sleeping on planes, **fly eastward on morning flights.**
- **Daylight** is the key to resetting your body clock. At the website for **Outside In** (www.bodyclock.com), you can get a customized plan of when to seek and avoid light.

---

frequent-flier program so you don't lose your miles before you use them. *Inside tip:* Award seats are offered almost a year in advance, but seats also open up at the last minute, so if your travel plans are flexible, you may strike gold. To play the frequent-flier game to your best advantage, consult the community bulletin boards on **FlyerTalk** (www.flyertalk.com) or go to Randy Petersen's **Inside Flyer** (www.insideflyer.com). Petersen and friends review all the programs in detail and post regular updates on changes in policies and trends.

ARRIVING AT THE AIRPORT

IMMIGRATION & CUSTOMS CLEARANCE   Foreign visitors arriving by air, no matter what the port of entry, should cultivate patience and resignation before setting foot on U.S. soil. U.S. airports have considerably beefed up security clearances in the years since the terrorist attacks of 9/11, and clearing Customs and Immigration can take as long as 2 hours.

People traveling by air from Canada, Bermuda, and certain Caribbean countries can sometimes clear Customs and Immigration at the point of departure, which is much faster.

LONG-HAUL FLIGHTS: HOW TO STAY COMFORTABLE

- Your choice of airline and airplane will definitely affect your legroom. Find more details about U.S. airlines at **www.seatguru.com**. For international airlines, the research firm Skytrax has posted a list of average seat pitches at **www.airlinequality.com**.
- Emergency exit seats and bulkhead seats typically have the most legroom. Emergency exit seats are usually left unassigned until the day of a flight (to ensure that someone able-bodied fills the seats); it's worth getting to the ticket counter early to snag one of these spots for a long flight. Many passengers find that bulkhead seating (the row facing the wall at the front of the cabin) offers more legroom, but keep in mind that bulkhead seats have no storage space on the floor in front of you.

- To have two seats for yourself in a three-seat row, try for an aisle seat in a center section toward the back of coach. If you're traveling with a companion, book an aisle and a window seat. Middle seats are usually booked last, so chances are good you'll end up with three seats to yourselves. And in the event that a third passenger is assigned the middle seat, he or she will probably be more than happy to trade for a window or an aisle.

- Ask about entertainment options. Many airlines offer seatback video systems where you get to choose your movies or play video games—but only on some of their planes. (Boeing 777s are your best bet.)

- To sleep, avoid the last row of any section or the row in front of an emergency exit, as these seats are the least likely to recline. Avoid seats near highly trafficked toilet areas. Avoid seats in the back of many jets—these can be narrower than those in the rest of coach. Or reserve a window seat so you can rest your head and avoid being bumped in the aisle.

- Get up, walk around, and stretch every 60 to 90 minutes to keep your blood flowing. This helps avoid **deep vein thrombosis,** or "economy-class syndrome." See the box "Avoiding 'Economy Class Syndrome,'" p. 26.

- Drink water before, during, and after your flight to combat the lack of humidity in airplane cabins. Avoid caffeine and alcohol, which will dehydrate you.

- If you're flying with kids, don't forget to carry on toys, books, pacifiers, and snacks and chewing gum to help them relieve ear pressure buildup during ascent and descent.

BY CAR

Nashville is a hub city intersected by three interstate highways. **I-65** runs north to Louisville, Kentucky, and south

to Birmingham, Alabama. **I-40** runs west to Memphis and east to Knoxville, Tennessee. **I-24** runs northwest toward St. Louis and southeast toward Atlanta. Downtown Nashville is the center of the hub, encircled by interstates 40, 65, and 265. Briley Parkway on the east, north, and west and I-440 on the south form a larger "wheel" around this hub.

If you're heading into downtown Nashville, follow the signs for I-65/24 and take either exit 84 or exit 85. If you're headed to Music Valley (Opryland Hotel), take I-40 east to the Briley Parkway exit and head north. If your destination is the West End/Music Row area, take I-40 around the south side of downtown and get off at the Broadway exit.

Here are some driving distances from selected cities: Atlanta, 250 miles; Chicago, 442 miles; Cincinnati, 291 miles; Memphis, 210 miles; New Orleans, 549 miles; and St. Louis, 327 miles.

Memphis lies at the southwestern tip of Tennessee, bordering Mississippi and Arkansas. **Interstate 40** connects Memphis with Nashville to the east and Little Rock, Ark., to the west. **Interstate 55** connects Memphis with Mississippi to the south and St. Louis, Mo., to the north. Both interstates intersect with **I-240,** which loops around the city's north, east and southern suburbs. The western edge of downtown Memphis is the Mississippi River.

For Memphis, here are some driving distances from other cities: Atlanta, 390 miles; Chicago, 534 miles; Little Rock 135 miles; New Orleans, 395 miles; St. Louis, 284 miles.

If you are a member of the **American Automobile Association (AAA)** and your car breaks down, call © **800/222-4357** for 24-hour emergency road service. The **local AAA office** in Nashville is at 2501 21st Ave. S., Suite 1 (© **615/297-7700),** and is open Monday to Friday 8:30am to 5:30pm and Saturday 9am to 1pm.

GETTING INTO NASHVILLE FROM THE AIRPORT

Nashville International Airport (𝒞 615/ 275-1675) is located about 8 miles east of downtown Nashville and is just south of I-40. It takes about 15 minutes to reach downtown Nashville from the airport. See "Getting Around Nashville" in chapter 4 for information on car-rental facilities at the Nashville airport. Many hotels near the airport offer a complimentary shuttle service, while others slightly farther away have their own fee shuttles; check with your hotel when you make your reservation.

The **Gray Line Airport Express** (𝒞 615/275-1180) operates shuttles between the airport and downtown and West End hotels. These shuttles operate from the airport every 15 to 20 minutes daily between 6am and 11pm; in addition to the hotels listed below, a few other hotels are on call. The downtown shuttle stops at the following hotels: Hilton, Union Station, Courtyard by Marriott (Fourth and Church), Holiday Inn Express, Renaissance Nashville Hotel, Nashville Sheraton, Westin Hermitage, and Doubletree Hotel Nashville. The West End shuttle stops at the following hotels: Loews Vanderbilt Plaza Hotel, Embassy Suites–West End, Holiday Inn Select, Courtyard by Marriott, Marriott-Vanderbilt, Guest House Inn, Hampton Inn–Vanderbilt, Hampton Inn and Suites–Elliston Place, and Days Inn–Vanderbilt. Rates are $11 one-way and $17 round-trip.

Metropolitan Transit Authority **buses** connect the airport and downtown Nashville. The no. 18 Elm Hill Pike bus runs between 8:13am and 5:33pm Monday to Friday (shorter hours and fewer departures on Saturday and Sunday). The adult, base fare is $1.45 each way, with exact change required, and the ride takes approximately 40 minutes. Buses from the airport leave at the ground-level curbside. Buses for the airport leave from

Shelter C at Deaderick Street and Fourth Avenue. For the most current schedule information, call 𝒞 615/862-5950 Monday to Friday 6:30am to 6pm and Saturday 8am to 1pm.

Metered **taxi fare** from the airport into downtown Nashville will cost you a $20 flat rate, or a few dollars more from the airport to West End hotels. Taxis are available on the ground level of the airport terminal. For information, call the Transportation Licensing Commission (TLC) at 𝒞 615/862-6777.

GETTING INTO MEMPHIS FROM THE AIRPORT

The **Memphis International Airport** (𝒞 901/922-8000) is located approximately 11 miles south of downtown Memphis off I-240. From the airport to East Memphis, it's about 9 miles. The route into either downtown or East Memphis is on I-240 all the way. Generally, allow about 20 minutes for the trip between the airport and downtown, and 15 minutes between the airport and East Memphis— up to an hour more during rush hour. See "Getting Around Memphis" in chapter 14 for information on car-rental facilities at the Memphis airport.

Although there is no direct bus service from the airport to downtown Memphis, it is possible (though impractical), with a change of bus en route, to get downtown on **Memphis Area Transit Authority (MATA)** buses (𝒞 901/274-6282). These buses, however, do not run very often and are not very convenient for visitors. The buses run every 1 to 2 hours until about 5:30pm Monday through Saturday, and until 5:15pm on Sunday, and the fare is $1.25. From the lower level at the airport, take no. 32, the East Parkway/Hollywood bus, and transfer to no. 10, the Lamar bus (which runs about every hour on weekdays, fewer times on Sat), or the no. 56, the Union/Kimball bus (running about every half-hour on weekdays), which will take you downtown. If you want to take the bus, the best bet is to call MATA or ask a bus driver for the latest schedule information.

A taxi from the airport to downtown Memphis will cost about $25; to East Memphis it will cost about $20. There are usually plenty of taxis around, but if you can't find one, call **Yellow/Checker Cab** (© 901/577-7777) or **City Wide Cab Company** (© 901/324-4202). The first mile is $3.20; after that, it's $1.50 per mile. Each additional passenger is 50¢ extra.

BY BUS

Greyhound Lines (© 800/231-2222) offers service to Nashville from around the country. These buses operate along interstate corridors or local routes. The fare between New York and Nashville is about $117 one-way and $206 round-trip; the fare between Chicago and Nashville is about $77 one-way and $152 round-trip. The Greyhound bus station is on the south side of downtown Nashville at 200 Eighth Ave. S.

Greyhound service between New York and Memphis costs about $63 one-way

and $136 round-trip; the fare between Chicago and Memphis is $82 one-way and $154 round-trip. The Greyhound bus station is in downtown Memphis, at 203 Union Ave.

From Atlanta, Georgia, round-trip fares are $139 to Memphis and $99 to Nashville.

BY TRAIN

Amtrak (© 800/872-7245) serves Memphis (but not Nashville) with a route that goes from Chicago through Memphis to New Orleans on the *City of New Orleans*. If you arrive in Memphis on an Amtrak train, you'll find yourself at **Central Station,** 545 S. Main St. (© **901/526-0052**), near Calhoun Street. This historic railway station has been completely renovated into a combination transportation center with public bus and Main Street Trolley connections and retail complex. However, the neighborhood around the station remains quite run-down. The area is not safe on foot, especially after dark. If arriving by train, you should take a cab or the Main Street Trolley to your hotel.

5 Money & Costs

It's always advisable to bring money in a variety of forms on a vacation: a mix of cash, credit cards, and traveler's checks. You should also exchange enough petty cash to cover airport incidentals, tipping, and transportation to your hotel before you leave home, or withdraw money upon arrival at an airport ATM.

Nashville and Memphis are moderately priced, compared with larger U.S. cities such as New York and Atlanta. However, costs for downtown parking, hotels, restaurants and gasoline have increased significantly in both cities in recent years, and continue to escalate as growth and development occurs at a brisk pace.

ATMs are readily available in both locations.

ATMS

Nationwide, the easiest and best way to get cash away from home is from an ATM (automated teller machine), sometimes referred to as a "cash machine," or "cashpoint." The **Cirrus** (© **800/424-7787;** www.mastercard.com) and **PLUS** (© **800/843-7587;** www.visa.com) networks span the country; you can find them even in remote regions. Go to your bank card's website to find ATM locations at your destination. Be sure you know your daily withdrawal limit before you depart.

Travel in the Age of Bankruptcy

Airlines go bankrupt, so protect yourself by **buying your tickets with a credit card.** The Fair Credit Billing Act guarantees that you can get your money back from the credit card company if a travel supplier goes under (and if you request the refund within 60 days of the bankruptcy). **Travel insurance** can also help, but make sure it covers against "carrier default" for your specific travel provider. And be aware that if a U.S. airline goes bust mid-trip, a 2001 federal law requires other carriers to take you to your destination (albeit on a space-available basis) for a fee of no more than $25, provided you rebook within 60 days of the cancellation.

Note: Many banks impose a fee every time you use a card at another bank's ATM, and that fee is often higher for international transactions (up to $5 or more) than for domestic ones (where they're rarely more than $2). In addition, the bank from which you withdraw cash may charge its own fee. To compare banks' ATM fees within the U.S., use **www.bankrate.com.** Visitors from outside the U.S. should also find out whether their bank assesses a 1% to 3% fee on charges incurred abroad.

CREDIT CARDS & DEBIT CARDS

Credit cards are the most widely used form of payment in the United States: **Visa** (Barclaycard in Britain), **Master-Card** (EuroCard in Europe, Access in Britain, Chargex in Canada), **American Express, Diners Club,** and **Discover.** They also provide a convenient record of all your expenses, and offer relatively good exchange rates. You can withdraw cash advances from your credit cards at banks or ATMs, but high fees make credit card cash advances a pricey way to get cash.

It's highly recommended that you travel with at least one major credit card. You must have a credit card to rent a car, and hotels and airlines usually require a credit card imprint as a deposit against expenses.

ATM cards with major credit card backing, known as **"debit cards,"** are an acceptable form of payment in most stores and restaurants. Debit cards draw money directly from your checking account.

TRAVELER'S CHECKS

Though credit cards and debit cards are more often used, traveler's checks are still widely accepted in the U.S. Foreign visitors should make sure that traveler's checks are denominated in U.S. dollars; foreign-currency checks are often difficult to exchange.

You can buy traveler's checks at most banks. Most are offered in denominations of $20, $50, $100, $500, and sometimes $1,000. Generally, you'll pay a service charge ranging from 1% to 4%.

The most popular traveler's checks are offered by **American Express** (© 800/807-6233; © 800/221-7282 for card holders—this number accepts collect calls, offers service in several foreign languages, and exempts Amex gold and platinum cardholders from the 1% fee); **Visa** (© 800/732-1322)—AAA members can obtain Visa checks for a $9.95 fee (for checks up to $1,500) at most AAA offices or by calling © 866/339-3378; and **MasterCard** (© 800/223-9920).

Be sure to keep a copy of the traveler's checks' serial numbers separate from your checks in the event that they are stolen or lost. You'll get a refund faster if you know the numbers.

House-Swapping

House-swapping is becoming a more popular and viable means of travel; you stay in their place, they stay in yours, and you both get an authentic and personal view of the area, the opposite of the escapist retreat that many hotels offer. Try **HomeLink International** (Homelink.org), the largest and oldest home-swapping organization, founded in 1952, with over 11,000 listings worldwide ($75 for a yearly membership). **HomeExchange.org** ($50 for 6,000 listings) and **InterVac.com** ($69 for over 10,000 listings) are also reliable.

6 Travel Insurance

The cost of travel insurance varies widely, depending on the cost and length of your trip, your age and health, and the type of trip you're taking, but expect to pay between 5% and 8% of the vacation itself. You can get estimates from various providers through **InsureMyTrip.com.** Enter your trip cost and dates, your age, and other information, for prices from more than a dozen companies.

For **U.K. citizens,** insurance is always advisable when traveling in the States. Travelers or families who make more than one trip abroad per year may find an annual travel insurance policy works out cheaper. Check **www.moneysuper market.com**, which compares prices across a wide range of providers for single- and multi-trip policies.

Most big travel agents offer their own insurance and will probably try to sell you their package when you book a holiday. Think before you sign. **Britain's Consumers' Association** recommends that you insist on seeing the policy and reading the fine print before buying travel insurance. **The Association of British Insurers** (© 020/7600-3333; www.abi. org.uk) gives advice by phone and publishes *Holiday Insurance*, a free guide to policy provisions and prices. You might also shop around for better deals: Try **Columbus Direct** (© 0870/033-9988; www.columbusdirect.net).

TRIP-CANCELLATION INSURANCE

Trip-cancellation insurance will help retrieve your money if you have to back out of a trip or depart early, or if your travel supplier goes bankrupt. Trip cancellation traditionally covers such events as sickness, natural disasters, and State Department advisories. The latest news in trip-cancellation insurance is the availability of **expanded hurricane coverage** and the **"any-reason"** cancellation coverage—which costs more but covers cancellations made for any reason. You won't get back 100% of your prepaid trip cost, but you'll be refunded a substantial portion. **Travel-Safe** (© **888/885-7233;** www.travelsafe. com) offers both types of coverage. Expedia also offers any-reason cancellation coverage for its air-hotel packages.

For details, contact one of the following recommended insurers: **Access America** (© 866/807-3982; www.access america.com); **Travel Guard International** (© 800/826-4919; www.travelguard.com); **Travel Insured International** (© 800/ 243-3174; www.travelinsured.com); and **Travelex Insurance Services** (© 888/ 457-4602; www.travelex-insurance.com).

MEDICAL INSURANCE

Although it's not required of travelers, health insurance is highly recommended. Most health insurance policies cover you if you get sick away from home—but check your coverage before you leave.

International visitors should note that unlike many European countries, the United States does not usually offer free or low-cost medical care to its citizens or visitors. Doctors and hospitals are expensive, and in most cases will require advance payment or proof of coverage before they render their services. Good policies will cover the costs of an accident, repatriation, or death. Packages such as **Europ Assistance's "Worldwide Healthcare Plan"** are sold by European automobile clubs and travel agencies at attractive rates. **Worldwide Assistance Services, Inc.** (✆ **800/777-8710;** www. worldwideassistance.com) is the agent for Europ Assistance in the United States.

Though lack of health insurance may prevent you from being admitted to a hospital in nonemergencies, don't worry about being left on a street corner to die: The American way is to fix you now and bill the living daylights out of you later.

If you're ever hospitalized more than 150 miles from home, **MedjetAssist** (✆ **800/527-7478;** www.medjetassistance. com) will pick you up and fly you to the hospital of your choice in a medically equipped and staffed aircraft 24 hours a day, 7 days a week. Annual memberships are $225 individual, $350 family; you can also purchase short-term memberships.

Canadians should check with their provincial health plan offices or call **Health Canada** (✆ **866/225-0709;** www.hc-sc.gc.ca) to find out the extent of their coverage and what documentation and receipts they must take home in case they are treated in the United States.

LOST-LUGGAGE INSURANCE
On flights within the U.S., checked baggage is covered up to $2,500 per ticketed passenger. On flights outside the U.S. (and on U.S. portions of international trips), baggage coverage is limited to approximately $9.05 per pound, up to approximately $635 per checked bag. If you plan to check items more valuable than what's covered by the standard liability, see if your homeowner's policy covers your valuables, get baggage insurance as part of your comprehensive travel-insurance package, or buy Travel Guard's "BagTrak" product.

If your luggage is lost, immediately file a lost-luggage claim at the airport, detailing the luggage contents. Most airlines require that you report delayed, damaged, or lost baggage within 4 hours of arrival. The airlines are required to deliver luggage, once found, directly to your house or destination free of charge.

7 Health

STAYING HEALTHY
GENERAL AVAILABILITY OF HEALTH CARE
Contact the **International Association for Medical Assistance to Travelers** (IAMAT) (✆ **716/754-4883** or, in Canada, 416/652-0137; **www.iamat.org**) for tips on travel and health concerns in the countries you're visiting, and for lists of local, English-speaking doctors. The United States

---

Healthy Travels to You
The following government websites offer up-to-date health-related travel advice.
- **Australia:** www.dfat.gov.au/travel
- **Canada:** www.hc-sc.gc.ca/index_e.html
- **U.K.:** www.dh.gov.uk/PolicyAndGuidance/HealthAdviceForTravellers/fs/en
- **U.S.:** www.cdc.gov/travel

Avoiding "Economy Class Syndrome"

Deep vein thrombosis, or as it's know in the world of flying, "economy-class syndrome," is a blood clot that develops in a deep vein. It's a potentially deadly condition that can be caused by sitting in cramped conditions—such as an airplane cabin—for too long. During a flight (especially a long-haul flight), get up, walk around, and stretch your legs every 60 to 90 minutes to keep your blood flowing. Other preventative measures include frequent flexing of the legs while sitting, drinking lots of water, and avoiding alcohol and sleeping pills. If you have a history of deep vein thrombosis, heart disease, or another condition that puts you at high risk, some experts recommend wearing compression stockings or taking anticoagulants when you fly; always ask your physician about the best course for you. Symptoms of deep vein thrombosis include leg pain or swelling, or even shortness of breath.

Centers for Disease Control and Prevention (© 800/311-3435; www.cdc.gov) provides up-to-date information on health hazards by region or country and offers tips on food safety. The website **www.trip prep.com**, sponsored by a consortium of travel medicine practitioners, **Travel Health Online,** may also offer helpful advice on traveling abroad. You can find listings of reliable clinics overseas at the **International Society of Travel Medicine** (www.istm.org).

WHAT TO DO IF YOU GET SICK AWAY FROM HOME

If you need a doctor in Nashville, call **Tri-Star Medline** at © 800/265-8624 or 615/342-1919; or contact the **Vanderbilt Medical Group Physician Referral Service** at © 615/322-3000.

In Memphis, call **Methodist Healthcare** at 1211 Union Ave. (© 901/5176-7000), or **The Regional Medical Center/Elvis Presley Trauma Center,** at 877 Jefferson Ave. (© 901/545-7100).

If you have dental problems in either city, a nationwide referral service known as **1-800-DENTIST** (© 800/336-8478) will provide the name of a nearby dentist or clinic.

You may want to ask the concierge at your hotel to recommend a local doctor—even his or her own. This will probably yield a better recommendation than any toll-free number would.

You can also try the emergency room at a local hospital. Many hospitals also have walk-in clinics for emergency cases that are not life-threatening; you may not get immediate attention, but you won't pay the high price of an emergency room visit. We list hospitals and emergency numbers under "Fast Facts," p. 52 and p. 158.

If you suffer from a chronic illness, consult your doctor before your departure. Pack **prescription medications** in your carry-on luggage, and carry them in their original containers, with pharmacy labels—otherwise they won't make it through airport security. Visitors from outside the U.S. should carry generic names of prescription drugs. For U.S. travelers, most reliable health-care plans provide coverage if you get sick away from home. Foreign visitors may have to pay all medical costs upfront and be reimbursed later. See "Medical Insurance," under "Travel Insurance," above.

8 Safety

STAYING SAFE

Nashville is a friendly city where travelers can feel safe both downtown and in outlying neighborhoods. Cautious tourists may want to be aware that the nightlife along Broadway downtown can become rowdy after dark.

Although Nashville and Memphis are friendly cities, crime is a problem, especially in Memphis, which had the highest violent crime rate in the U.S. in 2007. Although tourists aren't necessarily targeted, neither are they immune. Avoid walking or driving in unpopulated or inner-city areas alone, especially after dark. Be mindful of your surroundings, and take prudent precautions such as keeping valuables hidden and your car locked.

9 Specialized Travel Resources

TRAVELERS WITH DISABILITIES

Most disabilities shouldn't stop anyone from traveling in the U.S. There are more options and resources out there than ever before.

Almost all hotels and motels in Nashville offer wheelchair-accessible accommodations, but when making reservations be sure to ask. Additionally, the MTA public bus system in Nashville either has wheelchair-accessible regular vehicles or offers special transportation services for travelers with disabilities. To find out more about special services, call **Access Ride** (*C* **615/880-3970**).

The **Disability Information Office,** 25 Middleton St. (*C* **615/862-6492**), provides a referral and information service for visitors with disabilities. The *Nashville City Vacation Guide,* available either through this office or the Nashville Convention & Visitors Bureau, includes information on accessibility of restaurants, hotels, attractions, shops, and nightlife around Nashville. Similarly, the **Memphis Center for Independent Living,** 1633 Madison Ave. (*C* **901/ 726-6404,** v/tty 901/726-6521; www. mcil.org), is a consumer-oriented organization that helps people with disabilities.

Wheelchair Getaways of Tennessee (*C* **888/245-9944;** www.wheelchairgetaways.com) rents specialized vans with wheelchair lifts and other features for the disabled.

The **America the Beautiful— National Park and Federal Recreational Lands Pass—Access Pass** (formerly the **Golden Access Passport**) gives visually impaired or permanently disabled persons (regardless of age) free lifetime entrance to federal recreation sites administered by the National Park Service, including the Fish and Wildlife Service, the Forest Service, the Bureau of Land Management, and the Bureau of Reclamation. This may include national parks, monuments, historic sites, recreation areas, and national wildlife refuges.

The America the Beautiful Access Pass can only be obtained in person at any NPS facility that charges an entrance fee. You need to show proof of medically determined disability. Besides free entry, the pass also offers a 50% discount on some federal-use fees charged for such facilities as camping, swimming, parking, boat launching, and tours. For more information, go to www.nps.gov/fees_ passes.htm or call *C* **888/467-2757.**

Organizations that offer a vast range of resources and assistance to disabled travelers include **MossRehab** (*C* **800/ CALL-MOSS;** www.mossresourcenet. org); the **American Foundation for the Blind (AFB)** (*C* **800/232-5463;** www. afb.org); and **SATH (Society for Accessible Travel & Hospitality)** (*C* **212/ 447-7284;** www.sath.org). **AirAmbulance Card.com** is now partnered with SATH and allows you to preselect top-notch hospitals in case of an emergency.

Access-Able Travel Source (© 303/232-2979; www.access-able.com) offers a comprehensive database on travel agents from around the world with experience in accessible travel; destination-specific access information; and links to such resources as service animals, equipment rentals, and access guides.

Many travel agencies offer customized tours and itineraries for travelers with disabilities. Among them are **Flying Wheels Travel** (© 507/451-5005; www.flying wheelstravel.com) and **Accessible Journeys** (© 800/846-4537 or 610/521-0339; www.disabilitytravel.com).

Flying with Disability (www.flying-with-disability.org) is a comprehensive information source on airplane travel. **Avis Rent a Car** (© 888/879-4273) has an "Avis Access" program that offers services for customers with special travel needs. These include specially outfitted vehicles with swivel seats, spinner knobs, and hand controls; mobility scooter rentals; and accessible bus service. Be sure to reserve well in advance.

Also check out the quarterly magazine *Emerging Horizons* (www.emerging horizons.com), available by subscription ($17 year U.S.; $22 outside U.S.).

The "Accessible Travel" link at **Mobility-Advisor.com** (www.mobility-advisor.com) offers a variety of travel resources to disabled persons.

British travelers should contact **Holiday Care** (© 0845-124-9971 in U.K. only; www.holidaycare.org.uk) to access a wide range of travel information and resources for disabled and elderly people.

GAY & LESBIAN TRAVELERS

While lacking the vibrancy of many larger U.S. cities, both Nashville and Memphis have much to offer gay travelers.

To find out more about the Nashville gay and lesbian community, contact **Outloud Book Store**, 1703 Church St.

(© 615/340-0034; www.outloudonline.com). Nashville also has several gay and lesbian newspapers, including the entertainment weekly *Xenogeny* (© 615/831-1806).

In Memphis, volunteers staff the **Memphis Gay and Lesbian Community Center**, 892 S. Cooper (© 901/278-4297) nightly. For more information, look for the *Memphis Triangle Journal*, a free weekly newspaper that's available at local bookstores, libraries, and other locations.

The International Gay and Lesbian Travel Association (IGLTA) (© 800/448-8550 or 954/776-2626; www.iglta.org) is the trade association for the gay and lesbian travel industry, and offers an online directory of gay- and lesbian-friendly travel businesses and tour operators.

Many agencies offer tours and travel itineraries specifically for gay and lesbian travelers. **Above and Beyond Tours** (© 800/397-2681; www.abovebeyond tours.com) are gay Australia tour specialists. San Francisco–based **Now, Voyager** (© 800/255-6951; www.nowvoyager.com) offers worldwide trips and cruises and **Olivia** (© 800/631-6277; www.olivia.com) offers lesbian cruises and resort vacations.

Gay.com Travel (© 800/929-2268 or 415/644-8044; www.gay.com/travel or www.outandabout.com) is an excellent online successor to the popular *Out & About* print magazine. It provides regularly updated information about gay-owned, gay-oriented, and gay-friendly lodging, dining, sightseeing, nightlife, and shopping establishments in every important destination worldwide. British travelers should click on the "Travel" link at **www.uk.gay.com** for advice and gay-friendly trip ideas.

The Canadian website **GayTraveler** (www.gaytraveler.ca) offers ideas and advice for gay travel all over the world.

The following travel guides are available at many bookstores, or you can order them from any online bookseller: *Spartacus*

International Gay Guide, 35th Edition (Bruno Gmünder Verlag; www.spartacus world.com/gayguide) and *Odysseus: The International Gay Travel Planner, 17th Edition* (www.odyusa.com); and the **Damron** guides (www.damron.com), with separate, annual books for gay men and lesbians.

SENIOR TRAVEL

Senior travelers can expect discounts of several dollars off regular adult admission prices at most major tourist attractions in Nashville and Memphis.

Members of **AARP,** 601 E St. NW, Washington, DC 20049 (℗ **888/687-2277;** www.aarp.org), get discounts on hotels, airfares, and car rentals. AARP offers members a wide range of benefits, including *AARP: The Magazine* and a monthly newsletter. Anyone over 50 can join.

The U.S. National Park Service offers an **America the Beautiful—National Park and Federal Recreational Lands Pass—Senior Pass** (formerly the **Golden Age Passport**), which gives seniors 62 years or older lifetime entrance to all properties administered by the National Park Service—national parks, monuments, historic sites, recreation areas, and national wildlife refuges—for a one-time processing fee of $10. The pass must be purchased in person at any NPS facility that charges an entrance fee. Besides free entry, the America the Beautiful Senior Pass also offers a 50% discount on some federal-use fees charged for such facilities as camping, swimming, parking, boat launching, and tours. For more information, go to www.nps.gov/fees_passes.htm or call ℗ **888/467-2757.**

Many reliable agencies and organizations target the 50-plus market. **Elderhostel** (℗ **800/454-5768;** www.elderhostel. org) arranges worldwide study programs for those aged 55 and over. **ElderTreks** (℗ **800/741-7956** or 416/558-5000 outside North America; www.eldertreks.

com) offers small-group tours to off-the-beaten-path or adventure-travel locations, restricted to travelers 50 and older.

Recommended publications offering travel resources and discounts for seniors include the quarterly magazine *Travel 50 & Beyond* (www.travel50andbeyond. com) and the bestselling paperback *Unbelievably Good Deals and Great Adventures That You Absolutely Can't Get Unless You're Over 50 2005–2006, 16th Edition* (McGraw-Hill), by Joann Rattner Heilman.

FAMILY TRAVEL

Although not known specifically for their kid-friendly activities, both Nashville and Memphis offer plenty of fun options for families. For help in planning family vacations, check out the sample itineraries and hotel-and-attractions packages on the web sites of both cities' convention and visitors bureaus (www.visitmusic city.com and www.memphistravel.com).

To locate accommodations, restaurants, and attractions that are particularly kid-friendly, refer to the "Kids" icon throughout this guide.

Recommended family travel websites include **Family Travel Forum** (www. familytravelforum.com), a comprehensive site that offers customized trip planning; **Family Travel Network** (www.familytravel network.com), an online magazine providing travel tips; and **TravelWithYourKids. com** (www.travelwithyourkids.com), a comprehensive site written by parents for parents offering sound advice for long-distance and international travel with children.

You may also want to check out *Frommer's National Parks with Kids*.

WOMEN TRAVELERS

Check out the award-winning website **Journeywoman** (www.journeywoman. com), a "real life" women's travel-information network where you can sign up for a free e-mail newsletter and get advice on everything from etiquette and dress to safety. The travel guide *Safety and Security for Women Who Travel* by Sheila Swan and Peter Laufer ('Travelers' Tales Guides), offering common-sense tips on safe travel, was updated in 2004.

AFRICAN-AMERICAN TRAVELERS

Because Tennessee is so rich in African-American heritage, the convention and visitors bureaus in both cities offer free, specialized resources for travelers in black-history and multi-cultural heritage.

Black Travel Online (www.blacktravel online.com) posts news on upcoming events and includes links to articles and travel-booking sites. **Soul of America** (www.soulofamerica.com) is a comprehensive website, with travel tips, event and family-reunion postings, and sections on historically black beach resorts and active vacations.

Agencies and organizations that provide resources for black travelers include **Rodgers Travel** (© 800/825-1775; www. rodgerstravel.com); the **African American Association of Innkeepers International** (© 877/422-5777; www.africanamerican inns.com); and **Henderson Travel & Tours** (© 800/327-2309 or 301/650-5700; www.hendersontravel.com), which has specialized in trips to Africa since 1957.

Go Girl: The Black Woman's Guide to Travel & Adventure (Eighth Mountain Press) is a compilation of travel essays by writers including Jill Nelson and Audre Lorde. *The African-American Travel Guide* by Wayne C. Robinson (Hunter Publishing; www.hunterpublishing.com) was published in 1997, so it may be somewhat dated. *Travel and Enjoy Magazine* (© 866/266-6211; www.travelandenjoy. com) is a travel magazine and guide. The well-done *Pathfinders Magazine* (© 877/977-PATH; www.pathfinders travel.com) includes articles on everything from Rio de Janeiro to Ghana to upcoming ski, diving, golf, and tennis trips.

STUDENT TRAVEL

There are many universities and colleges in the Nashville area, but the main ones are **Vanderbilt University,** on West End Ave. (© 615/322-7311), a private four-year research-oriented university; **Tennessee State University,** 3500 John A. Merritt Blvd. (© 615/963-5000), a public four-year university; **Belmont University,** 1900 Belmont Blvd. (© 615/460-6000), a Baptist liberal arts university; and **Fisk University,** 1000 17th Ave. N. (© 615/329-8500), a private four-year African-American university.

There are about a dozen major colleges and universities in the Memphis area. The most prominent are **Rhodes College,** 2000 North Pkwy. (© 901/726-3000), which has a Gothic-style campus located opposite Overton Park; and the **University of Memphis,** on Central Avenue between Highland and Goodlett streets (© 901/678-2000), located on a large campus in midtown Memphis.

The **International Student Travel Confederation (ISTC)** (www.istc.org) was formed in 1949 to make travel around the world more affordable for students. Check out its website for comprehensive travel services information and details on how to get an **International Student Identity Card (ISIC),** which qualifies students for substantial savings on rail passes, plane tickets, entrance fees, and more. It also provides students with basic health and life insurance and a 24-hour helpline. The card is valid for a maximum of 18 months. You can apply for the card online or in person at **STA Travel** (© 800/781-4040 in North America; www.statravel.com), the biggest student travel agency in the world; check out the website to locate STA Travel offices worldwide. If you're no longer a student but are still under 26, you can get from the same people an **International Youth Travel Card (IYTC),** which entitles you to some discounts. **Travel CUTS** (© 800/592-2887; www.travelcuts.com) offers similar services for both Canadians and U.S. residents. Irish students may prefer to turn to **USIT** (✆ **01/602-1904**; www.usit.ie), an Ireland-based specialist in student, youth, and independent travel.

SINGLE TRAVELERS

On package vacations, single travelers are often hit with a "single supplement" to the base price. To avoid it, you can agree to room with other single travelers or find a compatible roommate before you go, from one of the many roommate-locator agencies.

Travel Buddies Singles Travel Club (✆ **800/998-9099**; www.travelbuddies worldwide.com), based in Canada, runs small, intimate, single-friendly group trips and will match you with a roommate free of charge. **TravelChums** (✆ **212/ 787-2621**; www.travelchums.com) is an Internet-only travel-companion matching service with elements of an online personals-type site, hosted by the respected New York–based Shaw Guides travel service.

Many reputable tour companies offer singles-only trips. **Singles Travel International** (✆ **877/765-6874**; www.singles travelintl.com) offers singles-only escorted tours to places like London, Alaska, Fiji, and the Greek Islands. **Backroads** (✆ **800/462-2848**; www.backroads.com) offers "Singles + Solos" active-travel trips to destinations worldwide.

For more information, check out Eleanor Berman's classic *Traveling Solo: Advice and Ideas for More Than 250*

Great Vacations, 5th Edition (Globe Pequot), updated in 2005.

VEGETARIAN TRAVEL

Happy Cow's Vegetarian Guide to Restaurants & Health Food Stores (www.happycow.net) has a restaurant guide with more than 6,000 restaurants in 100 countries. **VegDining.com** also lists vegetarian restaurants (with profiles) around the world. **Vegetarian Vacations** (www.vegetarian-vacations.com) offers vegetarian tours and itineraries. While many ethnic and vegetarian restaurants are available in both Memphis and Nashville, both cities stake their culinary identities to home cooking. That means you should always ask if the veggie dishes have been slow-simmered with meat (like turnip greens or green beans swimming in ham broth or bacon grease). And if you have a strong aversion to the ever-present aroma of barbecued pork meat, you may do best to avoid Memphis altogether.

TRAVELING WITH PETS

For travelers to Tennessee who just can't bear to leave their furry friends behind, the following websites offer information about pet-friendly accommodations and attractions:

- www.petswelcome.com
- www.pettravel.com
- www.travelpets.com

Also, all Motel 6 locations accept pets.

- www.motel6.com.

10 Sustainable Tourism/Ecotourism

Each time you take a flight or drive a car CO_2 is released into the atmosphere. You can help neutralize this danger to our planet through "carbon offsetting"—paying someone to reduce your CO_2 emissions by the same amount you've added. Carbon offsets can be purchased in the U.S. from companies such as

Carbonfund.org (www.carbonfund.org) and **TerraPass** (www.terrapass.org), and from **Climate Care** (www.climatecare. org) in the U.K.

Although one could argue that any vacation that includes an airplane flight can't be truly "green," you can go on holiday and still contribute positively to the environment. In addition to purchasing carbon offsets from the companies mentioned above, you can take other steps towards responsible travel. Choose forward-looking companies who embrace responsible development practices, helping preserve destinations for the future by working alongside local people. An increasing number of sustainable tourism initiatives can help you plan a family trip and leave as small a "footprint" as possible on the places you visit.

Responsible Travel (www.responsible travel.com), run by a spokesperson for responsible tourism in the travel industry, contains a great source of sustainable travel ideas.

You can find eco-friendly travel tips, statistics, and touring companies and associations—listed by destination under "Travel Choice"—at the TIES website, **www.ecotourism.org**. Also check out **Conservation International** (www. conservation.org)—which, with *National Geographic Traveler*, annually presents **World Legacy Awards** (www.wlaward.org) to those travel tour operators, businesses, organizations, and places that have made a significant contribution to sustainable tourism. **Ecotravel.com** is part online magazine and part ecodirectory that lets you search for touring companies in several categories (water-based, land-based, spiritually oriented, and so on).

In the U.K., **Tourism Concern** (www. tourismconcern.org.uk) works to reduce social and environmental problems connected to tourism and find ways of improving tourism so that local benefits are increased.

The **Association of British Travel Agents (ABTA)** (www.abtamembers.org/ responsibletourism) acts as a focal point for the U.K. travel industry and is one of the leading groups spearheading responsible tourism.

The **Association of Independent Tour Operators (AITO)** (www.aito.co.uk) is a group of interesting specialist operators leading the field in making holidays sustainable.

(Tips It's Easy Being Green

We can all help conserve fuel and energy when we travel. Here are a few simple ways you can help preserve your favorite destinations:

• Whenever possible, choose nonstop flights; they generally require less fuel than those that must stop and take off again.

• If renting a car is necessary on your vacation, ask the rental agent for the most fuel efficient one available. Not only will you use less gas, you'll save money at the tank.

• At hotels, request that your sheets and towels not be changed daily. You'll save water and energy by not washing them as often, and you'll prolong the life of the towels, too. (Many hotels already have programs like this in place.)

• Turn off the lights and air-conditioner (or heater) when you leave your hotel room.

Frommers.com: The Complete Travel Resource

It should go without saying, but we highly recommend **Frommers.com,** voted Best Travel Site by *PC Magazine.* We think you'll find our expert advice and tips; independent reviews of hotels, restaurants, attractions, and preferred shopping and nightlife venues; vacation giveaways; and an online booking tool indispensable before, during, and after your travels. We publish the complete contents of over 128 travel guides in our **Destinations** section covering nearly 3,600 places worldwide to help you plan your trip. Each weekday, we publish original articles reporting on **Deals and News** via our free **Frommers.com Newsletter** to help you save time and money and travel smarter. We're betting you'll find our new **Events** listings (http://events. frommers.com) an invaluable resource; it's an up-to-the-minute roster of what's happening in cities everywhere—including concerts, festivals, lectures, and more. We've also added weekly **Podcasts, interactive maps,** and hundreds of new images across the site. Check out our **Travel Talk** area featuring **Message Boards** where you can join in conversations with thousands of fellow Frommer's travelers and post your trip report once you return.

11 Staying Connected

TELEPHONES

Generally, hotel surcharges on long-distance and local calls are astronomical, so you're better off using your **cellphone** or a **public pay telephone.** Many convenience groceries and packaging services sell **prepaid calling cards** in denominations up to $50; for international visitors these can be the least expensive way to call home. Many public pay phones at airports now accept American Express, MasterCard, and Visa credit cards. **Local calls** made from pay phones in most locales cost either 25¢ or 35¢ (no pennies, please).

Most long-distance and international calls can be dialed directly from any phone. **For calls within the United States and to Canada,** dial 1 followed by the area code and the seven-digit number. **For other international calls,** dial 011 followed by the country code, city code, and the number you are calling.

Calls to area codes **800, 888, 877,** and **866** are toll-free. However, calls to area codes **700** and **900** (chat lines, bulletin boards, "dating" services, and so on) can be very expensive—usually a charge of 95¢ to $3 or more per minute, and they sometimes have minimum charges that can run as high as $15 or more.

For **reversed-charge or collect calls,** and for person-to-person calls, dial the number 0 then the area code and number; an operator will come on the line, and you should specify whether you are calling collect, person-to-person, or both. If your operator-assisted call is international, ask for the overseas operator.

For **local directory assistance** ("information"), dial 411; for long-distance information, dial 1, then the appropriate area code and 555-1212.

CELLPHONES

Just because your cellphone works at home doesn't mean it'll work everywhere in the U.S. (thanks to our nation's fragmented cellphone system). It's a good bet that your phone will work in major cities, but take a look at your wireless company's coverage map on its website before heading out; T-Mobile, Sprint, and Nextel are particularly weak in rural areas. If you need to stay in touch at a destination where you know your phone won't work, **rent** a phone that does from **InTouch USA** (© **800/872-7626;** www.intouch global.com) or a rental car location, but beware that you'll pay $1 a minute or more for airtime.

If you're not from the U.S., you'll be appalled at the poor reach of our **GSM (Global System for Mobile Communications) wireless network,** which is used by much of the rest of the world. Your phone will probably work in most major U.S. cities; it definitely won't work in many rural areas. To see where GSM phones work in the U.S., check out www.t-mobile.com/coverage/national_ popup.asp. And you may or may not be able to send SMS (text messaging) home.

VOICE-OVER INTERNET PROTOCOL (VOIP)

If you have web access while traveling, you might consider a broadband-based telephone service (in technical terms, **Voice over Internet Protocol,** or **VoIP**) such as Skype (www.skype.com) or Vonage (www.vonage.com), which allows you to make free international calls if you use their services from your laptop or in a cybercafe. The people you're calling must also use the service for it to work; check the sites for details.

INTERNET/E-MAIL WITHOUT YOUR OWN COMPUTER

To find cybercafes in your destination check **www.cybercaptive.com** and **www. cybercafe.com**.

Most major airports have **Internet kiosks** that provide basic Web access for a per-minute fee that's usually higher than cybercafe prices. Check out copy shops like **Kinko's** (FedEx Kinko's), which offers computer stations with fully loaded software (as well as Wi-Fi).

WITH YOUR OWN COMPUTER

More and more hotels, resorts, airports, cafes, and retailers are going Wi-Fi (wireless fidelity), becoming "hotspots" that offer free high-speed Wi-Fi access or charge a small fee for usage. Coffee shops, restaurants, and hotels/motels with free Wi-Fi are abundant in both Nashville and Memphis. Wi-Fi is even found in campgrounds, RV parks, and even entire towns. Most laptops sold today have built-in wireless capability. To find public Wi-Fi hotspots at your destination, go to **www.jiwire.com**; its Hotspot Finder

---

Tips **Hey, Google, did you get my text message?**

It's bound to happen: The day you leave this guidebook back at the hotel for an unencumbered stroll down Beale Street, you'll forget the address of the lunch spot you had earmarked. If you're traveling with a mobile device, send a text message to © **466453 (GOOGLE)** for a lightning-fast response. For instance, type "carnegie deli new york" and within 10 seconds you'll receive a text message with the address and phone number. This nifty trick works in a range of search categories: Look up weather ("weather philadelphia"), language translations ("translate goodbye in spanish"), currency conversions ("10 usd in pounds"), movie times ("harry potter 60605"), and more. If your search results are off, be more specific ("the abbey gay bar west hollywood"). For more tips and search options, see www.google.com/intl/en_us/mobile/sms/. Regular text message charges apply.

Online Traveler's Toolbox

Veteran travelers usually carry some essential items to make their trips easier. Following is a selection of handy online tools to bookmark and use.

- **Airplane Food** (www.airlinemeals.net)
- **Airplane Seating** (www.seatguru.com; and www.airlinequality.com)
- **Foreign Languages for Travelers** (www.travlang.com)
- **Maps** (www.mapquest.com)
- **Subway Navigator** (www.subwaynavigator.com)
- **Time and Date** (www.timeanddate.com)
- **Travel Warnings** (http://travel.state.gov, www.fco.gov.uk/travel, www.voyage.gc.ca, www.dfat.gov.au/consular/advice)
- **Universal Currency Converter** (www.xe.com/ucc)
- **Visa ATM Locator** (www.visa.com), **MasterCard ATM Locator** (www.mastercard.com)
- **Weather** (www.intellicast.com and www.weather.com)

holds the world's largest directory of public wireless hotspots.

For dial-up access, most business-class hotels in the U.S. offer dataports for laptop modems, and a few thousand hotels in the U.S. and Europe now offer free high-speed Internet access.

Wherever you go, bring a **connection kit** of the right power and phone adapters, a spare phone cord, and a spare Ethernet network cable—or find out whether your hotel supplies them to guests.

12 Packages for the Independent Traveler

Package tours are simply a way to buy the airfare, accommodations, and other elements of your trip (such as car rentals, airport transfers, and sometimes even activities) at the same time and often at discounted prices.

One good source of package deals is the airlines themselves. Most major airlines offer air/land packages, including **American Airlines Vacations** (② 800/321-2121; www.aavacations.com), **Delta Vacations** (② 800/654-6559; www.deltavacations.com), **Continental Airlines Vacations** (② 800/301-3800; www.covacations.com), and **United Vacations** (② 888/854-3899; www.unitedvacations.com). Several big **online travel agencies**—Expedia, Travelocity, Orbitz,

Site59, and Lastminute.com—also do a brisk business in packages.

For travel planning to Memphis, Northwest Airlines, which has a hub in Memphis, offers convenient packages. (From Europe, KLM airlines offers direct flights from Amsterdam to Memphis.) For travel to Nashville, Southwest Airlines offers similar packages into Nashville from major U.S. cities.

The convention and visitors bureaus' websites in Nashville and Memphis allow tourists to book vacation packages that include hotel and attractions options. For example, the Nashville Nights "Honky Tonk Heaven" package includes two hotel nights, and tours to Ryman Auditorium, the Tennessee State Capitol, Historic

---

Tips   **Ask Before You Go**

Before you invest in a package deal or an escorted tour:

- Always ask about the **cancellation policy.** Can you get your money back? Is there a deposit required?
- Ask about the **accommodations choices and prices** for each. Then look up the hotels' reviews in a Frommer's guide and check their rates online for your specific dates of travel. Also find out what types of rooms are offered.
- Request a complete **schedule** (escorted tours only).
- Ask about the **size** and demographics of the group (escorted tours only).
- Discuss what is included in the **price** (transportation, meals, tips, airport transfers, and more—escorted tours only).
- Finally, look for **hidden expenses.** Ask whether airport departure fees and taxes, for example, are included in the total cost—they rarely are.

Second Avenue, the Wildhorse Saloon, and the Hard Rock Cafe. All packages are customizable online, allowing you to book additional nights and add attractions to your itinerary.

Sweet Magnolia Tours is one of the few tour operators in Tennessee with offices in both Nashville and Memphis. In 2008, the company will begin offering specific vacation packages that combine the best of these two cities. The land-only packages include hotel and attractions. For more information, call © **866-320-5295** or 901-369-9838; www.sweetmagnolia tours.com.

For European travelers interested in touring Tennessee as well as Atlanta, Ga. And New Orleans, La., check out the following website: www.deep-south-usa.de.

Travel packages are also listed in the travel section of your local Sunday newspaper. Or check ads in the national travel magazines such as *Arthur Frommer's Budget Travel Magazine, Travel + Leisure, National Geographic Traveler,* and *Condé Nast Traveler.*

13 Escorted General-Interest Tours

Escorted tours are structured group tours, with a group leader. The price usually includes everything from airfare to hotels, meals, tours, admission costs, and local transportation.

Despite the fact that escorted tours require big deposits and predetermine hotels, restaurants, and itineraries, many people derive security and peace of mind from the structure they offer. Escorted tours—whether they're navigated by bus, motor coach, train, or boat—let travelers sit back and enjoy the trip without having to drive or worry about details. They take you to the maximum number of sights in the minimum amount of time with the least amount of hassle. They're particularly convenient for people with limited mobility and they can be a great way to make new friends.

On the downside, you'll have little opportunity for serendipitous interactions with locals. The tours can be jam-packed with activities, leaving little room for individual sightseeing, whim, or adventure—plus they often focus on the heavily touristed sites, so you miss out on many a lesser-known gem.

14 Getting Around Nashville & Memphis

BY PLANE

There is no plane service between Nashville and Memphis. You will have to rent a car and drive the three-hour distance between the two cities. Interstate 40, also known as "The Music Highway," has several interesting diversions along the way (see "Side Trips from Nashville," chapter 10).

BY CAR

As mentioned earlier, driving between Nashville and Memphis is the only practical way to see both cities. Interstate 40 connects the two. The speed limit is 70 mph for much of this stretch, which also offers access to clean rest stops and dozens of service stations and restaurants. For travel information at any time, dial 511 on your cell phone. While visiting each city, you'll need a car to get around. Public transportation in both cities is poor, and because attractions are spread out, you'll need a car to get beyond the downtown core in both Nashville and Memphis.

To limit frustration, try to avoid hitting the interstates around either city at morning or afternoon rush hour. Traffic tie-ups and lengthy delays are becoming increasingly common, especially in Nashville. Ongoing freeway construction and renovation projects further congest the roadways. To find out about lane closures and other headaches, call the Tennessee Department of Transportation's construction hotline at © 800/858-6349. Snow and ice storms may also make road conditions hazardous. For updates, call the state's inclement weather/road closure hotline (© 800/342-3258; www.tdot. state.tn.us/tdotsmartway).

If you're visiting from abroad and plan to rent a car in the United States, keep in mind that foreign driver's licenses are usually recognized in the U.S., but you should get an international one if your home license is not in English.

Check out **Breezenet.com,** which offers domestic car-rental discounts with some of the most competitive rates around.

BY TRAIN

International visitors planning to visit several U.S. cities can buy a **USA Rail Pass,** good for 5, 15, or 30 days of unlimited travel on **Amtrak** (© **800/USA-RAIL;** www.amtrak.com). The pass is available online or through many overseas travel agents. See Amtrak's website for the cost of travel within the western, eastern, or northwestern United States. Reservations are generally required and should be made as early as possible. Regional rail passes are also available.

BY BUS

Bus travel is often the most economical form of public transit for short hops between U.S. cities, but it's certainly not an option for everyone (particularly when Amtrak, which is far more luxurious, offers similar rates). **Greyhound** (© **800/ 231-2222;** www.greyhound.com) is the sole nationwide bus line. International visitors can obtain information about the **Greyhound North American Discovery Pass.** The pass can be obtained from foreign travel agents or through (www. discoverypass.com) for unlimited travel and stopovers in the U.S. and Canada.

15 Tips on Accommodations

Nashville and Memphis have a wealth of hotel options, most of which are large chains. It's worth noting that Memphis was the site of the first Holiday Inn, founded by local entrepreneur Kemmons Wilson. Today Memphis has a large corporate presence for the worldwide chain.

SURFING FOR HOTELS

In addition to the online travel booking sites **Travelocity, Expedia, Orbitz, Priceline,** and **Hotwire,** you can book hotels through **Hotels.com; Quikbook** (www.quikbook.com); and **Travelaxe** (www.travelaxe.net).

HotelChatter.com is a daily webzine offering smart coverage and critiques of hotels worldwide. Go to **TripAdvisor.com** or **HotelShark.com** for helpful independent consumer reviews of hotels and resort properties.

It's a good idea to **get a confirmation number** and **make a printout** of any online booking transaction.

SAVING ON YOUR HOTEL ROOM

The **rack rate** is the maximum rate that a hotel charges for a room. Hardly anybody pays this price, however, except in high season or on holidays. To lower the cost of your room:

- **Ask about special rates or other discounts.** You may qualify for corporate, student, military, senior, frequent flier, trade union, or other discounts.
- **Dial direct.** When booking a room in a chain hotel, you'll often get a better deal by calling the individual hotel's reservation desk rather than the chain's main number.
- **Book online.** Many hotels offer Internet-only discounts, or supply rooms to Priceline, Hotwire, or Expedia at rates much lower than the ones you can get through the hotel itself.
- **Remember the law of supply and demand.** Resort hotels are most crowded and therefore most expensive on weekends, so discounts are usually available for midweek stays. Business hotels in downtown locations are busiest during the week, so you can expect big discounts over the weekend.

- **Look into group or long-stay discounts.** If you come as part of a large group, you should be able to negotiate a bargain rate. Likewise, if you're planning a long stay (at least 5 days), you might qualify for a discount. As a general rule, expect 1 night free after a 7-night stay.
- **Sidestep excess surcharges and hidden costs.** Many hotels have the unpleasant practice of nickel-and-diming its guests with opaque surcharges. When you book a room, ask what is included in the room rate, and what is extra. Avoid dialing direct from hotel phones, which can have exorbitant rates. And don't be tempted by the room's minibar offerings: Most hotels charge through the nose for water, soda, and snacks. Finally, ask about local taxes and service charges, which can increase the cost of a room by 15% or more.
- **Book an efficiency.** A room with a kitchenette allows you to shop for groceries and cook your own meals. This is a big money saver, especially for families on long stays.
- **Consider enrolling in hotel "frequent-stay" programs,** which are upping the ante lately to win the loyalty of repeat customers. Frequent guests can now accumulate points or credits to earn free hotel nights, airline miles, in-room amenities, merchandise, tickets to concerts and events, discounts on sporting facilities—and even credit toward stock in the participating hotel, in the case of the Jameson Inn hotel group. Perks are awarded not only by many chain hotels and motels (Hilton HHonors, Marriott Rewards, Wyndham ByRequest, to name a few), but by individual inns and B&Bs as well. Many chain hotels partner with other hotel chains, car-rental firms, airlines, and credit card companies to give

Tips for Digital Travel Photography

- **Take along a spare camera—or two.** Even if you've been anointed the "official" photographer of your travel group, encourage others in your party to carry their own cameras and provide fresh perspectives—and backup. Your photographic "second unit" may include you in a few shots so you're not the invisible person of the trip.

- **Stock up on digital film cards.** At home, it's easy to copy pictures from your memory cards to your computer as they fill up. During your travels, cards seem to fill up more quickly. Take along enough digital film for your entire trip or, at a minimum, enough for at least a few days of shooting. At intervals, you can copy images to CDs. Many camera stores and souvenir shops offer this service, and a growing number of mass merchandisers have walk-up kiosks you can use to make prints or create CDs while you travel.

- **Share and share alike.** No need to wait until you get home to share your photos. You can upload a gallery's worth to an online photo sharing service. Just find an Internet café where the computers have card readers, or connect your camera to the computer with a cable. You can find online photo sharing services that cost little or nothing at **www.clickherefree. com.** You can also use America Online's Your Pictures service, or commercial enterprises that give you free or low-cost photo sharing: Kodak's EasyShare gallery (**www.kodak.com**), Snapfish (**www.snapfish.com**), or Shutterfly (**www.shutterfly.com**).

- **Add voice annotations to your photos.** Many digital cameras allow you to add voice annotations to your shots after they're taken. These serve as excellent reminders and documentation. One castle or cathedral may look like another after a long tour; your voice notes will help you distinguish them.

- **Experiment!** Travel is a great time to try out new techniques. Take photos at night, resting your camera on a handy wall or other support as your self-timer trips the shutter for a long exposure. Try close-ups of flowers, crafts, wildlife, or maybe the exotic cuisine you're about to consume. Discover action photography—shoot the countryside from trains, buses, or cars. With a digital camera, you can experiment and then erase your mistakes.

—From Travel Photography Digital Field Guide,
1st edition *(John Wiley & Sons, 2006)*

consumers additional incentive to do repeat business.

LANDING THE BEST ROOM

Somebody has to get the best room in the house. It might as well be you. You can start by joining the hotel's frequent-guest program, which may make you eligible for upgrades. A hotel-branded credit card usually gives its owner "silver" or "gold" status in frequent-guest programs for free. Always ask about a corner room. They're often larger and quieter, with more windows and light, and they often cost the same as standard rooms. When you make your reservation, ask if the hotel is renovating; if it is, request a room away from the construction. If you're a light sleeper, request a quiet room away from vending or ice machines, elevators, restaurants, bars, and discos. Ask for a room that has most recently been renovated or redecorated.

If you aren't happy with your room when you arrive, ask for another one. Most lodgings will be willing to accommodate you.

Tennessee can get quite warm in the summer months, so be sure to ask if your room has air-conditioning or ceiling fans. Do the windows open? If they do, and the nighttime entertainment takes place alfresco, you may want to find out when show time is over.

Suggested Nashville Itineraries

Nashville is spread out, with pockets of interesting neighborhoods, entertainment districts, and shopping areas scattered throughout the metro area, so having a car is important if you want to experience the breadth of all the city has to offer. However, the downtown area is relatively compact, making it feasible to hit several of Music City's high points right off the bat on your first day in town—and without too much driving. As with any destination, your interests will dictate what you choose to do and see. The itineraries below focus primarily on country music, fine arts, history and culture, and shopping and entertainment. The suggestions we've given you can be experienced during any season and regardless of most weather conditions.

1 The Best of Nashville in 1 Day

The day begins with a crash-course in the origins of American popular music, but it's a history lesson most pop-culture enthusiasts will love. The Country Music Hall of Fame and Museum is an endlessly entertaining and informative experience that will help you grasp Nashville's importance as a songwriting and recording mecca. A few blocks away is the hallowed hall where it all began: the Ryman Auditorium. Soak up the spirits of Hank Williams and Patsy Cline, and then stroll the lively strip along Broadway. Your afternoon continues with a visit to Nashville's best art museum: the Frist Center for the Visual Arts. The evening is yours to barhop or boot-scoot at the Wildhorse Saloon, Tootsie's Orchid Lounge, B.B. King Blues Club, or any other nightspot that strikes your fancy. **Start:** *Country Music Hall of Fame and Museum.*

❶ Country Music Hall of Fame and Museum 🎸🎸
Start your day downtown at the acclaimed Country Music Hall of Fame and Museum. It's chock-full of colorful exhibits and music, and seeing this will help you get your bearings for later exploration. See p. 96.

Walk north 4 blocks until, on your right, you see:
❷ Ryman Auditorium 🎸🎸
This sacred concert hall was a magnet for the so-called hillbilly and country music boom back in the 1940s and '50s. And

since you're going to attend a performance of the *Grand Ole Opry* while you're here, it will be nice to see the modest venue where it all began. See p. 99.

Walk south back to Broadway, and then turn left and continue past the honky-tonks almost to Third St. On your left, you'll see:
❸ Hatch Show Print
Take a trip back in time and get lost in the nostalgic aura of this long-time print shop, where posters of live concerts by virtually all of country music's greatest stars were created. See p. 117.

Nashville Suggested Itineraries

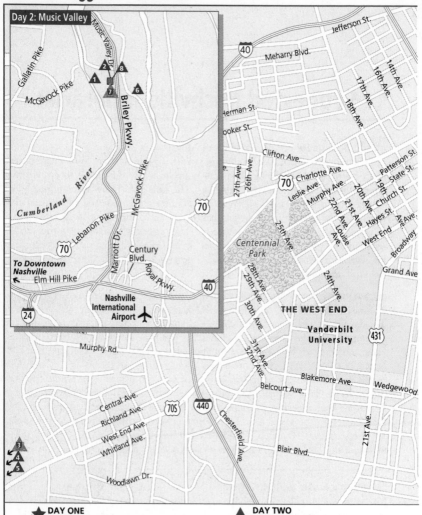

Day 2: Music Valley

To Downtown Nashville

Nashville International Airport

THE WEST END

Vanderbilt University

Centennial Park

★ **DAY ONE**
NASHVILLE IN 1 DAY

1 Country Music Hall of Fame and Museum
2 Ryman Auditorium
3 Hatch Show Print
4 Jack's Bar-B-Que
5 Frist Center for the Visual Arts
6 The District

▲ **DAY TWO**
MUSIC VALLEY

1 General Jackson Cruise
2 Homes of the Stars Tour
3 Martha's at the Plantation
4 Belle Meade Plantation
5 Cheekwood Botanical Garden and Museum
6 Opry Mills
7 Rainforest Café
8 Grand Old Opry

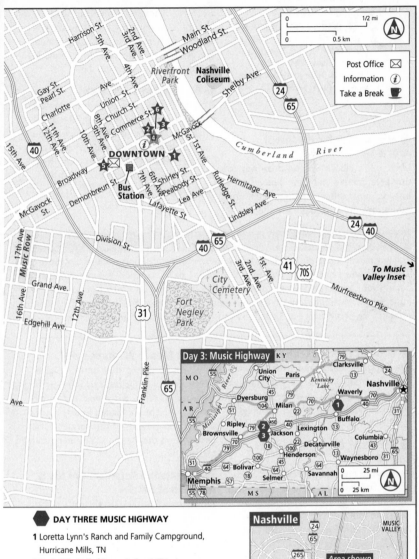

Day 3: Music Highway

<figure>
Map legend:
0 — 1/2 mi
0 — 0.5 km

Post Office ⊠
Information ⓘ
Take a Break ☕

Harrison St.
2nd Ave.
3rd Ave.
5th Ave.
Main St.
Woodland St.
Riverfront Park
Nashville Coliseum
Shelby Ave.
24
65
Gay St.
Pearl St.
4th Ave.
Church St.
Union St.
Commerce St.
McGavock St.
Cumberland River
Charlotte
11th Ave.
12th Ave.
8th Ave.
9th Ave.
10th Ave.
DOWNTOWN
Broadway
1st Ave.
40
15th Ave.
Demonbreun St.
Bus Station
7th Ave.
6th Ave.
Shirley St.
Peabody St.
Hermitage Ave.
Rutledge St.
Lafayette St.
Lea Ave.
Lindsley Ave.
24
40
Division St.
40
65
2nd Ave.
3rd Ave.
1st Ave.
41
705
To Music Valley Inset
Murfreesboro Pike
17th Ave.
Music Row
Grand Ave.
City Cemetery
16th Ave.
Edgehill Ave.
12th Ave.
31
Fort Negley Park
Franklin Pike
65
Ave.
</figure>

Day 3: Music Highway

KY
79
Clarksville
13
24
Nashville ★
MO
55
Union City
Paris
Kentucky Lake
Waverly
70
Dyersburg
45
79
1
40
31
AR
55
104
Milan
70
Buffalo
51
456
Ripley
79
40
Lexington
13
Brownsville
2
Jackson
22
Columbia
43
65
3
18
22
100
Decaturville
13
51
64
Bolivar
100
Henderson
64
Waynesboro
31
40
18
45
Selmer
Savannah
Memphis
57
55 78
MS
AL
0 — 25 mi
0 — 25 km

⬡ **DAY THREE MUSIC HIGHWAY**

1 Loretta Lynn's Ranch and Family Campground, Hurricane Mills, TN

2 Rockabilly Hall of Fame, Jackson, TN

3 Casey Jones Village, Jackson, TN

Nashville
24
65
265
Area shown
THE DISTRICT
DOWN-TOWN
Cumberland River
THE WEST END
MUSIC VALLEY
440
65
70
24
40
40

4 JACK'S BAR-B-QUE ⭐⭐
Slip in here and grab a Coke or a shredded-pork sandwich and some greasy fries. Jack's is a basic, no-frills dive. Make yourself at home. 416 Broadway. ☎ 615/254-5715. See p. 91.

5 Frist Center for the Visual Arts ⭐⭐⭐

Drive a few blocks west on Broadway to this breathtaking museum, housed in a historic post office building. First-rate exhibitions from throughout the world are shown here. The permanent ArtQuest Gallery is a wonderful, hands-on creativity center where children and adults alike can experiment with their own artwork. See p. 104.

6 Barhopping in the District

After a bit of rest and a bite to eat, browse the bars and colorful nightlife along Broadway and the surrounding area. You can hear live music most anywhere, from Tootsie's Orchid Lounge to B.B. King Blues Club. See chapter 9, "Nashville After Dark."

2 The Best of Nashville in 2 Days

Today you're heading out to Music Valley, the sprawling area northwest of downtown. The Opryland Hotel is the hub for much of the day's activities. You can book and board your Cumberland River cruise on the *General Jackson* showboat here, and do the same for a sightseeing tour of country music stars' homes. You'll be returning here tonight for a performance of the long-running Grand Ole Opry. *Start: Opryland Hotel.*

1 *General Jackson* Cruise

For a relaxing cruise along the Cumberland River that winds its way through downtown Nashville and the surrounding countryside, hop aboard this mighty paddlewheeler. See p. 114.

2 Homes of the Country Stars Tour ⭐

Get on the bus and get ready for a road trip to Brentwood and other elite gated communities, where chart-topping locals like Faith Hill and Tim McGraw, Martina McBride, Dolly Parton, and Alan Jackson live like royalty. See p. 112.

3 MARTHA'S AT THE PLANTATION ⭐⭐⭐
Call ahead and make lunch reservations at this wonderfully chic yet down-home restaurant, which is on the grounds of the Belle Meade Plantation. 5025 Harding Rd. ☎ 615/353-2828. See p. 86.

4 Belle Meade Plantation ⭐⭐

After lunch, take a tour of this elegant Greek Revival home built in 1853 on 30 tree-shaded acres. After you've traipsed through the antiques-laden formal house, saunter the grounds of this former horse farm to find the log cabin, creamery, and carriage house. See p. 100.

5 Cheekwood Botanical Garden & Museum of Art ⭐⭐

Drive almost to the outskirts of town to find this mansionlike museum set amidst a lush, 55-acre park with walking trails, landscaped gardens, and outstanding collections of American art and decorative furnishings from around the world. See p. 103.

6 Opry Mills

It's back to the Opryland area to get in a bit of shopping before tonight's performance. Check out the great factory outlet bargains while browsing for Music City trinkets or Tennessee Titans football souvenirs. See p. 120.

7 RAINFOREST CAFE ★★★

Have dinner with the monkeys, elephants, and tropical birds that spring to life at the Rainforest Cafe. Sure, it's kitschy and staged, yet somehow the Disney-esque mood of this place fits right in with all the other commercial excesses of Opryland. 353 Opry Mills Dr. ✆ 615/514-3000. See p. 88.

8 Grand Ole Opry ★★★

This is the ultimate for country music fans. Be prepared for a patriotic, toe-tappin' time and plenty of corny jokes. It's all part of the tradition here, where big-name acts share the stage with fading stars of yesteryear and new up-and-coming talents. See p. 126.

3 The Best of Nashville in 3 Days

You could spend another day in Nashville, but if your trip will take you to Memphis as well, follow these suggestions to get the most out of the Music Highway that links these two great Tennessee cities. Heading west to Memphis from Nashville, take a breather from the interstate at Hurricane Mills (I-40, exit 143). Drive a few miles deep into the wooded countryside, where you can sightsee and even spend the night at Loretta Lynn's Ranch and Family Campground. *Start: Leaving Nashville on I-40.*

1 Loretta Lynn's Ranch and Family Campground

The poor Coal Miner's Daughter bought this Graceland-esque mansion, an hour's drive from Nashville, when she made it big as the Queen of Country Music. Guests may tour her plantation home and the new 18,000-sq.-ft. Coal Miner's Daughter Museum, which are nestled on a leafy stream within her picturesque 3,500-acre farm. There's even a log-cabin replica of her Butcher Holler home place in Eastern Kentucky.

Before you get back onto the main highway, stop at Loretta's Country Kitchen and Gift Shop for a down-home buffet of fried chicken, mashed potatoes, biscuits, and all the trimmings. For more information, or to make campground reservations, call ✆ **931/296-7700; www. lorettalynn.com**.

2 Rockabilly Hall of Fame

An hour east of Memphis, you can stop by Carl Perkins's old hometown of Jackson, Tennessee. The rockabilly pioneer ("Blue Suede Shoes") died in 1998, but his memory lives on at the fledgling Rockabilly

Hall of Fame in the historic downtown district. In addition to the expected Sun Records memorabilia, including costumes, vinyl 78 records, photos, and instruments, a few eye-popping oddities are on display: the "paddles" from the defibrillator that supposedly shocked a dying Elvis at a Memphis hospital, and a wall of fame devoted to 8×10 glossies and newspaper clippings of game-show host Wink Martindale, who hails from these parts. For details, contact the Jackson/Madison County Convention and Visitors Bureau (✆ **800/498-4748**).

3 Casey Jones Village

While you're in Jackson, tour the train museum and sip a root beer float at Casey Jones Village (✆ **800/748-9588**), an old-time country store and soda fountain named for the legendary turn-of-the-20th-century railroad conductor who lost his life rescuing others in a fiery train wreck. Let the kids blow off some steam (so to speak) by climbing aboard a real locomotive. Then hop back in the car, hit the interstate, and go west another hour to reach Memphis.

4

Getting to Know Music City

Getting your bearings in a new city is often the hardest part of taking a trip, but in the following pages you'll find everything you need to know to get settled in after you arrive in town. This is the sort of nuts-and-bolts information that will help you familiarize yourself with Nashville.

1 Nashville Orientation

VISITOR INFORMATION

On the baggage-claim level of Nashville International Airport, you'll find the **Airport Welcome Center** (© **615/275-1675**), where you can pick up brochures, maps, and bus information, and get answers to any questions you may have about touring the city. This center is open daily from 6:30am to midnight. In downtown Nashville, you'll find the **Nashville Convention & Visitors Bureau Visitors Center,** Fifth Avenue and Broadway (© **800/657-6910** or 615/259-4700), the main source of information on the city and surrounding areas. The information center is located at the base of the radio tower of the Sommet Center and is open daily during daylight hours. Signs on interstate highways around the downtown area will direct you to the arena. Information is also available from the main office of the **Chamber of Commerce/Nashville Convention & Visitors Bureau,** in the lower level of the US Bank building at the corner of Fourth Avenue North and Commerce (© **615/259-4700**). The office is open Monday to Friday 8am to 5pm.

For information on the state of Tennessee, contact the **Tennessee Department of Tourism Development,** P.O. Box 23170, Nashville, TN 37202 (© **615/741-2158**).

CITY LAYOUT

Nashville was built on a bend in the Cumberland River; this and other bends in the river have defined the city's expansion over the years. The area referred to as **downtown** is located on the west side of the Cumberland and is built in a grid pattern. Numbered avenues run parallel to the river on a northwest-southeast axis. Streets perpendicular to the river are named. Though the grid pattern is interrupted by I-40, it remains fairly regular until you get to Vanderbilt University in the **West End** area.

Fun Fact **The King**

Elvis Presley may be more closely identified with Memphis than Nashville, but the King did, indeed, make his mark on the Music City. Elvis recorded more than 200 of his songs, including Christmas carols, at RCA's historic Studio B on Music Row.

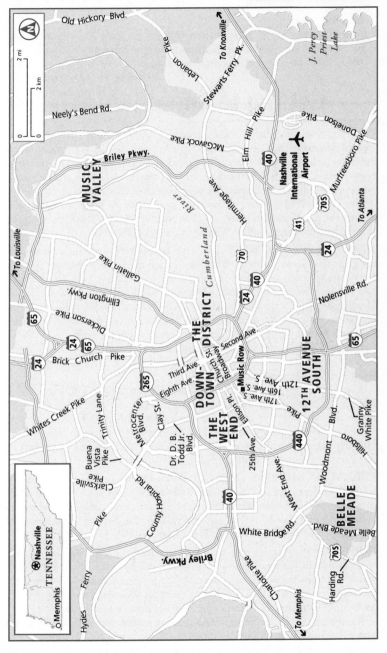

Impressions

Take of London fog 30 parts; malaria 10 parts; gas leaks 20 parts; dewdrops gathered in a brickyard at sunrise 25 parts; odor of honeysuckle 15 parts. Mix. The mixture will give you an approximate conception of a Nashville drizzle.

—O. Henry, "A Municipal Report,"
in *Strictly Business*, 1910

For the most part, Nashville is a sprawling modern city. Though there are some areas of downtown that are frequented by pedestrians, the city is primarily oriented toward automobiles. With fairly rapid growth in recent years, the city's streets and highways have been approaching their carrying capacity, and rush hours see plenty of long backups all around the city. The most important things to watch out for when driving around Nashville are the numerous divisions of the interstate highways that encircle the city. If you don't pay very close attention to which lane you're supposed to be in, you can easily wind up heading in the wrong direction.

MAIN ARTERIES & STREETS   The main arteries in Nashville radiate from downtown like spokes on a wheel. **Broadway** is the main artery through downtown Nashville and leads southwest from the river. Just after crossing I-40, Broadway forks, with the right fork becoming **West End Avenue.** West End Avenue eventually becomes **Harding Road** out in the Belle Meade area. If you stay on Broadway (the left fork), the road curves around to the south, becoming **21st Avenue** and then **Hillsboro Pike**.

Eighth Avenue is downtown's other main artery and runs roughly north-south. To the north, Eighth Avenue becomes **MetroCenter Boulevard;** to the south, it forks, with the right fork becoming **Franklin Pike** and the left fork becoming **Lafayette Road** and then **Murfreesboro Pike.**

There are also several roads that you should become familiar with out in the suburbs. **Briley Parkway** describes a large loop that begins just south of the airport, runs up the east side of the city through the area known as Music Valley, and then curves around to the west, passing well north of downtown. On the south side of the city, **Harding Place** connects I-24 on the east with Belle Meade on the west. Don't confuse Harding Place with Harding Road.

FINDING AN ADDRESS   Nashville's address-numbering system begins in downtown at Broadway and the Cumberland River and increases as you move away from this point. In the downtown area, and out as far as there are numbered avenues, avenues include either a north or south designation. The dividing line between north and south is the Broadway and West End Avenue corridor.

STREET MAPS   You can get a map of the city from the **Nashville Convention & Visitors Bureau Visitors Center,** Fifth Avenue and Broadway (℗ 615/259-4700), which is located below the radio tower of the Sommet Center. Maps can also be obtained in many hotel lobbies and at the **Airport Welcome Center** (℗ 615/275-1675) on the baggage-claim level at the Nashville International Airport.

If you happen to be a member of **AAA,** you can get free maps of Nashville and Tennessee from your local AAA office or from the Nashville office at 2501 Hillsboro Rd., Suite 1 (℗ 615/297-7700). They're open Monday to Friday 8:30am to 5:30pm and Saturday 9am to 1pm.

THE NEIGHBORHOODS IN BRIEF

While there are plenty of neighborhoods throughout the city, few are of real interest to most visitors. There are, however, named areas of the city that you'll want to be familiar with. There are also several outlying bedroom communities that may be of interest.

Downtown With the state capitol, the Tennessee State Museum, the Tennessee Center for the Performing Arts, the Tennessee Convention Center, and the Ryman Auditorium, downtown Nashville is a surprisingly vibrant area for a small Southern city. However, this is still almost exclusively a business and government district, and after dark the streets empty out, with the exception of the area known as The District.

The District With restored buildings housing interesting shops, tourist restaurants, nightclubs, and bars, this downtown historic district (along Second Ave. and Broadway) is the center of Nashville's nightlife scene. With each passing year, it becomes a livelier spot; pickup trucks and limousines jockey for space at night along Second Avenue. On Friday and Saturday nights, the sidewalks are packed with partiers who roam from dive bar to retro-disco to line-dance hootenanny.

The Gulch Just south of downtown lies this once-abandoned industrial area that's become the hottest real estate in town. Old warehouses are being razed and revamped, and gleaming high-rise condos and lofts are being developed, as upscale new hotels, restaurants, and clubs compete for space here.

Eighth Avenue South Just south of downtown and The Gulch, Eighth Avenue is an emerging district lined with antiques shops, corner cafes, and family-friendly eateries. If you're into leisurely bargain-shopping or are on a hunt for a one-of-a-kind antique, this no-frills, non-touristy area is great for browsing.

12th Avenue South What would have been unthinkable only a few years ago has come to pass. A once-blighted area south of downtown and The Gulch is enjoying a renaissance. Idealists, entrepreneurs, and young adults with dreams have been buying up and restoring old houses to set up shop. As a result, an interesting, off-the-beaten-path array of quirky boutiques and happening restaurants and night spots now dot the area roughly bordered by Linden and Kirkwood avenues.

Music Row Recording studios and record companies make this neighborhood, located around the corner of 16th Avenue South and Demonbreun Street (pronounced "De-*mon*-bree-in"), the center of the country music recording industry. The old Country Music Hall of Fame and Museum moved out of this neighborhood in the spring of 2001, leaving many of the country music souvenir shops vacant. However, if driving down the tree-lined boulevards to see stately homes converted into the offices of country music publishers, public relations agents, and the occasional gated recording studio excites you, by all means take a spin through the neighborhood.

Did You Know?

Nashville has the largest U.S. population of Kurds. With 8,000 ex-patriots living in Music City, it has earned the nickname "Little Kurdistan."

(Fun Fact **Nashville on the Rise**

What's with all the construction in downtown Nashville? For the past few years, the area has been awash in ambitious new construction projects. Music City USA may be rooted in pure country, but big-budget backers hope to attract affluent, hip city-slickers to live and work downtown.

Among the new developments slated to open in 2008:

• The Encore, an $80-million residential and retail high-rise at Third Avenue and Demonbreun

• The Pinnacle, a $110-million, 29-story residential building between Second and Third avenues

• Rolling Mill Hill, a five-building residential complex on First Avenue, just south of Broadway

---

The West End While tourists and barflies congregate in The District, the moneymakers and musicians of the Nashville scene gather in the West End, referred to by locals as the intellectual side of town. Located adjacent to Vanderbilt and Belmont universities, this upscale neighborhood is home to many small shops, lots of excellent (and often expensive) restaurants, and several hotels. Also known as **Hillsboro Village,** the area has a lively late-night dining scene fueled by the college crowd and well-heeled locals looking to see and to be seen. At the edge of the West End is the affluent **Belle Meade** community. Mansions abound in Belle Meade, and country stars own many of them. Two such historic mansions— Belle Meade Plantation and Cheekwood—are open to the public.

East Nashville Across the Cumberland River from downtown Nashville is this laid-back neighborhood of affordable restaurants, bars, coffeeshops and funky boutiques. Many homes in the area, which date back to the early 1900s, are being preserved and renovated by young families attracted to the area.

Music Valley This area on the east side of Nashville is where you'll find the Opryland Hotel, the Grand Ole Opry House, Opry Mills shopping center, and numerous other country-themed tourist attractions. There are very few decent restaurants in the area (except within Opry Mills and the Opryland Hotel itself).

Green Hills, South Nashville and Berry Hill Upscale shopping, trendy restaurants, affluent residential areas, and shiny new SUVs help define the suburban enclave of Green Hills. Among Nashvillians, Green Hills is considered to be a lively, happening neighborhood. Tourists might visit the vast Green Hills Mall that anchors the area.

---

2 Getting Around Nashville

BY PUBLIC TRANSPORTATION

BY BUS Although Nashville is served by the extensive and efficient **Metropolitan Transit Authority (MTA)** bus system, it is generally not practical for tourists. Call the Customer Service Center (© **615/862-5950**), which is open Monday to Friday 6:30am until 6pm. The MTA information center and ticket booth, located on Deaderick Street at Fifth Avenue, is open Monday to Friday 6:30am to 6:30pm and on Saturday 8am to 1pm. MTA bus stops are marked with blue-and-white signs; in the downtown area, signs include names and numbers of all the routes using that stop. All express buses are marked with an X following the route number.

Adult **bus fares** are $1.25 ($1.75 for express buses); children under 4 ride free. Exact change is required. You can purchase a weekly pass good for unlimited local rides from Sunday to Saturday for $17 per adult or $10 per youth age 19 and under; a picture ID is required. Seniors and riders with disabilities qualify for a 60¢ fare with an MTA Golden Age, Medicare, Tennesenior, or Special Service card. Call ℂ **615/ 862-5950** to register for this discount.

BY TROLLEY   For a quick way to get around downtown during weekdays, look for the LunchLINE shuttles. As a convenience to downtown workers, the Central Business Improvement District and Nashville Downtown Partnership offers a free trolley that loops through the heart of downtown weekdays from 11am to 1:30pm. Riders may hop on or off at any of the 15 stops. No tickets are required. Just look for the yellow LunchLINE signs.

The **downtown route** passes by many points of interest in downtown Nashville and is a good way to get acquainted with the city. For more information, look at this website: www.nashvilledowntown.com.

BY CAR

Because the city and its many attractions are quite spread out, the best way to get around Nashville is by car. It's surprisingly easy to find your way around the city and to find parking, even downtown. But bring plenty of cash. Parking can cost a few coins in the meter or upwards of $15 during special events. For helpful information, check out this website: www.parkitdowntown.com. The only time driving is a problem is during morning and evening rush hours. At these times, streets leading south and west out of downtown can get quite congested.

RENTAL CARS

All the major rental-car companies and several independent ones have offices in Nashville. Fortunately, most of the companies have desks conveniently located on the lower level at the Nashville International Airport. Major car-rental companies in Nashville include **Alamo Rent-A-Car,** at the airport (ℂ 800/327-9633 or 615/340-6546); **Avis Rent-A-Car,** at the airport (ℂ 800/831-2847 or 615/361-1212); **Budget Rent-A-Car,** at 1816 Church St., 1525 N. Gallatin Pike, and the airport (ℂ 800/ 763-2999 or 615/366-0822); **Dollar Rent-A-Car,** at the airport (ℂ 800/800-4000 or 615/367-0503); **Enterprise Rent-a-Car,** at the airport (ℂ 800/325-8007 or 615/ 275-0011); **Hertz,** at the airport (ℂ 800/654-3131 or 615/361-3131); **National Car Rental,** at the airport (ℂ 800/227-7368 or 615/361-7467); and **Thrifty Car Rental,**

⌐Fun Fact **Sand-Castle Nirvana**

Not only does Nashville Shores boast what it dubs the world's largest free-style slide—it's four stories (170 feet) high—but the outdoor recreation attraction also boasts an 8,000-square-foot, beach-style sandbox. The critical issue of sand wetness is constantly monitored, ensuring the best possible texture and consistency for building sand castles.

1201 Briley Pkwy. at Vultee Boulevard, and at the airport (© 800/367-2277 or 615/361-6050).

PARKING

In downtown Nashville, there are a variety of parking lots, ranging from $6 to more than $10 per day. Drop your money into the self-service machine at the end of the parking lot. Downtown parking is also available in other municipal and private lots and parking garages.

When parking on the street, be sure to check the time limit on parking meters. Also be sure to check whether you can park in a parking space during rush hour (4–5:30pm) or your car may be ticketed and towed. On-street parking meters are free after 6pm on weekdays, after noon on Saturday, and all day Sunday. For more information, check out www.parkitdowntown.com.

DRIVING RULES

A right turn at a red light is permitted after coming to a full stop, unless posted otherwise, but drivers must first yield to vehicles that have a green light or pedestrians in the walkway. Children under 4 years of age must be in children's car seats or other approved restraints when in the car.

Tennessee has a very strict DUI (driving under the influence of alcohol) law, and has a law that states a person driving under the influence with a child under 12 years of age in the vehicle may be charged with a felony.

BY TAXI

For quick cab service, call **American Music City Taxi** (© **615/262-0451**), **Checker Cab** (© **615/256-7000**), or **Allied and Nashville Cab** (© **615/244-7433**). The flag-drop rate is $3; after that it's $2 per mile, plus $1 for each additional passenger.

ON FOOT

Downtown Nashville is the only area where you're likely to do much walking around. In this area, you can visit numerous attractions, do some shopping, have a good meal, and go to a club, all without having to get in your car. The suburban strips can't make that claim.

FAST FACTS: **Nashville**

Airport See "Getting There," in chapter 2.

American Express In the airport area, the American Express Travel Service office is at 402 BNA Dr., Building 100, Suite 303 (© **800/528-4800** or 615/367-4900), and is open Monday to Friday 8:30am to 5pm.

Area Code The telephone area code in Nashville is **615**.

Business Hours Banks are generally open Monday to Thursday 9am to 4pm, Friday 9am to 5 or 6pm, and Saturday morning. Office hours in Nashville are usually Monday to Friday 8:30am to 5pm. In general, stores in downtown Nashville are open Monday to Saturday 10am to 6pm. Shops in suburban Nashville malls are generally open Monday to Saturday 10am to 9pm and Sunday 1 to 6pm. Bars in Nashville are frequently open all day long and are allowed to stay open daily until 3am, but might close between 1 and 3am.

Camera Repair Because camera repairs usually take several weeks, your best bet is to take your camera home with you. You can buy a few disposable cameras so you at least have some photos of your trip to Nashville.

Car Rentals See "Getting Around Nashville," earlier in this chapter.

Climate See "When to Go" in chapter 2.

Dentists If you should need a dentist while you're in Nashville, contact **Dental Referral Service** (① 800/243-4444).

Doctors If you need a doctor, call **Medline** (① 615/342-1919), available Monday to Friday 6:30am to 5pm; or contact the **Vanderbilt Medical Group Physician Referral Service** (① 615/322-3000) or **Columbia Medline** (① 800/265-8624).

Drugstores See "Pharmacies," below.

Emergencies Phone ① **911** for fire, police, emergency, or ambulance. If you get into desperate straits, call **Travelers' Aid** of the Nashville Union Mission, 639 Lafayette St. (① 615/255-2475). It's primarily a mission that helps destitute people, but if you need help in making phone calls or getting home, they might be able to help.

Eyeglass Repair If you have problems with your glasses, call **Horner Rausch,** which has 1-hour service. They have several locations. One is downtown at 968 Main St. (① 615/226-0251), and is open weekdays 9am to 6pm and Saturdays from 9am to 3pm. Another option is Eyeglasses Plus, 2135 N. Gallatin Rd. near Rivergate Mall (① 615/859-7888), where hours are Monday to Friday 9am to 5:45pm and Saturday 8am to 2:45pm.

Hospitals The following hospitals offer emergency medical treatment: **St. Thomas Hospital,** 4220 Harding Rd. (① 615/222-2111), and **Vanderbilt University Medical Center,** 1211 22nd Ave. S., in the downtown/Vanderbilt area (① 615/322-5000).

Hotlines The **Suicide Crisis Intervention** hotline number is ① 615/244-7444.

Information See "Visitor Information," earlier in this chapter.

Libraries The new **Main Library of Nashville and Davidson County** is at 615 Church St. (① 615/862-5800). It's open Monday to Thursday 9am to 8pm, Friday 9am to 6pm, Saturday 9am to 5pm, and Sunday 2 to 5pm.

Liquor Laws The legal drinking age in Tennessee is 21. Bars are allowed to stay open until 3am every day. Beer can be purchased at drug, grocery, or package stores, but wine and liquor are sold through package stores only.

Lost Property If you left something at the airport, call the **Airport Authority** at ① 615/275-1675; if you left something on an **MTA** bus, call ① 615/862-5969.

Luggage Storage/Lockers Hotels will usually store your bags for several hours or sometimes even several days. There is also a luggage-storage facility at the Greyhound Lines bus station at 200 Eighth Ave. S., although these are ostensibly for Greyhound passengers only. Call ① 615/255-6719.

Maps See "City Layout," earlier in this chapter.

Newspapers/Magazines The *Tennessean* is Nashville's morning daily and Sunday newspaper. The alternative weekly is the *Nashville Scene.*

Pharmacies (late-night) The following **Walgreens** pharmacies are open 24 hours a day: 518 Donelson Pike (© 615/883-5108); 5600 Charlotte Pike (© 615/356-5161); 3901 Hillsboro Pike (© 615/298-5340); 627 Gallatin Rd. (© 615/865-0010); or call © 800/925-4733 for the Walgreens nearest you.

Police For police emergencies, phone © **911.**

Post Office The post office located at 901 Broadway (© 800/275-8777) is convenient to downtown and the West End and will accept mail addressed to General Delivery. It's open Monday to Friday 8am to 5pm and on Saturday 8am to 2pm. There's also a post office in the downtown arcade at 16 Arcade (© 615/248-2287), which is open Monday to Friday 8:30am to 5pm.

Radio Nashville has more than 30 AM and FM radio stations. Some specialize in a particular style of music, including gospel, soul, big band, and jazz. Of course, there are several country music stations, including WSM (650 AM and 95.5 FM), the station that first broadcast the *Grand Ole Opry,* and the popular WSIX (97.9 FM). WPLN (90.3 FM) is Nashville's National Public Radio station, and WAY-FM (88.7 FM) plays contemporary Christian music. For eclectic college radio, tune to Vanderbilt University's WRVU (91.1 FM).

Restrooms Public restrooms can be found at the parking lot on First Avenue South in downtown Nashville and also at hotels, restaurants, and shopping malls.

Safety Even though Nashville is not a huge city, it has its share of crime. Take extra precaution with your wallet or purse when you're in a crush of people (such as a weekend night in The District)—pickpockets take advantage of crowds. Whenever possible at night, try to park your car in a garage, not on the street. When walking around town at night, stick to the busier streets of The District. The lower Broadway area, though popular with visitors, also attracts a rather unruly crowd to its many bars. See also "Safety," in Appendix A, "For International Visitors."

Taxes In Davidson County Tennessee, the combined state and local sales tax is 9.25%. This tax applies to goods as well as all recreation, entertainment, and amusements. However, in the case of services, the tax is often already included in the admission price or cost of a ticket. The Nashville hotel and motel room tax is 5%, which when added to the 9.25% makes for a total hotel room tax of 15.25% plus $2 city tax, per night. Car-rental taxes total 13.25%.

Taxis See "Getting Around Nashville," earlier in this chapter.

Television Local television channels include 2 (ABC), 4 (NBC), 5 (CBS), 8 (PBS), 17 (FOX), 30 (UPN), 39 (independent), and 58 (WB).

Time Zone Tennessee is in the central time zone—Central Standard Time (CST) or Central Daylight Time, depending on the time of year—making it 2 hours ahead of the West Coast and 1 hour behind the East Coast.

Transit Info Call © 615/862-5950 for information on the MTA bus system or trolleys.

Weather For the local forecast, call the **National Weather Service** (© 615/754-4633)

5

Where to Stay in Nashville

Nashville caters to tens of thousands of country music fans each year and so has an abundance of inexpensive and moderately priced hotels. Although prices have risen in recent years to match Nashville's rise as a tourist and convention destination, whatever your reason for being in Nashville, you'll likely find a hotel that's both convenient and fits your budget. If you're used to exorbitant downtown hotels, you'll be pleasantly surprised to learn that rooms in downtown Nashville are, for the most part, reasonably priced, although that is rapidly changing. With the frenzied construction of swank condo and loft complexes around every corner, downtown is being transformed into a more chic city center with ever-escalating prices for everything from hotel rooms to parking. Beyond downtown, new and moderately priced hotel chains have been mushrooming in the airport area along Elm Hill Pike, easily reached by heading east out of the city on I-40. If you want to be close to the city's best restaurants and wealthiest neighborhoods, book a room in a West End hotel.

Long gone are the days when you could easily nab a decent hotel room for under $100. Nashville is growing in popularity, and prices reflect that demand. When big events such as music festivals and conventions bring lots of tourists to the city, rates spike and rooms can be sold out all over town—even at otherwise more moderately priced chain properties in the Opryland and airport areas.

If you do want to splurge, consider a luxury hotel such as the Hermitage or Loews. However, for sheer visual impact, you can't beat the massive Opryland Hotel, which is shedding some of its Southern, Bible-belt clichés to appeal to more sophisticated tastes. A night here in a basic room will run you about $250 on average.

The rates quoted below are, for the most part, the published rates, sometimes called "rack rates" in hotel-industry jargon. At expensive business and resort hotels, rack rates are what you are most likely to be quoted if you walk in off the street and ask what a room will cost for that night. However, it's often not necessary to pay this high rate if you plan ahead or ask for a discount. It's often possible to get low corporate rates even if you aren't visiting on business. Many hotel and motel chains now have frequent-guest and other special programs that you can join. These programs often provide savings off the regular rates.

Virtually all hotels now offer non-smoking rooms (many properties are now entirely smoke-free) and rooms equipped for guests with disabilities. When making a reservation, be sure to request the type of room you need. While multi-line telephones are often the norm, charges for telephone calls vary widely. Some offer free local calls, while others do not. Many hotels have electronic in-room amenities such as flatscreen TVs, high-speed (often wireless) Internet access, and

Web-browser TV screens. Internet fees range from free access to about $12 per day. Increasingly, hotels have public computers in the their lobbies—a nice perk if you don't travel with a laptop but want to check your e-mail from time to time.

If you'll be traveling with children, always check into policies on children staying for free. Some hotels let children under 12 stay free, while others set the cutoff age at 18. Still others charge you for the kids, but let them eat for free in the hotel's restaurant.

The rates quoted here don't include the Tennessee sales tax (9.25%) or the Nashville room tax (5%), which together will add 14.25% onto your room bill. Keep this in mind if you're on a tight budget. And if you're driving to Nashville, don't overlook the cost of parking your car, which can cost up to $20 a night at downtown hotels. I have used the following rate definitions for price categories in this chapter (rates are for double rooms): **very expensive,** more than $175; **expensive,** $125 to $175; **moderate,** $75 to $125; **inexpensive,** under $75.

1 The Best Hotel Bets

- **Best Place to Splurge with Your Pet:** Not only is the posh **Hermitage,** 231 6th Ave. N. (© **888/888-9414** or 615/244-3121), one of the classiest and most romantic hotels in Tennessee, it also will accept—and even pamper—your pet. See below.
- **Best for Business Travelers:** Not only does the **Nashville Airport Marriott,** 600 Marriott Dr. (© **800/228-9290** or 615/889-9300), have rooms designed specifically with business travelers in mind, but it also has plenty of athletic facilities to help those same travelers unwind. Perhaps best of all, it's close to the airport and easy to find. See p. 67.
- **Best for Families:** With an indoor pool, a game room, and a tropical atrium complete with a stream running through it, the **Embassy Suites Nashville,** 10 Century Blvd. (© **800/362-2779** or 615/871-0033), is a good place to bring the kids. Parents might also appreciate having a bedroom (and a TV) all to themselves. The free buffet breakfast and in-room refrigerators also help cut expenses. See p. 67.
- **Most Like a Cruise Ship:** With the *Grand Ole Opry* and numerous theaters showcasing live country music nearby, an endless array of restaurants, bars, shops, and a world-class spa, the gargantuan **Opryland Hotel,** 2800 Opryland Dr. (© **888/777-OPRY** or 615/889-1000), is a cocoon of comfort and entertainment. See p. 64.

2 Downtown

VERY EXPENSIVE

The Hermitage Hotel ★★★ *Moments*   This historic downtown hotel, built in 1910 in the classic Beaux Arts style, is Nashville's grand hotel. Still fresh from an $18-million restoration, this is the city's top choice if you crave both space and elegance. The lobby, with its marble columns, gilded plasterwork, and stained-glass ceiling, is the most magnificent in the city. Afternoon tea is served here Thursday through Saturday. Guest rooms (all of which are suites) are recently upgraded, spacious, and comfortable, with down-filled duvets and pillows on the beds. All rooms feature large windows and marble-floored bathrooms with double vanities. Ask the staff to draw you a warm bath with a sprinkling of rose petals. North-side rooms have good views of the capitol.

Down in the lower level you'll find the Capitol Grille, which, with its vaulted ceiling, has the feel of a wine cellar. Also in the basement is a dark and woody lounge with an ornate plasterwork ceiling. Every floor has rooms for those with limited mobility.

231 6th Ave. N., Nashville, TN 37219. ⓒ **888/888-9414** or 615/244-3121. Fax 615/254-6909. www.thehermitage hotel.com. 123 suites. $299–$399 suite, $950 and up for 2-bedroom suites. AE, DC, DISC, MC, V. Valet parking $18 plus tax. Pets allowed ($25 daily fee). **Amenities:** Restaurant and lounge; 24-hr. concierge and room service; massage; babysitting; dry cleaning. *In room:* A/C, TV w/pay movies, dataport w/high-speed Internet access and Wi-Fi, hair dryer, iron, umbrella, DVD-CD player, rooms for those w/limited mobility.

Hilton Downtown Nashville 𝕽𝕽 One of Nashville's newest hotels boasts a bustling downtown location, with a palm-lined and Wi-Fi-equipped atrium lobby. Booking a room here is a good bet if you plan to spend time at LP Field (where the Tennessee Titans play) or the Country Music Hall of Fame and Museum, both of which are within short walking distance of the Hilton. Each suite comes equipped with a pullout sofa couch, two TVs, in-room movies and video games, microwave, refrigerator, coffeemaker, and more, making the Hilton a comfy-but-sophisticated place to hang your hat while in Music City. Suites include pillowtop mattresses, Egyptian cotton sheets, and curved shower curtains.

121 Fourth Ave. S., Nashville, TN 37201. ⓒ **800/HILTONS** or 615/620-1000. Fax 615/620-2050. www.nashvillehilton. com. 330 suites. $219–$459 double. AE, DC, DISC, MC, V. Valet parking $20. **Amenities:** 3 restaurants; 2 lounges; indoor pool; fitness center; car-rental desk; business center; laundry service; valet. *In room:* A/C, TV w/pay movies, dataport w/high-speed Internet access, fridge, coffeemaker, microwave.

EXPENSIVE

Courtyard Nashville Downtown 𝕽 This clean, inviting, and all non-smoking hotel is within easy walking distance to The Ryman and other downtown attractions, yet far enough away from the rowdy night-life of Broadway to offer a more peaceful environment. Rooms and public spaces are done in cheerful bright blues and pale yellows. The staff goes out of its way to offer friendly service. All guest rooms have new bedding, free high-speed Internet access, spacious work desks and task chairs, and multi-line telephones.

170 Fourth Ave. N. Nashville, TN 37219. ⓒ **888/687-9377** or 615/256-0900. Fax 615/256-0901. www.nashville hilton.com. 192 units, including 11 suites. $169–$209 double; $224 and up for suites. AE, DC, DISC, MC, V. Valet parking $20. (No self-parking.) **Amenities:** Restaurant. *In room:* A/C, TV w/pay movies, dataport w/high-speed Internet access, fridge, coffeemaker, microwave, hair dryer, iron.

Doubletree Hotel Nashville 𝕽𝕽 Of the high-rise hotels in downtown Nashville, this is one of the best choices if you're here on vacation. This Hilton property has a less hectic atmosphere than the Renaissance, for example, which is often uncomfortably crowded with conventioneers. Warm, contemporary décor features maple-colored wood paneling and comfy seating with free Wi-Fi in the elegant, second-floor lobby, where there's a full-service Starbucks cafe. Perks include fresh-baked cookies upon your check-in. Located a few blocks from The District, this hotel is also convenient for anyone in town on state government business. The corner rooms, with their sharply angled walls of glass, are the most appealing units in the hotel.

315 Fourth Ave. N., Nashville, TN 37219-1693. ⓒ **800/222-TREE** or 615/244-8200. Fax 615/747-4894. www. nashvilledoubletree.com. 337 units, including six suites. $129–$235 double; $299–$599 suite. AE, DC, DISC, MC, V. Valet parking $20. **Amenities:** Restaurant; lounge; indoor pool; exercise room; concierge; business center; room service; same-day dry cleaning. *In room:* A/C, TV w/pay movies, dataport w/high-speed Internet access, coffeemaker, hair dryer, iron.

Nashville Accommodations: Downtown, Music Row & the West End

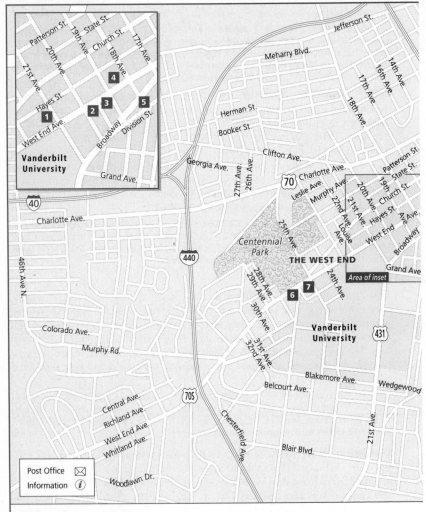

Best Western Music Row Inn **8**
Comfort Inn Downtown Music Row **9**
Courtyard by Marriott **2**
Courtyard Nashville Downtown **13**
Days Inn Vanderbilt Music Row **4**
Doubletree Hotel Nashville **12**
Embassy Suites Hotel **5**
Hampton Inn & Suites Downtown **17**
Hampton Inn Vanderbilt **3**

The Hermitage Hotel **11**
Hilton Nashville Downtown **16**
Holiday Inn Express **15**
Holiday Inn Select Vanderbilt **6**
Loews Vanderbilt Plaza Hotel **1**
Nashville Marriott at Vanderbilt **7**
Renaissance Hotel Nashville **14**
Union Station–A Wyndham Historic Hotel **10**

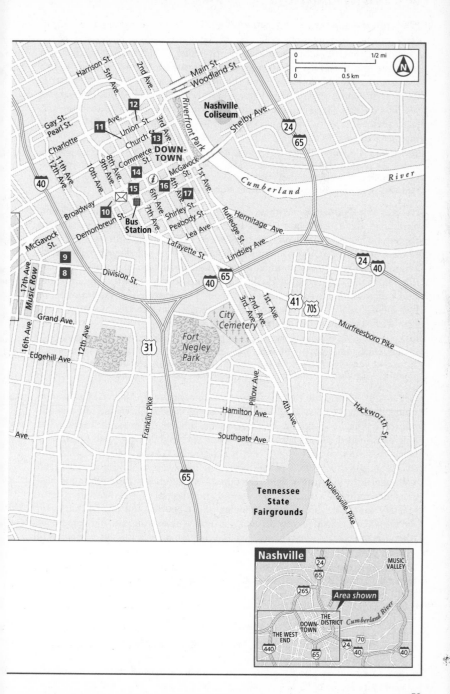

Hampton Inn and Suites Downtown ★★   Newly constructed in the summer of 2007, this user-friendly property is a bit off the beaten path—a block south of the Country Music Hall of Fame and Museum. Appealing to independent travelers who want convenience and style, the 6-story red brick inn offers relative proximity to area restaurants and clubs downtown and the nearby Gulch. Continental breakfast is served in the open, contemporary lobby, where there's plenty of natural sunlight and free Wi-Fi. Clean, modern rooms are equipped with comfy beds and crisp linens, and large, flatscreen TVs, as well as wet bars with fridges and microwaves. Free in-room Internet access and local calls are other value-added perks.

310 Fourth Ave. S., Nashville, TN 37201. ℂ **800/HAMPTON** or 615/277-5000. Fax 615/564-1700. www.hampton inn.com. 154 units, including 34 suites. $189–$359 double; suites $259 and up. AE, DC, DISC, MC, V. Free self-parking. **Amenities:** Indoor pool and whirlpool; fitness room; coin-operated laundry. *In room:* A/C, TV w/pay movies, dataport w/high-speed Internet access, fridge, coffeemaker, microwave, hair dryer, iron.

Holiday Inn Express ★   With an inviting, spacious lobby and simple yet elegant furnishings, this above-ordinary property offers a slightly less expensive alternative to the historic Union Station Hotel across the street. In fact, rooms with westward views of the Union Station's Gothic beauty are an added plus—and though you'll still be able to see and hear the trains rumbling down the railroad tracks, they're not right outside your window as they are at Union Station. This hotel is across the street from the Frist Center for the Arts and a short hike (about 5 blocks straight down Broadway) to bars and nightclubs in The District. Rooms are bright, clean, and reasonably spacious. Free Wi-Fi and continental breakfast are other amenities.

920 Broadway, Nashville, TN 37203. ℂ **800/258-2466** or 615/244-0150. Fax 615/244-0445. www.holiday-inn.com. 287 units, including 14 suites. $149–$179 double; $244–$299 suite. AE, DISC, MC, V. Self-parking $14. **Amenities:** Outdoor pool; exercise room; business center. *In room:* A/C, TV, dataport w/high-speed Internet access, fridges and microwaves in suites and in all rooms on the sixth and seventh floors, coffeemaker, hair dryer, iron.

Renaissance Nashville Hotel   Because it's connected to the Nashville Convention Center, this large, modern hotel is usually filled with conventioneers and consequently can feel crowded and chaotic. However, it does offer all the expected luxuries. The king rooms (especially the corner kings, which have slightly larger bathrooms) are a better choice than rooms with two beds, which are a bit cramped. However, whichever style room you choose, you'll at least have a comfortable chair in which to relax, and walls of glass let in plenty of light. The upper floors (24th and 25th) offer additional amenities, including a concierge, private lounge, bathrobes, express checkout, complimentary continental breakfast and evening hors d'oeuvres, and evening turndown service. There's a Starbucks in the lobby, as well as several lounges and restaurants. Although the hotel is nonsmoking, you'll likely have to walk through a gauntlet of smokers once you step outside the front lobby.

611 Commerce St., Nashville, TN 37203. ℂ **800/327-6618** or 615/255-8400. Fax 615/255-8202. www.renaissance hotels.com. 673 units. $169–$229 double; $300–$500 suite. AE, DC, DISC, MC, V. Valet parking $23; self-parking $6.

⌜Tips⌝ Boots Made for Walking

If you're staying at the Opryland Hotel, comfortable walking shoes are a must. Even if you opt for the valet parking, the distances between drop-off points and your room can be daunting. Each member of the bell staff at Opryland walks an average of 12 miles a day.

> ### (Kids) Family-Friendly Hotels
>
> **Guest House International Inn and Suites, Music Valley** (p. 66)   With an indoor pool and a garden atrium, there is plenty to keep the kids distracted here. The two-room suites also provide kitchenettes and lots of space.
>
> **Hyatt Place Opryland** (p. 66)   Teens and tweens can appreciate a place with huge, in-room plasma TVs with plug-and-play capability. This completely refurbished property also offers spacious rooms with beds as well as comfy leather ottomans and pull-out sofas so the family can spread out.
>
> **Opryland Hotel** (p. 64)   The kids can wander all over this huge hotel's three tropical atriums, exploring waterfalls, hidden gardens, fountains, whatever, and then head for one of the pools. There are also enough restaurants under this one roof (the property encompasses nine under glass) to keep everyone in the family happy.

Amenities: 2 restaurants; 2 bars; indoor pool; exercise room; indoor whirlpool; sauna; concierge; business center; sundries shop; 24-hr. room service; massage; valet; laundry service; sundeck. *In room:* A/C, TV w/pay movies, dataport w/high-speed Internet access, coffeemaker, hair dryer, iron.

Union Station: A Wyndham Historic Hotel ✿ (Moments)   Housed in the Romanesque Gothic former Union Station railway terminal, built in 1900, this hotel is a grandly restored National Historic Landmark. Following a $10-million renovation completed in 2007, all guest rooms and public spaces have been updated. The lobby is the former main hall of the railway station and has a vaulted ceiling of Tiffany stained glass. In contrast to the historic atmosphere, décor in the public spaces such as the lobby is contemporary. Although guest rooms offer exterior views, some also have the disadvantage of overlooking the railroad tracks, a plus for railroad buffs but perhaps less endearing to those who can't sleep with the clang-and-roar that continues day and night. Take a tip that I learned the hard way: Go ahead and splurge on valet parking, because self-parking is inconvenient and down several flights of outdoor stairs.

1001 Broadway, Nashville, TN 37203. (C) **800/996-3426** or 615/726-1001. Fax 615/248-3554. www.wyndham.com. 125 units. $169–$239 double; $349–$499 suite. AE, DC, DISC, MC, V. Valet parking $20. **Amenities:** Restaurant and lounge; exercise room; business center; limited room service; same-day dry cleaning. *In room:* A/C, TV w/pay movies, dataport w/high-speed Internet access, coffeemaker, hair dryer, iron.

3 Music Row & the West End

For locations of hotels in this section, see the "Nashville Accommodations: Downtown, Music Row & the West End" map on p. 58.

VERY EXPENSIVE

Loews Vanderbilt Plaza Hotel ✿✿✿   This posh high-rise across the street from Vanderbilt University maintains an air of quiet sophistication, which makes it the most luxurious West End hotel. European tapestries and original works of art adorn the travertine-floored lobby. In addition, the hotel houses the upscale Kraus commercial art gallery. The lower guest rooms, with angled walls that slope inward, are among the hotel's most charming, with a wall of curtains lending a romantic coziness. Service is

---

Fun Fact **Nashville Notables**

Music stars Amy Grant and Vince Gill aren't the only celebrities who hang their hats in Nashville. Other superstar locals include Nicole Kidman, Keith Urban, Kid Rock, Reese Witherspoon, Sheryl Crow, Ashley Judd, Jack White, Michael McDonald, Kirk Whalum, and Donna Summer. Among the city's best-known former residents are Oprah Winfrey, Al Gore, and Fred Thompson, former senator turned actor *(Law and Order)* and early 2008 presidential candidate.

---

gracious and attentive. Concierge-level rooms are more spacious and upscale and include complimentary breakfast and evening hors d'oeuvres in an elegant lounge with a view of the city. One level below the lobby, you'll find a Ruth's Chris Steakhouse.

2100 West End Ave., Nashville, TN 37203. ✆ 800/23-LOEWS or 615/320-1700. Fax 615/320-5019. www.loews vanderbilt.com. 340 units. $199–$399 double; $700–$1,800 suite. AE, DC, DISC, MC, V. Valet parking $24; self-parking $19. Pets allowed; no deposit required if paying by credit card, although guests are liable for damage caused by pets. **Amenities:** 2 restaurants; exercise room; spa; concierge; business center; 24-hr. room service; massage; babysitting; valet; laundry service; concierge-level rooms; shoe-shine service. *In room:* A/C, TV and CD player, fax, dataport w/high-speed Internet access, minibar, coffeemaker, hair dryer, iron, safe, umbrella.

EXPENSIVE

Embassy Suites Hotel ★★ *Finds*   In the city's trendy West End/Vanderbilt University district, this property combines gracious service and impeccable decor. A sunny garden atrium features lush plants, cascading waterfalls, and overstuffed furniture arranged in cozy nooks. The spacious, tastefully appointed suites have comfy sleeper sofas, easy chairs, work desks, and lamps. With value-added touches including a generous, cooked-to-order breakfast (included in the room rate) and free shuttle service to downtown and other locales within a 2-mile radius of the hotel, this is a good choice for those who want to feel pampered without paying an arm and a leg. Downstairs is an Omaha Steak House.

1811 Broadway, Nashville, TN 37203. ✆ 800/362-2779 or 615/320-8899. Fax 615/320-8881. www.embassysuites.com. 208 units. $129–$239 double. Rates include cooked-to-order breakfast. AE, DC, DISC, MC, V. Valet parking $17; self-parking $13. **Amenities:** Restaurant; lounge; exercise room; sauna; limited room service; coin-op laundry; same-day dry cleaning. *In room:* A/C, TV w/pay movies, dataport and Wi-Fi, kitchenette (microwave, minibar, and sink), coffeemaker, hair dryer.

Nashville Marriott at Vanderbilt ★★   This rose-colored high-rise hotel rivals the nearby Loews in terms of elegance and sophistication. Upper rooms at the 11-story property offer bird's-eye views of both the Vanderbilt football stadium and the Parthenon in nearby Centennial Park. The location is also ideal for those who want to be in the thick of things. It's within a corner of an upscale shopping complex (P.F. Chang's China Bistro is among the tenants) and close to all the West End action. (The downside is that during peak dinner hours and weekends, the hotel parking lot and garage can become a tangled traffic jam.) Guests visiting here on business will appreciate the spacious rooms, which are decorated in soothing cream colors and include well-lighted work desks and multi-line phones.

2555 West End Ave., Nashville, TN 37203. ✆ 800/228-9290 or 615/321-1300. Fax 615/321-1400. www.marriott. com. 307 units. $149–$359 double; $350–$459 suite. AE, DC, DISC, MC, V. Valet parking $20, plus tax; self-parking $16. **Amenities:** Restaurant; lounge; indoor pool; fitness center; concierge; 24-hr. room service; valet; laundry service. *In room:* A/C, TV w/pay movies, dataport w/high-speed Internet access and Wi-Fi, coffeemaker, hair dryer, iron. Safe-deposit boxes available at front desk.

MODERATE

Courtyard by Marriott ⊛   This seven-story hotel on West End Avenue fills the price and service gap between the Loews Vanderbilt Plaza and the less-expensive motels listed below. Guest rooms are none too large, but those with king beds were conceived with the business traveler in mind. All the rooms have coffeemakers, and the medium-size bathrooms have a moderate amount of counter space. For the most part, what you get here is a good location close to Music Row at prices only slightly higher than those at area motels. A breakfast buffet is available daily (at an additional charge of $6.95 plus tax), and the hotel offers a whirlpool and an exercise room.

1901 West End Ave., Nashville, TN 37203. ⓒ **800/245-1959** or 615/327-9900. Fax 615/327-8127. www.marriott. com. 223 units. $99–$169 double; $199–$239 suite. AE, DC, DISC, MC, V. Valet parking $14, self-parking $12. **Amenities:** Lounge; outdoor pool; exercise room; business center; coin-op laundry; laundry service; same-day dry cleaning. *In room:* A/C, TV, fax, dataport w/high-speed Internet access and Wi-Fi, coffeemaker, hair dryer, iron.

Hampton Inn Vanderbilt *Value*   This reliable chain motel is located just 1 block from Vanderbilt University and 6 blocks from both Music Row and the Parthenon. Open while undergoing a top-to-bottom renovation, this property reportedly ranks as one of the Hampton chain's busiest in the country. Guest rooms are modern and comfortable. You'll find the king rooms particularly spacious. There are quite a few good restaurants within walking distance.

1919 West End Ave., Nashville, TN 37203. ⓒ **800/HAMPTON** or 615/329-1144. Fax 615/320-7112. www.hampton inn.com. 171 units. $119–$189 double. Rates include cooked breakfast. AE, DC, DISC, MC, V. Free parking. **Amenities:** Outdoor pool; exercise room; valet; laundry service; same-day dry cleaning. *In room:* A/C, TV, dataport with free high-speed Internet access and Wi-Fi, coffeemaker, hair dryer, iron.

Holiday Inn Select Vanderbilt   With the Vanderbilt University football stadium right outside this 12-story hotel's back door, it isn't surprising that this is a favorite with Vanderbilt alumni and football fans. However, if you stay here, you're also right across the street from Centennial Park and the Parthenon, making it a good option for families with children. Couples and business travelers will do well to ask for a king room. If you ask for a room on the park side of the hotel, you may be able to see the Parthenon from your room. All the rooms here have small private balconies. Wi-Fi is available in the lobby.

2613 West End Ave., Nashville, TN 37203. ⓒ **800/HOLIDAY** or 615/327-4707. Fax 615/327-8034. www.holiday-inn. com. 300 units. $109–$179 double. AE, DC, DISC, MC, V. Free self-parking. **Amenities:** Restaurant; lounge; outdoor pool; business center; concierge; tour desk; coin-op laundry; laundry service; same-day dry cleaning. *In room:* A/C, TV w/pay movies, dataport and high-speed Internet, coffeemaker, hair dryer, iron.

INEXPENSIVE

Best Western Music Row ⊛   This casual, no-frills motel stays booked most of the time with cost-conscious tourists who appreciate its affordability and easy access to both downtown and Music Row. Bargain-priced rooms are standard, although the suites offer significantly more space for a few extra dollars. Live music is performed nightly (except Sundays) in the lounge.

1407 Division St., Nashville, TN 37203. ⓒ **800/228-5151** or 615/242-1631. Fax 615/244-9519. www.bestwestern. com. 103 units. $70–$130 double. Rates include continental breakfast. Free local calls. AE, DC, DISC, MC, V. Free self-parking. Pets up to 25 pounds $10 per day. **Amenities:** Lounge; outdoor pool. *In room:* A/C, TV, dataport and free Wi-Fi, unstocked fridge, microwave, coffeemaker, hair dryer, iron, safe.

Comfort Inn Downtown–Music Row ⊛   If you want to stay right in the heart of Music Row and near downtown, try this popular motel. In the lobby, you'll find walls covered with dozens of autographed photos of country music stars who have stayed here in years past. The rooms are fairly standard, though they are all quite clean and comfortable. Free local calls and in-room Internet access are other pluses. The seven suites all have whirlpool tubs.

1501 Demonbreun St., Nashville, TN 37203. ✆ **800/552-4667** or 615/255-9977. Fax 615/242-6127. www.comfort innnashville.com. 144 units. $79–$89 double; $119–$149 suite. Rates include free continental breakfast. AE, DC, DISC, MC, V. Free self-parking, with mobile-home and bus spaces available. Pet deposit $10 per day. **Amenities:** Outdoor pool; nearby golf course; nearby lighted tennis courts; business center; in-room massage; dry cleaning. *In room:* A/C, TV, dataport and Wi-Fi, unstocked fridge, microwave, coffeemaker, hair dryer and iron on request.

Days Inn Vanderbilt/Music Row   If you're looking for a decent room and a bargain, consider this motel that dates back to the 1960s. Rooms are refurbished every few years, but prices have remained modest by Nashville standards. Local calls and in-room Internet access are both free, making this place an especially good choice if you're on a budget. Music Row and Vanderbilt University are both within walking distance, and the hotel has free shuttle service to the nearby medical center.

1800 West End Ave., Nashville, TN 37203. ✆ **800/329-7466** or 615/327-0922. Fax 615/327-0102. www.daysinn. com. 151 units. $65–$109 double. Rates include continental breakfast. AE, DC, DISC, MC, V. Free parking. **Amenities:** Outdoor pool; exercise room; complimentary shuttle to nearby medical center. *In room:* A/C, TV, dataport and free Wi-Fi, coffeemaker, hair dryer, iron on request.

4 The Music Valley Area

If you plan to spend any amount of time at either the Opryland Hotel or the Opry Mills mall, staying in the Music Valley area will be your best bet. It will also be much more convenient if you plan to attend the Grand Ole Opry, where the second of two nightly shows can sometimes extend past midnight. After a night of all that barn-raising music, who wants to get in their car and drive across town to get to their hotel?

VERY EXPENSIVE

Opryland Hotel 🌟🌟🌟 *Kids*   What Graceland is to Memphis, Opryland is to Nashville. In other words, whether you're an Elvis fan or not, you owe it to yourself to visit the mansion at least once. Ditto for Opryland. Whether you're into country music or not, a tour of this palatial property with its 85-foot water fountains, tropical foliage, and winding "rivers," has become almost obligatory. The Opryland has the look and feel of a cruise ship and it does attract thousands of visitors daily (on top of the numbers who are actually staying at this massive hotel). The most impressive of the hotel's numerous areas is the Cascade Conservatory, which consists of two linked atriums. Waterfalls splash across rocky outcroppings, and fountains dance with colored lights and lasers. Bridges and meandering paths and a revolving gazebo bar add a certain quaint charm. Elsewhere at Opryland, the Magnolia lobby resembles an elegant antebellum mansion, with its classically proportioned double staircase worthy of Tara itself.

The hotel's stunning new spa, Relâche, provides an extensive array of salon and fitness services. Scented candles flicker and soothing music wafts through the dim corridors and 12 treatment rooms, where guests can indulge in raw-earth stone pedicures, warming sugar-spice facials, and pink-pearl firming body massages. There is also a 25-meter indoor pool (in addition to outdoor pools) and a state-of-the-art fitness center with an arsenal of cardio machines and other exercise equipment.

Nashville Accommodations: Music Valley & the Airport Area

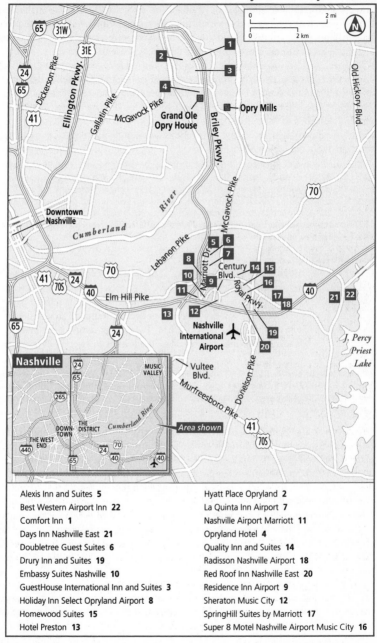

Alexis Inn and Suites **5**	Hyatt Place Opryland **2**
Best Western Airport Inn **22**	La Quinta Inn Airport **7**
Comfort Inn **1**	Nashville Airport Marriott **11**
Days Inn Nashville East **21**	Opryland Hotel **4**
Doubletree Guest Suites **6**	Quality Inn and Suites **14**
Drury Inn and Suites **19**	Radisson Nashville Airport **18**
Embassy Suites Nashville **10**	Red Roof Inn Nashville East **20**
GuestHouse International Inn and Suites **3**	Residence Inn Airport **9**
Holiday Inn Select Opryland Airport **8**	Sheraton Music City **12**
Homewood Suites **15**	SpringHill Suites by Marriott **17**
Hotel Preston **13**	Super 8 Motel Nashville Airport Music City **16**

Opryland's standard guest rooms, while not overly spacious, are comfortable and convenient. All the rooms have been updated with new furnishings including queen beds with pillow-top mattresses and fine linens. Rooms with atrium views (which cost $75 extra) are charming, but keep in mind that musical events occurring in the lobby below your window might not be as quaint if you want to hit the sack early. Gift shops, cafes, and food specialty stores are scattered throughout Opryland. From family-style Italian dining and a build-your-own burger joint to upscale steak and seafood restaurants, that old cliché rings true: There's something here for all tastes and budgets. And don't be too cheap to unscrew the water bottles in your room; Opryland has recently begun charging overnight hotel guests an additional $10 per day resort fee, which includes the H_2O and Wi-Fi.

2800 Opryland Dr., Nashville, TN 37214-1297. (© 888/777-OPRY or 615/889-1000. Fax 615/871-5728. www.gaylord hotels.com. 2,881 units. $199–$274 double; $319–$3,500 suite. AE, DC, DISC, MC, V. Valet parking $18, plus tax; self-parking $10, plus tax. **Amenities:** 14 restaurants and lounges; 2 outdoor pools and 1 indoor pool; golf club; fitness center; off-premises children's daycare; game/video room; concierge; tour desk; car-rental desk; business center; 20 retail shops; spa/salon; 24-hr. room service; laundry service; dry cleaning. *In room:* A/C, TV w/pay movies, dataport w/high-speed Internet access and Wi-Fi; kitchen or kitchenette in suites, minibar or unstocked fridge in some units, coffeemaker, hair dryer, iron, safe.

MODERATE

Guest House International Inn & Suites This four-story red brick hotel is especially popular with vacationing families. It's next door to a McDonald's and within walking distance of the Opryland Hotel, but a free shuttle will take you there (as well as to and from the airport) so you don't have to dodge the traffic on foot. Suites feature sleeper-sofas in addition to a king-size bed. Four larger family suites have two queen-size beds and two full-size sleeper sofas, in addition to two vanity areas and kitchenettes.

2420 Music Valley Dr., Nashville, TN 37214. (© 800/214-8378 or 615/885-4030. Fax 615/329-4890. www.guesthouse intl.com 184 units. $99–$129 double. Rates include continental breakfast. AE, DC, DISC, MC, V. Free self-parking, including covered garage. Pets accepted (no deposit). **Amenities:** Lounge; indoor pool; outdoor hot tub; exercise room. *In room:* A/C, TV, dataport w/high-speed Internet access (some rooms have Wi-Fi), coffeemaker, hair dryer, iron.

Hyatt Place Opryland 🐸🐸 This mid-rise hotel is located just off Music Valley Drive and is your most comfortable choice in the area if you aren't willing to splurge on the Opryland Hotel. Completely renovated in 2007, this former Amerisuites property has the hip appeal and contemporary décor of a boutique hotel. The sleek standard rooms are not only larger and less expensive than those at Opryland, they're also equipped with 42-inch-screen plasma TVs with plug-n-play capability. Cushy, oversized sofa-sleepers and wet bars offer plenty of room to stretch out and make yourself at home. Beyond the lobby, a sunny breakfast kitchen area features morning breakfast served on white china with real silverware. Continental breakfast with freshly brewed Starbucks coffee is complimentary each morning, with hot-cooked entrees and picnic items such as sandwiches available for purchase.

220 Rudy's Circle, Nashville, TN 37214. (© 888-HYATTHP or 615/872-0422. Fax 615/872-9283. www.hyatt.com. 123 units. $99–$189. Rates include continental breakfast. AE, DISC, MC, V. Free parking. **Amenities:** Small outdoor pool; exercise room; coin-op laundry; laundry service; same-day dry cleaning. *In room:* A/C, TV, Wi-Fi, kitchenette, unstocked fridge, coffeemaker, hair dryer, iron, safe.

INEXPENSIVE

A number of national and regional chain motels, generic but dependable, can be found in the area (see appendix D for toll-free reservation numbers), including **Days**

Inn, 2460 Music Valley Dr. (✆ **615/889-0090**), charging $50 to $90 double (with an outdoor pool and an adjacent miniature-golf course); and **Comfort Inn,** 2516 Music Valley Dr. (✆ **615/889-0086**), charging $75 to $90 for a double.

5 The Airport Area

Business travelers may find the plethora of airport hotels most conveniently located for their needs. But even leisure travelers including those with families may find many of these resort-style properties appealing for their broad array of amenities.

EXPENSIVE

Embassy Suites Nashville ✿ *Kids*   This all-suite hotel makes a great choice and a good value for families, as well as business travelers. Not only do you get a two-room suite, but cooked-to-order breakfast and evening cocktails are also included in the rates. These rooms are spacious, modern, and tastefully decorated in warm colors. The centerpiece of the hotel is its large atrium, which is full of tropical plants, including palm trees. A rocky stream runs through the Wi-Fi accessible atrium, and there are caged tropical songbirds adding their cheery notes to the pleasant atmosphere.

10 Century Blvd., Nashville, TN 37214. ✆ **800/EMBASSY** or 615/871-0033. Fax 615/883-9987. www.embassy suites.com. 296 units. $99–$179 suite. Rates include cooked-to-order breakfast. AE, DC, DISC, MC, V. Free parking. **Amenities:** Restaurant and bar; indoor pool; exercise room; hot tub; sauna; game room; concierge; 24-hour business center; limited room service; complimentary airport shuttle; complimentary evening manager's reception; gift shop. *In room:* A/C, TV w/pay movies, Wi-Fi, wet bar, fridge, microwave, coffeemaker, hair dryer, iron.

Holiday Inn Select Opryland/Airport   If you're looking for someplace convenient to the airport, this Holiday Inn just off the Briley Parkway is a good bet. The lobby features two back-to-back atria, one of which houses the reception desk, a car-rental desk, and a couple of seating areas, while the other contains the swimming pool, a lobby lounge area, and a terraced restaurant. Guest rooms are fairly standard but feature big TVs and plenty of counter space in the bathrooms. The king rooms have a bit more space and are designed with business travelers in mind. On the 14th-floor executive level, you'll receive a complimentary breakfast and other upgraded amenities.

2200 Elm Hill Pike, Nashville, TN 37214. ✆ **800/HOLIDAY** or 615/883-9770. Fax 615/391-4521. www.holiday-inn. com. 382 units. $109–$140 double. AE, DC, DISC, MC, V. Free parking. **Amenities:** Restaurant; 2 lounges; indoor pool; exercise room; indoor hot tub; sauna; video-game room; car-rental desk; business center; limited room service; valet; coin-op laundry; laundry service; airport shuttle. *In room:* A/C, TV w/pay movies, Wi-Fi, some rooms have fridges and microwaves, coffeemaker, hair dryer, iron, safe.

Hotel Preston ✿   One of the airport area's most unexpected surprises is this 11-story boutique hotel. In-room perks such as lava lamps, pet fish, rubber duckies, art kits, and milk and cookies are available upon request at check-in. Beds feature luxurious linens with pillowtop mattresses and a menu of pillows from which to choose. The room also have comfy chairs, well-lighted work desks, Aveda bath products, and in-room Starbucks coffee and Tazo teas.

733 Briley Pkwy., Nashville, TN 37217. ✆ **877/361-5500** or 615/361-5900. Fax 615/367-4468. www.hotelpreston. com. 196 units. $129–$159 double; $169 suite. AE, DC, DISC, MC, V. Free parking. **Amenities:** Restaurant and lounge; outdoor pool; valet; laundry service; complimentary airport and Opryland-area shuttle. *In room:* A/C, TV w/pay movies, dataport w/high-speed Internet access, coffeemaker, hair dryer, iron, CD player.

Nashville Airport Marriott ✿✿ *Kids*   This is one of the airport area's most resort-like hotels, featuring lots of recreational facilities, not the least of which is an indoor/outdoor pool. If you want to stay in shape while you're away from home, this is an excellent choice. The hotel grounds cover 17 landscaped and wooded acres, though the proximity to the highway keeps the grounds rather noisy. Traffic sounds are not a problem if you book an upper-level room. All the guest rooms are being updated with contemporary décor and flatscreen TVs. For business travelers, there are large work desks and a concierge level. Families will do well to ask for a lower-level poolside room; for extra space, try one of the corner rooms, which are 30% larger than standard rooms. The casual restaurant serves a wide range of pasta, poultry dishes, and generous salads, and has a pleasant view of the woods outside. Updated in spring 2008, with more contemporary décor and flatscreen TVs.

600 Marriott Dr., Nashville, TN 37214-5010. ℭ **800/228-9290** or 615/889-9300. Fax 615/889-9315. www. marriott.com. 398 units. $119–$199 double; $450–$650. AE, DC, DISC, MC, V. Free parking. **Amenities:** Restaurant; lounge; indoor/outdoor pool; tennis courts; health club; whirlpool; sauna; concierge; tour desk; limited room service; babysitting; valet; laundry service; complimentary airport shuttle; picnic area; basketball court; volleyball court. *In room:* A/C, TV w/pay movies, dataport and high-speed Internet and Wi-Fi access, coffeemaker, hair dryer, iron.

Residence Inn Airport ✷✷   This sprawling, extended-stay Marriott property feels more like a suburban apartment complex than a chain hotel. Studios are a real bargain, considering they include a queen-size bed, sofa-sleeper, and full kitchen with refrigerator, stove, and sink. (For a few dollars more, two-story lofts include two bedrooms.) All rooms are nonsmoking. Rates also include free in-room Internet access (but not local calls) and daily hot breakfast. And you can bring your pet.

2300 Elm Hill Pike, Nashville, TN 37214. ℭ **800/331-3131** or 615/889-8600. Fax 615/871-4970. www.marriott.com. 168 units. $109–$159 double. AE, DC, DISC, MC, V. Free parking. **Amenities:** Outdoor pool; fitness room; valet; coin-operated laundry; laundry service. *In room:* A/C, TV w/pay movies, dataport with free high-speed Internet access, coffeemaker, hair dryer, iron.

Sheraton Music City ✷✷   Big, elegant, and set on 23 acres in a modern business park near the airport, this large convention hotel (second in size only to Opryland) has a commanding vista of the surrounding area. Classic Georgian styling sets the tone and conjures up the feel of an antebellum mansion. In the elegant lobby, you'll find marble floors and burnished paneling and free Wi-Fi. Public areas including the indoor pool and restaurant areas were upgraded in late 2006. Comfortable guest rooms feature sleighbeds, work desks, and three telephones. And here's good news for big-dog owners: Pets up to 80 pounds are accepted with a security deposit but no daily fee. The hotel reserves 20 rooms on the ground-floor level specifically for pet owners.

777 McGavock Pike, Nashville, TN 37214-3175. ℭ **800/325-3535** or 615/885-2200. Fax 615/231-1134. www. sheratonmusiccity.com. 410 units. $109–$189 double; $300–$600 suite. AE, DC, DISC, MC, V. Valet parking $7; free self-parking. **Amenities:** Restaurant; lounge; outdoor pool in quiet central courtyard; indoor pool; health club with whirlpool and exercise equipment; concierge; valet; laundry service; complimentary airport shuttle. *In room:* A/C, TV, dataport and high-speed Internet access, coffeemaker, hair dryer, iron.

INEXPENSIVE TO MODERATE

National and regional chain motels in the area are increasing exponentially. Some good choices include the following (see appendix C for toll-free reservation numbers): **Alexis Inn and Suites,** 600 Ermac Dr. (ℭ **615/889-4466**), charging $59–$109; **Doubletree Guest Suites,** 2424 Atrium Way (ℭ **615/889-8889**), charging $129 to $179 for a double; **Drury Inn & Suites,** 555 Donelson Pike (ℭ **615/902-0400**), charging $109 to $130; **Homewood Suites,** 2640 Elm Hill Pike (ℭ **615/884-8111**), charging $109 to $159; **Quality Inn and Suites,** 2521 Elm Hill Pike (ℭ **615/391-3919**), charging $108 to $120 for a double; **La Quinta Inn Airport,** 2345 Atrium

Way (© **615/885-3000**), charging $79 to $115 for a double; **Radisson-Nashville Airport,** 1112 Airport Center Dr. (© **615/889-9090**), charging $99 to $145 for a double; and **SpringHill Suites by Marriott,** 1100 Airport Center Dr. (© **615/884-6111**), charging $94 to $134 for a double.

Other budget bets include such old standbys as **Best Western Airport,** 701 Stewart's Ferry Pike (© **615/889-9199**), charging $60 to $70 for a double; **Days Inn–Nashville East,** 3445 Percy Priest Dr. (© **615/889-8881**), charging $59 to $72 for a double; **Red Roof Inn–Nashville East,** 510 Claridge Dr. (© **615/872-0735**), charging $50 to $60 for a double; and **Super 8 Motel–Nashville/Airport/Music City,** 720 Royal Pkwy. (© **615/889-8887**), charging $58 to $78 for a double.

6

Where to Dine in Nashville

The rest of the country may make fun of Southern cooking, with its fatback and chitlins, collard greens, and fried everything, but there is much more to Southern food than these tired stereotypes. You'll find that Southern fare, in all its diversity, is a way of life here in Nashville. This is not to say that you can't get good Italian, French, German, Japanese, Chinese, or even Thai—you can. However, as long as you're below the Mason-Dixon line, you owe it to yourself to try a bit of country cookin'. Barbecue and fried catfish are two inexpensive staples well worth trying (see "Barbecue" and "Music Valley & East Nashville" sections later in this chapter for restaurants serving these specialties). If you enjoy good old-fashioned American food, try a "meat-and-three" restaurant, where you get your choice of three vegetables with your meal. However, to find out what Southern cooking is truly capable of, try someplace serving New Southern or New American cuisine. This is the equivalent of California cuisine, but made with traditional, and not-so-traditional, Southern ingredients.

Nashville is well represented by scores of popular chain restaurants, including a disproportionate number of upscale steakhouses: **Morton's of Chicago,** 641 Church St. (© **615/259-4558**); **Fleming's Prime Steakhouse and Wine Bar,** 2525 West End Ave. (© **615/342-0131**); **Ruth's Chris Steak House,** 2100 West End Ave. (© **615/320-0163**); and **Stoney River Legendary Steaks,** 3015 West End Ave. (© **615/340-9550**).

However, I like to find worthy independent places to recommend. Happily, Nashville is bursting at the seams with them. In this chapter I've only been able to scratch the surface.

For these listings, I have classified restaurants in the following categories (estimates do not include beer, wine, or tip): **expensive,** if a complete dinner would cost $30 or more; **moderate,** where you can expect to pay between $15 and $30 for a complete dinner; and **inexpensive,** where a complete dinner can be had for less than $15.

1 The Best Dining Bets

- **Best Spot for a Romantic Dinner:** The sumptuous country-French ambience and top-tier service alone would qualify **Zola,** 3001 West End Ave. (© **615/320-7778**), as a perfect setting for an intimate meal with that certain someone. Award-winning chef Debra Paquette's creative cuisine makes it deliciously ideal. Start with gourmet cheeses accompanied by orange-apricot bread and apple crackers, then sample the signature paella or the pistachio salmon with black-bean bread pudding and spicy banana yogurt. See p. 82.
- **Best Spot for a Business Lunch:** **Capitol Grille,** 231 Sixth Ave. N. (© **615/345-7116**), at the Hermitage Hotel, is very popular with the downtown business set.

Why? It could be the prime spot next to the state capitol, or the traditional ambience, or perhaps the secret is in the exclusive wine list, grilled steaks, and espresso fudge cake.

- **Best for Kids:** It's not everywhere that you get to eat in a restaurant next to a full-size trolley car, and anyway, isn't spaghetti one of the major food groups? For less than most restaurants charge for a round of drinks, the whole family can eat at **The Old Spaghetti Factory,** 160 Second Ave. N. (© **615/254-9010**), in the heart of The District. See p. 79.

- **Best for Big Families:** You'll think it's Sunday dinner at Grandma's when you enter the cozy Victorian home that houses **Monell's.** You'll share a big table with family and fellow travelers, passing dishes of old-fashioned Southern staples such as fried chicken, mashed potatoes, and greens. Monell's, 1235 Sixth Ave. N. © **615/248-4747,** downtown. See p. 79.

- **Best Soul Food:** One of Nashville's oldest minority-owned restaurants, **Swett's** is still the benchmark for home-style comfort foods such as pork chops, slow-simmered green beans, cornbread, and macaroni and cheese. That first bite of banana pudding may bring tears to your eyes. Swett's Restaurant, 2725 Clifton Ave. © **615/329-4418.** www.swettsrestaurant.com.

2 Restaurants by Cuisine

AMERICAN

Elliston Place Soda Shop ☆ (Music Row & the West End, $, p. 83)

Germantown Café ☆☆ (Downtown, The District & 12th Avenue South, $, p. 76)

Green Hills Grille (Green Hills & South Nashville, $$, p. 85)

Harper's ☆☆ (Green Hills and South Nashville, $, p. 85)

Margot Café & Bar ☆☆ (Music Valley & the Airport, $$, p. 88)

Monell's ☆ (Downtown, The District & 12th Avenue South, $, p. 79)

Pancake Pantry ☆ (Music Row & the West End, $, p. 84)

Paradise Park Trailer Resort (Downtown p. 79)

Rainforest Café ☆☆☆ (Music Valley & the Airport, $$, p. 88)

Tin Angel ☆ (West End, $, p. 85)

The Yellow Porch ☆ (South Nashville, $$, p. 86)

BARBECUE

Bar-B-Cutie ☆ (Music Valley & the Airport, $, p. 90)

Jack's Bar-B-Que ☆ (Downtown, The District & 12th Avenue South, $, p. 91)

Mary's Old-Fashioned Bar-B-Q ☆ (South Nashville, $, p. 91)

Whitt's Barbecue ☆ (Belle Meade & Environs, $, p. 91)

BURGERS

Blackstone Restaurant & Brewery ☆ (Music Row & the West End, $$, p. 80)

Bobbie's Dairy Dip ☆ (South Nashville, $, p. 83)

Rotier's ☆ (Music Row & the West End, $, p. 84)

CARIBBEAN

Calypso ☆ (Music Row & the West End, $, p. 92)

Rainforest Café ☆☆☆ (Music Valley & the Airport, $$, p. 88)

DELICATESSEN

Noshville ☆☆ (Music Row & the West End, $, p. 84)

FRENCH

Margot Café & Bar ✹✹ (Music Valley & the Airport, $$, p. 88)

Marche Artisan Foods ✹✹ (East Nashville, $, p. 87)

FUSION

Mirror ✹✹ (Downtown, The District & 12th Avenue South, $$, p. 78)

Zola ✹✹ (Music Row & the West End, $$, p. 82)

GERMAN

Gerst Haus ✹✹ (Downtown, The District & 12th Avenue South, $, p. 78)

ITALIAN

The Old Spaghetti Factory (Downtown, The District & 12th Avenue South, $, p. 79)

JAPANESE

Goten ✹ (Music Row & the West End, $$, p. 81)

MEDITERRANEAN

Kalamata's ✹ (South Nashville, $, p. 86)

MEXICAN

La Hacienda Taqueria ✹ (Green Hills & South Nashville, $, p. 86)

Las Paletas ✹ (12th Avenue South, $, p. 78)

NEW AMERICAN/NEW SOUTHERN

Acorn ✹ (Music Row & the West End), $$$, p. 80)

Blackstone Restaurant & Brewery ✹ (Music Row & the West End, $$, p. 80)

Bound'ry ✹✹✹ (Music Row & the West End, $$, p. 80)

Cabana ✹ (West End, $$, p. 81)

Capitol Grille ✹✹✹ (Downtown, The District & 12th Avenue South, $$$, p. 73)

F. Scott's Restaurant and Jazz Bar ✹✹✹ (South Nashville, $$$, p. 85)

The Mad Platter ✹ (Downtown, The District & 12th Avenue South, $$, p. 77)

Martha's at the Plantation ✹✹✹ (South Nashville, $$, p. 86)

The Merchants ✹ (Downtown, The District & 12th Avenue South, $$$, p. 73)

Midtown Café ✹ (Music Row & the West End, $$, p. 82)

Sunset Grill ✹✹ (Music Row & the West End, $$, p. 82)

Watermark ✹✹ (Downtown, $$$, p. 76)

PIZZA

DaVinci's Gourmet Pizza ✹ (Music Row & the West End, $, p. 83)

Mafiaoza's (Downtown, The District & 12th Avenue South, $, p. 78)

SEAFOOD

Aquarium (Music Valley & the Airport, $$, p. 87)

Caney Fork Fish Camp (Music Valley, $$, p. 88)

Chappy's On Church ✹ (The West End, $$, p. 76)

Jimmy Kelly's ✹ (Music Row & the West End, $$, p. 81)

SOUTHERN

Arnold's Country Kitchen ✹✹ (South Nashville, $, p. 78)

Cock of the Walk ✹ (Music Valley & the Airport, $, p. 90)

Harper's ✹✹ (Green Hills & South Nashville, $, p. 85)

Loveless Café ✹✹ (Belle Meade & Environs, $, p. 86)

Prince's Hot Chicken Shack ✹ (Music Valley, $, p. 91)

South Street ✹ (Music Row & the West End, $$, p. 84)

Swett's Restaurant ✹✹✹ (Belle Meade, $, p. 87)

White Trash Café (South Nashville, $, p. 80)

STEAKS
- Jimmy Kelly's (Music Row & the West End, $$, p. 81)
- Nick & Rudy's 🐦 (Music Row & the West End, $$$, p. 82)
- Old Hickory Steakhouse 🐦🐦🐦 (Music Valley, $$$, p. 88)

- The Palm Restaurant (Downtown, The District & 12th Avenue South, $$$, see below)
- Stock-Yard Restaurant (Downtown, The District & 12th Avenue South, $$$, see below)

3 Downtown Area, The Gulch & 12th Avenue South

EXPENSIVE

Capitol Grille 🐦🐦🐦 NEW AMERICAN/NEW SOUTHERN   New chef Tyler Brown is maintaining the high standards at the posh Hermitage hotel's Capitol Grille, where polished service attracts politicians, power-lunchers, and theatergoers from the nearby Tennessee Performing Arts Center. Diners rave about his Carolina-influenced dishes, including Low-Country oyster stew. Other standouts are the salad of mixed lettuces and radishes with a honey-roasted peanut-ginger-peach vinaigrette; and the Niman Ranch pork chop with brown sugar rub. Grilled salmon and steaks are also on the menu, along with tempting sweets such as English toffee croissant bread pudding (served with maple ice cream and caramel sauce), and the unusual Mission fig cheesecake, made with goat cheese, figs, hazelnuts, and sorghum *crème fraiche*.

In the Hermitage, 231 Sixth Ave. N. 📞 615/345-7116. www.thehermitagehotel.com. Reservations recommended. Main courses $25–$35. AE, DC, DISC, MC, V. Daily 5:30–10pm; Mon–Sat 6:30–10:30am and 11:30am–2pm; Sun 6:30–10am and 11am–2pm.

The Merchants 🐦 NEW AMERICAN/NEW SOUTHERN   Housed in a restored brick building amid the funky bars of lower Broadway, this classy restaurant is another favorite power-lunch spot and after-work hangout for the young executive set. The restaurant's first floor is a café and bar, while the upstairs is the more formal dining room. Dinner here might begin with lively tequila shrimp. From there, you could move on to beef tenderloin pan-seared with apples, Jack Daniel's, and maple syrup; or perhaps lamb chops with herbs, bourbon, and a cranberry demiglace. The Merchants also boasts an extensive wine list.

401 Broadway. 📞 615/254-1892. www.merchantsrestaurant.com. Reservations recommended. Main courses $12–$35. AE, DC, DISC, MC, V. Mon–Thurs 11am–10pm; Fri–Sat 11am–11pm; Sun 5–9pm.

The Palm Restaurant STEAKS   Currently the "in" place to see and to be seen, The Palm is an upscale enclave, located within the cushy confines of the Hilton Suites downtown. Conspicuous consumption is a hallmark here, where a 36-oz. New York strip for two comes with a $60 price tag. Chops include thick cuts of lamb, pork, and veal, while beef eaters may opt for everything from prime rib to aged porterhouse. Salads, pasta, chicken, and fish dishes should appease diners who don't do beef. String beans, creamed spinach, mashed potatoes, and other sides are served family style. Celebs favor the private dining rooms, though if you keep your eyes peeled, you may see a Tennessee Titan or two, or the occasional country music star.

1140 Fifth Ave. S. 📞 615/742-7256. www.thepalm.com. Reservations recommended. Main courses $15 lunch; $18–$38 dinner. AE, DC, DISC, MC, V. Mon–Fri 11am–11pm; Sat 5–11pm; Sun 5–10pm.

Stock-Yard Restaurant STEAKS   If The Palm seems too pretentious, head a few blocks uptown to the old Nashville Union Stockyard building where local old-money

Nashville Dining: Downtown Area, Music Row & the West End

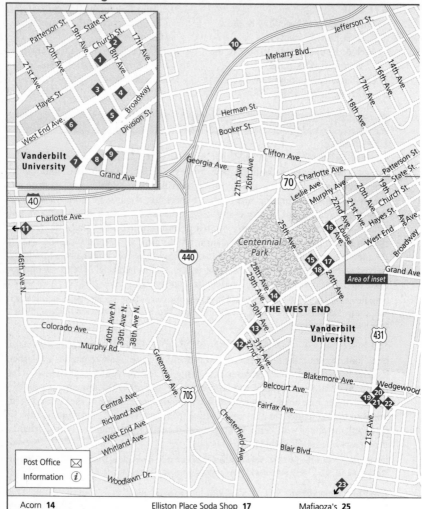

Acorn **14**	Elliston Place Soda Shop **17**	Mafiaoza's **25**
Arnold's Country Kitchen **29**	F. Scott's Restaurant **23**	Merchants **38**
Blackstone Restaurant and Brewery **3**	Germantown Café **31**	Midtown Café **4**
	Gerst Haus **36**	Mirror **24**
Bobby's Dairy Dip **11**	Goten **6**	Monell's **30**
Bound'ry **8**	Harper's **10**	Nashville Farmer's Market **30**
Cabana **19**	Jack's Bar-B-Que **37**	Nick and Rudy's **7**
Calypso **15**	Jackson's in the Village **21**	Noshville **5**
Capitol Grill **34**	Jimmy Kelly's **16**	The Old Spaghetti Factory **35**
Chappy's On Church **2**	Las Paletas **26**	The Palm Restaurant **40**
DaVinci's Gourmet Pizza **1**	Mad Platter **32**	Pancake Pantry **20**

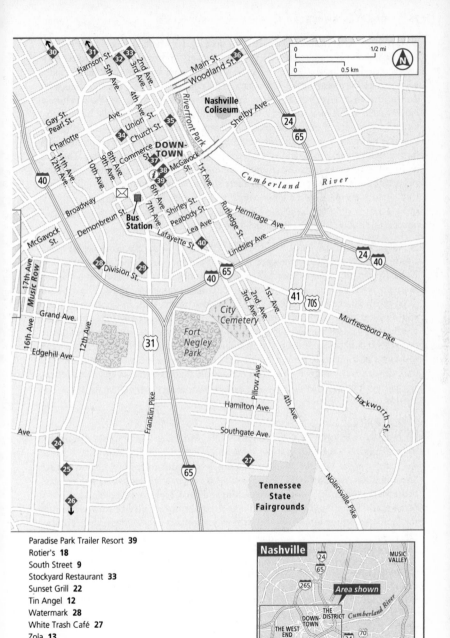

Paradise Park Trailer Resort **39**
Rotier's **18**
South Street **9**
Stockyard Restaurant **33**
Sunset Grill **22**
Tin Angel **12**
Watermark **28**
White Trash Café **27**
Zola **13**

types have gathered to slice slabs of beef for decades. It's where Dad comes for Father's Day, or Son on his graduation. What you get is a very impressive foyer, complete with crystal chandelier, marble floor, and an alcove containing a wine display that includes what may be the oldest bottles of Madeira in the country (from 1776 to 1792). A window off the foyer gives you a glimpse into the meat-storage room, so you can have a look at what you'll soon be served. For a steakhouse, this place actually has a pretty limited assortment of steaks, but most diners stop at the first offering—the prime rib. If you're not a steak eater but still would like to visit this Nashville tradition, you'll find several seafood, pork, and chicken dishes, as well as a few pasta plates. There's a nightclub downstairs from the restaurant in case you feel like dancing off some calories after dinner. The restaurant offers a free shuttle to hotels within a 15-mile radius. Call ahead for a space on the buses, which seat between 14 and 45 people.

901 Second Ave. N. ⓒ **615/255-6464.** www.stock-yardrestaurant.com. Reservations highly recommended. Main courses $21–$45. AE, DC, DISC, MC, V. Mon–Thurs 5–10pm; Fri–Sat 5–11pm; Sun 5–9pm.

Watermark ☆☆ NEW AMERICAN/SOUTHERN   When executive chef Joe Shaw, a protégé of Birmingham's renowned Frank Stitt, opened this fine-dining spot in The Gulch in late 2005, Nashvillians had high expectations. Shaw delivered, but his departure two years later did little to dampen Watermark's immense appeal. The sophisticated urban dining room and bar is a sleek, modern space, done in blacks and whites. Exquisite preparations of Southern-influenced delicacies include the stone-ground grits soufflé with goat cheese and apple-smoked bacon butter sauce; and the sweet potato ravioli with ham hock pot liquor. Local and regional products, such as artisanal cheeses and farm-fresh produce, enliven the flavors brought to the table by experienced wait staff. Be sure to save room for blackberry crisp with almond brittle ice cream for dessert.

507 12th Ave. S. ⓒ **615/254-2000.** Reservations recommended. Main courses $18–$29. AE, DISC, MC, V. Mon–Thurs 5:30–9pm; Fri–Sat 5:30–10pm.

MODERATE

Chappy's on Church ☆ CAJUN/CREOLE   Mississippi Gulf Coast restaurateur John Chapman lost his 20-year-old restaurant, Chappy's, during Hurricane Katrina. Relocating to Nashville, he set up shop in this yellow brick corner building on Church Street in 2006. An old New Orleans vibe, with French streetlamps and stained glass, pervades the romantic, two-tiered restaurant and bar. Creole soups, seafood, grits, and bread pudding are among chef Chapman's signature dishes. Elevate your spirits with the Sunday-morning champagne brunch, which features live Southern gospel music.

1721 Church St. ⓒ **615/322-9932.** www.chappys.com. Reservations recommended. Main courses $19–$32. AE, DISC, MC, V. Mon–Fri 11am–2pm and 5–10pm; Sat–Sun 11am–10pm (brunch until 3pm).

Germantown Café ☆☆ AMERICAN   For a stunning view of the Nashville skyline at sunset, stake out a dinner table at this pristine bistro in the Germantown neighborhood just north of downtown. Sip a cocktail and pore over the eclectic menu, which includes artful interpretations of crab cakes, French onion soup, and even fried green tomatoes with goat cheese. Grilled fish entrees, such as the herb-crusted skate, are excellent, as are the tasso-stuffed chicken and the substantial mustard-marinated pork tenderloin served with a savory plum sauce. As for side dishes, the garlic mashed potatoes are out of this world. Service is polished and gracious.

1200 Fifth Ave. N. ⓒ **615/242-3226.** www.germantowncafe.com. Reservations recommended. Main courses $9–$19 at dinner; $5–$12 at lunch. AE, DC, DISC, MC, V. Mon–Fri 11am–2pm and 5–11pm; Sat 5–11pm; Sun brunch 10:30am–2pm.

Best Tennessee-Based Eateries

All three of these homegrown Tennessee chains have multiple locations throughout the state and beyond.

BACK YARD BURGERS: Founded in Cleveland, Miss., in 1987, BYB is a fast-food chain specializing in gourmet-quality, home-style grilled burgers, spicy seasoned fries, and hand-dipped milkshakes. Today, it's a publicly traded company, based in Memphis, with more than 200 locations nationwide, including several in Memphis and Nashville. My favorite drive-through indulgence: Savory chicken sandwich, topped with fresh tomatoes and lettuce, and an extra-thick chocolate milkshake. © **800/333-9566;** www.backyardburgers.com.

CRACKER BARREL OLD COUNTRY STORE: A sure bet on any road trip through Tennessee, Cracker Barrels are ubiquitous along interstates. You'll recognize them by the rows of wooden rocking chairs on the brown buildings' wide porches. The Lebanon, Tenn.-based restaurant chain is the real McCoy, serving hearty portions of consistently good, home-style food at breakfast, lunch, and dinner. Chock full of old farm equipment, kitchen gadgets, and other antiques, the eateries all have crackling stone fireplaces that are especially welcoming in cold winter weather. You can also browse for old-fashioned candy in the gift stores, and even rent audio books for your travels.

There are more than 570 restaurants in 41 states, including multiple locations in Memphis and Nashville. Best breakfast bet: Fried ham, biscuits and gravy, scrambled eggs, and Southern-style grits swimming in butter. © **800/333-9566;** www.crackerbarrel.com.

J. ALEXANDER'S: Based in Nashville, J. Alexander's operates contemporary, full-service American restaurants in more than a dozen central U.S. states, with two locations in Nashville and one in Memphis. Unlike BYB and Cracker Barrel, J. Alexander's has a relaxing yet upscale atmosphere and offers a full bar with wines available by the glass or bottle. Signature dishes: Baby-back ribs, prime beef, and cilantro shrimp. My choice: Rattlesnake pasta.

In Nashville: 2609 West End Ave., © **615/340-9901;** and 3401 West End Ave. © **615/269-1900.** In Memphis: 2670 N. Germantown Parkway, Cordova (in the suburbs, near Wolfchase Galleria mall), © **901/381-9670;** www.jalexanders.com.

The Mad Platter ✿ NEW AMERICAN/NEW SOUTHERN   For many years now, the Mad Platter has been one of Nashville's trendiest restaurants. Located in an old brick corner store in a historic neighborhood of restored Victorian houses, the Mad Platter feels like a cozy upscale library, with bookshelves crammed with knickknacks and old copies of *National Geographic*. The ambience is reserved, not pretentious, and service is personable, if a bit slow at times. The menu, including vegetarian options, changes daily. Appetizers might include a Gorgonzola-and-asparagus Napoleon, as well as a prosciutto roulade stuffed with truffle mousse. Recent entrees have included grilled duck breast basted with a pomegranate molasses and a rack of lamb *moutarde*. Don't you dare leave without trying the best-named dessert in all of Nashville: Chocolate Elvis is an obscenely rich, fudgy cake that, put simply, takes the cake.

1239 Sixth Ave. N. (€) 615/242-2563. Reservations recommended. Main courses $18–$28. AE, DC, DISC, MC, V. Mon–Fri 11am–2pm; Tues–Sat 5:30–11pm; Sun 5–9pm.

Mirror ⟨★★ FUSION   Mirror serves one of the best vodka cucumber martinis in town, a feat that befits this ultra-hip bar and restaurant in the 12th Avenue South district. Metallic furniture, pale blue walls, and gauze curtains define the casual, chic setting. Spanish sherry is a must when ordering from the extensive tapas menu, including olives, tuna ceviche (raw fish dish marinated in citrus juice and spices), and crispy prosciutto-wrapped cipollini onions. I highly recommend the warm goat cheesecake with mesclun greens, asparagus, tomatoes, and mushroom ragout. Entrees include light options (salmon spring rolls, carrot/ginger soufflé) and heartier seared duck or rosemary-marinated filet mignon with truffle mashed potatoes, spinach, and sherry-spiked mushroom sauce.

2317 12th Ave. South. (€) 615/383-8330. www.eatdrinkreflect.com. Tapas $1–$3.50; main courses $13–$21. AE, MC, V. Mon–Wed 5–10pm; Thurs–Sat 5–11pm.

INEXPENSIVE

In addition to the restaurants listed here, you can get quick, inexpensive meals at the **Nashville Farmers Market,** 900 Eighth Ave. N. (€ **615/880-2001**), adjacent to the Bicentennial Capitol Mall State Park. It's open from 9am to 6pm 7 days a week, year-round except winter, when it closes at 5pm.

Arnold's Country Kitchen ⟨★★ SOUTHERN   Plan to arrive early to grab a parking spot in the cracked and busted lot next to Arnold's, a soul-food landmark for more than two decades. Be prepared to stand in line and to share a table with strangers too, if you plan to eat your buffet meal on the premises. But don't worry; over fried green tomatoes, barbecued pork, fried chicken, and knee-weakening mashed potatoes, you're always among friends.

605 8th Ave. S. (€) 615/256-4455. Main courses $6.50. MC, V. Hours Mon–Fri 10:30am–2:30pm.

Gerst Haus ⟨★★ GERMAN   This beloved Nashville landmark is best known for its beer hall atmosphere, German food, and more recently, salads, catfish, and steaks. From its plum perch across the street from the Coliseum, chances are the Gerst Haus will be endearing new fans of hearty Bavarian fare for generations to come. Open for lunch and dinner.

301 Woodland St. (€) 615/244-8886. Main courses $9–$16. AE, MC, V. Sun–Thurs 11am–10pm; Fri–Sat 11am–11pm.

Las Paletas ★ ICE CREAM/MEXICAN   Sweet indulgences such as these *paletas* (traditional Mexican popsicles) are sublime when they're both delicious *and* wholesome—made fresh daily without preservatives or syrupy artificial additives. The small, unmarked storefront at the edge of the 12th Avenue South corridor offers several dozen flavors on any given day: Rose-petal, hibiscus, tamarind, watermelon, or prune are delicate tastes, while jalapeno and chili-cucumber are bright and bold on the palate. At only $2.50 a pop, you can afford to try more than one.

2907 12th Ave. S. (€) 615/386-2101. Popsicles $2.50. Tues–Sat noon–6pm. Hours are seasonal; call ahead.

Mafiaoza's PIZZA   With a toasty fire crackling in the pizza ovens and the dim roar of a lively cocktail crowd, this pizzeria in the trendy 12th Avenue South district has

---

Kids Family-Friendly Restaurants

Elliston Place Soda Shop (p. 83) Bring the kids by for a burger and a shake and tell them how their mom and dad or grandma and grandpa used to hang out in a place just like this one when they were love-struck teenagers.

The Old Spaghetti Factory (see below) Kids love spaghetti and here, that's all there is to it. Adults will enjoy the Victorian decor. And kids will also love the old trolley car in the middle of the dining room.

Rainforest Café (p. 88) Entertaining for the whole family, this theme cafe offers basic American sandwiches and entrees with a faint tropical flair—served in a jungle atmosphere complete with roaring elephants, chest-thumping gorillas, and thunderous, simulated rainstorms.

---

built a loyal following. An outdoor patio gives patrons a great place to hang while throwing back a few beers or bottles of vino. Skip the soggy, tomato-laden bruschetta but try the meaty pasta dishes and thin-crust pizzas, sold by the slice or whole pie.

2400 12th Ave. S. ℂ 615/269-4646. www.mafiaozas.com. Main courses $6.75–$25. AE, DISC, MC, V. Tues–Fri 4pm–3am; Sat–Sun 11am–3pm.

Monell's ★ *Finds* AMERICAN Dining out doesn't usually involve sitting at the same table with total strangers, but be prepared for just such a community experience at Monell's. Housed in a restored brick Victorian home, this very traditional boardinghouse-style lunch spot feels as if it has been around for ages, which is just what the proprietors want you to think. A meal at Monell's is meant to conjure up family dinners at Grandma's house, so remember to say "please" when you ask for the mashed potatoes or peas. The food is good, old-fashioned home cookin' most of the year, and everything is all-you-can-eat. In December (the 1st through the 23rd), Monell's gets fancy and offers reservation-only Victorian dinners ($40).

1235 Sixth Ave. N. ℂ 615/248-4747. Main courses $9–$16. MC, V. Mon–Fri 10:30am–2pm; Fri 5–8:30pm; Sat 8:30am–1pm and 5–8:30pm; Sun 8am–4pm.

The Old Spaghetti Factory *Value Kids* ITALIAN With its ornate Victorian elegance, you'd never guess that this restaurant was once a warehouse. Where boxes and bags were stacked, diners now sit surrounded by burnished wood. There's stained and beveled glass all around, antiques everywhere, and plush seating in the waiting area. The front of the restaurant is a large and very elegant bar. Now if they'd just do something about that trolley car someone parked in the middle of the dining room. A complete meal—including a salad, bread, spumoni ice cream, and a beverage—will cost you less than a cocktail in many restaurants. A great spot to bring the family, this is one of the cheapest places to get a meal in The District.

160 Second Ave. N. ℂ 615/254-9010. www.osf.com. Main courses $4.60–$10. AE, DISC, MC, V. Mon–Fri 11:30am–2pm; Mon–Thurs 5–10pm; Sat noon–11pm; Sun noon–10pm.

Paradise Park Trailer Resort AMERICAN Funny how fried bologna and Spam-and-cheese sandwiches taste so mighty good with Guns N Roses blaring in the background. But they do at this cheap, 24-hour diner that looks and feels like a trailer park

in the wrong part of town. The could-care-less staff wear T-shirts reading "Best Mul-
lett in Town," a thought for you to ponder as you sink back into your plastic lawn
chair and decide whether to cap off your paper-plate meal with the Twinkie or the
Moon Pie, both of which are on the menu. Paradise Park also serves bacon and eggs
and pancakes for breakfast.

411 Broadway. ☎ 615/251-1515. www.paradiseparkonline.com. Main courses $6–$9. MC, V. Daily 24 hours.

White Trash Cafe SOUTHERN   Southern plate lunches and country breakfasts
are the mainstays of this hole-in-the-wall strategically located near the Nashville Flea
Market at the Tennessee State Fairgrounds. A squat, cinderblock building whose fore-
boding entrance is littered with hubcaps, discarded plumbing fixtures, and other junk-
yard gems, fits right in with the rest of the run-down neighborhood. Inside,
surrounded by tacky toys and knick-knacks, locals including well-to-do music-indus-
try types hunker over tables laden with warm, homemade yeast rolls, fried chicken,
cabbage casserole, and other mouthwatering hillbilly vittles.

1914 Branford Ave. ☎ 615/383-0109. Main courses $6.50–$7.50. MC, V. Mon–Fri 7am–3pm; Sat 7am–2pm.

4 Music Row & the West End

For locations of restaurants in this section, see the "Nashville Dining: Downtown,
Music Row & the West End" map on p. 74.

EXPENSIVE

Acorn ⚘ NEW AMERICAN   In a tree-shaded neighborhood near Centennial Park,
Acorn offers evocative lighting, contemporary artwork, and a treehouse-view patio.
Though a tad overpriced, the food is first-rate. I loved the wasabi-encrusted seared
tuna with pureed sesame carrots and Japanese vegetables. Also popular are the acorn-
squash-stuffed ravioli with cream sauce, chervil shrimp bisque, and pear and spinach
salad studded with sugar-cinnamon walnuts. Tapas, quiche, and sandwiches make the
late-night menu a notch above the typical bar food usually available at this hour.

114 28th Ave. N. ☎ 615/320-4399. www.theacornrestaurant.com. Reservations recommended. Main courses
$18–$32. AE, DC, DISC, MC, V. Daily 5pm–midnight.

MODERATE

Blackstone Restaurant & Brewery ⚘ BURGERS/NEW AMERICAN   At this
glitzy brewpub, brewing tanks in the front window silently crank out half a dozen different beers ranging from a pale ale to a dark porter. Whether you're looking for a
quick bite of pub grub (pizzas, soups, pub-style burgers) or a more formal dinner (a
meaty pork loin well complemented by apple chutney and a smidgen of rosemary, garlic, and juniper berries), you'll be satisfied with the food here, especially if you're into
good microbrews. Fish and chips can't be beat, especially when washed down by a St.
Charles Porter ale. This place is big, and you'll have the option of dining amid a pub
atmosphere or in one of the sparsely elegant dining areas.

1918 West End Ave. ☎ 615/327-9969. www.blackstonebrewpub.com. Sandwiches, pizza, and main courses
$8–$20. AE, DC, DISC, MC, V. Mon–Thurs 11am–midnight; Fri–Sat 11am–1am; Sun noon–10pm.

Bound'ry NEW AMERICAN/NEW SOUTHERN   With its colorful murals and
chaotic angles (seemingly inspired by Dr. Seuss), this Vanderbilt-area eatery is a fun
yet sophisticated bastion of trendiness, popular with everyone from college students

to families to businesspeople in suits. Add some jazz to the wild interior design and you have a very energetic atmosphere. The menu is wildly eclectic and international, from tapas such as pork egg rolls with chipotle-juniper barbecue sauce to fried calamari served with anchovy aioli. In addition to signature salads such as the Bound'ry, which combines endive and radish relish with crispy ham, tomatoes, and black-eyed peas, "large platter" entrees include vegetarian dishes such as polenta stacked with eggplant, portobello mushrooms, and cheeses to meaty pork chops and steaks, including the 16-oz. porterhouse. Wine and beer choices are quite extensive here.

911 20th Ave. S. © 615/321-3043. www.pansouth.net. Reservations recommended, except Fri–Sat after 6:30pm when it's first come, first served. Tapas $4.75–$11; main courses $15–$30. AE, DC, DISC, MC, V. Restaurant daily 5pm–1am. Bars daily 4pm–2:30am.

Cabana *✿* NEW AMERICAN/NEW SOUTHERN   Ultra-cool Cabana boasts one of the liveliest after-dark scenes of all the West End's restaurant/lounges. Co-owned by restaurateur Randy Rayburn (Midtown, Sunset Grill), Cabana has a sprawling, 2,900-square-foot outdoor patio that's in use year-round. Gorgeous young people hover at the bar, or mingle in chic private cabanas equipped with flatscreen TVs. Food here is affordable and, above all, fun. Nosh on homemade potato chips with Gorgonzola dipping sauce. Then dive into top-notch interpretations on Tennessee sliders (miniature fried-ham sandwiches) or the childlike chicken-wing lollipops, and frosty root beer floats with freshly baked cookies on the side.

1910 Belcourt Ave. © 615/577-2262. www.cabananashville.com. Reservations. Main courses $6–$12. AE, DISC, MC, V. Mon–Sat 4pm–3am; Sun 4pm–2am.

Goten *✿* JAPANESE   Glass brick walls and a high-tech Zen-like elegance set the mood at this West End Japanese restaurant, situated across the street from Vanderbilt University. The valet parking is a clue that this restaurant is slightly more formal than other Japanese restaurants in Nashville. Don't come here expecting watery bowls of miso soup and a few noodles. Hibachi dinners are the specialty, with the menu leaning heavily toward steaks, which are just about as popular in Japan as they are in Texas. However, if you are more a sushi person, don't despair; the sushi bar here is Nashville's best, and you can get slices of the freshest fish in town. A sister restaurant, **Goten 2**, is at 209 10th Ave. S. (© **615/251-4855**).

110 21st Ave. S. © 615/321-4537. www.nashvillecity.com. Reservations recommended. Main courses $10–$20. AE, DC, DISC, MC, V. Mon–Fri 11am–2pm; Sun–Thurs 5–10pm; Fri–Sat 5–11pm.

Jimmy Kelly's STEAKS/SEAFOOD   Tradition is the name of the game at Jimmy Kelly's, so if you long for the good old days of gracious Southern hospitality, be sure to schedule a dinner here. The restaurant is in a grand old home with neatly trimmed lawns and a valet-parking attendant (it's free) waiting out front. Inside you'll almost always find the dining rooms and bar bustling with activity as waiters in white jackets navigate from the kitchen to the tables and back. Though folks tend to dress up for dinner here, the several small dining rooms are surprisingly casual. The kitchen turns out well-prepared traditional dishes such as chateaubriand in a burgundy-and-mushroom sauce and blackened catfish (not too spicy, to accommodate the tastes of middle Tennessee). Whatever you have for dinner, don't miss the cornbread—it's the best in the city.

217 Louise Ave. © 615/329-4349. www.jimmykellys.com. Reservations recommended. Main courses $18–$36. AE, DC, MC, V. Mon–Sat 5–11pm.

Midtown Café ✿ NEW AMERICAN/NEW SOUTHERN   Located just off West End Avenue, this small, upscale restaurant conjures up a very romantic atmosphere with indirect lighting and bold displays of art. The design has been pulling in Nashvillians for years. Rich and flavorful sauces are the rule here, with influences from all over the world. The dinner tasting menu is a good way to sample the fare. Be sure to start a meal here with the lemon-artichoke soup, which is as good as its reputation around town. From there, consider moving on to crab cakes served with cayenne hollandaise and available either as an appetizer or an entree. Lunches here are much simpler than dinners, with lots of sandwiches on the menu. However, a few of the same dishes from the dinner menu are available, including the crab cakes.

102 19th Ave. S. ✆ 615/320-7176. www.midtowncafe.com. Dinner reservations recommended. Main courses $12–$35. AE, DC, DISC, MC, V. Mon–Fri 11am–2:30pm; Sun–Sat 5–10pm.

Nick & Rudy's ✿ STEAK   This clubby favorite is one of the few locally owned steakhouses strong enough to stand out against all the new chains. Oysters and French onion soup are menu mainstays, along with generous steaks, chops, seafood, chicken, and pork dishes. There's no extra charge for the Old World charm, and tableside preparations of Caesar's salad and bananas Foster make mealtimes memorable here.

204 21st Ave. S. ✆ 615/329-8994. www.nickandrudys.com. Reservations recommended. Main courses $16–$28. AE, DC, DISC, MC, V. Mon–Fri 11am–2pm; Mon–Sat 5–10pm.

Sunset Grill ✿✿ NEW AMERICAN/NEW SOUTHERN   In the West End neighborhood of Hillsboro Village, the Sunset Grill is that rare breed of restaurant that's both critically acclaimed in the national press and an enduring customer favorite with the locals. The decor is minimalist and monochromatic with original paintings to liven things up a bit. The menu changes daily, with an emphasis on seafood preparations. After all these years, I can't resist the Sonoma Salad, a scrumptious combination of mixed field baby greens, tart apples, almonds, and blue cheese in a pink wine-garlic vinaigrette. Others may prefer the ostrich carpaccio, spicy voodoo pasta, or Szechwan duck. Desserts, such as coconut sushi or butterscotch-habanero bread pudding, show creative panache. On Sundays, Sunset offers half-price wine specials. With more than 300 varieties by the bottle and more than 100 by the glass, you have plenty of choices.

2001 Belcourt Ave. ✆ 615/386-FOOD. www.sunsetgrill.com. Reservations recommended. Main courses $7–$42. AE, DC, DISC, MC, V. Tues–Fri 11am–4:45pm; Mon–Thurs 4:45–10pm; Fri–Sat 4:45pm–midnight; Sun 4:45–11pm.

Zola ✿✿ ⟨Value⟩ FUSION   Chef-owner Debra Paquette has been consistently named one of Nashville's best chefs, and Zola's wine list has received a *Wine Spectator* Award of Excellence for the last few years. Rustic country-French decor lends warmth to the restaurant, where service is friendly and polished. The exotic menu is laced with Mediterranean appetizers such as Moroccan spiced scallops with sweet potato and pistachio griddle cakes, passion fruit sauce, and pomegranate glaze. The specialty of the

---

⟨*Tips*⟩ **Would You Like Fries with That?**

Desperately craving a chicken-salad sandwich on pumpernickel but don't see any parking spaces near the always jam-packed Noshville? The deli has free valet parking during the weekday lunch rush.

Tips **Tired of Waiting?**

The Pancake Pantry may be a breakfast-lover's first choice, but the daunting lines can aggravate appetites as well as patience. Across the street, the brew pub **Boscos** and bakery **Provence** both do a delectable brunch (see listings in this chapter). Next door, barflies looking for hangover relief flock to laid-back **Jackson's in the Village** (1800 21st Ave. S. at Belcourt Ave. (© **615/385-9968**), for Bloody Marys and fried eggs.

---

house is Grandma Zola's Paella, steaming risotto studded with fresh fish, juicy scallops, ham, artichokes, shrimp, and homemade Spanish sausage drizzled with a tangy green aioli. Zola's French Laundry is a deliciously different mélange of arugala, radicchio, diced green apples, toasted hazelnuts, Stilton cheese, and cured orange peel drenched in a champagne vinaigrette.

3001 West End Ave. © 615/320-7778. www.zolarestaurant.com. Reservations highly recommended. Main courses $17–$32. AE, DC, DISC, MC, V. Mon–Thurs 5:30–10pm; Fri–Sat 5:30–11pm.

INEXPENSIVE

Bobbie's Dairy Dip ✯ ICE CREAM/BURGERS   Scrumptious black-bean veggie burgers with guacamole and salsa may be the most unexpected find at this nostalgic, pink-and-green neon, drive-in ice cream stand that's been around for decades. Beefy burgers, sloppy chili dogs, and greasy, fresh-cut fries are also preferred preludes to creamy, hand-dipped milkshakes, hot-fudge sundaes, and other cool treats.

5301 Charlotte Pike. © 615/463-8088. Main courses $7–$9. AE, DISC, MC, V. Daily 11am–10pm. Open seasonally.

DaVinci's Gourmet Pizza ✯ PIZZA   Frequently voted the best pizza in Nashville, this casual neighborhood place is in a renovated brick house in a nondescript neighborhood. As you step through the front door, you'll likely be hit with the overpowering aromas of fragrant pizzas baking in the oven. The pizzas here are all made from scratch and include some very interesting creations. The oysters-Rockefeller pizza is made with smoked oysters, while the Southwestern comes with salsa, roasted chicken, and cilantro. With such offerings as potato pizza, vegetarians are catered to as well. To wash your pizza down, there are lots of imported and domestic beers. In the summer, there's outdoor seating in the flower-dotted front yard.

1812 Hayes St. (at 19th Ave., 1 block off West End Ave.). © 615/329-8098. Pizzas $6.50–$22. AE, DC, DISC, MC, V. Mon–Fri 11am–2pm; Sun–Thurs 4:30–9pm; Fri–Sat 4:30–10pm.

Elliston Place Soda Shop ✯ *Kids* ICE CREAM/AMERICAN   One of the oldest eating establishments in Nashville, the Elliston Place Soda Shop has been around since 1939, and it looks it. The lunch counter, black-topped stools, and signs advertising malted milks and banana splits all seem to have been here since the original opening. It's a treat to visit this time capsule of Americana, with its red-and-white tiled walls, old beat-up Formica tables, and individual booth jukeboxes. The soda shop serves plate lunches of an entree and veggies, with four different specials of the day. Of course, you can also get club sandwiches, steaks, and hamburgers, and the best chocolate shakes in town.

2111 Elliston Place. © 615/327-1090. Main courses $2–$6. MC, V. Mon–Fri 7am–7pm; Sat 7am–5pm.

Tips **Curbside Service**

If you're planning to drive-and-dine in the West End, carry some cash for valet parking. Most restaurants offer the complimentary service, but tips are expected.

Noshville ✦✦ DELICATESSEN   There's only so much fried chicken and barbecue you can eat before you just have to have a thick, juicy Reuben or a bagel with hand-sliced lox. When the deli craving strikes in Nashville, head for Noshville. The deli cases in this big, bright, and antiseptic place are filled to overflowing with everything from beef tongue to pickled herring to corned beef to chopped liver. Make mama happy: Start your meal with some good matzo-ball soup. Then satisfy the kid inside you by splurging on a hefty, two-fisted chocolate-and-vanilla-iced shortbread cookie.

1918 Broadway. © 615/329-NOSH. www.noshville.com. Main courses $6–$16. AE, DC, DISC, MC, V. Mon 6:30am–2:30pm; Tues–Thurs 6:30am–9pm; Fri 6:30am–10:30pm; Sat 7:30am–10:30pm; Sun 7:30am–9pm.

Pancake Pantry ✦ AMERICAN   *The New York Times, Bon Appetit,* and long lines even in all kinds of foul weather attest to the immense popularity of this satisfying but otherwise non-extraordinary eatery in Nashville's West End. College students, country-music stars, NFL players, tourists, and locals alike queue up outside the redbrick building for the chance to sit inside and sip a cup of coffee and cut into a stack of steamy flapjacks. With such varied wait times, it's worth noting that the Pancake Pantry also includes lunch items among its extensive breakfast menu.

1796 21st Ave. S. © 615/383-9333. Main courses $5–$15. AE, DC, DISC, MC, V. Mon–Fri 6am–3pm; Sat–Sun 6am–4pm.

Rotier's ✦ BURGERS   If you're a fan of old-fashioned diners, don't miss Rotier's. This little stone cottage is surrounded by newer buildings but has managed to remain a world unto itself. Sure, it looks like a dive from the outside, and the interior doesn't seem to have been upgraded in 40 years, but the food is good and the prices great. The cheeseburger here is said to be the best in the city, and the milkshakes are pretty good, too. For bigger appetites, there is that staple of Southern cooking—the "meat-and-three." You get a portion of meat (minute steak, pork chops, fried chicken, whatever) and three vegetables of your choice. They also do daily blue-plate specials and cheap breakfasts.

2413 Elliston Place. © 615/327-9892. www.rotiers.net. Sandwiches/main courses $4.25–$16. MC, V. Mon–Fri 10:30am–10pm; Sat 9am–10pm.

South Street ✦ SOUTHERN   The flashing neon sign proclaiming "authentic dive bar," a blue-spotted pink cement pig, and an old tire swing out front should clue you in that this place doesn't take itself too seriously. In fact, this little wedge-shaped eatery is as tacky as an episode of *Hee Haw,* but with Harleys often parked out front. On the menu, you'll find everything from fried pickles to handmade nutty buddies (candy bars). However, the mainstays are crispy catfish, pulled pork barbecue, smoked chicken, ribs, and steaks with biscuits. If you're feeling flush, you can opt for the $43 crab-and-slab dinner for two (two kinds of crab and a "slab" of ribs).

907 20th Ave. S. © 615/320-5555. www.pansouth.net. Main courses $9–$13. AE, DC, DISC, MC, V. Mon–Sat 11am–3am; Sun 11am–midnight.

Tin Angel *★* AMERICAN   A mainstay in the West End, Tin Angel is a best-kept secret among locals and college students. The pressed-tin ceiling, dark wood paneling and crackling fireplace lend a hearth-worthy warmth to the bistro that's known for its soups, fresh salads, and pasta dishes. If you're looking to avoid (other) tourists like yourself, it's also a pleasant place to enjoy a leisurely Sunday brunch, with service that's un-frenzied and friendly.

3201 West End Ave. © 615/298-3444. www.tinangel.net. Reservations recommended. Main courses $10–$15. AE, DISC, MC, V. Mon–Thurs 11am–10pm; Fri 11am–11pm; Sat 5–11pm; Sun 11am–3pm.

5 Southeast Nashville, Green Hills & Berry Hill

EXPENSIVE

F. Scott's Restaurant & Jazz Bar *★★★* *Finds* NEW AMERICAN   Chic and urbane, F. Scott's is an unexpected gem tucked amidst the shopping center hinterlands surrounding the Green Hills area. The classic movie-palace marquee out front announces in no uncertain terms that this place is different. Inside, everything is tastefully sophisticated yet comfortable and cozy. The restaurant's seasonally inspired menu is among the most creative in the city. Although the menu changes frequently, you might start with an appetizer of tender scallops, wild mushrooms, and spinach in a crispy phyllo cup with sun-dried tomatoes, bacon, and a white-truffle *beurre blanc* (warm butter sauce). The salad course of mesclun greens in a curried apple vinaigrette topped with goat cheese, cashews, and carrot shards, served in a crispy papadam cup, couldn't be tastier. Daring but universally delicious entrees vary from chile-braised short ribs with pineapple-plantain potato cakes, to pan-roasted Arctic char with butternut squash spaetzle and green beans, and Singapore noodles with julienned beef, leeks, peppers, and onions. The wine list here is very good, although expensive. Live jazz in the lounge nightly provides another incentive to keep sophisticates coming back. There's also free valet parking.

2210 Crestmoor Rd. © 615/269-5861. www.fscotts.com. Reservations recommended. Main courses $28–$30. AE, DC, DISC, MC, V. Sun 11am–2pm and 5:30–9pm; Mon–Thurs 5:30–10pm; Fri–Sat 5:30–11pm.

MODERATE

Green Hills Grille AMERICAN/SOUTHWESTERN   Located a few blocks past the Mall at Green Hills, this modern Santa Fe–style restaurant was an instant hit with Nashvillians when it opened several years ago. Although suburban strip malls surround it, both its interior decor and menu manage to do a decent job of conjuring up the new Southwest. While most dishes here tend to cater to spicy-food-lovers, enough tamer offerings are available to satisfy those who aren't fire-eaters. For the former, there is "rattlesnake" pasta, and for the latter, there is mild tortilla soup. Spinach-and-artichoke dip makes a good starter. You can't go wrong with an overstuffed black-bean burrito or a juicy cheeseburger. The Green Hills Grille is popular both with businesspeople and families, so you can show up in either jeans or a suit.

2122 Hillsboro Dr. © 615/383-6444. www.greenhillsgrille.com. Reservations not accepted; call-ahead wait list. Main courses $8–$15. AE, DISC, MC, V. Mon–Thurs 7am–10pm; Fri 7am–11pm; Sat 10am–11pm; Sun 10am–10pm. Brunch Sat–Sun 10am–1pm.

INEXPENSIVE

Harper's *★★* *Finds* AMERICAN/SOUTHERN   If the thought of slow-simmered turnip greens, crispy fried chicken, tender sweet potatoes, and fluffy yeast rolls makes your mouth water, wipe off your chin and immediately head to the Jefferson Street district for Nashville's best soul food. Be sure to save room for a slice of pie or a heaping bowl of banana pudding. Popular with white-collar professionals and blue-collar laborers alike, Harper's attracts a friendly, diverse clientele. Unlike seamier soul-food haunts, this immaculate cafeteria accepts credit cards but (thankfully) does not allow smoking.

2610 Jefferson St. ⓒ **615/329-1909.** Main courses $4–$7. AE, DISC, MC, V. Mon–Fri 6am–8pm; Sat–Sun 11am–6pm.

La Hacienda Taqueria ★★ *Moments* MEXICAN   Ethnic eateries and Mexican restaurants have flooded the outskirts of Nashville in recent years, but this former taco stand rises above the rest. Now a family-friendly, full-service restaurant, it's adorned with rustic handmade wood tables and oversized chairs, and colorful wall murals. Crisp, hot tortilla chips, potent salsa, and chunky guacamole are exceptional, as are the enchiladas, flautas, rice, and refried beans. The menu includes tasty little crisp tacos with a long list of fillings, including *chorizo* and beef tongue. There are also fajitas with chicken, beef, or shrimp. You can get Salvadoran *pupusas* (corn tortillas), and just about everything comes with fresh house-made tortillas. Wash it all down with a glass of *tamarindo*.

2615 Nolensville Rd. ⓒ **615/256-6142.** www.lahaciendainc.com. Main courses $7–$20. AE, DISC, MC, V. Mon–Thurs 10am–9pm; Fri–Sat 9am–10pm; Sun 9am–9pm.

6 Belle Meade & Environs

MODERATE

Loveless Café ★★ *Moments* SOUTHERN   For some of the best country cooking in the Nashville area, take a trip out past the city's western suburbs to this old-fashioned roadhouse and popular Nashville institution. People rave about the cooking here—and with good reason. The country ham with red-eye gravy, Southern fried chicken, and homemade biscuits with homemade fruit jams are made just the way Granny used to make them back when the Loveless opened nearly 40 years ago. This restaurant may be a little out of the way, but it's well worth it if you like down-home cookin'—and if you're prepared to endure a long wait to get one of the few available tables inside.

8400 Tenn. 100, about 7½ miles south of Belle Meade and the turnoff from U.S. 70 S. ⓒ **615/646-9700.** www.loveless cafe.com. Main courses $7–$17. Reservations recommended. Daily 7am–9pm.

Martha's at the Plantation ★★★ AMERICAN/NEW SOUTHERN   Fried green tomatoes with horseradish sauce, salmon and artichoke quiche, and herbed chicken-breast salad are indicative of the lunch menu at this delightful restaurant on the grounds of Belle Meade Plantation. The second-floor room is bright and airy; fresh flowers adorn the cloth-covered tables, and lots of windows frame the leafy treetops outside. Regional favorites include buttermilk-battered fried chicken with milk gravy, baked cheese grits, and savory cheddar olive spread. A summer favorite is the fresh fruit platter with pink poppyseed dressing and cheese straws. Wash it down with a crisp sauvignon blanc or tea-flavored punch. And save room for either sugar cookies with minty lemon sorbet, or the wicked fudge pie with vanilla-bean ice cream.

5025 Harding Rd. ⓒ **615/353-2828.** www.marthasattheplantation.com. Main courses $8–$12. AE, DISC, MC, V. Daily 11am–2pm.

The Yellow Porch ★ AMERICAN   In the cute Berry Hill neighborhood south of Nashville, next to a gas station and just across a busy, multi-lane highway, lies this irresistible little bistro. Look for the rocking chair garden planter out front. Service is cordial, and the atmosphere is casual. Salads are excellent. Try the port-poached, sun-dried cherry salad with baby greens, spiced walnuts, and balsamic vinaigrette. Also tempting is the antipasti plate with Genoa salami, Tennessee prosciutto, cheeses, hummus, sundried tomato pesto, and Greek olives. Steaks include a tequila-marinated porterhouse with poblano skillet corn, tomatillo salsa, and mole sauce, while myriad vegetarian options include Mediterranean vegetarian lasagna.

734 Thompson Lane. ✆ 615/386-0260. www.theyellowporch.com. Main courses $13–$25. AE, DISC, MC, V. Mon–Sat 11am–3pm and 5–10pm.

INEXPENSIVE
Kalamata's ✸ MEDITERRANEAN   Risk the road rage that usually comes with a traffic-choked drive out to the Green Hills neighborhood for this oasis of sumptuous Mediterranean cuisine. Its setting may be a nondescript suburban shopping center, but the food is consistently fresh and flavorful. Leafy green salads are flecked with feta cheese and olives, while the creamy hummus—laced with a drizzle of olive oil—is out of this world when dipped alongside soft pita bread and crispy falafel.

3764 Hillsboro Rd. ✆ 615/383-8700. www.bigfatgreekolives.com. Main courses $5–$12. AE, DISC, MC, V. Mon–Thurs 11am–8pm; Fri–Sat 11am–9pm.

Swett's Restaurant ✸✸✸ SOUTHERN   Southern soul food is doled out, cafeteria style, in the city's oldest minority-owned restaurant, which has been in business since 1954. Fresh-cooked collard greens, sweet potatoes, buttered corn, pork-laden green beans, and crumbly cornbread keep the place packed from lunchtime until after supper. Entrees include juicy fried chicken as well as beef, pork, and fish dishes, but I can make a meal on the wicked macaroni and cheese. Wash it down with sweet iced tea—and save room for banana pudding.

2725 Clifton Ave. ✆ 615/329-4418. www.swettsrestaurant.com. Main courses $5.75. AE, DISC, MC, V. Daily 11am–8pm.

7 Music Valley & East Nashville

Music Valley includes the Opryland Hotel and Opry Mills, both of which offer a plethora of eateries—food-court buffets to sit-down restaurants. While the airport area is mostly devoid of commendable places to grab more than a quick bite, the flourishing East Nashville neighborhood has excellent bars, bistros and cafes.

MODERATE
Aquarium SEAFOOD   The novelty of dining amidst 20,000 gallons of water teeming with tropical fish ensures family traffic at this Opry Mills eatery-as-entertainment venue. While the overpriced menu includes burgers, sandwich wraps, soups, and salads, specialties are platters of seafood (broiled, grilled, blackened, or fried). Despite its fun atmosphere, service can be so-so.

516 Opry Mills Dr. ✆ 615/514-3474. www.nashvilleaquarium.com. Main courses $16–$28. AE, DISC, MC, V. Mon–Thurs 11am–10pm; Fri 11am–11pm; Sat 10:30am–11pm; Sun 10:30am–9pm.

Marche Artisan Foods ✸✸ FRENCH   Part market, part bistro and deli, this vegetarian-friendly restaurant serves breakfast, lunch, and dinner. A sunny spot with big picture windows for people-watching, the cafe is owned by **Margot McCormack**, of Margot Café, right around the corner. McCormack's attention to detail and freshness is evident in every aspect of the meals served here, from the fresh-cut summer zinnias in glass jars on the marble tables, to artisanal breads and crisp biscotti, fluffy omelets, luscious salads, and creamy quiches. Before you feast, sip coffee or champagne as you browse the edible goods that abound: Imported olive oils, pestos, and pastas are artfully displayed around wooden farmhouse tables.

1000 Main St. ⓒ **615/262-1111.** www.marcheartisanfoods.com. Main courses $7–$10, dinner $12–$17. AE, DISC, MC, V. Tues–Fri 7am–7pm; Sat 8am–5pm; Sun 9am–4pm.

Margot Café & Bar ⭐⭐ AMERICAN/FRENCH   Chef-owner Margot McCormack's cozy brick cafe in East Nashville is a charmer, especially during Sunday brunch, when diners with prized reservations queue up to sip mimosas or the coffee that's served in individual French-press carafes. On the menu are mouthwatering breads, pastries, and breakfast dishes such as the creamy chicken-artichoke casserole. Tables and banquettes are close together, creating a convivial atmosphere among the clientele, which ranges from upscale professionals to casually clad coeds. Service is exceedingly friendly and efficient.

1017 Woodland St. ⓒ **615/227-4668.** Reservations strongly recommended. Main courses $13–$25. AE, MC, V. Tues–Sat 6–10pm; Sun 11am–2pm.

Old Hickory Steakhouse ⭐⭐⭐ STEAKS   Opryland is in the process of revamping all of its restaurants, including the seafood restaurant Cascades and the family-style Italian place, Volare Ristorante. No changes were needed at the Old Hickory Steakhouse, which is the property's best fine-dining restaurant. Its antebellum mansion décor, replete with a library lounge serving single-malt whiskeys and rare cognacs, reflects Old South grandeur. The menu is much more cosmopolitan than the setting implies, however. Delicious steaks, including certified Angus beef and lean bison cuts, are grilled perfectly to diners' specifications. Succulent Atlantic salmon with bacon ravioli is the best steak-alternative entrée. A tantalizing array of sheep, cow, and goat cheese from throughout the U.S. and Western Europe is served tableside, from a glass-encased cart, along with plump fresh fruits. Service is impeccable, making Old Hickory worth the drive to Music Valley from wherever you might be.

2800 Opryland Dr. ⓒ **615/871-6848.** www.gaylordopryland.com. Reservations recommended. Main courses $23–$40. AE, DISC, MC, V. Sun–Thurs 5–10pm; Fri–Sat 5–11pm.

Rainforest Café ⭐⭐⭐ (Kids) AMERICAN/CARIBBEAN   Lush waterfalls, live birds, and brilliantly colored fish in floor-to-ceiling aquariums provide a feast for the senses at this popular theme restaurant. Indulge in huge platters of oversized burgers, fish sandwiches, and rich entrees such as pasta alfredo. Then save room for the flaming chocolate volcano dessert, which is sure to turn heads when the safari-clad wait staff parades it to your table.

353 Opry Mills Dr. ⓒ **615/514-3000.** www.rainforestcafe.com. Reservations recommended. Main courses $10–$30. AE, DC, DISC, MC, V. Mon–Thurs 11am–9:30pm; Fri–Sat 10:30am–10:30pm; Sun 10:30am–8:30pm.

INEXPENSIVE

Caney Fork Fish Camp SEAFOOD   Two-fisted fried catfish sandwiches, barbecued pork ribs, and comfort-food favorites like meatloaf and mashed potatoes fill the bill at this cavernous, log cabin/lodge-like restaurant near the Opryland Hotel. Fireplaces, a waterfall and small pond, and big-screen TVs augment the outdoorsy camp décor, with fishing nets, rods, lures, and an old 1939 pick-up truck adding visual interest.

2400 Music Valley Dr. ⓒ **615/724-1200.** www.caneyforkfishcamp.com. Main courses $8–$18. AE, DISC, MC, V. Sun–Thurs 11am–10pm; Fri–Sat 11am–11pm.

Nashville Dining: Music Valley & East Nashville

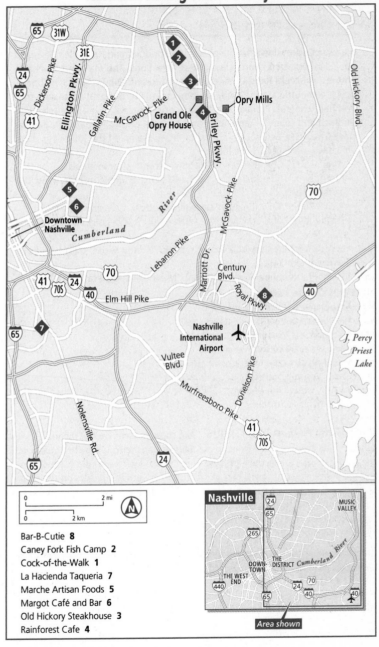

Bar-B-Cutie **8**
Caney Fork Fish Camp **2**
Cock-of-the-Walk **1**
La Hacienda Taqueria **7**
Marche Artisan Foods **5**
Margot Café and Bar **6**
Old Hickory Steakhouse **3**
Rainforest Cafe **4**

The Cheeses Of Old Hickory

Madison County, Iowa, has its picturesque bridges, and Nashville's Opryland has its unexpected, world-class cheese selections. The massive convention and resort hotel's flagship, fine-dining restaurant, Old Hickory Steakhouse, offers a mouthwatering array of more than 100 pungent soft, semi-soft, and hard cheeses. Popular as a before- or after-meal course, the selections on the menu sound as tantalizing as they taste, given the rhapsodic descriptions listed (see below). On a recent visit, we sampled the following, all of which we can highly recommend:

- Aged Gouda Cow (Holland) "Explosive, crunchy, caramelized"
- Montgomery Cheddar Cow (England) "Dry, crumbly, robust, long balanced finish"
- Pierre Robert Cow (France) "Decadent, buttery, silky smooth"
- Rogue River Blue Cow Milk Blue (Oregon) "Spicy, moist, soaked in pear brandy"
- Shropshire Blue Cow Milk Blue (England) "Fudgy, warm, tangy, delicious, sweet cream flavor"
- Wabash Cannonball Goat (Indiana) "Musky, tart, mineral, goaty"

5 Best Cheese Names
- Purple Haze Goat (California)
- Primadonna Cow (Switzerland)
- Gorgonzola Cremificato Cow (Italy)
- Brillat Savarin Cow (France)
- Roaring 40's Cow Milk Blue (Australia)

Source: Old Hickory Steakhouse, Opryland

Cock of the Walk ☞ SOUTHERN   No, roosters aren't on the menu. The restaurant takes its unusual name from an old flatboatman's term for the top boatman. This big, barnlike eatery near the Opryland Hotel is well known around Nashville for having the best seafood in town. Like the catfish fillets and dill pickles on the menu, the shrimp and chicken are fried in peanut oil. Rounding out the hearty platters are sides such as beans and turnip greens brought to the table in big pots.

2624 Music Valley Dr. ℂ 615/889-1930. www.cockofthewalkrestaurant.com. Reservations accepted for groups of 20 or more. Main courses $9–$12. AE, DISC, MC, V. Mon–Thurs 5–9pm; Fri–Sat 5–10pm; Sun 11am–9pm.

8 Barbecue and Hot Chicken
INEXPENSIVE

Bar-B-Cutie ☞ BARBECUE   If you're out by the airport and have an intense craving for barbecue, head to Bar-B-Cutie. Just watch for the sign with the bar-b-doll cowgirl in short shorts. Bar-B-Cutie has been in business since 1948 and, while there is mesquite-grilled chicken available, you'd be remiss if you didn't order the pork shoulder or baby-back ribs. There's another Bar-B-Cutie at 5221 Nolensville Rd. (ℂ **615/834-6556**), on the south side of town.

501 Donelson Pike. ☎ **888/WE-BARBQ** or 615/872-0207. www.bar-b-cutie.com. Full meals $5–$10. AE, DC, MC, V. Sun–Thurs 10am–9pm; Fri–Sat 10am–10pm.

Jack's Bar-B-Que BARBECUE   When the barbecue urge strikes in The District, don't settle for cheap imitations; head to Jack's, where you can get pork shoulder, Texas beef brisket, St. Louis ribs, and smoked turkey, sausage, and chicken. There's another Jack's at 334 W. Trinity Lane (☎ **615/228-9888**), in north Nashville.

416 Broadway. ☎ **615/254-5715**. www.jacksbarbque.com. Main courses $3–$9.50. AE, DISC, MC, V. Summer Mon–Sat 10:30am–10pm. Winter Mon–Wed 10:30am–3pm; Thurs–Sat 10:30am–10pm. Open Sundays only for Tennessee Titans home games.

Mary's Old Fashioned Bar-B-Q ✿ BARBECUE   Short-rib or cornmeal-dusted fried fish sandwiches are served on white bread at this Jefferson Street landmark. Ask for hot sauce, onions, and pickles, if you like. Service is take-out only.

1108 Jefferson St. ☎ **615/256-7696**. Meals $5–$7. Mon–Thurs 8am–midnight. Fri–Sat 8am–2am; Sun 2–10pm.

Prince's Hot Chicken Shack ✿ SOUTHERN   Grease will soak through the brown paper bag in which your fiery, deep-fried chicken is unceremoniously served. That's to be expected here at this proud but run-down joint in a dicey part of town. Line up at the counter with the diverse local clientele to pick your poison—mild, medium, or extra-hot sauce? If you need a cool-down, pray you've got enough change for the Coke machine.

123 Ewing Dr. ☎ **615/226-9442**. Meals $6.50–$8. Tues–Thurs noon–midnight; Fri–Sat noon–4am.

Whitt's Barbecue BARBECUE   Walk in, drive up, or get it delivered. Whitt's serves some of the best barbecue in Nashville. There's no seating here, so take it back to your hotel or plan a picnic. You can buy barbecued pork, beef, and even turkey by the pound, or order sandwiches and plates with the extra fixins. The pork barbecue sandwiches, topped with zesty coleslaw, get my vote for best in town. Among the many other locations are those at 2535 Lebanon Rd. (☎ **615/883-6907**), and 114 Old Hickory Blvd. E. (☎ **615/868-1369**).

5310 Harding Rd. ☎ **615/356-3435**. www.whittsbarbecue.com. Meals $3–$8; barbecue $6.60 per pound. AE, DC, DISC, MC, V. Mon–Sat 10:30am–8pm.

9 Cafes, Bakeries & Pastry Shops

When you just need a quick pick-me-up, a rich pastry, or some good rustic bread for a picnic, there are several good cafes, coffeehouses, and bakeries scattered around the city. Downtown, in the sunny lobby of the Country Music Hall of Fame and Museum, you can order cocktails or coffee with lunch at **SoBro Grill,** 222 5th Ave. S. (☎ **615/254-9060;** www.sobrogrill.com). The stretch of 12th Avenue South is where you'll find the funky **Frothy Monkey,** 2509 12th Ave. S. (☎ **615/292-1808;** www.frothymonkeynashville.com), a bungalow with hardwood floors and a skylight, not to mention free wireless access. **Portland Brew,** 2605 12th Ave. S. (☎ **615/ 292-9004**) and 1921 Eastland (☎ **615/262-9088;** www.portlandbrewcoffee.com), is another locally owned spot whose owners were inspired by coffee shops they encountered in Oregon.

An African word meaning "village" was the inspiration for the name of the **Kijiji Coffee House and Deli,** 1207 Jefferson St. (☎ **615/321-0403;** www.kijijicoffee. com), a popular hangout near Fisk University. Live jazz and poetry readings are held here and at a newly opened second location downtown, at 121 Second St. N. (© 615/ 734-3400).

Bongo Java, 2007 Belmont Blvd. (© 615/385-JAVA; www.bongojava.com), located near Belmont University, is located in an old house on a tree-lined street. It has good collegiate atmosphere, but parking during peak hours can pose a challenge. Nearby in the West End, where coffee shops and cafes are ubiquitous, two of my favorites are **Grins** (pronounced "greens") **Vegetarian Café,** at 25th Ave. and Vanderbilt Place (© 615/322-8571); and **Fido,** 1812 21st Ave. S. (© 615/385-7959), an artsy former pet shop and musicians' hangout that is one of the friendliest Wi-Fi spots in the neighborhood. You can link to both places through Bongo Java's website, listed above.

Across the street from Fido you'll find **Provence Breads & Café** 🍴, 1705 21st Ave. S. (© 615/386-0363; www.provencebreads.com), a European-style coffeehouse which bakes crusty French baguettes along with the most delectable tarts and cookies in town. Gourmet sandwiches and salads, along with brunch items, are on the extensive menu. Provence also has a stylish bistro in the downtown library, 601 Church St. (© 615/644-1150).

Sweet 16th—A Bakery, 311 N. 16th St. (© 615/226-8367; www.sweeth16th. com), is a charming bakery anchoring a trendy residential neighborhood in East Nashville. Heavenly aromas fill the cheerful, immaculate shop, which has a few window seats for those who like to savor their pastries over coffee. From fresh scones and iced éclairs to festive cookies and decadent brownies, this sweet spot has it all.

Out near the Nashville zoo you'll find **Aurora Bakery,** 3725 Nolensville Rd. (© 615/837-1933). Grab sandwiches and picnic fare for the family while browsing one of Nashville's most extensive selection of baked goods, including breads, pastries, cookies, and cakes. Ask for a free taste of the moist *tres leches* (milk) cake, a Mexican specialty.

Tea houses in Nashville include **Loose Leaf Tea Bar** (223 Donelson Pike; © 615/ 889-0044; www.teafortwoandmore.com); **Tea Time Nashville** (2814 12th Ave. S; © 615/497-7292; www.teatimenashville.com); and **Savannah Tea Company** (2206 8th Ave. S.; © 615/383-1832).

And, finally, **Calypso,** 2424 Elliston Place (© 615/321-3878) is an inexpensive chain with multiple locations that features Caribbean-inspired salads and sandwiches, including good vegetarian options such as Boca burgers.

7

Exploring Nashville

Nashville, Music City, the Country Music Capital of the World. There's no question why people visit Nashville. But you may be surprised to find that there's more to see and do here than just chase country stars. Sure, you can attend the *Grand Ole Opry,* linger over displays at the **Country Music Hall of Fame,** take a tour past the homes of the country legends, and hear the stars of the future at any number of clubs. However, the state capital of Tennessee also has plenty of museums and other attractions that have nothing to do with country music. Although the **Van Vechten Art Gallery** at **Fisk University** is temporarily closed for renovations, the city has many other enriching cultural attractions, including the impressive **Frist Center for the Visual Arts** and **Cheekwood Botanical Garden**—not to mention Nashville's full-size reproduction of the **Parthenon.** So even if you've never heard of Marty Stuart or Martina McBride, you'll find something to keep you busy while you're in town. However, if you own every album ever released by George Jones or The Judds, you'll be in hog heaven on a visit to Nashville.

1 On the Music Trail

For information on the *Grand Ole Opry* and other country music performance halls, theaters, and clubs, see chapter 9, "Nashville After Dark." For information on country music gift shops, see chapter 8, "Shopping in Nashville." If you want to drive by some homes of the country stars, pick up a copy of the "Homes of the Stars" map, sold at the **Ernest Tubb Record Shop,** 417 Broadway (© **615/255-7503**), and other country music souvenir shops around town. At the **Visitors Center** in the **Sommet Entertainment Center,** you can also get a booklet with more information on the homes of the stars. With celebrity books all the rage these days, it's not surprising that **Davis-Kidd Booksellers,** 2121 Green Hills Village Dr. (inside The Mall at Green Hills; © **615/385-2645**), brings in country music stars for book signings several times a year. Call them for a schedule.

Cooter's Place and General Store Actor Ben Jones, who starred as Cooter in the late-1970s TV show *The Dukes of Hazzard,* owns this "good-ole-boys" hang-out, where you can buy Confederate flags and other Southern knick-knacks. A museum dedicated to the cult TV hit displays props, records, costumes, posters, and scripts related to the show and its stars. It's popular with tourists year-round, but especially each summer, when Nashville hosts the annual CMT DukesFest charity event at the Tennessee State Fairgrounds and the Music City Motorplex, featuring appearances by former cast members John Schneider, Catherine Bach, and others. In 2007 more than 60,000 fans attended DukesFest, which also includes stunt-car driving, wrestling, and

Nashville Attractions: Downtown & Music Row

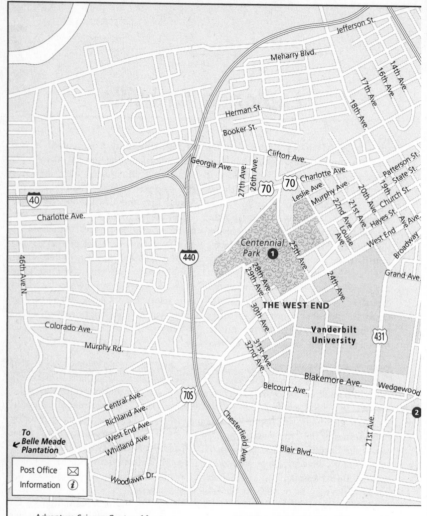

Adventure Science Center **14**

Belmont Mansion **2**

Bicentennial Mall Capitol State Park **3**

Country Music Hall of Fame and Museum **11**

Fort Nashborough **6**

Frist Center for the Visual Arts **10**

Historic RCA Studio B **13**

Lane Motor Museum **15**

Musicians Hall of Fame and Museum **12**

Nashville Coliseum **7**

Parthenon **1**

Ryman Auditorium and Museum **8**

Sommet Center **9**

Tennessee State Capitol **4**

Tennessee State Museum **5**

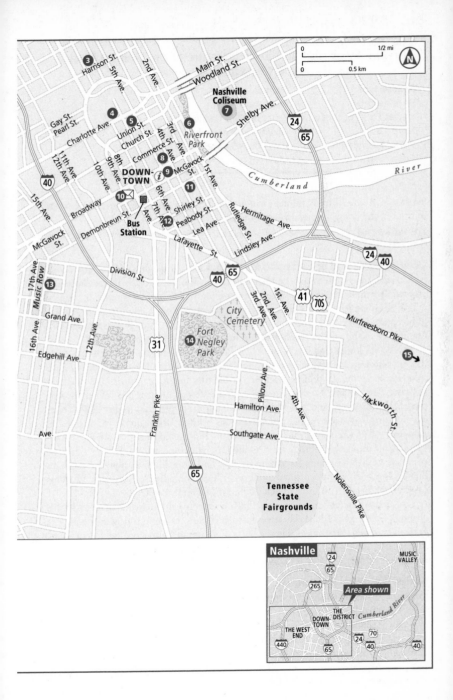

Fun Fact Symbolism in the Architecture of the Country Music Hall of Fame & Museum

Architecture	Symbol
Dark windows	Piano keys
Upward arch of roof	Fin of a 1950s Cadillac
Spire	Country's WSM radio tower
Tiered rotunda	Vinyl 78s, 45s, and CDs
From overhead	Museum resembles a bass clef

---

live music. Allow 20 to 30 minutes to tour the museum and have your picture taken in front of the orange General Lee car out front.

2613 McGavock Pike. ⓒ 615/872-8358. www.cootersplace.com. Free. Daily 9am–7pm. Take McGavock Pkwy to Music Valley Dr.

Country Music Hall of Fame and Museum ⓚⓚ   Although it's more Patsy Montana than Carrie Underwood, country music fans should not miss this wonderfully entertaining museum. Here, you can immerse yourself in the deep roots of country music. Savvy multimedia exhibits let visitors absorb bluegrass, country swing, rockabilly, Cajun, honky-tonk, and contemporary country music through personalized CD listening posts, interactive jukeboxes, and multi-media computer stations.

Elvis's gold-leafed Cadillac (a gift from Priscilla) is a top draw, but on my many return visits here, I always relish revisiting these artifacts: a crude banjo made of hand-split oak and groundhog hide; black-and-white film footage of Stan Laurel mugging with the Cumberland Ramblers in 1935; Jimmie Rodgers' guitar and trademark railroad brakeman's cap; and Bill Monroe's walking cane, personal Bible (with a joker playing card bookmark tucked inside), and his beloved 1923 Gibson F-5 mandolin. And, as if all of this wasn't more than a visitor could stand, the museum also showcases such down-home objects d'art as the kitschy cornfield from TV's *Hee Haw*—complete with Junior Samples' denim overalls and Lulu Roman's plus-size gingham dress. The museum's next major exhibition is "Family Tradition: The Hank Williams Legacy," which will run from March 2008 until December 2009.

If you want to arrange a visit to the old RCA recording studio (see separate entry, this chapter), where Elvis laid down a few hits, you'll need to sign up here at the Hall of Fame. The studio itself is located in the Music Row area of Nashville. Allow 2 to 3 hours.

222 Fifth Ave. S. (at Demonbreun). ⓒ 800/852-6437 or 615/416-2001. www.countrymusichalloffame.com. Admission $18 adults, $16 seniors, military, and college students; $9.95 children 6–17. Daily 9am–5pm.

Grand Ole Opry Museum ⓚ   Adjacent to the Grand Ole Opry House, these exhibits are tributes to the performers who have appeared on the famous radio show over the years: Patsy Cline, Hank Snow, George Jones, Jim Reeves, Marty Robbins, and other longtime stars of the show. There are also about a dozen other exhibits on more recent performers such as Martina McBride, Reba McEntire, and Clint Black. These museums are best visited in conjunction with a night at the *Opry*, so you might want to arrive early. Allow 20 to 30 minutes (just right for browsing prior to attending a performance of the *Grand Ole Opry*).

Nashville Attractions: Music Valley

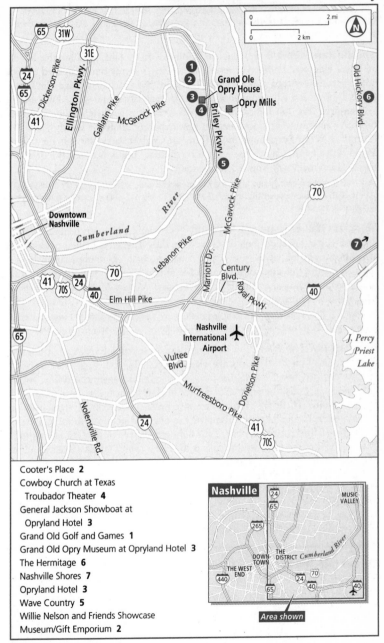

Cooter's Place **2**
Cowboy Church at Texas
  Troubador Theater **4**
General Jackson Showboat at
  Opryland Hotel **3**
Grand Old Golf and Games **1**
Grand Old Opry Museum at Opryland Hotel **3**
The Hermitage **6**
Nashville Shores **7**
Opryland Hotel **3**
Wave Country **5**
Willie Nelson and Friends Showcase
Museum/Gift Emporium **2**

2804 Opryland Dr. ℂ 615/871-OPRY. www.gaylordopryland.com. Free admission. Daily 10am to varied closing hours depending on performance schedule. Closes for special events; call ahead. At the Grand Ole Opry House (it's within the same complex).

Historic RCA Studio B ✿   Dubbed "Home of 1,000 Hits," this humble building on Music Row was a hotbed of recording activity from the time it opened in 1957, until the early 1970s (it closed in 1977). Guided tours include vintage film footage, photo displays, and a lingering look inside the legendary studio where Elvis recorded his immortal "Are You Lonesome Tonight?" Other hits cut here include The Everly Brothers' "All I Have to Do is Dream"; Roy Orbison's "Only the Lonely"; and Dolly Parton's "I Will Always Love You." Tours are available only through the Country Music Hall of Fame and Museum, which shuttles visitors between the downtown museum and the Music Row recording studio.

Music Row (Departures from Country Music Hall of Fame and Museum, 222 Fifth Ave. S.) ℂ **800/852-6437** or 615/416-2001. www.countrymusichalloffame.com. Admission $13 adults, $11 youth. (Discounted tickets available for both museum and studio tour.) Daily 9am–5pm.

Musicians Hall of Fame and Museum   Ever wonder who was behind the haunting steel-guitar hook on Bob Dylan's "Lay Lady Lay?" Nashville's newest music museum answers that mystery, as it pays tribute to the back-up musicians behind the stars. So whether you crave details on the bio of Jimi Hendrix's bass player, or want to see the snare drum used on Red Hot Chili Peppers' *Mothers' Milk* and *Blood Sugar Sex Magik*, this is the place.

301 6th Ave. S. ℂ **615/244-3263**. www.musicianshalloffame.com. Admission $15 adults, $13 seniors and students, $12 military, $9.95 children 7–12, free to children 6 and under. Mon–Thurs 10am–6pm; Fri–Sat 10am–5pm.

Opryland Hotel ✿ *(Moments*   Hotels aren't usually tourist attractions, but this one is an exception. With 2,881 rooms, the place is beyond big, but what makes it worth a visit are the three massive atria that form the hotel's three main courtyards. Together these atria are covered by more than 8 acres of glass to form vast greenhouses full of tropical plants. There are rushing streams, roaring waterfalls, bridges, pathways, ponds, and fountains. There are also plenty of places to stop for a drink or a meal. In the evenings, live music and a laser light show can be seen in the Cascades Atrium.

The largest of the three atriums here is the Delta, which covers 4½ acres and has a quarter-mile-long "river," a 110-foot-wide waterfall, an 85-foot-tall fountain, and an island modeled after the French Quarter in New Orleans. On this island are numerous shops and restaurants, which give the hotel the air of an elaborate shopping mall. You can take boat rides on the river and, at night, catch live music in a nightclub on the island. Allow 20 to 30 minutes.

⌠*Fun Fact* **Music Row**

Nashville's Music Row has lots of high-profile recording studios and music publishing offices. Ocean Way Nashville Studio, on 17th Ave. S., boasts a Who's Who roster of artists who've cut records there. Not just country stars, they run the gamut from Harry Connick, Jr., and Sheryl Crow to Matchbox Twenty and Yo-Yo Ma. Among Music City clients are Faith Hill, Toby Keith, Montgomery Gentry, Willie Nelson, and George Strait.

Traveling Between Downtown and Music Valley

A cab ride from downtown to the Opryland Hotel costs about $25. A trolley serves Music Valley attractions, but a car is really the best way to get around. If you're staying as a guest at Opryland, you'll have access to daily, round-trip shuttle service to downtown tourist sites, including the Wildhorse Saloon and The Ryman Auditorium.

2800 Opryland Dr. ℭ 615/889-1000. www.gaylordopryland.com. Free admission. Daily 24 hours. Parking $10. Take I-40 to exit 215 and take Briley Pkwy. (155 North) to exit 12. Turn left at the second traffic light into the Gaylord Opryland complex.

Willie Nelson & Friends Showcase Museum/Gift Emporium *(Overrated*   Less a museum than a souvenir shop with a few dusty exhibits in a big back room, this tourist site for die-hard Willie fans features many of his old guitars, gold and platinum records, movie posters, and even his pool table. It's a hodgepodge that includes areas devoted to fellow Outlaws Waylon Jennings, Johnny Cash, and Kris Kristofferson, as well as an extensive collection of B-movie Western star Audie Murphy's memorabilia. Unexpected finds, like a ticket stub from Elvis Presley's final concert, can be jarring. The museum displays are tucked behind saloonlike doors of a gift shop that hawks everything from shot glasses, T-shirts, and swizzle sticks to feathery dream catchers and dolphin figurines. Allow 20 to 30 minutes.

2613A McGavock Pike. ℭ 615/885-1515. www.willienelsongeneralstore.com. Admission $5 adults, $4.50 seniors, $3 children 6–12, free for children under 6. Daily 9am–5pm (closing hours sometimes vary). Closed Dec 25 and Jan 1. Take McGavock Pkwy. to Music Valley Dr.

IN THE DISTRICT

All downtown attractions are accessible from the downtown trolley.

Ryman Auditorium & Museum 👀★   If you're as enamored with music history as I am, you could devote several hours to a self-guided tour of this National Historic Landmark where you're free to stand onstage—even belt out a few bars if the spirit moves you—or sit in the hardwood "pews," and wander the halls upstairs and down, looking at memorabilia in glass showcases. However, the typical tourist may be satisfied with a quick walk through the stately redbrick building. In either case, the best way to experience the Ryman is to attend a performance here. The site of the *Grand Ole Opry* from 1943 to 1974, the Ryman Auditorium is known as the "Mother Church of Country Music," the single most historic site in the world of country music. Originally built in 1892 as the Union Gospel Tabernacle by riverboat captain Tom Ryman, this building served as an evangelical hall for many years. By the early 1900s, the building's name had been changed to honor its builder and a stage had been added. That stage, over the years, saw the likes of Enrico Caruso, Katharine Hepburn, Will Rogers, and Elvis Presley. The *Grand Ole Opry* began broadcasting here in 1943. For the next 31 years, the Ryman Auditorium was host to the most famous country music radio show in the world. However, in 1974, the *Opry* moved to the then-new Grand Ole Opry House in the Music Valley area. Since its meticulous renovation in 1994, the Ryman has regained its prominence as a temple of bluegrass and country music. Its peerless acoustics make it a favored venue of rock's best singer-songwriters and classical musicians, as well. Acts as diverse as Yo-Yo Ma, Coldplay, and

Keith Urban have performed here. In 2005, director Jonathan Demme filmed Neil Young's performance for the concert film *Prairie Wind.* Allow at least an hour for a self-guided tour.

116 Fifth Ave. N. (between Commerce and Broadway) ℂ 615/458-8700 or 615/889-3060. www.ryman.com. Self-guided tours admission $13 adults, $6.25 children 4–11, free for children under 4; add $3.75 for backstage tour. Daily 9am–4pm. Closed Thanksgiving, Dec 25, and Jan 1.

2 More Attractions

HISTORIC BUILDINGS

Belle Meade Plantation ⭐⭐ Belle Meade was built in 1853 after this plantation had become famous as a stud farm that produced some of the best racehorses in the South. Today, the Greek Revival mansion is the centerpiece of the affluent Belle Meade region of Nashville and is surrounded by 30 acres of manicured lawns and shade trees. A long driveway leads uphill to the mansion, which is fronted by six columns and a wide veranda. Inside, the restored building has been furnished with 19th-century antiques that hint at the elegance and wealth that the Southern gentility enjoyed in the late 1800s.

Tours led by costumed guides follow a theme (for example, holidays, aspects of plantation life, and so on) that changes every 3 months. These themed tours provide fascinating glimpses into the lives of the people who once lived at Belle Meade. Also on the grounds are a large carriage house and stable that were built in 1890 and that now house a large collection of antique carriages. During your visit, you can also have a look inside a log cabin, a smokehouse, and a creamery that are here on the grounds. Belle Meade's parklike grounds make it a popular site for festivals throughout the year.

In addition, **Martha's at the Plantation** (ℂ 615/353-2828), a simple yet stylish restaurant above the gift shop, is drawing raves for chef Martha Stamp's American/Southern dishes such as chicken salad, crawfish, quiches, and caramel cakes. A best-selling cookbook author, Stamp has also been featured in *Southern Living* and *Victorian* magazines, as well as on the TV show *Martha Stewart Living.* Sunday brunch is among the locals' favorites at Martha's at the Plantation, open daily 11am to 2pm. Allow a full morning or afternoon to soak up everything here.

5025 Harding Rd. ℂ 800/270-3991 or 615/356-0501. www.bellemeadeplantation.com. Admission $14 adults, $11 seniors, $6 children 6–12, free for children under 6. Mon–Sat 9am–5pm; Sun 11am–5pm. (Last tour starts at 4pm.) Closed Thanksgiving, Dec 25, Jan 1, and Easter. Take 70 South to Belle Meade Blvd. to Deer Park Drive and follow the signs.

Belmont Mansion ⭐ Built in the 1850s by Adelicia Acklen, then one of the wealthiest women in the country, this Italianate villa is the city's most elegant historic home open to the public, and its grand salon is one of the most elaborately decorated rooms in any antebellum home in Tennessee. Belmont Mansion was originally built as a summer home, yet no expense was spared in its construction. On your tour of the

---

Fun Fact **Make Mine a Shower**

Portly President Howard Taft once got stuck in a bathtub at Belle Meade Plantation while visiting Nashville. The subsequent installation of a shower at Belle Meade prompted Taft to have a shower installed at the White House.

> **Tips** **Shutterbugs, Take Note**
>
> Unlike many museums and historic mansions, photography *is* permitted inside the Belmont Mansion. So click away!

mansion, you'll see rooms filled with period antiques, artwork, and marble statues. This museum also has an excellent gift shop full of reproduction period pieces. Allow at least 90 minutes to tour the mansion.

1900 Belmont Blvd. © 615/460-5459. www.belmontmansion.com. Admission $10 adults, $3 children 6–12, free for children under 6. Mon–Sat 10am–4pm; Sun 1–4pm. (Last tour starts at 3:15pm.) Closed major holidays. Take Wedgewood Ave. off 21st Ave. S. (an extension of Broadway), turn right on Magnolia Ave., left on 18th Ave. S., then left on Acklen.

Fort Nashborough   Though it's much smaller than the original, this reconstruction of Nashville's first settlement includes several buildings that faithfully reproduce what life in this frontier outpost was like in the late 18th century. The current fort looks oddly out of place in modern downtown Nashville, but if you're interested in Tennessee's early settlers, this site is worth a brief look. Allow 30 minutes or more if you've got kids who want to play here.

170 First Ave. N. (between Church and Commerce). No phone. Free admission. Daily 9am–4pm. On the edge of Riverfront Park on the banks of the Cumberland River.

The Hermitage ✮   Though you may not know it, you probably see an image of one of Nashville's most famous citizens dozens of times every week. Whose face pops up so frequently? It's Andrew Jackson, whose visage appears on the $20 bill, and who is the man who built The Hermitage, a stately Southern plantation home. Jackson moved to Tennessee in 1788 and became a prosecuting attorney. He served as the state's first congressman and later as a senator and judge. However, it was during the War of 1812 that he gained his greatest public acclaim as the general who led American troops in the Battle of New Orleans. His role in that battle helped Jackson win the presidency in 1828 and again in 1832.

Though The Hermitage now displays a classic Greek Revival facade, this is its third incarnation. Originally built in the Federal style in 1821, it was expanded and remodeled in 1831, and acquired its current appearance in 1836. Recordings that describe each room and section of the grounds accompany tours through the mansion and around it. In addition to the main house, you'll also visit the kitchen, the smokehouse, the garden, Jackson's tomb, an original log cabin, the spring house (a cool storage house built over a spring), and, nearby, the Old Hermitage Church and Tulip Grove mansion. You can tour the museum and grounds in a few hours.

Old Hickory Blvd., Nashville. © 615/889-2941. www.thehermitage.com. Admission $15 adults, $13 seniors, $11 for students 13–18; $7 children 6–12, free for children under 6. Daily 9am–5pm. Closed Thanksgiving, Dec 25, and 3rd week of Jan. Take I-40 east to exit 221, then head north 4 miles.

The Parthenon   Centennial Park, as the name implies, was built for the Tennessee Centennial Exposition of 1897, and this full-size replica of the Athens Parthenon was the exposition's centerpiece. The original structure was only meant to be temporary, however, and by 1921 the building, which had become a Nashville landmark, was in an advanced state of deterioration. In that year, the city undertook reconstruction of

Who Was Patsy Montana?

No, she wasn't the godmother of contemporary teen idol Miley Cyrus/Hannah Montana—even though her real-life dad is Billy Ray ("Achey-Break Heart") Cyrus. Patsy Montana was one of the first bona fide, female country-music stars. Her Depression-era radio hit, "I Want to Be a Cowboy's Sweetheart," made her the first non-pop female singer ever to sell a million records. Born in a log cabin in the Ozark Mountains near Hope, Ark., in 1908, Patsy Montana was an icon of her day—known as much for her yodeling and fringed cowgirl outfits and wholesome, girl-next-door good looks. Montana died in 1996, the same year she was inducted into the Country Music Hall of Fame. You can learn more about Patsy Montana's colorful career at the Country Music Hall of Fame and Museum.

its Parthenon and by 1931 a new, permanent building stood in Centennial Park. The building now duplicates the floor plan of the original Parthenon in Greece. Inside stands the 42-foot-tall statue of Athena Parthenos, the goddess of wisdom, prudent warfare, and the arts. Newly gilded with 8 pounds of gold leaf, she is the tallest indoor sculpture in the country.

In addition to this impressive statue, there are original plaster castings of the famous Elgin marbles—bas-reliefs that once decorated the pediment of the Parthenon. Inside the air-conditioned galleries, you'll find an excellent collection of 19th- and 20th-century American art. The Parthenon's two pairs of bronze doors, which weigh in at 7½ tons per door, are considered the largest matching bronze doors in the world. Allow about 30 minutes.

Centennial Park, West End Ave. (at West End and 25th Aves.). © 615/862-8431. www.parthenon.org. Admission $5 adults, $2.50 seniors and children. Oct–Mar Tues–Sat 9am–4:30pm; Apr–Sept Tues–Sat 9am–4:30pm, Sun 12:30–4:30pm. (Closed Sundays after Labor Day.)

Tennessee State Capitol   The Tennessee State Capitol, completed in 1859, is a classically proportioned Greek Revival building that sits on a hill on the north side of downtown Nashville. The capitol is constructed of local Tennessee limestone and marble that slaves and convict laborers quarried and cut. Other notable features include the 19th-century style and furnishings of several rooms in the building, a handful of ceiling frescoes, and many ornate details. President and Mrs. James K. Polk are both buried on the capitol's east lawn. You can pick up a guide to the capitol at the Tennessee State Museum. It won't take long to admire it from the outside.

Charlotte Ave. (between Sixth and Seventh Aves.). © 615/741-2692. Free admission. Mon–Fri 9am–5pm. Closed all state holidays.

Travellers Rest Historic House Museum   Built in 1799, Travellers Rest, as its name implies, once offered gracious Southern hospitality to travelers passing through a land that had only recently been settled. Judge John Overton (who, along with Andrew Jackson and General James Winchester, founded the city of Memphis) built Travellers Rest. Overton also served as a political advisor to Jackson when he ran for president. Among the period furnishings you'll see in this restored Federal-style farmhouse is the state's largest public collection of pre-1840 Tennessee-made furniture. Allow an hour to tour the museum, and more if you want to wander the grounds and outbuildings.

636 Farrell Pkwy. ℭ 615/832-8197. www.travellersrestplantation.org. Admission $10 adults, $9 seniors, $5 students 13–18, $3 children 6–12, free for children under 6. Mon–Sat 10am–4pm; Sun 1–4pm. Closed Thanksgiving, Dec 25, and Jan 1. Take I-65 to exit 78B (Harding Place West), go west to Franklin Pike, turn left, and then follow the signs.

MUSEUMS

Adventure Science Center *(Kids)*   It's hard to say which exhibit kids like the most at the Center. There are just so many fun interactive displays from which to choose in this modern, hands-on museum. Though the museum is primarily meant to be an entertaining way to introduce children to science, it can also be fun for adults. Kids of all ages can learn about technology, the environment, physics, and health as they roam the museum pushing buttons and turning knobs. On weekends there are almost always special shows and demonstrations, and throughout the year the museum schedules special exhibits. In the **Sudekum Planetarium,** there are regular shows that take you exploring through the universe. Allow 2 hours.

800 Ft. Negley Blvd. ℭ 615/862-5160. www.adventuresci.com. Admission $9 adults, $7 seniors and children 3–12, free for children under 3. Mon–Sat 10am–5pm; Sun 12:30–5:30pm. (Open Fri–Sat until 7pm from Memorial Day Labor Day.) Closed Thanksgiving, Dec 25, and Jan 1. Fourth Ave. S. to Oak St., to Bass St. to Fort Negley.

Cheekwood Botanical Garden & Museum of Art ⋆⋆ *(Kids)*   Once a private estate, Cheekwood today has much to offer both art lovers and garden enthusiasts. The museum and gardens are situated in a 55-acre park that's divided into several formal gardens and naturally landscaped areas. The museum itself is housed in the original Cheek family mansion, which was built in the Georgian style with many architectural details brought over from Europe. Among the mansion's most outstanding features is a lapis lazuli fireplace mantel. Within the building are collections of 19th- and 20th-century American art, Worcester porcelains, antique silver serving pieces, Asian snuff bottles, and a good deal of period furniture. The grounds are designed for strolling, and there are numerous gardens, including Japanese, herb, perennial, dogwood, magnolia, iris, peony, rose, and azalea—and there are greenhouses full of orchids. Kids will enjoy romping around the grassy meadows on the museum grounds. Don't miss the glass bridge that rewards hikers along the wooded sculpture trail. You'll also find a gift shop and good restaurant, The Pineapple Room, on the grounds. Allow a couple of hours to tour the museum, or up to a full day if you plan to explore the grounds and garden as well.

1200 Forrest Park Dr. (8 miles southwest of downtown). ℭ 615/356-8000. www.cheekwood.org. Admission $30 per household, $10 adults, $8 seniors, $5 college students and children 6–17, free for children under 6. Tues–Sat

---

Value **Everybody Loves a Bargain**

The Nashville Visitors Center has made it fun and easy to get the most out of a trip to Music City with the Total Access Attraction Pass. For $45, you can choose any four of the following: Adventure Science Center, Belle Meade Plantation, Belmont Mansion, Cheekwood, Country Music Hall of Fame and Museum, The Delta Riverboat Company at Gaylord Opryland, Frist Center for the Visual Arts, General Jackson Showboat, The Hermitage, Musicians Hall of Fame and Museum, Nashville Shores Water Park, Nashville Zoo at Grassmere, Ryman Auditorium, and Travellers Rest Plantation and Museum. For more information, call ℭ 800/657-6910 or 615/259-4700, or go online to www.visitmusiccity.com.

9:30am–4:30pm; Sun 11am–4:30pm. Closed Thanksgiving, Dec 25, Jan 1, and 2nd Sat in June. Take West End Ave. to Belle Meade Blvd. and turn left; then left at Page Road and left on Forest Park Dr.

The Frist Center for the Visual Arts ✺✺✺ *Kids*   Opened in 2001, the Frist Center for the Visual Arts brings world-class art exhibits to the historic downtown post office building. The nonprofit center does not maintain a permanent collection but rather presents exhibitions from around the globe. Among the works slated to be shown in 2008 include paintings by Claude Monet, Henri Matisse, and Salvador Dali; stained-glass lamps by Louis Comfort Tiffany; and bronze sculptures by Auguste Rodin. Upstairs, the **ArtQuest Gallery** ✺ encourages visitors to explore a range of art experiences through more than 30 interactive multimedia stations. Creative kids and likeminded adults could spend hours here.

The Frist is free to visitors 18 and under, making it an excellent value. Seniors get half-price admission the third Monday of each month, when musical activities such as sing-alongs are held.

919 Broadway. ℂ 615/244-3340. www.fristcenter.org. Admission $8.50 adults, $7.50 seniors, free for children under 18. (Admission prices may be charged for special exhibitions.) Mon–Wed 10am–5:30pm; Thurs–Fri 10am–9pm; Sat 10am–5:30pm; Sun 1–5:30pm. Closed Thanksgiving, Dec 25, and Jan 1. Between Ninth and 10th Aves. next to the Union Station Hotel.

Lane Motor Museum   This unexpected find features about 150 unusual cars and motorcycles. Most are European vehicles from the 1950s through the 1970s. Mechanics and car buffs alike will enjoy ogling the candy-colored Citroens and one-of-a-kind prototypes, such as a 1928 Martin Aerodynamic Car, and a 1946 Hewson Rocket. One of the museum's main missions is to keep all the cars in its collection, from Fiats to Lamborghinis, in good running order.

702 Murfreesboro Pike ℂ 615/742-7445. www.lanemotormuseum.com. Admission $5 adults, $3 seniors, free to youth (18 and under). Thurs–Mon 10am–5pm. Closed Thanksgiving, Dec. 25, and Jan. 1.

Tennessee State Museum *Kids*   Kids always rush to find the 3,000-year-old Egyptian mummy on display, but along the way maybe they will gain a better understanding of Tennessee history during a visit to this museum beneath the Tennessee Performing Arts Center. The museum showcases Native American artifacts as well as objects from 18th-century century pioneer life. You'll see Daniel Boone's rifle and a powder horn that once belonged to Davy Crockett, along with exhibits on presidents Andrew Jackson and James K. Polk.

Fun Fact   **Planes, Trains & Automobiles**

Constructed during the Depression, Nashville's main post office is home to the Frist Center for the Visual Arts. Classical and Art Deco architectural styles are prominent within the marble and gray-pink granite building, which is on the National Register of Historic Places. Intricate grillwork celebrates icons of American progress: an airplane, a locomotive, a ship, and an automobile. Among other achievements represented in the icons: scientific research (microscope, test tube, and flask), harvesting (sheaf of wheat and sickle), industry (cogwheels), publishing (book press), sowing (hand plow), metalwork (hammer and anvil), the pursuit of knowledge (lamp of learning resting on books), and nautical endeavors (dolphin and propeller).

Fun Fact African-American Heritage

Fisk University was founded in 1866 as a liberal arts institution committed to educating newly freed slaves. Prominent 20th-century cultural figures such as educator W.E.B. Dubois, artist Aaron Douglas, and poet Nikki Giovanni attended the school. Fisk is perhaps best known for its Jubilee Singers, an African-American singing group that preserved spirituals, or slave songs, from extinction. The choir's 1873 tour of the U.S. and Europe helped finance the construction of Fisk University. **Jubilee Hall,** one of the oldest structures on the campus, is a Victorian Gothic gem listed on the register of National Historic Landmarks. Now used as a dormitory, the building houses a floor-to-ceiling portrait of the original Jubilee Singers, commissioned by Queen Victoria of England as a gift to Fisk. To see the hall, make arrangements ahead of time (© 615/329-8500).

Visitors may view pre–Civil War artifacts including full-scale replicas of old buildings and period rooms, a log cabin, a water-driven mill, a woodworking shop, an 18th-century print shop, and an 1855 parlor. Although the lower level of the museum is devoted mostly to the Civil War and Reconstruction, exhibits change; visitors are advised to call ahead to see what is currently on display. One block west on Union Street, you'll find the museum's Military Branch, which houses displays on Tennessee's military activity from the Spanish-American through Viet Nam wars. Allow 2 to 3 hours.

Fifth Ave. (between Union and Deaderick Sts.). © 800/407-4324 or 615/741-2692. www.tnmuseum.org. Free admission; donations encouraged. Tues–Sat 10am–5pm. Closed Easter, Thanksgiving, Dec 25, and Jan 1.

PARKS, PLAZAS & BOTANICAL GARDENS

To celebrate the 200th anniversary of Tennessee statehood, Nashville constructed the impressive **Bicentennial Capitol Mall State Park** (© 615/741-5280), north of the state capitol. The mall, which begins just north of James Robertson Parkway and extends (again, north) to Jefferson Street between Sixth and Seventh avenues, is a beautifully landscaped open space that conjures up the countryside with its limestone rockeries and plantings of native plants. As such, it is a very pleasant place for a leisurely stroll. The western edge of the park offers fantastic views of the capitol.

However, this mall is far more than just a park. It is also a 19-acre open-air exhibition of Tennessee history and geography and a frame for the capitol, which sits atop the hill at the south end of the mall. Also at the south end of the mall is a 200-foot-long granite map of the state, and behind this are a gift shop/visitor center, a Tennessee rivers fountain, and an amphitheater used for summer concerts. Along Sixth Avenue, you'll find a walkway of Tennessee counties, with information on each county (beneath the plaques, believe it or not, are time capsules). Along Seventh Avenue is the Pathway of History, a wall outlining the state's 200-year history. Within the mall, there are also several memorials.

Known together as "The Warner Parks" (© 615/370-8051; www.nashville.gov), Edwin Warner Park and Percy Warner Park offer beautiful scenery, miles of hiking and equestrian trails, picnic areas, and outdoor recreation sites. **Percy Warner Park** (2500 Old Hickory Blvd.), is the crown jewel of Nashville green spaces. Named for Percy

Warner, a local businessman and avid outdoorsman, the wooded hills and rolling meadows extend for more than 2,000 acres. Though popular with bicyclists, be aware that they must share the winding, paved roads with vehicular traffic. Perfect for picnics and other outdoor pursuits, the park offers clean shelters, restrooms, and even a 27-hole golf course. **Edwin Warner Park,** 50 Vaughn Road (on Old Hickory Blvd. near Highway 100), also has lovely picnic areas, scenic overlooks, and a dog park.

After visiting this park, it seems appropriate to take a stroll around **Centennial Park,** located on West End Avenue at 25th Avenue. This park, built for the 1896 centennial celebration, is best known as the site of the Parthenon, but also has many acres of lawns, colorful playground equipment, 100-year-old shade trees, and a small lake.

See also the entry for Cheekwood Botanical Garden & Museum of Art on p. 103.

NEIGHBORHOODS
THE DISTRICT

The District, encompassing several streets of restored downtown warehouses and other old buildings, is ground zero for the Nashville nightlife scene. It's divided into three areas. Second Avenue between Broadway and Union Street, the heart of The District, was originally Nashville's warehouse area and served riverboats on the Cumberland River. Today, most of the old warehouses have been renovated and now house a variety of restaurants, nightclubs, souvenir shops, and other shops. Anchoring Second Avenue at the corner of Broadway is the **Hard Rock Cafe,** and a few doors up the street is the **Wildhorse Saloon,** a massive country music dance hall. Along Broadway between the Cumberland River and Fifth Avenue, you'll find several of country music's most important sites, including the **Ryman Auditorium** (home of the *Grand Ole Opry* for many years), **Tootsie's Orchid Lounge** (where Opry performers often dropped by for a drink), **Gruhn Guitars,** and the **Ernest Tubb Record Shop.** Along this stretch of Broadway, you'll also find **Robert's Western World,** the entrance to the **Gaylord Entertainment Center,** and the **Nashville Convention & Visitors Bureau Visitors Center.** The third area of The District is Printer's Alley, which is off Church Street between Third and Fourth avenues. Though not as lively as it once was during the days of Prohibition and speakeasies, the alley is an interesting place for an afternoon or early-evening stroll. At night, a few clubs still offer live music.

MUSIC ROW

Located along 16th and 17th avenues between Demonbreun Street and Grand Avenue, Music Row is the very heart of the country music recording industry and is home to dozens of recording studios and record-company offices. Demonbreun, which suffered a few years ago when the old country music museum closed (and the new Hall of Fame opened downtown), is enjoying a resurgence as shops, pubs, and restaurants begin to fill the void. The neighborhood is a combination of old restored homes and modern buildings that hint at the vast amounts of money generated by the country music industry. This is one of the best areas in town for spotting country music stars, so keep your eyes peeled. Anchoring the Music Row "turnaround" (a circular roadway at the entrance to the area) is *Musica.* The 40-foot-tall bronze sculpture of six nude figures was considered a bit shocking when it was unveiled in the fall of 2003. After all, Nashville is located in the buckle of the Bible Belt.

THE GULCH

The Gulch is a rapidly growing area just south of downtown that's being developed at a furious pace. An increasing cluster of buzz-worthy restaurants such as **Watermark** and **Radius 10** have ramped up the area's cache with the in-crowd. Construction of $250,000 condominium and loft towers and other mixed-use high-rises is proceeding at breakneck pace.

8TH AVENUE SOUTH AND 12TH AVENUE SOUTH
If you want to get off the tourist trail for the afternoon, head south a few miles from downtown to the funky little neighborhood known as 12th Avenue South. Twentysomethings have been buying and refurbishing the area bungalows. The area, roughly bounded by Linden and Kirkwood avenues, is also home to some of Nashville's hippest new restaurants and boutiques. There are a couple of clothing stores, including **Serendipity Emporium** and **Katy K's Ranch Dressing,** as well as a cool unisex hair salon called **Trim.** Start your sojourn with a bite to eat at **Mirror** or **Mafiaoza's,** browse the boutiques, and end the trip with a gourmet Popsicle from **Las Paletas.**

EAST NASHVILLE/FIVE POINTS
Across the Cumberland River from downtown Nashville lies the endearing neighborhood known as Five Points in East Nashville. From downtown, take the Woodland Street bridge east and follow it a mile or so to this gentrified, turn-of-the-last-century neighborhood that's home to some of the city's hippest bistros and clubs, including **Margot Cafe, Family Wash,** and **Lipstick Lounge.**

A DAY AT THE ZOO
Nashville Zoo at Grassmere *(Kids)*   This 80-acre zoo just south of downtown has it all, from giraffes, elephants and alligators to meerkats, rainbow-colored lorikeets, and African wild hogs. In the naturalistic habitats, you'll see river otters, bison, elk, black bear, gray wolves, bald eagles, and cougars, as well as other smaller animals. In the park's aviary, you can walk among many of the state's songbirds, and at the Cumberland River exhibit expect to see fish, reptiles, and amphibians. Kids can ride wood-carved cougars and other critters on the zoo's colorful new carousel. Allow 2 to 3 hours. *Tip:* To beat the crowds, try visiting the zoo during off-peak times of the day. Best bets are any weekday around 1pm, or Sunday morning at 9am.

3777 Nolensville Pike. © **615/833-1534.** www.nashvillezoo.org. Admission $13 adults, $11 seniors, $8 children 3–12, free for children under 3. Parking $2. Apr–Oct 15 daily 9am–6pm; Oct 16–Mar daily 9am–4pm. Closed Thanksgiving, Dec 25, and Jan 1. (Nolensville Rd./Harding Place.) Follow Fourth Ave. south to Nolensville Pike to U.S. 11 and turn on Zoo Rd.

3 Especially for Kids

Even if your child is not a little Tim McGraw or Faith Hill in training, Nashville is full of things for kids to see and do. In addition to the attractions listed below, see also the listings in this chapter for Cheekwood Botanical Garden & Museum of Art (p. 103), Adventure Science Center (p. 103), the Frist Center for the Visual Arts (p. 104), the Nashville Zoo at Grassmere (see above), and the Tennessee State Museum (p. 104).

Grand Old Golf & Games & Valley Park Go-Karts   With three miniature-golf courses, a go-kart track, and game room, this place, located near the Opryland Hotel, is sure to be a hit with your kids. You can easily spend the whole day here.

2444 Music Valley Dr. © **615/871-4701.** www.grandoldgolf.net. Fees 1 course $6.50, 2 courses $7.50, 3 courses $8.50; half-price for children 10 and under. Fees for go-karts $7 for single seat, $8 for double seat. May–Sept Mon–Thurs 10am–11pm, Fri–Sat 10am–midnight, Sun noon–11pm; Oct–Nov daily noon–9pm; Dec–Feb daily noon–5pm; Mar–Apr daily 11am–10pm. All open hours are weather-permitting. Take Briley Pkwy. to McGavock Pike to Music Valley Dr.

Nashville Shores   Tucked on the pristine shores of Percy Priest Lake about 10 miles outside of Nashville, this massive water park and family recreation destination offers white-sand beaches, jet-ski and boat rentals, eight water slides, and even kayaking areas. Other activities include lake cruises, miniature golf, volleyball, basketball, and horseshoes.

Tips **Picnic It**

To reserve a picnic shelter in any of Nashville's city parks, call ℂ 615/862-8408.

4001 Bell Road. ℂ 615/889-7050. www.nashville shores.com. Mon–Sat 10am–6pm; Sun 11am–6pm. Admission $22 adults (48 inches and taller); $17 for 47 inches and shorter and seniors 55 and older, and military.

Wave Country   This water park is located just off Briley Parkway about a mile from the old Opryland USA and is a summertime must for kids of all ages. There's a huge freshwater wave pool, three water flumes and two speed slides. Pack a picnic, and make an afternoon of it.

2320 Two Rivers Pkwy. (off Briley Pkwy.). ℂ 615/885-1052. Admission $8 adults, $7 children 5–12, free for children under 5; half price for children after 4pm. Memorial Day to Labor Day daily 10am–6pm.

4 Strolling Around Nashville

If you'd like a bit more information on some of these sites or would like to do a slightly different downtown walk, pick up a copy of the *Nashville City Walk* brochure at the Visitors Center in the Gaylord Entertainment Center. This brochure, produced by the Metropolitan Historical Commission, outlines a walk marked with a green line painted on downtown sidewalks. Along the route are informational plaques and green metal silhouettes of various characters from history.

WALKING TOUR   DOWNTOWN NASHVILLE

Start:	Riverfront Park at the intersection of Broadway and First Avenue. (There's a public parking lot here.)
Finish:	Printer's Alley.
Time:	Anywhere from 3 to 8 hours, depending on how much time you spend in the museums, shopping, or dining.
Best Times:	Tuesday through Friday, when both the Tennessee State Museum and the Tennessee State Capitol are open to the public.
Worst Times:	Sunday, Monday, and holidays, when a number of places are closed. Or anytime the Titans have a home football game, which makes traffic and parking a mess.

Though Nashville is a city of the New South and sprawls in all directions with suburbs full of office parks and shopping malls, it still has a downtown where you can do a bit of exploring on foot. Within the downtown area are the three distinct areas that comprise The District, a historic area containing many late-19th-century commercial buildings that have been preserved and now house restaurants, clubs, and interesting shops. Because Nashville is the state capital, the downtown area also has many impressive government office buildings.

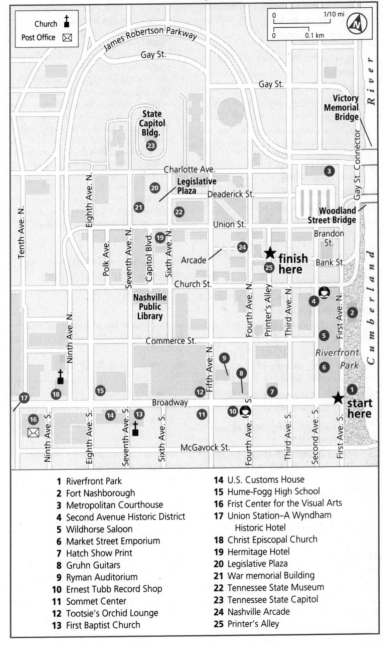

Walking Tour: Downtown Nashville

Church ✝
Post Office ✉

| 0 | | 1/10 mi |
| 0 | 0.1 km | |

1 Riverfront Park
2 Fort Nashborough
3 Metropolitan Courthouse
4 Second Avenue Historic District
5 Wildhorse Saloon
6 Market Street Emporium
7 Hatch Show Print
8 Gruhn Guitars
9 Ryman Auditorium
10 Ernest Tubb Record Shop
11 Sommet Center
12 Tootsie's Orchid Lounge
13 First Baptist Church

14 U.S. Customs House
15 Hume-Fogg High School
16 Frist Center for the Visual Arts
17 Union Station–A Wyndham
Historic Hotel
18 Christ Episcopal Church
19 Hermitage Hotel
20 Legislative Plaza
21 War memorial Building
22 Tennessee State Museum
23 Tennessee State Capitol
24 Nashville Arcade
25 Printer's Alley

Start your tour at the intersection of Broadway and First Avenue, on the banks of the Cumberland River, at:

❶ Riverfront Park

The park was built as part of Nashville's bicentennial celebration, and is where the Nashville Trolleys start their circuits around downtown and out to Music Row. If you should grow tired of walking at any time during your walk, just look for a trolley stop and ride the free trolley back to the park.

Walk north along the river to:

❷ Fort Nashborough

This is a reconstruction of the 1780 fort that served as the first white settlement in this area.

Continue up First Avenue to Union Street and turn left. Across the street is the:

❸ Metropolitan Courthouse

This imposing building, which also houses the Nashville City Hall, was built in 1937. It incorporates many classic Greek architectural details. Of particular interest are the bronze doors, the etched-glass panels above the doors, and the lobby murals. At the information booth in the lobby, you can pick up a brochure detailing the building's many design elements.

If you now head back down Second Avenue, you'll find yourself in the:

❹ Second Avenue Historic District

Between Union Avenue and Broadway are numerous Victorian commercial buildings, most of which have now been restored. Much of the architectural detail is near the tops of the buildings, so keep your eyes trained upward.

❺ Wildhorse Saloon

This is Nashville's hottest country nightspot. In the daylight hours, you can snap a picture of the comical, cowboy-booted horse statue near the front entrance.

TAKE A BREAK
Second Avenue has several excellent restaurants where you can stop for lunch or a drink. **The Old Spaghetti Factory,** 160 Second Ave. N. (© 615/254-9010), is a cavernous place filled with Victorian antiques. There's even a trolley car parked in the middle of the main dining room. A couple of doors down is **B.B. King Blues Club & Grill,** at 152 Second Ave. N. (© 615/256-2727), a bluesy bar with a juke-joint atmosphere where you can sample Southern food or grab a burger.

There are several interesting antiques and crafts stores along Second Avenue, but first take note of a couple of Nashville's best watering holes. Several doors down from The Old Spaghetti Factory you'll find:

Also along this stretch of the street is the:

❻ Market Street Emporium

The emporium holds a collection of specialty shops.

At the corner of Second Avenue and Broadway, turn right. Between Third and Fourth avenues, watch for:

❼ Hatch Show Print

The oldest poster shop in the United States still prints its posters on an old-fashioned letterpress printer. The most popular posters are those advertising the *Grand Ole Opry.*

Cross Fourth Avenue and you'll come to:

❽ Gruhn Guitars

This is the most famous guitar shop in Nashville; it specializes in used and vintage guitars.

Walk up Fourth Avenue less than a block and you will come to the new main entrance of:

❾ Ryman Auditorium

The *Grand Ole Opry* was held here from 1943 to 1974. The building was originally built as a tabernacle to host evangelical revival meetings, but because of its good acoustics and large seating capacity, it became a popular setting for theater and music performances.

After leaving the Ryman Auditorium, walk back down to the corner of Broadway and Fourth Avenue.

TAKE A BREAK
If you didn't stop for lunch on Second Avenue, now would be a good time. Directly across the street is **The Merchants** restaurant, at 401 Broadway (✆ **615/254-1892**), a favorite Nashville power-lunch spot. The atmosphere is sophisticated and the cuisine is New American.
   In the same block as The Merchants, you'll find the:

⑩ Ernest Tubb Record Shop
This store was once the home of the *Midnite Jamboree,* a country music radio show that took place after the *Grand Ole Opry* was over on Saturday nights.

Continue up the block to the corner of Fifth Avenue and you'll come to the main entrance to the new:

⑪ Sommet Center
Right at the corner (inside what used to be known as the Nashville Arena) is the Sommet (formerly) Gaylord Center. Inside is the Nashville Convention & Visitors Bureau Visitors Center. If you haven't already stopped in for information or to check out the gift shop, now would be a good time.

Back across Broadway, you'll find:

⑫ Tootsie's Orchid Lounge
Grand Ole Opry musicians used to duck in here, one of the most famous bars in Nashville, before, during, and after the show at the Ryman. There's live country music all day long at Tootsie's.

From this corner, head up Broadway, and at the corner of Seventh Avenue, you'll find the:

⑬ First Baptist Church
This modern building incorporates a Victorian Gothic church tower built between 1884 and 1886. The church's congregation wanted a new church but didn't want to give up the beautiful old tower. This is the compromise that was reached.

Across Seventh Avenue is the:

⑭ U.S. Customs House
Now leased as private office space, this Victorian Gothic building was built in 1877 and displays fine stonework and friezes. The imposing structure, with its soaring tower and arched windows, could be in any European city.

Directly across the street is:

⑮ Hume-Fogg High School
Built between 1912 and 1916, the building incorporates elements of English Tudor and Gothic design.

Two blocks farther up Broadway, you'll see a decidedly different style of architecture, the:

⑯ Frist Center for the Visual Arts
This breathtaking art museum is housed in the historic U.S. Post Office building, designed with elements of both neoclassical and Art Deco architectural styling.

The post office shares a parking lot with:

⑰ Union Station Hotel
This Victorian Romanesque Revival building was built in 1900 as Nashville's main passenger railroad station, but in 1986 it was renovated and reopened as a luxury hotel. The stone exterior walls incorporate many fine carvings, and the lobby is one of the most elegant historic spaces in Nashville.

Head back the way you came and cross over to the opposite side of Broadway at Ninth Avenue. Here you'll find:

⑱ Christ Episcopal Church
Constructed between 1887 and 1892, the building is in the Victorian Gothic style and is complete with gargoyles. This church also has Tiffany stained-glass windows.

Continue back down Broadway and at Seventh Avenue, turn left and walk up to Union Street and turn right. In 1 block, you'll come to the:

⑲ Hermitage Hotel

This is Nashville's last grand old hotel; newly renovated and lovingly restored in 2002, the lobby exudes Beaux Arts extravagance, with a stained-glass skylight and marble columns and floor.

Across Union Street from the Hermitage Hotel is:

⑳ Legislative Plaza

This large public plaza is a popular lunch spot for downtown office workers.

Fronting onto this plaza is the:

㉑ War Memorial Building

This neoclassical building was built in 1925 to honor soldiers who died in World War I. The centerpiece is an atrium holding a large statue titled *Victory*. This building also houses the Tennessee State Museum Military Branch.

On the opposite side of the plaza is the:

㉒ Tennessee State Museum

In the basement of the same building that houses the Tennessee Performing Arts Center, this museum contains an extensive and well-displayed collection of artifacts pertaining to Tennessee history.

Returning to the Legislative Plaza and continuing to the north across Charlotte Street will bring you to the:

㉓ Tennessee State Capitol

This Greek Revival building was built between 1845 and 1859. Be sure to take a look inside, where you'll find many beautiful architectural details and works of art.

If you walk back across the Legislative Plaza and take a left on Union Street and then a right on Fifth Avenue (cross to the far side of the street), you'll come to the west entrance of the:

㉔ Nashville Arcade

This covered shopping arcade was built in 1903 and is modeled after an arcade in Italy. Only a few such arcades remain in the United States, and unfortunately, no one has yet breathed new life into this one. Still, you can mail a letter here or buy a bag of fresh-roasted peanuts.

Walk through the arcade and continue across Fourth Avenue. The alley in front of you leads to:

㉕ Printer's Alley

For more than a century, this has been a center for evening entertainment. Today, things are much tamer than they once were, but you can still find several nightclubs featuring live music.

5 Organized Tours

CITY & HOMES-OF-THE-STARS TOURS

Gray Line of Nashville, 2416 Music Valley Dr. (© **800/251-1864** or 615/883-5555; www.graylinenashville.com), offers more than half a dozen different tours ranging in length from 3½ hours to a full day. On the popular, 3-hour tour of the stars' homes, you'll ride past the current or former houses and mansions of such chart-toppers as Hank Williams, Sr., Dolly Parton, Kix Brooks and Ronnie Dunn (separate homes), Trisha Yearwood, Martina McBride, and Alan Jackson. Other themed tours focus exclusively on historical sites, honky-tonks and nightlife, and other specialty areas. Adult tour prices range from $35 for the "Homes of the Country Stars" bus tour to $85 for a dinner cruise on the General Jackson showboat.

Johnny Walker Tours, 2416 Music Valley Dr. (© **800/722-1524** or 615/834-8585), has merged with Gray Line Tours. However, the company still sells group tours and individual vacation packages.

For a fun and campy tour of Nashville aboard a gaudy pink bus, try **Nash Trash Tours** (© **800/342-2132** or 615/226-7300; www.nashtrash.com), narrated by the spandex-clad "Jugg" sisters. Sheri Lynn and Brenda Kay dish the dirt on all your favorite country stars. Throw in a few risqué jokes, plenty of music, and a policy that

Nashville Name Game

Can you identify these country stars and legends by their real first/last names?

Audrey Faith Perry	(Faith Hill)
Alvis Edgar	(Buck Owens)
Virginia Pugh	(Patsy Cline)
Eileen Regina Edwards	(Shania Twain)
Floyd Elliot Wray	(Colin Raye)
Waylon Albright	(Shooter Jennings)
Sarah Ophelia Colley Cannon	(Minnie Pearl)
Patricia Lynn	(Trisha Yearwood)
Maurice Woodward	(Tex Ritter)
Ernest Jennings	(Tennessee Ernie Ford)
William Neal Browder	(T.G. Sheppard)
Anthony Graham	(T. Graham Brown)
Randy Bruce Traywick	(Randy Travis)
Patricia Lee Ramey	(Patty Loveless)
Ruby Blevins	(Patsy Montana)
Lonnie Melvin	(Mel Tillis)
Loretta Webb	(Loretta Lynn)
Loretta Lynn Morgan	(Lorrie Morgan)
Little Jimmy Dickens	(James Cecil Dickens)
Kitty Wells	(Eileen Muriel Deason)
Kathleen Alice	(Kathy Mattea)
Louis Marshall	(Grandpa Jones)
Troyal Brooks	(Garth Brooks)
Virginia Patterson Hensley	(Patsy Cline)
Brenda Gail Webb Gatzimos	(Crystal Gayle)

Bonus: Which country star's middle name is also his wife's maiden name? (Vince Grant Gill married Amy Grant)

Double Bonus: Which singer/songwriter named one of her daughters after Minnie Pearl? (Amy Grant's daughter is Sarah Cannon Chapman)

allows passengers to bring aboard coolers (with alcohol, if desired), and it all makes for a trashy good time in Music City. Because the 90-minute tours can become rowdy, they're not advised for young children (those under 13 are not allowed.) Hours vary, but generally speaking, tours are offered Tuesdays through Saturdays. Call in advance for current times and to make reservations, which are required. Tickets, which cost $32 for adults, $30 for seniors, and $20 for youth ages 13 to 18, do not include 9.25% sales tax or tip for the bus driver. (Rates are discounted from Jan. 1–Feb. 15.) Bring plenty of extra cash if you want to buy any of the commemorative souvenirs the sisters hawk. Note: The bus is not wheelchair-accessible.

For groups such as family reunions, churches, and students who would like to learn more about the African-American history of Nashville, contact Bill Daniel at **Nashville Black Heritage Tours,** in nearby Smyrna, TN (© **615/890-8173**).

RIVERBOAT TOURS

The Opryland Hotel, 2800 Opryland Dr. (© 615/883-2211; www.oprylandhotel. com), operates the paddle-wheeler—the *General Jackson* (© 615/458-3900)—on the Cumberland River. Tours depart from a dock near the Opryland Hotel. At 300 feet long, the *General Jackson* showboat recalls the days when riverboats were the most sophisticated way to travel. You go on this cruise for the paddle-wheeler experience, not necessarily for the food (not so great) and entertainment that go along with it. During the summer, the Southern Nights Cruise offers a three-course dinner and dancing under the stars to live bands. Fares for this trip cost $73 for adults. Midday cruises are also available mid-April to mid-October and cost $45 for adults. Discounted rates are available for cruise and buffet only, without entertainment. In addition, special-event cruises with such themes as Valentine's Day, Mardi Gras, tailgating, and the holidays are offered year-round. Prices vary. Call for details.

6 Outdoor Activities

BOAT RENTALS   In the summer, a wide variety of boats, from canoes and paddleboats to personal watercraft and pontoon boats, can be rented at **Four Corners Marina** on Percy Priest Lake, 4027 Lavergne Couchville Pike, Antioch (© 615/641-9523). This grocery store sells bait, tackle, and fishing licenses year-round. The gorgeous lake, only a few miles east of downtown, is surrounded by a series of parks, trees, and natural beauty rather than commercial and residential development.

At Kingston Springs, about 20 miles west of Nashville off I-40, you can rent canoes from **Tip-a-Canoe,** 1279 U.S. 70, at Harpeth River Bridge (© 800/550-5810 or 615/254-0836; www.tip-a-canoe.com), or bring your own. Canoe trips of varying lengths, from a couple of hours up to 5 days, can be arranged. Rates start at $45 per canoe, which includes the shuttle upriver to your chosen put-in point. Trips lasting 5 days cost $125. The Harpeth River is a meandering, scenic river of mostly Class I water with some Class II—and a few spots where you'll have to carry the canoe.

GOLF   Three area courses consistently get praised by Nashville golfers. The **Hermitage Golf Course,** 3939 Old Hickory Blvd. (© 615/847-4001; www.hermitage golf.com), is a challenging 36-hole public course about 20 minutes east of downtown. Greens fees are $49 to $69 and can be booked in advance online. The Vanderbilt **Legends Club of Tennessee,** 1500 Legends Club Lane, Franklin (© 615/791-8100; www.legendsclub.com), is a bit farther out of town but offers a 36-hole course designed by Tom Kite and Bob Cupp. Greens fees for the Legends Club are $36 to $85. For many golfing visitors, however, the **Opryland's Gaylord Springs Golf Links,** 18 Springhouse Lane (© 615/458-1730; www.gaylordsprings.com), is most convenient. This par-72, 18-hole course is set on the bank of the Cumberland River. The course boasts not only challenging links, but also an antebellum-style clubhouse that would have made Rhett Butler feel right at home. Greens fees range from $40 to $90 for 18 holes. For the most serious enthusiasts, The Golf Institute at Gaylord Springs offers high-tech analysis of golfers' swings, two indoor hitting bays for year-round instruction, and on-site customized club fittings and repair workshop.

HORSEBACK RIDING   If you want to go for a ride through the Tennessee hills, there are a couple of nearby places where you can rent a horse. The **Ramblin' Breeze/A Cowboy Town,** 3665 Knight Rd., Whites Creek (© 615/876-1029;

www.acowboytown.com), 7 miles north of downtown Nashville, rents horses for $20 an hour ($15 for children ages 7–12). **Ju-Ro Stables,** 735 Carver Lane, Mt. Juliet (✆ 615/773-7433; www.jurostables.com), is located about 15 minutes from Nashville on I-40 east, at the Mt. Juliet exit, and charges $15 an hour for rides around Old Hickory Lake ($44 for moonlight rides).

SWIMMING   Though most of the hotels and motels listed in this book have pools, if you'd rather go jump in a lake, head for **Percy Priest Lake.** You'll find this large man-made reservoir just east of downtown Nashville at exit 219 off I-40. Stop by the information center to get a map showing the three designated swimming areas.

7 Spectator Sports

AUTO RACING   NASCAR racing is a Southern institution, and every Saturday aspiring stock-car drivers race their cars at the **Music City Motorplex** (✆ 615/726-1818; www.musiccitymotorplex.com) on the Tennessee State Fairgrounds. The race season, which runs from April through November, also includes several pro series races, as well as a celebrity charity race. Saturday admission is $10, while tickets to the pro races run $60 and up.

The **Music City Raceway,** 3302 Ivy Point Rd., Goodlettsville (✆ 615/876-0981; www.musiccityraceway.com), is the place to catch National Hot Rod Association (NHRA) drag-racing action. The drag strip, known as Nashville's "Playground of Power," has races on Tuesdays, Fridays, Saturdays, and some Sundays between March and October. Admission is $10.

BASEBALL   The **Nashville Sounds** (✆ 615/242-4371; www.nashvillesounds. com), a Triple-A team affiliate of the Milwaukee Brewers, play at Greer Stadium, 534 Chestnut St., off Eighth Avenue South. Admission ranges from $6 general to $10 for reserved box seats ($5–$9 for children).

FOOTBALL   Perennial playoff favorites the **Tennessee Titans** draw loyal crowds to the 68,000-seat LP Field on the banks of the Cumberland River. The stadium is at 1 Titans Way, Nashville, TN 37213 (✆ 615/565-4200; www.titansonline.com).

GOLF TOURNAMENTS   Vanderbilt Legends Club (✆ 615/791-8100) hosts an annual LPGA event each spring. Call for prices and dates.

HOCKEY   Nashville's own NHL hockey team, the **Nashville Predators** (✆ 615/770-PUCK; www.nashvillepredators.com), plays at the Gaylord Entertainment Center on lower Broadway in downtown Nashville. Ticket prices range from $10 to $95.

HORSE SHOWS   Horse shows are important events on the Nashville area's calendar. The biggest and most important horse show of the year is the **Annual Tennessee Walking-Horse National Celebration** (✆ 931/684-5915; www.twhnc.com). This show takes place 40 miles southeast of Nashville in the town of Shelbyville and is held each year in late August. Advance reserved ticket prices range from $7 to $20, while general-admission tickets are $5 to $12.

The city's other big horse event is the annual running of the **Iroquois Steeplechase** (✆ 615/322-7284) on the second Saturday in May. This is one of the oldest steeplechase races in the country and is held in Percy Warner Park in the Belle Meade area. Proceeds from the race benefit the Vanderbilt Children's Hospital. Tickets are $12 at the gate or $10 in advance.

8

Shopping in Nashville

Nashville is a great shopping city, so be sure to bring your credit cards. Whether you're looking for handmade stage outfits costing thousands of dollars or a good deal on a pair of shoes at a factory-outlet store, you'll find plenty of spending opportunities in Nashville.

1 The Nashville Shopping Scene

As in most cities of the South, the shopping scene in Nashville is spread out over the width and breadth of the city. Most of the city's best shopping can be found in the many large new shopping malls scattered around the newer suburbs. However, there are also many interesting and exclusive shops in the West End area. In downtown Nashville, you'll find gift and souvenir shops, antiques stores, and musical instrument and record stores that cater to country musicians and fans. Second Avenue North, in the historic downtown area known as The District, is becoming a souvenir and gallery district, though it still has a few antiques stores.

Country music fans will appreciate plenty of opportunities to shop for Western wear. There are dozens of shops specializing in the de rigueur attire of country music. You probably can't find a better selection of cowboy boots anywhere outside Texas, and if your tastes run to sequined denim shirts or skirts, you'll find lots to choose from.

2 Nashville Shopping A to Z

ANTIQUES

For the best antiques browsing, drive just south of downtown to the corner of Eighth Avenue South and Douglas Street, where several large antiques shops are clustered.

ART & HOME FURNISHINGS

The Arts Company   Many of Nashville's most promising artists, working divergent media such as painting, sculpture, and photography, display and sell their pieces at this prominent downtown gallery. 415 5th Ave. N. ℰ **615/254-2040**. www.theartscompany.com.

Cumberland Art Gallery   With an emphasis on regional artists, this well-regarded gallery deals in sculptures, paintings, photographs, and works on paper in a wide variety of styles. 4107 Hillsboro Circle. ℰ **615/297-0296**. www.artnet.com/cumberland.html.

Curious Heart Emporium ✶   Quirky gifts such as offbeat refrigerator magnets, photography books, stuffed animals, children's toys, whimsical folk art, and artsy home décor create an eclectic mix at this unusual shop. There are two locations, including one near the Loveless Café southwest of town on Highway 100. Berry Hill, 2832 Bransford Ave. and at 8414 Highway 100. ℰ **615/298-7756**. www.curiousheartemporium.com.

Finer Things   It's a short drive from downtown, but if you have an appreciation of unusual and highly imaginative fine contemporary crafts and art, consider Finer Things. It's an eclectic, out-of-the-way gallery worth a look. 1898 Nolensville Rd. ℰ 615/244-3003. www.finerthingsgallery.com.

Hatch Show Print   This is the oldest letterpress poster print shop in the country and not only does it still design and print posters for shows, but it also sells posters to the public. Reprints of old circus, vaudeville, and *Grand Ole Opry* posters are the most popular. 316 Broadway. ℰ 615/256-2805. www.hatchshowprint.com.

Local Color Gallery   This gallery specializes in works by Tennessee artists. Watercolors and other paintings comprise the largest portion of the works on sale here, but you'll also find ceramics and sculptures. 1912 Broadway. ℰ 615/321-3141. www.localcolornashville.com.

Woodcuts   If you're interested in artworks by African-American artists, this is the place to visit in Nashville. Prints, posters, notecards, and greeting cards make up the majority of the offerings here, though they also do framing. The shop is adjacent to Fisk University. 1613 Jefferson St. ℰ 615/321-5357. www.woodcutsfineart.com.

BOOKS

BookMan BookWoman ✿   Widely regarded (and rightfully so) as Nashville's best used bookstore, this Vandy-area favorite has tens of thousands of books, including hardcover and collectors' editions. Their inexpensive paperbacks encompass nearly every genre, including mysteries, science fiction, photography, and children's books. 1713 21st Ave. S. ℰ 615/383-6555. www.bookmanbookwoman.com.

Borders   This multilevel bookstore, part of a national chain, dominates a busy intersection near the Vanderbilt University campus. Thousands of books, CDs, and an extensive selection of DVDs draw shoppers, as do frequent author book signings. 2501 West End Ave. ℰ 615/327-9656. www.bordersstores.com.

Davis-Kidd Booksellers ✿   For the best and biggest selection of books in Nashville, go to the Green Hills area, where you'll find this welcoming, well-stocked and locally owned store. With an active roster of book signings and other community-oriented events, a good second-floor cafe, and an array of unique gift items, Davis-Kidd gets my pick as the best bookstore chain in Tennessee. (Other locations are in Memphis and Jackson.) 4007 Hillsboro Pike. ℰ 615/385-2645. www.daviskidd.com.

Elder's Bookstore   This dusty old shop looks as if some of the antiquarian books on sale were stocked back when they were new. Every square inch of shelf space is jammed full of books, and there are more stacks of books seemingly everywhere you turn. This place is a book collector's dream come true. And who needs a fancy, in-store Starbucks cafe when you've got the retro Elliston Soda Shop right next door? 2115 Elliston Place. ℰ 615/327-1867. www.eldersbookstore.com.

CRAFTS

The American Artisan   Stocking only the finest of contemporary American handicrafts from around the country, American Artisan is Nashville's best place to shop for original fine crafts. These include intricate baskets, elaborate ceramic pieces, colorful kaleidoscopes, one-of-a-kind jewelry, and beautiful wood furniture. All exhibit the artist's eye for creativity. 4231 Harding Rd. ℰ 615/298-4691. www.american-artisan.com.

Nashville Shopping

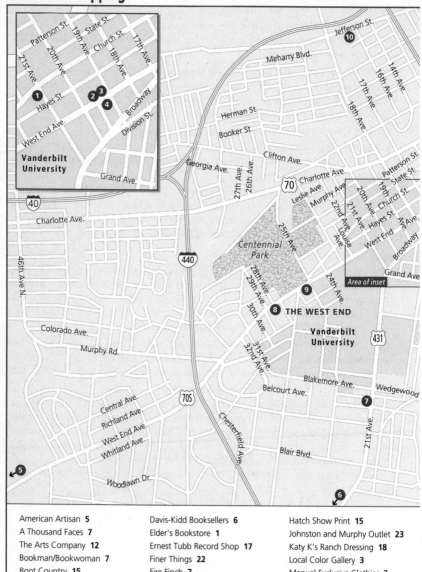

American Artisan **5**
A Thousand Faces **7**
The Arts Company **12**
Bookman/Bookwoman **7**
Boot Country **15**
Borders **9**
Coco **5**
Cotten Music Center **7**
Cumberland Art Gallery **6**

Davis-Kidd Booksellers **6**
Elder's Bookstore **1**
Ernest Tubb Record Shop **17**
Finer Things **22**
Fire Finch **7**
Fork's Drum Closet **19**
The Great Escape **4**
Grimey's **20**
Gruhn Guitars **14**

Hatch Show Print **15**
Johnston and Murphy Outlet **23**
Katy K's Ranch Dressing **18**
Local Color Gallery **3**
Manuel Exclusive Clothier **2**
Nashville Farmer's Market **11**
Pangaea **7**
The Peanut Shop **13**
Posh Boutique **7**

CLOSED
due to
accidental demolition

WEGEN BISSIGEN
EICHHÖRNCHEN GESCHLOSSEN

CERRADO

CABRAS

Κλειστό
Μετεωρίτες

プール POOL CLOSED 閉
も 鎖
ELECTRIC EELS 中

Hotel
closed for
facelifting

FERMÉ POUR
RAISON
DE GRÈVE
DES BONNES

FECHADO!
POR CAUSA DE
ATAQUES DOS CROCODILOS

I don't speak sign language.

A hotel can close for all kinds of reasons.
Our Guarantee ensures that if your hotel's undergoing construction, we'll
let you know in advance. In fact, we cover your entire travel experience.
See www.travelocity.com/guarantee for details.

travelocity®
You'll never roam alone.

©2007 Travelocity.com LP. CST # 2056372-50.

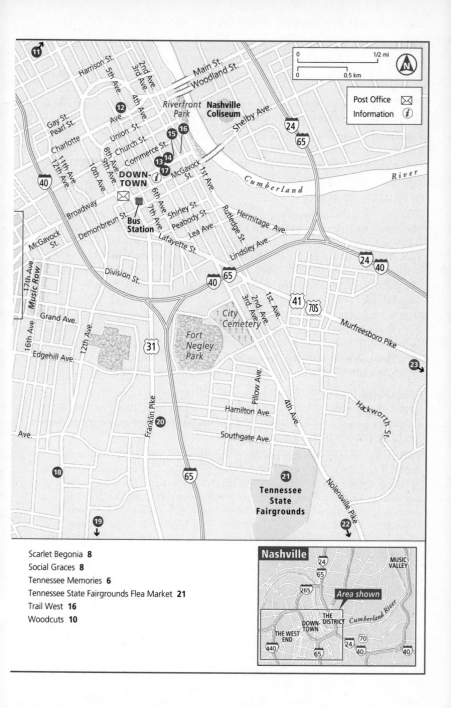

Pangaea ⟨★★⟩   From hand-carved soaps and South American textiles to one-of-a-kind Elvis icons, this eclectic boutique in Nashville's trendy Hillsboro Village area has interesting gifts to suit a variety of tastes, if not budgets. (They also sell cool clothes.) Items are on the pricey side, but for a unique shopping experience adjacent to scores of hip coffee shops and galleries, even window-shopping at Pangaea is time well spent. 1721 21st Ave. S. ℂ 615/269-9665. www.pangaeanashville.com.

Tennessee Memories   Located in the Fashion Square shopping plaza next to the Mall at Green Hills, this small store is filled with crafts (including pottery and baskets) and gourmet food products from around the state. 2182 Bandywood Dr. ℂ 615/298-3253. www.tennesseememories.com.

DEPARTMENT STORES

Dillard's   Dillard's is recognized as one of the nation's leading department stores. They carry many leading brands and have stores at several malls around Nashville. **Bellevue Center Mall,** 7624 U.S. 70 S. (ℂ 615/662-1515); **Mall at Green Hills,** 2126 Abbott Martin Rd. (ℂ 615/297-0971); **Hickory Hollow Mall,** 5248 Hickory Hollow Pkwy. (ℂ 615/731-6600); **Rivergate Mall,** 1000 Rivergate Pkwy., Goodlettsville (ℂ 615/859-2811); and **Cool Springs Galleria,** 1796 Galleria Blvd. (ℂ 615/771-7101).

Macy's   Formerly Hecht's, this is one of Nashville's upscale department stores and is well known for its personable employees and wide selection of fine lines. **Cool Springs Galleria,** 1790 Galleria Blvd. (ℂ 615/771-2100); **Bellevue Center,** 7616 U.S. 70 S. (ℂ 615/646-5500); **Hickory Hollow Mall,** 917 Bell Rd. (ℂ 615/731-5050); and **Rivergate Mall,** 1000 Two Mile Pkwy., Goodlettsville (ℂ 615/859-5251).

DISCOUNT SHOPPING

Johnston & Murphy Outlet   Located across the road from the airport, this outlet mall offers good shopping for all kinds of discounted shoes. Genesco Park, 1415 Murfreesboro Rd. ℂ 615/367-4443. www.johnstonmurphy.com.

Opry Mills   For bargains on everything from Bibles to fine crystal, look no farther than this mammoth "shoppertainment" venue in the Music Valley. Among the dozens of factory-outlet stores here are those by such well-known apparel retailers as Ann Taylor, Banana Republic, Gap, Guess, Levi's, and Tommy Hilfiger. Bargain shoes and handbags can be found at Dexter, Etienne Aigner, G.H. Bass, Off Broadway Shoe Warehouse, Reebok, and Nike. The mall is open Monday through Saturday from 10am to 9:30pm, and Sunday from 11am to 7pm. 433 Opry Mills Dr. ℂ 615/514-1000. www.oprymills.com.

FASHIONS

See also "Western Wear" below.

WOMEN'S

Coco   This ladies' boutique sells designer sportswear, dresses, and accessories, and features such lines as Ellen Tracy and Emmanuel. Both the fashions and the clientele tend to be upscale. 4239 Harding Rd. ℂ 615/292-0362. www.coco-online.com.

Posh Boutique   Trendy clothes and footwear by the likes of Diesel, Chinese Laundry, and Miss Sixty attract a young, affluent clientele. That's not to say you can't scour the place for occasional bargains. 1809 21st Ave. S. ℂ 615/383-9840. www.poshonline.com.

Scarlett Begonia Ethnic fashions, jewelry, and fine crafts from around the world prove that there is life beyond country Nashville. The emphasis here is on South American clothing, and the quality is much higher than you'll find in the average import store. 2805 West End Ave. ✆ 615/329-1272. www.scarlettbegonia.com.

FINE GIFTS/SOUVENIRS

Nashville abounds in shops purveying every manner of country-themed souvenirs. The greatest concentrations of these shops are in the Music Row and Music Valley (Opryland Hotel) areas, where several of the stores specialize in particular country music performers. Several of the gift shops, including Cooter's and the Willie Nelson Museum on McGavock Pike (Music Valley), also have backroom museums where you can see music memorabilia. These museums are, however, really just an excuse to get you into the big souvenir shop out front, but if you're a fan, you'll enjoy touring the exhibits and maybe picking up a souvenir. See "On the Music Trail" in chapter 7 for further information.

A Thousand Faces 🎯 Beautifully crafted one-of-a-kind gifts including jewelry, artwork, and home decor are packed inside every square inch of this vibrant West End boutique that's perfect for leisurely browsing. 1720 21st Ave. S. ✆ 615/298-3304. www.athousandfaces.com.

Fire Finch Eclectic, primitive-style artwork and other interesting, upscale gift items are sold in this atmospheric store. And yes, you might see a finch or two, too. A second location opened in 2007 in Printer's Alley downtown. It's at 305 Church St. (✆ 615/942-5271). 1818 21st Ave. S. ✆ 615/385-5090. www.firefinch.net.

Social Graces Designer stationery sets, invitations, handmade paper, and an assortment of luxurious writing gifts and accessories are lavishly displayed here. As part of a full day of shopping, the relatively quiet, contemplative atmosphere at this store makes a nice change of pace from some of the West End's livelier shops. 1704 21st Ave. S. ✆ 615/383-1911. www.socialgracesonline.com.

FLEA MARKETS

Tennessee State Fairgrounds Flea Market This huge flea market is held the fourth weekend of every month (except December, when it's the third weekend), attracting more than 1,000 vendors selling everything from cheap jeans to handmade crafts to antiques and collectibles. You'll find the fairgrounds just a few minutes south of downtown. Tennessee State Fairgrounds, Fourth Avenue. ✆ 615/862-5016. www.tennesseestatefair.org.

FOOD

Nashville Farmer's Market 🎯 Located across the street from the Bicentennial Mall, this large indoor farmer's market has 100 farm stalls, as well as 100 flea-market stalls. There are also more than a dozen prepared food vendors and gourmet- and imported-food stalls, selling everything from Jamaican meat patties to hundreds of different hot sauces. The market is open daily 8am to 7pm in summer; 9am to 6pm the rest of the year. 900 Eighth Ave. N. ✆ 615/880-2001. www.nashvillefarmersmarket.gov.

The Peanut Shop If you've been trudging around downtown Nashville all day and need a quick snack, consider a bag of fresh-roasted peanuts. This tiny shop in the Arcade (connecting Fourth Ave. N. and Fifth Ave. N.) has been in business since 1927 and still roasts its own peanuts. In fact, there are more styles of peanuts sold here than

you've probably ever seen in one place. A true Nashville institution. 19 Arcade. ℂ 615/
256-3394. www.nashvillenut.com.

MALLS/SHOPPING CENTERS

Cool Springs Galleria   South of Nashville off I-65 (at the Moore's Lane exit) is one
of the city's newest shopping malls. Here you'll find four major department stores,
including the upscale Parisian store, and more than 100 specialty stores, such as Yan-
kee Candle. This mall is a 10 to 15 minute drive from downtown Nashville. 1800 Galleria Blvd. ℂ 615/771-2128. www.coolspringsgalleria.com.

Hickory Hollow Mall   More than 180 specialty shops, a food court, Ruby Tuesday's
restaurant as well as four department stores—Macy's, Sears, JCPenney, and Dillard's—
are housed in this shopping mall. You'll find the mall south of downtown at exit 60
off I-24 East. 5252 Hickory Hollow Pkwy., Antioch ℂ 615/731-MALL. www.hickoryhollowmall.com.

The Mall at Green Hills   The Mall at Green Hills is among Nashville's busiest
malls. Among its shops are Brooks Brothers, Ann Taylor, and Pottery Barn, along with
anchor stores Macy's and Dillard's. Surrounding the mall are several more small plazas
full of interesting shops and restaurants. Hillsboro and Abbott Martin roads. ℂ 615/298-5478.
www.mallatgreenhills.com.

Opry Mills _(Kids_   Miles of retail sales, not to mention live music during special events,
await customers at Nashville's premier shopping mall, a vast extravaganza of department stores, specialty boutiques, restaurants, and entertainment venues that's laid out
in an oval, racetrack formation. At this mall, you can try your hand at rock climbing,
see a first-run movie, or visit the IMAX 3-D Theatre, and top it all off with a chocolate soda at Ghirardelli's old-time ice cream parlor. Among Opry Mill's 200 tenants
are anchors Bass Pro Shops Outdoor World, Barnes & Noble, Apple Barn Cider Bar
and General Store, Off Broadway Shoe Warehouse, Old Navy, and Rainforest Cafe. If
you want to shop 'til you drop, this is the place to do it. 433 Opry Mills Dr. ℂ 615/514-
1000. www.oprymills.com.

Rivergate Mall   If you're looking for shopping in northern Nashville, head up I-65
North to exit 95 or 96. The Rivergate Mall includes four department stores and more
than 155 boutiques, specialty shops, and restaurants. 1000 Two Mile Pkwy. ℂ 615/859-
3456. www.rivergate-mall.com.

MUSIC

Ernest Tubb Record Shop _(★ (Moments_   Whether you're looking for a reissue of an
early Johnny Cash album or the latest from Garth Brooks, you'll find it at Ernest
Tubb. These shops sell exclusively country music recordings on CD, cassette, and a
handful of vinyl records by the likes of Loretta Lynn and Jimmie Davis. There's
another location out near Opryland, at 2416 Music Valley Dr. (ℂ **615/889-2474**);

Fun Fact Kids' Stuff

Don't overlook music attractions as shopping sources. For instance, in addition
to an extensive selection of books and CDs, the **Country Music Hall of Fame and
Museum** (see Chapter 7) features a wondrous kids' corner, with hundreds of
goodies, from kazoos and coin purses, to rooster-headed pencil sharpeners,
and cowboy-hatted rubber duckies.

Fun Fact **The One & Only**

So just who was Ernest Tubb, anyway? One of Nashville's earliest country recording stars, this native Texan known to friends as "E. T." scored a big hit with "Walkin' the Floor Over You" in 1941. The beloved entertainer, who in gratitude to his audiences had the word "Thanks" emblazoned on the back of his guitar, earned a slew of industry awards, played Carnegie Hall, and was inducted into the Country Music Hall of Fame. After a long and successful career as one of the pioneers in country music, he died in Nashville in 1984.

---

this is where the *Midnite Jamborees* are held each Saturday night at midnight. 417 Broadway. ✆ 615/255-7503. www.ernesttubb.com.

The Great Escape This old store adjacent to the Vanderbilt campus caters to the record and comic book needs of college students and other collectors and bargain-seekers. The used records section has a distinct country bent, but you can also find other types of music as well. This is a big place with a great selection, including records, CDs, comic books, video games, and so on. An outlet store a few blocks away, open only on Friday and Saturday, is at 1907 Broadway (no phone). Another Great Escape can be found at 111 N. Gallatin Pike. 1925 Broadway. ✆ 615/327-0646. www.the greatescapeonline.com.

Grimey's 🐦🐦 New and "pre-loved" (don't call them used) CDs are bought and sold at this independently owned record store and community clearinghouse for all things related to the local music scene. You can buy T-shirts, posters, concert memorabilia, and other cool stuff, and get a leg up on everything that's going on around town. 1604 8th Ave. S. ✆ 615/254-4801. www.grimeys.com.

MUSICAL INSTRUMENTS

Cotten Music Center High-end acoustic stringed instruments have kept this West End music store in business since 1961. For $15,000 you could buy a vintage 1945 D18 Martin. Guitar accessories are also for sale, and the shop offers repair service too. 1815 21st Ave. S. ✆ 615/383-8947. www.cottenmusic.com.

Fork's Drum Closet Drums and other percussion instruments fill this large shop near the far end of 12th Avenue South. It's also a great place to hang—in hopes of networking with other working musicians. 2701 12th Ave. S. ✆ 615/383-8343. www.forksdrum closet.com.

Gibson Bluegrass Showcase Nightly music is offered at this combination performance stage and retail store, where Gibson-brand guitars are sold, and where the company's bluegrass stringed instruments including dobros, mandolins, and banjos are crafted and shipped worldwide. Free bluegrass jams are open to all comers beginning at 7pm Mondays and Wednesdays. Tuesday is Songwriters' Night. Local bands usually perform Thursdays and Fridays. Call for schedule. In Opry Mills, 161 Opry Mills Dr. ✆ 615/514-2233. www.gibson.com.

Gruhn Guitars Nashville's biggest guitar dealer (and one of the largest in the world) stocks classic used and collectible guitars as well as reissues of musicians' favorite instruments. If you're in the market for a 1953 Les Paul or a 1938 Martin D-28, this is the place to hit. 400 Broadway. ✆ 615/256-2033. www.gruhn.com.

WESTERN WEAR

In addition to places listed below, you can pick up clothing at the Wildhorse Saloon and other shops in The District. There are also clothing stores in Music Valley and on Music Row.

Boot Country   Cowboy boots, more cowboy boots, and still more cowboy boots. That's what you'll find at this boot store. Whether you want a basic pair of work boots or some fancy python-skin show boots, you'll find them here. There are other locations in Cool Springs Mall and Rivergate Mall. 304 Broadway. ℂ **615/259-1691.**

Katy K's Ranch Dressing (★★ (Finds   Can't afford a custom-made rhinestone blazer from Manuel's (see below), that well-known tailor to the country stars? Then head south of downtown to find this one-of-a-kind boutique (look for the shapely cowgirl cutout on the building's stone facade), where you can pick up some vintage Manuel suits and spangled gowns by Nudie's of Hollywood. It's all here, from Western wear, including designer boots, belt buckles, hats, and shirts—what the owners cleverly call "Ranch Dressing"—to rockabilly and punk fashions. It's a kick. 2407 12th Ave. S. ℂ **615/ 297-4242.** www.katyk.com.

Manuel Exclusive Clothier (★   This is where the stars get their threads. If you're a fan of country music, you've already seen plenty of Manuel's work, though you probably didn't know it at the time. Manuel has dressed Johnny Cash, Merle Haggard, Lorrie Morgan, Bob Dylan, the Rolling Stones, Emmylou Harris, Dolly Parton, Trisha Yearwood, and Pam Tillis. Unless you're an established performer, you probably won't be able to afford anything here, but it's still great fun to have a look at the pricey duds Manuel creates. Everything is impeccably tailored, with the one-of-a-kind pieces often covered with rhinestones. 1922 Broadway. ℂ **615/321-5444.**

Trail West   For all your Western-wear needs, this store is hard to beat. They handle the Brooks & Dunn Collection plus all the usual brands of hats, boots, and denim. There are other locations at 2416 Music Valley Dr. across from the Opryland Hotel (ℂ **615/883-5933**), and at 312 Broadway (ℂ **615/251-1711**). 214 Broadway. ℂ **615/ 255-7030.**

9

Nashville After Dark

Live music surrounds you in Nashville. Not only are there dozens of clubs featuring live country and bluegrass music, as you'd expect, but there's also a very lively rock scene. Jazz, blues, and folk clubs are also part of the mix, as are nightclubs and songwriters' showcases. And, of course, there's the granddaddy of them all, the long-running country music radio broadcast known as the *Grand Ole Opry.*

Some of this music can be found in unexpected places: street corners, parking lots, parks, or hotel lounges. Like Memphis, the city overflows with talented musicians who play where they can, much to the benefit of visitors to Nashville.

If I've given you the impression that Nashville is a city of live popular music only, let me point out the city's well-rounded, if lesser known, performing arts organizations. Nashville boasts a vibrant symphony orchestra, opera company, ballet company, the state's largest professional theater company, and several smaller community theaters.

The *Nashville Scene* is the city's arts-and-entertainment weekly. It comes out on Thursday and is available at restaurants, clubs, convenience stores, and other locations. Just keep your eyes peeled. Every Friday, the *Tennessean,* Nashville's morning daily, publishes the *Opry* lineup, and on Sunday it publishes a guide to the coming week's entertainment. Nashville nightlife happens all around town but predominates in two main entertainment areas—The District and Music Valley. **The District,** an area of renovated warehouses and old bars, is the livelier of the two. Here you'll find the Wildhorse Saloon and two dozen other clubs showcasing bands on any given weekend night. On the sidewalks, people are shoulder to shoulder as they parade from one club to the next, and in the streets, stretch limos vie for space with tricked- out pickup trucks. Within The District, Second Avenue is currently the main drag—where you'll find the most impressive of the area's clubs. However, there was a time shortly after the Civil War when Printer's Alley was the center of downtown Nashville nightlife.

Within a few blocks of The District, you'll also find the **Tennessee Performing Arts Center** and several other clubs.

Music Valley offers a more family-oriented, suburban nightlife scene. This area on the east side of Nashville is where you'll find the *Grand Ole Opry* Nashville Palace, and Texas Troubadour Theatre, we well as the Opryland Hotel, which has bars featuring live music. The **Five Points** neighborhood of East Memphis, just south of Music Valley, also has a growing number of excellent cafes and bars showcasing local talent.

Tickets to major concerts and sporting events can be purchased through **Ticketmaster** (© 615/255-9600), which maintains a desk at the Tennessee Performing Arts Center box office. A service charge is added to all ticket sales. Finally, for a comprehensive list of live music, performing arts, and sports events, visit **www.nowplayingnashville.com.**

1 The Country Music Scene

IN MUSIC VALLEY

General Jackson Showboat ✦   If you'd like to combine some evening entertainment with a cruise on the Cumberland River, try the *General Jackson*. This huge reproduction paddle-wheeler brings back the glory days of river travel. Comedy and country music with a strong patriotic undercurrent keep the predominately bus-tour clientele happy. During the summer, the Southern Nights Cruise offers dancing under the stars to live bands; dinner is optional. 2812 Opryland Dr. ✆ 615/889-6611, ext. 1000. Tickets $20 night cruises, $52 dinner cruises.

Grand Ole Opry ✦✦✦ *(Moments*   The show that made Nashville famous, the *Grand Ole Opry* is the country's longest continuously running radio show and airs every weekend from a theater adjacent to the Opryland Hotel. Over the years the Opry has had several homes, including the Ryman Auditorium in downtown Nashville. In late 2003 the 4,400-seat Grand Ole Opry House got its first major refurbishment since 1974, when the program was moved from the Ryman to its current home in the Music Valley. Through it all, the *Opry* remains a comforting mix of country music and gentle humor that has endured for nearly three-quarters of a century. Over the decades, the program has featured nearly all the greats of country music. Nearly all *Grand Ole Opry* performances sell out, and though it's often possible to get last-minute tickets, you should try to order tickets as far in advance as possible. The *Opry's* lineup of performers for Friday and Saturday nights are announced each Wednesday prior to the shows, which are staged at the Opry House in Music Valley from March through October, and at the Ryman Auditorium downtown from November through February. 2804 Opryland Dr. ✆ 800/SEE-OPRY or 615/871-OPRY. www.opry.com. Tickets vary; call for prices.

Nashville Palace   Open nightly from 5pm to 1:30am for live country-and-western music, a dance floor, and a full restaurant, this venue features acts familiar to fans of the *Grand Ole Opry*. Tuesday and Wednesday are Talent Nights (winners from both nights compete on Thursday nights), so be on the lookout for the next Randy Travis, who got his start here. The Palace is easy to find, located directly opposite the Opryland Hotel entrance. 2400 Music Valley Dr. ✆ 615/889-1540. www.nashvillepalace.net. Cover $5.

Texas Troubadour Theatre/Cowboy Church ✦✦   Although the original jamboree started at Ernest Tubb's downtown record shop on Broadway, the Music Valley location now hosts the weekly **Ernest Tubb** *Midnite Jamboree*. Recent headliners have included Bill Anderson, the Osborne Brothers, and Connie Smith, but to find out who's scheduled during your visit, log onto the Ernest Tubb Record Shop's website at www.etrecordshop.com. If you're looking for a down-home dose of gospel music ministry the morning after, make it to the Cowboy Church on time: The old-timey,

---

(Tips) Sitting Pretty

What's the difference between the *Grand Ole Opry* at Opryland and the Ryman Auditorium? Plenty, but the most practical piece of information is this: The long pews at the Opry are padded, while the ones at the Ryman are hard, well-worn wood. But don't despair over your derriere; inexpensive plastic seat cushions can be purchased at the Ryman's lobby gift shop.

> **Fun Fact Songs & Albums Recorded in Music City**
>
> Elvis Presley's "Heartbreak Hotel" in 1956
> The Everly Brothers' "Bye Bye Love" in 1957
> Brenda Lee's "Rockin' Around the Christmas Tree" in 1958
> Roy Orbison's "Oh, Pretty Woman" in 1964
> Bob Dylan's *Blonde on Blonde* in 1966
> Robert Night's "Everlasting Love" in 1967
> Joan Baez's "The Night They Drove Old Dixie Down" in 1971
> Kansas's "Dust in the Wind" in 1978
> R.E.M.'s *Document* in 1987
> Vanessa Williams's "Save the Best for Last" in 1992
> Matchbox Twenty's *Mad Season* in 2000
> India.Arie's *Acoustic Soul* in 2001
> Jimmy Buffett's *License to Chill* in 2004
> Bon Jovi's *Lost Highway* in 2007
> Kings of Leon's *Because of the Times* in 2007
> White Stripes' *Icky Thump* in 2007

nondenominational services kick off Sundays at 10am sharp (📞 **615/859-1001;** www.nashvillecowboychurch.org). Come as you are or don your best Stetson and bolo tie. Either way, you'll fit right in with the eclectic, all-ages congregation of locals and tourists alike that packs the pews every week for a patriotic praise-and-worship service. Music Valley Village, 2416 Music Valley Dr. 📞 615/889-2474.

IN THE DISTRICT

In addition to the clubs mentioned here, you'll find several small bars along lower Broadway, in an area long known as **Honky-tonk Row** or **Honky-tonk Highway.** The teeming, 2-block strip between Fourth and Fifth avenues is a nostalgic neon hootenanny of country-music sights, sounds, and occasionally some good old-fashioned rabble-rousing.

Legends Corner *(Value)* Today's starving artists are tomorrow's country music superstars, and this beloved dive in The District sets the stage for such happily-ever-after scenarios. Die-hard bar-hoppers insist that Legends Corner has downtown's best live local music and one of the friendliest staffs in all of Music City. Nostalgic memorabilia on the walls adds a quaint, down-home charm. And you can't beat the price: The tip jar gets passed around the room like a collection plate, enabling the rowdy crowds to help support the struggling pickers and grinners who've put Nashville on the map. 428 Broadway. 📞 615/248-6334. www.legendscorner.com. No cover. Ages 21 and older only after 6pm.

Robert's Western World 🎸 Located just a couple of doors down from the famous Tootsie's, this former Western-wear store helped launch the career of BR549. These days, Brazilbilly rocks the house most Friday and Saturday nights. 416 Broadway. 📞 615/244-9552. www.robertswesternworld.com. No cover.

Ryman Auditorium 🎸🎸 *(Moments)* Once the home of the *Grand Ole Opry,* this historic theater was renovated a few years back and is once again hosting performances with a country and bluegrass music slant. The Ryman was showcased in the documentary

Nashville After Dark

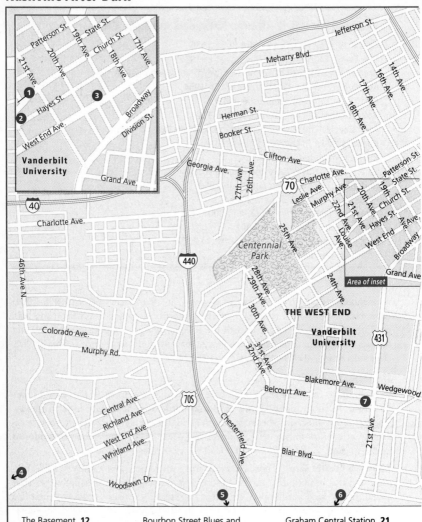

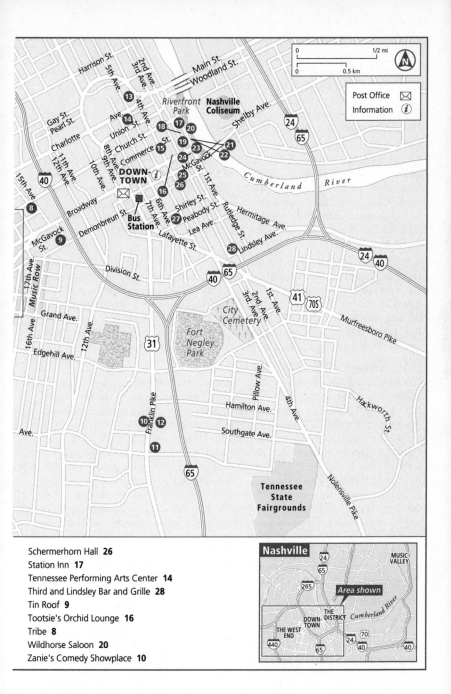

Schermerhorn Hall **26**
Station Inn **17**
Tennessee Performing Arts Center **14**
Third and Lindsley Bar and Grille **28**
Tin Roof **9**
Tootsie's Orchid Lounge **16**
Tribe **8**
Wildhorse Saloon **20**
Zanie's Comedy Showplace **10**

Down From the Mountain, a film version of the all-star bluegrass concert performed there featuring music from the movie soundtrack *O Brother, Where Art Thou?* In 2003, the venue was the site of a star-studded memorial concert for the late Johnny Cash. Today, musicians of all genres revere the intimate auditorium, where the acoustics are said to be better than Carnegie Hall's. In recent years, acts as diverse as Beck, Yo-Yo Ma, Coldplay, Al Green, and India.Arie have played to packed houses at this National Historic Landmark. 116 Fifth Ave. N. ✆ **615/254-1445** or 615/889-6611. www.ryman.com. Tickets $18–$43.

Tootsie's Orchid Lounge ★ *(Value)* This rowdy country dive has been a Nashville tradition since the days when the *Grand Ole Opry* was still performing in the Ryman Auditorium around the corner. Back then, *Opry* stars used to duck into Tootsie's for a drink. Today, you can see signed photos of the many stars who have downed a few here. Free live country music spills out onto the sidewalks daily 10am to 3am, and celebrities still occasionally make the scene. 422 Broadway. ✆ **615/726-0463.** www.tootsies. net. No cover.

Wildhorse Saloon Run by the same company that gave Nashville the Opryland Hotel and stages the *Grand Ole Opry,* this massive, three-story dance hall attracts everyone from country music stars to line-dancing senior citizen groups. In recent years, the saloon has tried to reach beyond its boot-scootin' roots to a more mainstream crowd by booking rock bands such as recent headliners Todd Rundgren and Styx. Because the club closes for private parties from time to time, be sure to call first before you head out. 120 Second Ave. N. ✆ **615/251-1000.** www.wildhorsesaloon.com. Cover varies.

ELSEWHERE AROUND NASHVILLE

The Bluebird Cafe ★★ *(Moments)* For a quintessential Nashville experience, visit this unassuming 100-seat club that remains one of the nation's premier venues for up-and-coming as well as established songwriters. Surprisingly, you'll find the Bluebird not in The District or on Music Row but in a suburban shopping plaza across the road from the Mall at Green Hills. There are usually two shows a night. Between 6 and 7pm, there is frequently music in the round, during which four singer-songwriters play some of their latest works. After 9pm, when more established acts take the stage, there's a cover charge. This is the place in Nashville to catch the music of people you'll be hearing from in coming years. Because the club is so small, reservations (taken noon–5pm) are recommended. 4104 Hillsboro Rd. ✆ **615/383-1461.** www.bluebirdcafe.com. No cover for early shows, but there is a minimum $7 order per person at tables. Cover fees vary ($8–$20) for late shows after 9pm.

⸤*Tips* **Shhh!**

That's the slogan of **The Bluebird Cafe.** So save your hell-raising for elsewhere. Once the audition-winning songwriters step onstage, the Bluebird becomes pin-drop quiet. For musicians the world over, playing here is the country music equivalent of Carnegie Hall. Reserving one of the venue's 21 tables takes persistence. Weekend shows often sell out days in advance. The Bluebird advises patrons to start calling on Monday "and keep hitting the redial button until you get through!" If you can't get reservations, there's usually standing-room-only (on a first-come, first-served basis) at the bar or at benches.

Did You Know?

BR549, the well-known country-rock band that hails from Nashville, took its name from Junior Samples' used car commercial skit on the old TV show *Hee Haw*. BR549 was the phone number to call for a great deal on a junker.

Douglas Corner Café   Though it has the look and feel of a neighborhood bar, this is one of Nashville's top places for songwriters trying to break into the big time—it's the city's main competition for The Bluebird Cafe. The club also has occasional shows by performers already established. It's located a few minutes south of downtown, near all the antiques shops. 2106 Eighth Ave. S. ⓒ **615/298-1688**. www.douglascorner.com. Cover fee up to $7.

Station Inn 🐦   For decades widely regarded as one of the best bluegrass venues around, this humble little dive still thrives in the shadow of the rapidly developing Gulch district south of Broadway in downtown. Live music is on tap 7 nights a week. Seating is first-come, first-served, so plan to arrive early if up-and-coming stars such as The Grascals are booked. A relatively more laid-back antidote to the boozy bars on Broadway, the Station Inn has a strict no-smoking policy. 402 12th Ave. S. ⓒ **615/255-3307**. www.stationinn.com. Cover $7 Tues–Sat; free Sun.

2 The Rest of the Club & Music Scene: Rock, Blues & Jazz

The Basement   This eclectic, live music venue hosts an array of alternative, rock, and indie artists. Look for it in the same unassuming little building that houses Grimey's New and Preloved Music, one of the best record stores in town. Like the Station Inn in the Gulch, this club has gone smoke-free (except for the outdoor patio). 1604 Eighth Ave. S. ⓒ **615/254-8006**. www.thebasementnashville.com.

Exit/In   Mercifully free of the glitz of the bigger nightspots in The District; this battered old building has long been a local favorite of alternative-rock and even the fast-growing alternative country genre. Music ranges from rock to blues to reggae and a little country; there's usually live music 6 nights a week. 2208 Elliston Place. ⓒ **615/321-3340**. www.exitin.com. Cover varies.

Graham Central Station   Tucked in the middle of all the action on Second Avenue North, this entertainment complex includes four floors of music and seven different clubs under one roof (in fact, there is even a party on the roof when the weather's good). Top 40 and Bell Bottoms (Old School dance hits) get their own floors, but there's also a karaoke bar, a South Beach-style lounge, and a live-music showcase. Basically, this place covers all the bases. 128 N. Second Ave. ⓒ **615/251-9593**. www.grahamcentralstationnashville.com. Cover fee up to $12.

JAZZ & BLUES

The **Tennessee Jazz & Blues Society** publishes a free monthly newsletter featuring news and event listings of interest to music buffs of these genres (www.jazzblues.org). If you're here in the summer, check to see who's playing at the society's concert series at Belle Meade Plantation (ⓒ **615/356-0501**).

B.B. King Blues Club 🐦🐦   Nashville can consider itself lucky to have landed one of the legendary blues guitarist's few clubs. The original, launched in Memphis more than a decade ago, has become Beale Street's crown jewel (satellite locations are in Los Angeles, New York City, and Orlando). B.B. himself inaugurated the Music City spot with a sold-out, standing-room-only show in September 2003. Since then, locals and tourists craving another alternative to Nashville's pervasive country music bars have ensured this authentic blues bar has a solid future in The District. 152 Second Ave. © 615/256-2727. www.nashville.bbkingclubs.com. Cover $5–$7 (usually $50–$200 for B.B.'s increasingly infrequent, but always sold-out, concerts).

Bourbon Street Blues and Boogie Bar If you're wandering around in The District wishing you could hear some wailing blues guitar, head over to Printer's Alley and check out the action at this smoky club. Live blues and a Cajun-American menu are on tap seven nights a week. 220 Printers Alley. © 615/242-5837. www.bourbonstreetblues.com. Cover $5–$10.

F. Scott's Restaurant Live jazz is presented nightly at this suburban outpost of chic. An extensive wine list and upscale dinner menu enhance its appeal for culture vultures. Free valet parking is an added perk at this classy establishment, located a stone's throw from the Mall at Green Hills. 2210 Crestmoor Rd. © 615/269-5861. www.fscotts.com. No cover.

3rd & Lindsley Bar & Grill Eight blocks south of Broadway, in a new office complex surrounded by old warehouses, you'll find Nashville's premier bar and grill. The atmosphere may lack the rough edges and smoke that you'd expect of a blues club, but the music encompasses everything from Americana and soul to rock. Good pub grub is available for either lunch or dinner. 818 3rd Ave. S. © 615/259-9891. www.3rdandlindsley.com. Cover fee up to $20.

FOLK & CELTIC

Mulligan's Pub This small pub in the heart of The District is always packed at night and definitely has the feel of an Irish pub. There's good Irish food, cold pints, and live Irish and American folk music Thursday to Saturday nights. 117 Second Ave. N. © 615/242-8010. www.mulliganspubandrestaurant.com. No cover.

GAY & LESBIAN DANCE CLUBS AND BARS

Lipstick Lounge ⊛ The periwinkle and cherry-red corner house in an East Nashville residential area entertains patrons with Karaoke, trivia contests, an oxygen bar, and frequent live music. Along with a full breakfast menu, inventive cocktails, and

---

GOOD, GODLY FUN

Grammy-winning contemporary Christian music star Michael W. Smith founded **Rocketown** (401 Sixth Ave. S.; © 615/843-4001; www.rocketown.com) in 2003 to provide a place for kids, teens, and young adults to hang out and have fun in a safe, drug- and alcohol-free environment. A nonprofit outreach and entertainment complex spanning more than 40,000 square feet, Rocketown offers everything from a challenging skate park and hip coffeehouse to a fully equipped concert hall. Although many of the club's activities are geared toward adolescents and teens, concerts are all-ages events. The live-music venue, which has three stages, showcases many of today's top up-and-coming rock bands and singer-songwriters. Who knows? Maybe this is where the next Newsboys, Casting Crowns, or MercyMe will emerge.

More Nightlife

An ever-increasing array of nightspots keep Nashville jumping after dark. Redevelopment is bustling in The Gulch. Across the street from the venerable bluegrass venue the **Station Inn** is **Sambuca**, 601 12th Ave. S. (℃ **615/ 248-2888**), a Dallas-based newcomer with an eclectic menu and nightly live music—with an emphasis on jazz. Next door are a few more relatively new hipster hangouts: **Ru San's**, 505 12th Ave. S. (℃ **615/252-8787**), is a vibrant, ultra-modern, Atlanta-based sushi bar; while **City Hall**, 405 12th Ave. S. (℃ **244-2115**), has become a popular party and live music venue. It backs up to another trendy nightspot: **Bar Twenty3**, 503 12th Ave. S. (℃ **615/963- 9998**), an urban warehouse environment where you can wash down cocktails with everything from empanadas to bite-sized beef Wellingtons.

Farther south of downtown, **Rumours Wine Bar**, 2304 12th Ave. S. (℃ **615/292-9400**), is a cozy house converted into a festive bar that offers more than 50 by-the-glass wines along with good eats, an artsy patio, and lots of whimsical metal sculptures.

Meanwhile, in the West End, **Virago**, 1811 Division St. (℃ **615/320-5149**), is still the Vanderbilt University area's most sizzling sushi bar and a late-night gathering place—at least for the young, beautiful, and thirsty. Another upscale West-End restaurant that's better known for its after-hours vibe than its Mediterranean-inspired menu is **Layla Rul**, 909 20th Ave. S. (℃ **615/620-6015**).

an upstairs pool table, this is a beloved lesbian lounge where everyone can feel at home. 1400 Woodland St. ℃ **615/226-6343.** www.thelipsticklounge.com.

Tribe ⚜ A cosmopolitan dance club, Tribe attracts fashionable men and women, gay and straight. Music videos and a pool table provide diversions away from the dance floor, but the energetic crowds don't usually disperse until late into the night and early morning. 1517A Church St. ℃ **615/329-2912.** www.tribenashville.com. No cover.

A COMEDY CLUB

Zanies Comedy Showplace   This is Nashville's oldest, if not only, comedy club and has shows Wednesday through Sunday nights. Most weekend headliners have TV and movie track records. Cover is sometimes slightly higher for big-name comedians. 2025 Eighth Ave. S. ℃ **615/269-0221.** www.zanies.com. Cover $20 (plus minimum of 2 drink or food orders).

3 The Bar & Pub Scene

The Nashville bar scene is for the most part synonymous with the Nashville restaurant scene; an establishment has to serve food in order to serve liquor. So, in addition to the places listed below, if you want a cocktail, step into almost any moderately priced or expensive restaurant. The first thing you're likely to see is a bar.

BARS

The Beer Sellar   As the name implies, this downtown mainstay is all about the brew. By the bottle or on tap, there's a vast selection of beers that draws a rowdy crowd

---

Fun Fact **Out-Standing**

The Dixie Chicks' "Wide Open Spaces" now rivals Tammy Wynette's "Stand By Your Man" as one of the top-selling country music songs of all time.

---

of fun-loving types. The dark but homey basement bar has a kickin' jukebox, too. 107 Church St. (*C*) 615/254-9464. www.beersellar.net.

Buffalo Billiards   Formerly Havana Lounge, this popular night spot in an old warehouse in the middle of The District offers 27 pool tables, darts, and an eclectic menu of food and drink. 154 Second Ave. N. (*C*) 615/313-7665. www.buffalobilliards.com/nashville.

Family Wash   A cozy former East Nashville Laundromat has become a landmark beer joint known for having the best pub grub in town. While chilling to the live nightly music, sample some hearty shepherd's pie or roasted chicken with mashed potatoes and gravy. 2038 Greenwood Ave. (*C*) 615/226-6070. www.familywash.com.

The Gerst Haus   Though ostensibly a German restaurant, this place is more like a lively beer hall than anything else. They serve their own amber lager, and on weekends there is a live polka band in the evenings. 228 Woodland St. (*C*) 615/244-8886.

Jimmy Kelly's   This place is straight out of the Old South and might have you thinking that you've stepped onto the set of a Tennessee Williams play. Jimmy Kelly's is primarily a restaurant and the bar isn't very large, but you'll feel as though you're part of a Nashville tradition when you have a drink here. The place is always lively, and the clientele tends to be older and well-to-do. 217 Louise Ave. (*C*) **615/329-4349.** www.jimmykellys.com.

The Old Spaghetti Factory   Sure it's touristy, but the drinks are cheap. If you think Victoriana is the height of romance, you won't want to miss out on bringing a date here. It's hard to believe that this elegant room was once a warehouse. 160 Second Ave. N. (*C*) 615/254-9010. www.osf.com.

Radius 10   A ritzy rendezvous spot for happy-hour specials, late-night drinks and dinner, this high-profile eatery in The Gulch offers stunning views of the nearby Nashville skyline. Celebrity locals like Nicole Kidman and Keith Urban have been known to nosh here. After sipping Snickers-flavored or blueberry-lemon drop martinis, try the Kobe beef short ribs or sashimi-grade tuna—served with a side shot glass of coconut-pineapple smoothie. 1103 McGavock St. (*C*) 615/259-5105. www.radius10.com.

The Tin Roof   American pub fare, a casual atmosphere, and a thriving happy-hour scene make this Music Row bar a refreshing antidote to the crowded dives along Broadway downtown. Music industry execs, session musicians, and college kids frequent this club, where there always seems to be a party. 1516 Demonbreun St. (*C*) 615/313-7103.

BREWPUBS

Big River Grille & Brewing Works   With a weird, retro-contemporary atmosphere that harkens back to a friendly '70s fern bar, this vast pub, part of a small Chattanooga-based chain, does a brisk food business. Handcrafted "boutique" beers include lagers, pilsners, and stouts, along with a seasonal brew that changes throughout the year. On a weekends, this place stays packed. 111 Broadway. (*C*) 615/251-4677. www.bigrivergrille.com.

Blackstone Restaurant & Brewery   Nashville's most upscale brewpub draws a lot of business travelers who are staying in nearby hotels. Casual comfort is the setting here, with cushioned chairs, a fireplace, and marbled bar. The food, including wood-fired pizzas and pretzels, is consistently good. But the beer is the main focus. Choose from a variety of brews including several that change with the seasons. There's also a six-pack sampler. 1918 West End Ave. (*C*) **615/327-9969.** www.blackstonebrewery.com.

Boscos *&*   With locations in Memphis and Nashville, Tennessee-based Boscos has built a reputation as the best brewpub around. Here in Music City, Boscos occupies a cavernous but congenial space in Hillsboro Village. Either inside the vivacious brew pub or outside on the lovely teakwood deck, patrons can wash down fresh fish dishes, gourmet pizzas, and stuffed mushrooms with a choice of more than half a dozen beers on tap. The bar sometimes serves cask-conditioned ales. 1805 21st Ave. S. (*C*) **615/385-0050.** www.boscosbeer.com.

4 The Performing Arts

THE TENNESSEE PERFORMING ARTS CENTER (TPAC)

A major renovation completed in fall 2003 gave the drab, utilitarian **Tennessee Performing Arts Center (TPAC),** 505 Deaderick St. ((*C*) **615/782-4000;** www.tpac.org), a much-needed makeover. Glass walls and an electronic marquee now illuminate the formerly nondescript, concrete exterior of Nashville's premier performance facility. The center houses three theaters: the Andrew Johnson, the James K. Polk, and the Andrew Jackson, whose expanded lobby now dazzles patrons with a 30-foot waterfall and other aesthetic touches. The three spaces can accommodate large and small productions (ticket prices range $10–$45). Resident companies based here include the **Nashville Ballet** ((*C*) **615/297-2966;** www.nashvilleballet.com), which each year stages two full-length ballets and two programs of selected pieces; and the **Nashville Opera** ((*C*) **615/832-5242;** www.nashvilleopera.org), which mounts four lavish productions annually.

TPAC, as locals know it, is also home to two theater companies. The **Tennessee Repertory Theatre** ((*C*) **615/244-4878;** www.tnrep.org) is the state's largest professional theater company. Its five seasonal productions run from September to May and include dramas, musicals, and comedies. TPAC's other resident theater company is **Circle Players** ((*C*) **615/332-PLAY;** www.circleplayers.net), Nashville's oldest nonprofit volunteer arts group. This company does six productions per season and seems to take more chances on lesser-known works than the Rep does.

In addition to productions by Nashville's main performing arts companies, TPAC also hosts various acts and an annual **"Broadway Series"** ((*C*) **615/782-4000**) that brings first-rate touring productions such as *My Fair Lady* and *Spamalot* to Nashville between October and June. Tickets to TPAC performances are available either at the TPAC box office or through **Ticketmaster** ((*C*) **615/255-9600**).

The **Nashville Symphony** ((*C*) **615/783-1200;** www.nashvillesymphony.org), which presents a mix of classical and pops concerts, as well as a children's series, has a stunning new home in the **Schermerhorn Hall** (corner of Fourth Ave. S. at Demonbreun). The acoustically superior 1,872-seat venue features 30 soundproof overhead windows, making it the only major concert hall in the world featuring natural light.

OTHER VENUES & SERIES AROUND THE CITY

Looking beyond TPAC, you'll find a wide array of performances in the **Great Performances at Vanderbilt** series ((*C*) **615/322-2471;** www.vanderbilt.edu), which is staged at Vanderbilt University's Ingram Hall, Blair School of Music, 24th Avenue South at Children's Way (tickets $10–$26). Each year, this series includes more than a dozen internationally acclaimed performing arts companies from around the world. In 2007–2008, acts ranged from Australia's contemporary BalletLab to the cutting-edge Kronos Quartet. The emphasis is on chamber music and modern dance, but touring theater productions are also scheduled.

The **Nashville Municipal Auditorium,** 417 Fourth Ave. N. (© **615/862-6390;** www.nashvilleauditorium.com), was for many years the site of everything from circuses to revivals. Today the aging, dome-roofed venue plays host to everyone from Bob Dylan to Bob the Builder. Plus, there's always the occasional rodeo, boxing match, or monster-truck mash. A stone's throw away, the newly renamed **Sommet Center** (previously the Gaylord Entertainment Center), 501 Broadway (© **615/770-2000;** www.sommetcenter.com), is now the venue of choice for major rock and country music concerts, ice shows, the Arena Football League's Kats, and NHL hockey courtesy of the Nashville Predators. Thanks to the recent purchase of the team by a group of Nashville investors, the Predators' future in Nashville seems secure.

The "Music City J.A.M. (Jazz and More)" festival is one of the premier live, outdoor music events. It takes place Saturday and Sunday over Labor Day weekend at downtown Nashville's **Riverfront Park.** Every Thursday night from June to August, Grammy-nominated jazz saxophonist Kirk Whalum serves as emcee for the all-star, family-oriented program, which includes gospel, jazz, soul, reggae, and blues acts. Admission is $25 for a 2-day pass or $15 for a single-day pass. For more information, call Ticketmaster Outlets (© **615/255-3588**). The **Frist Center for the Arts** offers Frist Fridays on the last Friday of every month (May–Sept). Free admission includes live music and appetizers outside on the courtyard, along with entry into the Frist's galleries (5:30–9pm). For more information, call © **615/244-3340.**

Farther away, the verdant grounds of **Cheekwood Botanical Garden & Museum of Art,** 1200 Forrest Park Dr. (© **615/356-8000;** www.cheekwood.org), are the site of annual summer concerts by the Nashville Symphony each June.

In addition, I highly recommend the **Belcourt Theatre,** 2102 Belcourt Ave. (© **615/383-9140;** www.belcourt.org), where you can catch the latest art-house film releases and other cinematic fare that's all but ignored by today's modern multiplexes. From October through December, the theater stages a weekend classics matinee series called "The Best Old Movies for Families." Vintage gems including the Marx Brothers' *Duck Soup,* old Hollywood musicals, and Frank Capra's *It's a Wonderful Life* were featured in the 2007 series. Live entertainment, including musical events and occasional lectures/discussions, are also staged occasionally at The Belcourt—fitting, as the venue was one of the early homes of the *Grand Ole Opry.*

If you enjoy dinner theater, you may want to check out **Chaffin's Barn Dinner Theatre,** 8204 Tenn. 100 (© **800/282-BARN** or 615/646-9977; www.dinnertheatre. com), housed in a big old Dutch-colonial barn 20 minutes outside of Nashville (dinner and show $40 adults, $20 children 12 and under; show only $33 adults, $25 children). The dinner is an all-you-can-eat country buffet (think fried catfish, ham, green beans, and fruit cobblers and berry shortcakes). Recent stage shows have run the gamut from *Chicago* and *Lend Me A Tenor* to *Arsenic and Old Lace.* Performances are Tuesday through Saturday. Reservations are required and must be paid for 24 hours in advance. To reach Chaffin's Barn, take I-40 west to Exit 199 (Old Hickory Blvd.) and head south to Old Harding Road (Tenn. 100), turn right, and continue for 4 miles.

⌒Tips Know Before You Go

Opry bound? Be aware that not all country stars are members of the grand ol' gang. So if you're hoping to see, say, George Strait, Wynonna, or the Dixie Chicks, look elsewhere. Many fans might not realize that *Opry* members are invited performers who must agree to a certain number of *Opry* appearances. Consequently, due to scheduling conflicts or other concerns, not every country singer who's a household name is represented.

But plenty of them are. The *Opry*'s stellar roster includes Trace Adkins, Bill Anderson, Dierks Bentley, Clint Black, Garth Brooks, Jim Ed Brown, Roy Clark, John Conlee, Skeeter Davis, Diamond Rio, Little Jimmy Dickens, Joe Diffie, Holly Dunn, The Gatlin Brothers, Vince Gill, Billy Grammer, Tom T. Hall, Emmylou Harris, Jan Howard, Stonewall Jackson, Alan Jackson, George Jones, Hal Ketchum, Alison Krauss, Patty Loveless, Loretta Lynn, Martina McBride, Del McCoury, Reba McEntire, Lorrie Morgan, The Osborne Brothers, Brad Paisley, Dolly Parton, Charley Pride, Jeanne Pruett, Del Reeves, Riders In The Sky, Ricky Van Shelton, Jean Shepard, Ricky Skaggs, Ralph Stanley, Marty Stuart, Pam Tillis, Randy Travis, Travis Tritt, Ricky Van Shelton, Steve Wariner, The Whites, and Trisha Yearwood.

10

Side Trips from Nashville

After you've had your fill of Nashville's country music scene, it may be time for a change of scenery—and a taste of the real country. Heading out in any direction from Nashville, you'll hit the Tennessee hills. These are the hills famous for their walking horses and sour-mash whiskey. They also hold historic towns and Civil War battlefields that are well worth visiting.

1 Franklin, Columbia & Scenic U.S. 31

Franklin is 20 miles south of Nashville; Columbia is 46 miles south of Nashville.

South of Nashville, U.S. 31 leads through the rolling Tennessee hills to the historic towns of Franklin and Columbia. This area was the heart of the middle Tennessee plantation country, and there are still many antebellum mansions along this route. Between Nashville and Franklin, you'll pass by more than a dozen old plantation homes, with still more to the south of Franklin.

ESSENTIALS
GETTING THERE The start of the scenic section of U.S. 31 is in Brentwood at exit 74 off I-65. Alternatively, you can take I-65 straight to Franklin (exit 65) and then take U.S. 31 back north to Nashville. From Columbia, you can head back north on U.S. 31, take U.S. 412/Tenn. 99 east to I-65, or head west on Tenn. 50 to the **Natchez Trace Parkway.** This latter road is a scenic highway administered by the National Park Service.

VISITOR INFORMATION In Franklin, stop in at the tiny **Williamson County Visitor Information Center,** 209 E. Main St. (© **615/591-8514**), open daily except holidays.

EXPLORING HISTORIC FRANKLIN
At the visitor center—housed in a former doctor's office built in 1839—you can pick up information about various historic sites around the area, including a map to the historic homes along U.S. 31 and a self-guided walking-tour map of Franklin. A 15-block area of downtown and quite a few other buildings around town have been listed on the National Register of Historic Places. Today, nearly the entire town has been restored—both commercial buildings around the central square and residential buildings in surrounding blocks—giving the town a charming 19th-century air. The best thing to do in Franklin is just stroll around admiring the restored buildings, browsing through the many antiques stores and malls. In addition to downtown antiques malls, there are others at the I-65 interchange.

Franklin is best known in Tennessee as the site of the bloody Battle of Franklin during the Civil War. During this battle, which took place on November 30, 1864, more

Side Trips from Nashville

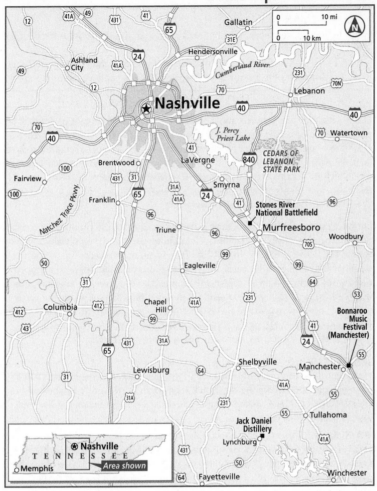

than 6,000 Confederate and 2,000 Union soldiers were killed. Each year on November 30, there are special activities here to commemorate the battle. Among the events are costumed actors marching through town and, after dark, a bonfire. Contact the Visitor Information Center for details.

To learn more about the town's Civil War history, visit the following historic homes.

Carnton Plantation 🐾   Recently, this somber tourist attraction gained greater visibility as the backdrop for Robert Hicks' best-selling historic novel, *The Widow of the South* (2006). Built in 1826 by Randal McGavock, a former mayor of Nashville, Carnton Plantation is a beautiful neoclassical antebellum mansion with a Greek Revival portico. During the Battle of Franklin, one of the bloodiest battles of the Civil War, this plantation home served as a Confederate hospital, and today you can still see the blood stains on floors throughout the house. The interior of the stately old home

Tuneful Tidbit

"There is no richer, more illuminating showcase of musical roots in the country than in this 220-mile stretch of highway."

—Esteemed rock music critic Robert Hilburn of the *Los Angeles Times*, describing the 3-hour drive between Nashville and Memphis along I-40

is almost completely restored and houses many McGavock family pieces and other period furnishings. Two years after the battle, the McGavock family donated 2 acres of land to be used as a cemetery for Confederate soldiers who had died during the Battle of Franklin. There are almost 1,500 graves in the McGavock Confederate Cemetery, which makes this the largest private Confederate cemetery in the country.

1345 Carnton Lane. ☎ 615/794-0903. www.carnton.org. Admission $10 adults, $9 seniors, $5 children 6–12. Mon–Sat 9am–5pm, Sun 1–5pm. Closed major holidays.

Carter House   Built in 1830, the Carter House served as the Union army command post during the Battle of Franklin. Throughout the bloody fight, which raged all around the house, the Carter family and friends hid in the cellar. Today, you can still see many bullet holes in the main house and various outbuildings on the property. In addition to getting a tour of the restored home, you can spend time in the museum, which contains many Civil War artifacts. A video presentation about the battle that took place here will provide you with a perspective for touring the town of Franklin.

1140 Columbia Ave. ☎ 615/791-1861. www.carter-house.org. Admission $8 adults, $7 seniors, $4 children. Apr–Oct Mon–Sat 9am–5pm, Sun 1–5pm; Nov–Mar Mon–Fri 9am–4pm, Sun 1–4pm. Closed major holidays.

COLUMBIA

Heading south from Franklin on U.S. 31 for about 26 miles will bring you to the town of Columbia. Along the way, you'll see a dozen or so historic antebellum homes, and in Columbia itself, more old homes and three districts listed on the National Register of Historic Places.

James K. Polk House   This modest home was where James K. Polk, the 11th president of the United States, grew up and where he lived when he began his legal and political career. Though Polk may not be as familiar a name as those of some other early presidents, he did achieve two very important goals while in office: Polk negotiated the purchase of California and settled the long-standing dispute between the United States and England over where to draw the border of the Oregon Territory. The house is filled with antiques that belonged to Polk's parents when they lived here and to Polk and his family during their time in the White House. There's even a lock of former U.S. President Andrew Jackson's hair.

301 W. Seventh St., Columbia. ☎ 931/388-2354. www.jameskpolk.com. Admission $7 adults, $6 seniors, and $4 students 6–18 (maximum of $20 per family for parents with children under 18). Apr–Oct Mon–Sat 9am–5pm, Sun 1–5pm; Nov–Mar Mon–Sat 9am–4pm, Sun 1–5pm. Closed major holidays.

2 Distilleries, Walking Horses & a Civil War Battlefield

Though Tennessee was last to secede from the Union, the Civil War came early to the state, and 3 years of being on the front lines left Tennessee with a legacy written in blood. More Civil War battles were fought here than in any other state except Virginia, and the bloodiest of these was the Battle of Stones River, which took place 30 miles south of Nashville near the city of Murfreesboro. Today this battle is commemorated at the **Stones River National Battlefield.**

In the 2 decades that followed the war, Tennessee quickly recovered and developed two of the state's most famous commodities—Tennessee sippin' whiskey and Tennessee walking horses. Another 45 miles or so south of Murfreesboro, you can learn about both of these time-honored Tennessee traditions.

For those of you who are not connoisseurs of sour-mash whiskeys, Tennessee whiskey is *not* bourbon. This latter whiskey, named for Bourbon County, Kentucky, where it was first distilled, is made much the same way, but it is not charcoal-mellowed the way fine Tennessee sour-mash whiskey is.

Stones River National Battlefield   On New Year's Eve 1862, what would become the bloodiest Civil War battle west of the Appalachian Mountains began just north of Murfreesboro along the Stones River. Though by the end of the first day of fighting the Confederates thought they were assured a victory, Union reinforcements turned the tide against the rebels. By January 3, the Confederates were in retreat and 23,000 soldiers lay dead or injured on the battlefield. Today, 351 acres of the battlefield are preserved. The site includes a national cemetery and the Hazen Brigade Monument, which was erected in 1863 and is the oldest Civil War memorial in the United States. In the visitor center you'll find a museum full of artifacts and details of the battle.

3501 Old Nashville Hwy., Murfreesboro. ✆ 615/893-9501. www.nps.gov/stri. Free admission. Daily 8am–5pm. Closed Dec 25. Take I-24 south from Nashville for about 30 miles to exit 78B.

Continue on I-24 to exit 105. Drive southwest for 10 miles to Tullahoma and follow signs to:

Jack Daniel's Distillery ✈   Old Jack Daniel (or Mr. Jack, as he was known hereabouts) didn't waste any time setting up his whiskey distillery after the Civil War came to an end. Founded in 1866, this is the oldest registered distillery in the United States and is on the National Register of Historic Places. It's still an active distillery; you can tour the facility and see how Jack Daniel's whiskey is made and learn how it gets such a distinctive earthy flavor. There are two secrets to the manufacture of Mr. Jack's famous sour-mash whiskey. The first of these is the water that comes gushing—pure, cold, and iron-free—from Cave Spring. The other is the sugar maple that's used to make the charcoal. In fact, it is this charcoal, through which the whiskey slowly drips, that gives Jack Daniel's its renowned smoothness.

After touring the distillery, you can glance in at the office used by Mr. Jack and see the safe that did him in. Old Mr. Jack kicked that safe one day in a fit of anger and wound up getting gangrene for his troubles. One can only hope that regular doses of Tennessee sippin' whiskey helped ease the pain of his last days. If you want to take home a bottle of Jack Daniel's, they can be purchased here at the distillery, but nowhere else in this county, which is another of Tennessee's dry counties. (No tastings at the end of the tour I'm afraid.)

182 Lynchburg Hwy, Lynchburg. ✆ 931/759-6319. www.jackdaniels.com. Free admission. Daily 9am–4:30pm. Tours at regular intervals throughout the day. Reservations not accepted. Closed Thanksgiving, Dec 24–25, Dec 31, and Jan 1. Take Tenn. 55 off I-24 and drive 26 miles southwest to Lynchburg.

Tennessee Walking Horse Museum   The Tennessee walking horse, named for its unusual high-stepping walking gait, is considered the world's premier breed of show horse, and it is here in the rolling hills of middle Tennessee that most of these horses are bred. Using interactive videos, hands-on exhibits, and other displays, this museum

Tennessee Jammin'

If you're a rock-and-roots music fan planning a Tennessee road trip, don't miss the Bonnaroo Music & Arts Festival in Manchester, about 60 miles southeast of Nashville. This wild, four-day outdoor concert event—held every June and rapidly becoming one of the hottest live music events in the country—conjures up a laid-back, hippie vibe on a grassy, 700-acre farm not far from Jack Daniel's and George Dickel's noted whiskey distilleries (in Lynchburg and Tullahoma, respectively).

Bring your camping gear and sense of free-spirited abandon to Bonnaroo. In between sets by such diverse headliners such as Pearl Jam, Kanye West, Robert Plant and Alison Kraus, The Swell Season, Broken Social Scene, and B.B. King, browse the eccentric village scene for other entertaining diversions and eye-popping people-watching. For more information, visit www.bonnaroo.com.

presents the history of the Tennessee walking horse. Though the exhibits here will appeal primarily to equine enthusiasts, there is also much for the casual visitor to learn and enjoy. The annual Tennessee Walking Horse National Celebration, held each August here in Shelbyville, is one of middle Tennessee's most important annual events. Tennessee walkers can also be seen going through their paces at various other annual shows in the Nashville area.

183 Main St., Lynchburg. (C) **931/759-5747.** www.twhnc.com. Free admission. Tues–Sat 10am–noon and 1–4pm. Closed major holidays.

AN UNFORGETTABLE LUNCH STOP IN LYNCHBURG

Miss Mary Bobo's Boarding House (★ SOUTHERN   You'll feel as if you should be wearing a hoop skirt or top hat when you see this grand white mansion, with its columns, long front porch, and balcony over the front door (but casual, contemporary clothes are just fine). Miss Mary Bobo's, housed in an antebellum-style mansion built slightly postbellum (in 1866), opened for business as a boardinghouse back in 1908, and though it no longer accepts boarders, it does serve the best lunch for miles around. Be prepared for filling portions of good, Southern home cooking, and remember, lunch here is actually midday dinner. Miss Mary's is very popular, and you generally need to book a weekday lunch 2 to 3 weeks in advance; for a Saturday lunch, you'll need to make reservations at least 2 to 3 *months* in advance.

Main St., Lynchburg. (C) **931/759-7394.** www.jackdaniels.co.uk/lynchburg/boarding.asp. Reservations required well in advance. Set menu $11 adults, $5 children under 10. No credit cards. Lunch seatings Mon–Fri 1pm; Sat 11am and 1pm.

11

The Best of Memphis

Memphis spawned several of the most important musical forms of the 20th century, yet Nashville stole the Tennessee limelight with its country music. Ask the average American what makes Memphis special, and he or she *might* be able to tell you that this is the city of Graceland, Elvis Presley's mansion.

What they're less likely to know is that Memphis is also the birthplace of the blues, rock 'n' roll, and soul music. Memphis is where W. C. Handy put down on paper the first written blues music, where The King made his first recording, and where Otis Redding and Al Green expressed the music in their souls.

Many fans of American music (and they come from all over the world) know Memphis. Walking down Beale Street today, sitting in the Sun Studio Cafe, or waiting to pass through the wrought-iron gates of Graceland, you're almost as likely to hear French, German, and Japanese as you are to hear English. British, Irish, and Scottish accents are all common in a city known throughout the world as the birthplace of the most important musical styles of the 20th century. For these people, a trip to Memphis is a pilgrimage. The Irish rock band U2 came here to pay homage and wound up infusing their music with Americana on the record and movie *U2: Rattle and Hum.* Lead singer Bono, when interviewed for the city's new Soulsville museum, called the city's musical heritage "extraordinary."

Pilgrims come to Memphis not only because Graceland, the second most-visited home in America (after the White House), is here. They come because Beale Street was once home to Handy—and later, B.B. King, Muddy Waters, and others—who merged the gospel singing and cotton-field work songs of the Mississippi Delta into a music called the blues. They come because Sun Studio's owner, Sam Phillips, in the early 1950s began recording several young musicians who experimented with fusing the sounds of "hillbilly" (country) music and the blues into an entirely new sound. This uniquely American sound, first known as rockabilly, would quickly become known as rock 'n' roll, the music that has written the soundtrack for the baby-boom generation.

1 Frommer's Most Unforgettable Travel Experiences

- **Remembering Reverend Martin Luther King from the Balcony of the Lorraine Motel:** Mournful gospel hymns play softly in the background as visitors approach the place where the civil rights leader was assassinated in 1968. This is the conclusion of a visit to the inspiring **National Civil Rights Museum,** 450 Mulberry St. (© **901/521-9699**), built on the site of this once-segregated motel. See p. 205.

• **Standing at the Sun Studio Microphone that Elvis Used for His First Recordings:** It's worth the tour admission price just to handle the microphone in this famed recording studio at 706 Union Ave. (℃ **800/441-6249**). It launched the career of Elvis Presley and created a sound that would come to be called rock 'n' roll. See p. 202.

• **Getting Your First Glimpse of the "Jungle Room":** Sure, you've probably heard about the hideously gaudy decor inside Graceland mansion, 3734 Elvis Presley Blvd. (℃ **800/238-2000**), but nothing prepares you for that first face-to-faux-fur encounter in the green-and-gold den Elvis created to remind him of Hawaii. See p. 199.

2 The Best Splurge Hotels

• **The Peabody Memphis,** 149 Union Ave. (℃ **800/PEABODY** or 901/529-4000): Steeped in tradition and brimming with gracious hospitality, this is one of the most elegant hotels in the South. Of course, you'll also be sharing the lobby with the famous Peabody ducks. See p. 164.

• **The Madison Hotel,** 79 Madison Ave. (℃ **866/44-MEMPHIS** or 901/333-1200): This sophisticated boutique hotel was built in a historic bank building downtown. Warm and intimate, it's a romantic retreat that offers spectacular sunsets from the rooftop garden. See p. 161.

• **Hilton Memphis,** 939 Ridge Lake Blvd., (℃ 800/774-1500 or 901/684-6664): This is a modern, artsy skyscraper at the edge of East Memphis and Germantown. Book an upper room and enjoy spectacular views of the Memphis area. See p. 169.

3 The Best Moderately Priced Hotels

• **Sleep Inn–Downtown at Court Square,** 40 N. Front St. (℃ **800/753-3946** or 901/522-9700): With a terrific downtown location between Court Square and the Mississippi River, and the Main Street Trolley at your door, this clean, comfy motel is an affordable gem. See p. 168

• **Elvis Presley's Heartbreak Hotel at Graceland,** 3677 Elvis Presley Blvd.

(℃ **877/777-0606** or 901/332-1000): If you're an Elvis fan, this one's a no-brainer. Operated by Graceland and mere steps away from The King's mansion, this modest hotel has kitsch to spare. Elvis is everywhere, from the breakfast nook to the outdoor pool. See p. 173.

4 The Most Unforgettable Dining Experiences

• **Chomping on Dry Ribs at The Rendezvous,** 52 S. Second St. (℃ **901/523-2746**): It's dark, it's noisy, and the waiters are intentionally surly, but oh, those barbecued ribs! "Wet" (cooked with liquid sauce) or "dry" (rubbed with a dry blend), the spice-slathered,

succulent pork won't disappoint. This place is an institution. See p. 184.

• **Indulging in a Full-Course Gourmet Meal at Erling Jensen—The Restaurant,** 1044 S. Yates (℃ **901/763-3700**): Food and wine connoisseurs can expect to be coddled at this pricey bastion of fine dining in East Memphis. Danish-born chef Jensen is a true artist whose culinary creations never fail to delight discerning diners. See p. 187.

- **"Lookin' Good and Eatin' Good" (as goes their slogan) at the Beauty Shop,** 966 S. Cooper (© **901/272-7111**): Be it a basic burger and pepper-dusted spicy fries or more inventive Thai Cobb Salad, this Cooper-Young beauty parlor turned restaurant is a hoot. And yes, you can nosh under an honest-to-gosh, '60s-style hair dryer seat. See p. 185.

5 The Best Things to Do for Free (Or Almost)

- **Walkin' in Memphis:** The paved trails and grassy expanse of Tom Lee Park downtown provide breathtaking views of the Mississippi River and Memphis skyline. Take a brisk walk or loll on a bench and watch the barges glide by on their way to New Orleans. See p. 207.

- **Browsing for Bargains at A. Schwab Dry Goods Store:** Need Elvis aviator sunglasses? Voodoo candles? Sombreros or screwdrivers? Underpants or overalls? It's all here, and then some, at A. Schwab Dry Goods Store, 163 Beale St. (© **901/ 523-9782**). Opened in 1876 and little-changed since then, this beloved old-time dime store and antiques museum has creaky wooden floors, cheap prices, and a mind-boggling array of stuff you won't find anywhere else. See p. 226.

- **Shopping for the Tackiest Elvis Souvenir in the World:** The hip-swinging Elvis clock has become all too familiar, so why not try some stick-on Elvis sideburns, an Elvis temporary tattoo, an Elvis Christmas ornament, Elvis playing cards, an Elvis nightlight, or a little plastic tray displaying a photo of Elvis with President Richard Nixon. See "Shopping A to Z" in chapter 18.

12

Suggested Memphis Itineraries

Many of Memphis's must-see sites are located downtown and in nearby South Memphis. Therefore, it's feasible to tackle a good chunk of the city's best in a single, action-packed day. As with any destination, the seasons and your personal interests will dictate how you proceed. Besides musical attractions, Memphis has much to offer in terms of culture and history. In the spring, summer, and fall, take advantage of the longer days and get outdoors to enjoy some of the city's many parks and natural attractions. Of course, rainy or wintry days make museums, galleries, and antiques shops more practical diversions. Fortunately, most of the city's popular attractions may be enjoyed during any time of year.

1 The Best of Memphis in 1 Day

Today you will get a taste of the musical legends that put Memphis on the map at the city's best music museums before getting a chance to reflect on the sociopolitical context of the 1950s. Start your day where rock 'n' roll was born: *at Sun Studio.*

❶ Sun Studio ✰✰
Start your day where it all began: In the early 1950s, a shy, teenaged truck driver named Elvis Presley sauntered into Sam Phillips's tiny recording studio, asked to cut a birthday song for his mama, and ultimately launched the birth of rock 'n' roll. See p. 202.

❷ Soulsville USA: The Stax Museum of American Soul Music ✰✰✰
Albert King; Al Green; Earth, Wind & Fire; Isaac Hayes; and The Staples Singers are just a handful of the musical greats whose inspiring stories unfold in this rousing, interactive museum. The funky music reverberating throughout will make you want to sing, dance, stomp, and shout. See p. 201.

❸ FOURWAY RESTAURANT ✰✰✰
After getting funkified by the vibes at Stax, head down the block and hang with the locals at this family-oriented soul food restaurant. Crispy, piping-hot fried chicken, turnip greens, and candied yams with cornbread and butter are the perfect preludes to silky lemon meringue pie. But there's a lot of other comfort food, too. 998 Mississippi Blvd. ✆ **901/507-1519.** See p. 192.

Drive back downtown and park at the National Civil Rights Museum:

❹ National Civil Rights Museum ⭐⭐⭐

After spending the morning rocking to the sounds of Memphis music, put some social and political context behind what you've seen and heard. The National Civil Rights Museum is an absorbing and deeply moving experience, as it traces the cruel history of oppression and discrimination in the American South. See p. 205.

❺ South Main Street Arts District

Walk north back toward Beale Street, window shopping at boutiques and stepping inside cozy art galleries that line this revitalized historic district.

At the corner of Beale Street, turn right.

❻ Beale Street ⭐⭐

This legendary strip, revered the world over as the birthplace of the blues, can be a rowdy, neon booze-fest after dark. But during the day, it's a sea of curious tourists taking pictures, listening to live music at the outdoor W. C. Handy Park, and shopping for souvenirs. Join them. A. Schwab's, a 130-year-old general store, has the best bargains around. See p. 198.

Walk west back toward Main Street and walk to the nearest trolley stop.

 7 BLUES CITY CAFÉ
Grab a bite at this juke joint and diner that's my pick as the best of the Beale Street eats. Spicy tamales, lip-smackin' slabs of pork barbecue ribs, as well as cold beer, burgers, and rich gumbo are on the menu. With its weather-beaten booths and rural Mississippi shack-inspired decor, the mojo here is laid-back. 138 Beale St., ✆ 901/526-3637. See p. 193.

❽ Main Street Trolley

Take a ride on one of Memphis's antique restored trolley cars. They're old, they're creaky, their hard wooden seats are uncomfortable, and they're slow. But for a dollar or two you can sit back, relax, and ride the clanging, cumbersome streetcars from one end of downtown to the other, getting glimpses of the Pyramid, the Mississippi River, and other local landmarks. See p. 156.

Hop off the trolley at Pembroke Square for the:

❾ Center for Southern Folklore

Step inside the one-of-a-kind Center for Southern Folklore. Part coffeehouse, part outsider and folk art gallery, and part intimate performance space, the center is a beloved, locally owned nonprofit that celebrates the region's rich diversity. See p. 234.

2 The Best of Memphis in 2 Days

Okay, you're goin' to Graceland. If you're an Elvis Presley zealot, you probably couldn't wait until Day 2 to head to the home of the King, so you've already tried to squeeze it into Day 1. Fair enough. True fans should not miss seeing his homey (in a *Beverly Hillbillies* sort of way) mansion and taking the complete tour of all that's offered here. Tourists with no more than a mild interest in Elvis, though, might want to skip the full shebang and do a simple drive-by of the place instead. From here, you'll head back to Midtown and East Memphis for some fine art interspersed with flora and fauna. Cap off your day of critters and culture with a little rest and relaxation in the bohemian Cooper Young neighborhood.

Suggested Memphis Itineraries

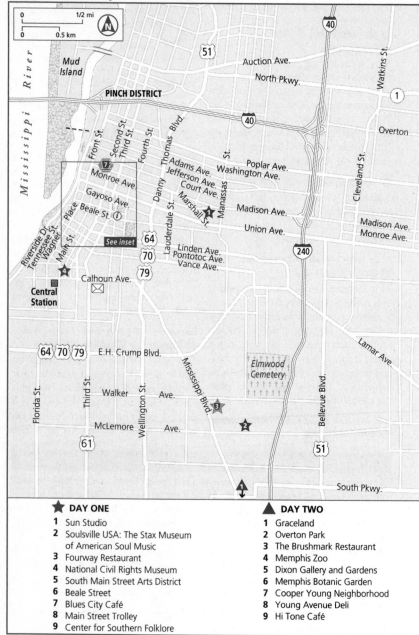

★ **DAY ONE**

1 Sun Studio
2 Soulsville USA: The Stax Museum
   of American Soul Music
3 Fourway Restaurant
4 National Civil Rights Museum
5 South Main Street Arts District
6 Beale Street
7 Blues City Café
8 Main Street Trolley
9 Center for Southern Folklore

▲ **DAY TWO**

1 Graceland
2 Overton Park
3 The Brushmark Restaurant
4 Memphis Zoo
5 Dixon Gallery and Gardens
6 Memphis Botanic Garden
7 Cooper Young Neighborhood
8 Young Avenue Deli
9 Hi Tone Café

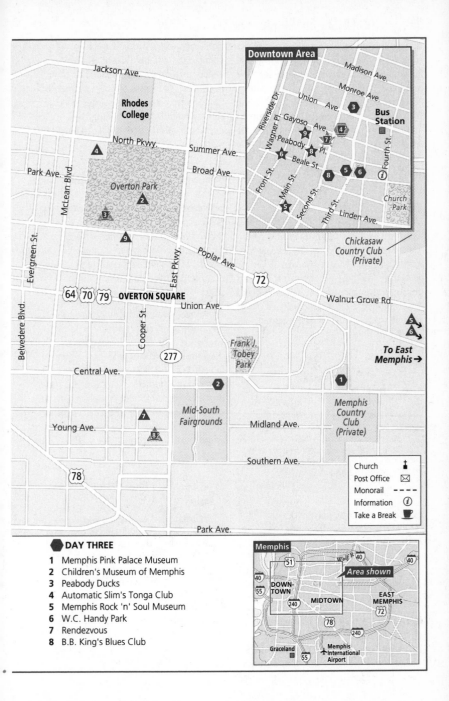

DAY THREE

1 Memphis Pink Palace Museum
2 Children's Museum of Memphis
3 Peabody Ducks
4 Automatic Slim's Tonga Club
5 Memphis Rock 'n' Soul Museum
6 W.C. Handy Park
7 Rendezvous
8 B.B. King's Blues Club

❶ Graceland ★★

The blue-and-white living room where he and Priscilla entertained guests. The mirrored, yellow TV room where Elvis liked to unwind. His paisley pool room. You'll see it all and more on a tour of the mansion where Elvis lived—and where he died. Across the street from the house you can tour his Austin Powers–ish airplanes, watch Elvis movies, and even admire his car collection. See p. 199.

❷ Overton Park

Back in Midtown, Overton Park is a beautiful setting that's home to the Memphis Zoo, the Memphis College of Art, and the Brooks Museum of Art. Visit the museum to get an overview of art through the ages. From Medieval and Impressionist to contemporary, a range of styles and media are represented. See p. 207.

> **❸ BRUSHMARK RESTAURANT**
> Before or after browsing the masterpieces in the Brooks Museum of Art, take some refreshment in the Brushmark Restaurant. Sit outside on the terrace, order a light lunch, and enjoy the lush views of the wooded park surroundings. 1934 Poplar Ave., ℭ 901/544-6225. See p. 194.

❹ Memphis Zoo ★★

The two soulful, cuddly panda bears from China are the reigning stars of this world-class zoo. But there are plenty of other animals and exhibits to see. From snakes and lions to elephants and monkeys, this is where the wild things are. See p. 206.

❺ Dixon Gallery and Gardens ★

In East Memphis, you'll find the next two stops on your itinerary: The Dixon Gallery and Gardens and the Memphis Botanic Garden are right across the street

from each other. Impressionist works are a highlight of the Dixon, a posh residence-turned-museum. Shaded by towering trees, the meticulously landscaped grounds are perfect for strolling. It's especially gorgeous in the spring, when the dogwoods and azaleas are in bloom. See p. 204.

❻ Memphis Botanic Garden ★

Nature enthusiasts will find much to love in this oasis of fragrant roses, iris beds, herb gardens, and acres of other flowering plants, majestic trees, and paved walking trails. The Japanese Garden of Tranquility, with its goldfish ponds, lanterns, and angular evergreens, is a favorite of romantics. See p. 208.

❼ Cooper-Young Neighborhood

Drive back toward Midtown and explore the bohemian area known as Cooper-Young. If you like felines, peek inside the **House of Mews,** 933 S. Cooper St. (ℭ 901/272-3777), a storefront converted into a homelike sanctuary for stray cats awaiting adoption. Shop for gifts at specialty boutiques or step into one of the great restaurants and bars clustered around this intersection. See p. 155.

> **❽ YOUNG AVENUE DELI**
> Flop a spell at this artsy coffee shop (2119 Young Ave., ℭ 901/278-0034,) and enjoy the eccentric people-watching in this offbeat area of town. Or walk half a block to cull the bins at **Goner Records** for vinyl rarities or other cheesy finds (p. 229).

❾ Hi Tone Café

Tonight, head back over to the Overton Park area to see what's happening and who's playing at this hip nightclub. 1913 Poplar, ℭ **901/278-8663.**

3 The Best of Memphis in 3 Days

Today begins with a bit of kids' stuff that will appeal to the child in all of us. You'll start at the Pink Palace Museum before heading over to the Children's Museum of Memphis. Then it's downtown to catch the ceremonious march of the Peabody ducks. The remainder of today you're downtown, taking in the Memphis Rock 'n' Soul Museum, W. C. Handy Park on Beale Street, and (I saved the best for last!) barbecued ribs at The Rendezvous. Tonight, say farewell to the city in style by taking in some smoldering live music at B.B. King Blues Club.

❶ Pink Palace Museum 🟊

Grocery store owner and entrepreneur Clarence Saunders, who pioneered the self-service grocery store with the Piggly Wiggly chain at the beginning of the 20th century, lived in this pink marble home. Today, it's a museum packed with educational exhibits, along with a planetarium and an IMAX Theatre. See p. 205.

❷ Children's Museum of Memphis 🟊

A fire engine for climbing, a castle for dreaming, a kid-sized city with a bank for cashing play checks, and a grocery store for filling shopping carts are among the favorites at this Midtown museum, located next to the Liberty Bowl Stadium. See p. 210.

❸ Peabody Ducks

Sure, it's touristy, but you owe it to yourself to see what all the fuss is about. If you can make it by 11am, you'll get to see the ducks waddle out of the elevator and into the lobby fountain. But if not, they'll be here all afternoon. They make their return trip to the ducky penthouse at 5pm. See p. 165.

> ### ☕ ❹ AUTOMATIC SLIM'S TONGA CLUB 🟊🟊
> Head downtown for lunch at this hip, artsy restaurant. Great food and drinks, along with a vibrant clientele, always keep this hangout buzzing. 83 S. Second St., ☏ 901/525-7948. See p. 182.

❺ Memphis Rock 'n' Soul Museum 🟊

On the plaza outside the FedEx Forum you'll find the entrance to this museum that traces the importance of Memphis in the history of rock music, soul, and rhythm-and-blues. Browse the exhibits, jam to the classics, and learn something new about your favorite musical heroes. See p. 201.

❻ W. C. Handy Park

Listen for the sounds of a bluesy rock band, or look for the statue of the early 20th century trumpeter, which dominates this open-air park and amphitheater. Take a load off at one of the benches, watch the crowds go by, and start tapping your feet to the beat. See p. 208.

> ### ☕ ❼ THE RENDEZVOUS RESTAURANT 🟊🟊
> Make a beeline back down toward Union Avenue, find the alley across from The Peabody, and let your nose lead the way to the source of the sizzling pork barbecue aromas that pervade the area. Feast on The Rendezvous' famous spice-dusted ribs, or try a chopped pork sandwich. 52 S. Second St., ☏ 901/523-2746. See p. 184.

❽ B.B. King Blues Club 🟊🟊

Kick back and surrender to the blues tonight, taking in whatever act happens to be playing at B.B. King's namesake nightclub on Beale Street. See p. 234.

13

Getting to Know
the Home of the Blues

When you hit town, you may be surprised and even a bit baffled by Memphis.
The city is spread out, so getting around
can be confusing and frustrating at first.

Read this chapter, and your first hours in
town should be less confusing. I've also
compiled a lot of useful information that
will help you throughout your stay.

1 Orientation

VISITOR INFORMATION

The city's main visitor information center, located downtown at the base of Jefferson
Street, is the **Tennessee State Welcome Center,** 119 N. Riverside Dr. (© **901/543-
6757**). It's open daily 24 hours but staffed only between 8am and 7pm (until 8pm in
the summer months). Inside this large information center, you'll find soaring statues
of both Elvis and B.B. King.

At the airport, you'll find information boards with telephone numbers for contacting hotels and numbers for other helpful services.

CITY LAYOUT

Memphis, built on the east bank of the **Mississippi River,** lies just above the Mississippi state line. Consequently, growth has proceeded primarily to the east and, to a
lesser extent, to the north. The inexorable sprawl of the suburbs has pushed the limits of the metropolitan area far to the east, and today the area known as **East Memphis** is the city's business and cultural center. Despite the fact that the city has a fairly
small and compact downtown area, the sprawl of recent years has made getting around
difficult for both residents and visitors. Traffic congestion on main east-west avenues
is bad throughout the day, so you're usually better off taking the interstate around the
outskirts of the city if you're trying to cross town.

In general, the city is laid out on a grid with a north-south axis. However, there are
many exceptions, including downtown, which was laid out with "streets" parallel to
the river and "avenues" running perpendicular to the river. Throughout the city you'll
find that, for the most part, avenues run east-west and streets run north-south.

MAIN ARTERIES & STREETS Memphis is circled by **I-40,** which loops around
the north side of the city, and **I-240,** which loops around the south side. **Poplar
Avenue** and **Sam Cooper Boulevard/North Parkway** are the city's main east-west
arteries. Poplar, heavily lined with businesses, is narrow, congested, and accident-prone.

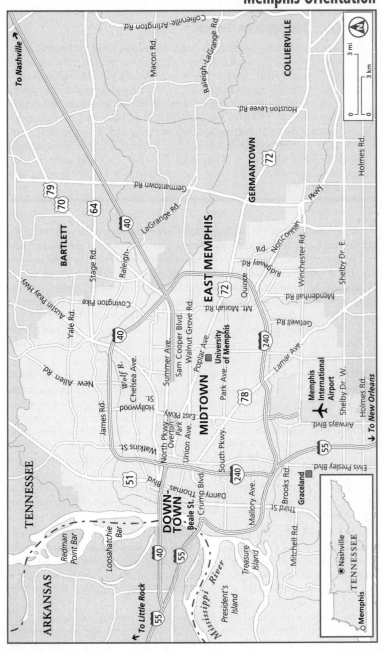

Fun Fact **Memphis on Screen**

Award-winning director John Sayles' latest film may be set in the fictional town of Harmony, Ala., in 1950, but much of the cast, character, and story line about race relations and roots music in the Deep South are pure Memphis. Smoke-filled juke joints, still common to many parts of the Mississippi Delta region, provide much of the film's evocative atmosphere. *Honeydripper,* which premiered at the 2007 Memphis Independent Film Festival, stars Danny Glover, Stacy Keach, Charles S. Dutton, and Vondie Curtis-Hall. Filling in at the last minute for rhythm-and-blues legend Ruth Brown (who died unexpectedly before fulfilling the role) is Mable John, a former recording artist at Stax, Memphis's legendary record label that spawned hits by Otis Redding and countless others.

If you don't want to take the interstate, **Sam Cooper Boulevard** is an alternative route into downtown, as is **Central Avenue** between Goodlett Road in the east and Lamar Avenue in the west. **Union Avenue** is the dividing line between the north and south sides of the city. Other important **east-west roads** include Summer Avenue and Park Avenue. Major **north-south arteries** include (from downtown heading eastward) Third Street/U.S. 61, I-240, Elvis Presley Boulevard/U.S. 51, Airways Boulevard/East Parkway, and Mendenhall Road. Lamar Avenue is another important road.

Out in **East Memphis,** the main east-west arteries are Poplar Avenue and Winchester Road. The main north-south arteries are Perkins Road/Perkins Road Extended, Mendenhall Road, Hickory Hill Road, and Germantown Road.

FINDING AN ADDRESS   Your best bet for finding an address in Memphis will always be to call the place first and ask for directions or the name of the nearest main cross street. Though address numbers increase the farther you get from downtown, they do not increase along each block in an orderly fashion. It is nearly impossible to determine how many blocks out an address will be. However, there are some general guidelines to get you in the vicinity of where you're going. If an address is in the hundreds or lower, you should be downtown. If the address is an avenue or other east-west road in the 2000-to-4000 range, you'll likely find it in midtown; if the number is in the 5000-to-7000 range, you should be out in East Memphis. If the address is on a street, it will likely have a north or south prefix included. Union Avenue is the dividing line between north and south.

STREET MAPS   Because the streets of Memphis can seem a bit baffling at times, you'll definitely need a good map. The **Tennessee State Welcome Center,** 119 N. Riverside Dr. (© **901/543-6757**), offers a simple map; you can also buy a more detailed one at any bookstore, pharmacy, or gas station. If you arrive at the airport and rent a car, the rental company will give you a basic map that will at least get you to your hotel or to the information center.

If you happen to be a member of **AAA,** you can get free maps of Memphis and the rest of Tennessee either from your local AAA office or from the Memphis office at 5138 Park Ave., Memphis, TN 38117 (© **901/761-5371**); it's open Monday to Friday 8:30am to 5:30pm, and Saturdays from 9am to 1pm.

THE NEIGHBORHOODS IN BRIEF

More important than neighborhoods in Memphis are the city's general divisions. These major divisions are how the city defines itself.

Downtown The oldest part of the city, downtown is constructed on the banks of the Mississippi River. After years of efforts toward revitalization, this area has finally turned the corner to become one of the most vibrant cities in the New South. Historic **Beale Street** remains the city's main entertainment district. Elsewhere downtown, a mushrooming array of restaurants, hot night spots, and cultural attractions await around every corner.

Midtown This is primarily a residential area, though it's also known for its numerous hospitals. Though a far cry from bustling Beale Street, the **Overton Square** area is midtown's main entertainment area and is the site of several decent restaurants. South of Overton Square, you'll find the hip

Cooper-Young neighborhood—basically a single intersection with trendy eateries, coffeehouses, and interesting boutiques. Midtown is also where you will find **Overton Park,** which envelops the Memphis Zoo and Aquarium, and the Memphis Brooks Museum of Art. There are many large, stately homes on parklike blocks surrounding Overton Park.

East Memphis Heading still farther east from downtown brings you to East Memphis, which lies roughly on either side of I-240 on the east side of the city. This is among the most affluent areas within the city limits. It's characterized by multilane highways, scads of malls and shopping centers (seemingly at every major intersection), office complexes, and a few high-rise hotels.

2 Getting Around Memphis

BY PUBLIC TRANSPORTATION

BY BUS The **Memphis Area Transit Authority (MATA; ☎ 901/274-MATA;** www.matatransit.com) operates citywide bus service, but I do not recommend it for tourists. Compared to other major cities, public transportation here is poor and does not offer convenient connections between most hotels and tourist sites. Bus stops are indicated by green-and-white signs. For schedule information, ask a bus driver or call the MATA number above. The standard fare is $1.50 and exact change is required. Transfers from bus to bus cost 10¢, but there's no transfer fee to the trolley. MATA offers a 50% discount for travelers with disabilities and senior citizens with ID cards. (*Note:* To qualify for the discounted fare, however, you need to show a Medicare card

---

Go, Cat, Go!

Elvis Presley finally has his own Tennessee license plate. Graceland unveiled the automotive honor in February 2008, placing the very first plate, hot off the assembly line, onto the King's purple 1956 Eldorado Cadillac. The white plates feature Elvis' signature in black cursive writing, along with a color caricature of the 50s'-era Elvis playing a guitar. Profits from the plates will benefit the Elvis Presley Memorial Trauma Center at The Regional Medical Center. "The Med," as it's known, is a major Memphis hospital with the only Level-1 trauma center in a five-state region.

Fun Fact   **Local Legends**

Everybody—or at least those who saw Tom Hanks play a dedicated overnight delivery man in the film *Castaway*—knows that Memphis is the world head-quarters for FedEx, but did you know its founder, Fred Smith, is also a budding movie mogul? His production company's hits (and misses) include *My Dog Skip, The Sisterhood of the Traveling Pants, Racing Stripes, Insomnia,* and *Dude, Where's My Car?*

Most recently, the entrepreneur's daughter, Molly Smith, teamed up as producing partner with Oscar-winning actress Hillary Swank for the 2007 romantic comedy *P.S. I Love You.* Incidentally, the film's supporting cast includes Kathy Bates, another beloved hometown heroine and Academy Award–winning actress.

or obtain a MATA ID card by bringing two forms of identification to the MATA Customer Service Center at 444 N. Main St., open Mon–Fri 7am–7pm.)

BY STREETCAR   The **Main Street Trolley** (© **901/577-2640**) operates renovated 1920s trolley cars (and modern reproductions) on a circular route that includes Main Street from the Pyramid to the National Civil Rights Museum and Central Station and then follows Riverside Drive, passing the Tennessee State Visitors Center. It's a unique way to get around the downtown area. The fare is $1 each way, with a special lunch-hour rate of 50¢ between 11am and 1:30pm. An all-day pass is $3.50; exact change is required, and passengers may board at any of the 20 stations along Main Street. Trolleys are wheelchair-accessible.

BY CAR

Memphis is a big sprawling city, and the best—and worst—way to get around is by car. A car is nearly indispensable for traveling between downtown and East Memphis, yet traffic congestion can make this trip take far longer than you'd expect (45 min. isn't unusual). East-west avenues and almost any road in East Memphis at rush hour are the most congested. Parking downtown is not usually a problem, but stay alert for tow-away zones and watch the time on your meter. Out in East Memphis, there is usually no parking problem. When driving between downtown and East Memphis, you'll usually do better to take the interstate.

CAR RENTALS   For tips on saving money on car rentals, see "Getting Around Nashville" in chapter 4.

All the major car-rental companies and several independent companies have offices in Memphis. Some are located near the airport only, and some have offices both near the airport and in other areas of Memphis. Be sure to leave yourself plenty of time for returning your car when you head to the airport to catch your return flight. None of the companies has an office in the airport itself, so you'll have to take a shuttle van from the car drop-off point to the airport terminal.

Most major car-rental companies in Memphis are clustered around the airport area and include **Alamo/National Rent-A-Car,** 2680 Rental Rd. (© **800/462-5266** or 901/398-8888); **Avis,** 2520 Rental Rd. (© **800/577-1521** or 901/345-6129); **Budget Rent-A-Car,** 2650 Rental Rd. (© **800/527-0700** or 901/398-8888); **Dollar**

Rent-A-Car, 2600 Rental Road (© **866/434-2226** or 901/346-3290); **Enterprise Rent-a-Car,** 2909 Airways Blvd. (© **866/799-7965** or 901/396-3736); **Hertz,** 2560 Rental Rd. (© **800/654-3131** or 901/345-5680); and **Thrifty Car Rental,** 2680 Rental Rd. (© **877/283-0898** or 901/345-0170).

PARKING   Parking in downtown Memphis is a lot more expensive than it used to be. There are plenty of parking lots behind the Beale Street clubs; these charge big bucks. Metered parking on downtown streets is becoming increasingly scarce; if you're lucky enough to snag a spot close to your destination, be sure to check the time limit on the meter. Downtown parking is also available in municipal and private lots and parking garages. Again, most require a stiff fee. The good news is, many of the automated parking kiosks now accept credit and debit cards for payment, eliminating the need to carry a lot of change.

In midtown, where parking is rarely a problem, there is a free lot in Overton Square between Madison Avenue and Monroe Avenue.

DRIVING RULES   A right turn at a red light is permitted after coming to a full stop, unless posted otherwise, but drivers must first yield to vehicles that have a green light or pedestrians in the walkway. Children under 4 years of age must be in a child's car seat or other approved child restraint when in the car.

Tennessee has a very strict DUI (driving under the influence of alcohol) law, and anyone caught driving under the influence with a child under 12 years of age in the car may be charged with a felony.

BY TAXI

For quick cab service, call **Checker/Yellow Cab** (© **901/577-7777**) or **City Wide Cab Company** (© **901/324-4202**), or have your hotel or motel call one for you. The first mile is $3; after that, it's $1.80 per mile. Each additional passenger is $1 extra.

ON FOOT

Downtown Memphis is walkable, though the only areas that attract many visitors are the Beale Street area and Main Street from the National Civil Rights Museum north to the Pyramid. The rest of the city is not walkable.

FAST FACTS: **Memphis**

Airport The **Memphis International Airport** (© **901/922-8000**; www.mscaa. com) serves the Memphis area; see "Getting There," in chapter 12.

American Express There is no American Express office in Memphis, but its representative is **American and International Travel Services,** at 5124 Poplar Ave. (© **901/754-6970**), open Monday to Friday 8:30am to 5pm. There is a national number for American Express (© **800/528-4800**) and for American Express travel assistance (© **800/YES-AMEX**).

Area Code The telephone area code in Memphis is **901.**

Babysitters Contact **Annie's Nannies** (© **901/755-1457**).

Business Hours Banks are generally open Monday to Thursday 8:30am to 4pm, with later hours on Friday. Office hours in Memphis are usually Monday to Friday 8:30am to 5pm. In general, stores located in downtown Memphis are open

Monday to Saturday 10am to 5:30pm. Shops in suburban Memphis malls are generally open Monday to Saturday 10am to 9pm and on Sunday 1 to 5 or 6pm. Bars are allowed to stay open until 3am, but may close between 1 and 3am.

Car Rentals See "Getting Around Memphis," above.

Climate See "When to Go," in chapter 12.

Dentists Contact **Dental Referral Service** (© 800/917-6453).

Doctors If you should find yourself in need of a doctor, call the referral service at **Methodist/LeBonheur Healthcare** (see "Hospitals," below).

Driving Rules See "Getting Around Memphis," above.

Drugstores See "Pharmacies," below.

Emergencies For police, fire, or medical emergencies, phone © **911.**

Eyeglass Repair Contact **Eyemasters,** with several locations. The most convenient may be inside Oak Court Mall, at 4465 Poplar Ave. (© **901/683-1689**).

Hospitals Major hospitals in the downtown/midtown areas are **Methodist Healthcare** at 1211 Union Ave. (© **901/516-7000**), and The **Regional Medical Center/Elvis Presley Trauma Center,** at 877 Jefferson Ave. (© **901/545-7100**).

Hotlines The **Crisis Counseling and Suicide Prevention** number is © **901/ 274-7477,** and the **Memphis Sexual Assault Resource Center** number is © **901/ 272-2020.**

Information See "Visitor Information," above.

Libraries The modern, user-friendly main branch of the **Memphis/Shelby County Public Library** is at 3030 Poplar Ave. Elsewhere around town, there are more than 20 other branches (© **901/415-2700**).

Liquor Laws The legal drinking age in Tennessee is 21. Bars are allowed to stay open until 3am every day. Beer can be purchased at a convenience, grocery, or package store, but wine and liquor are sold through package stores only.

Lost Property If you left something at the airport, call the **airport police** at © **901/922-8298.** If you left something on a **MATA bus,** call © **901/274-6282.**

Luggage Storage/Lockers There are lockers in the Greyhound station at 203 Union Ave.

Maps See "City Layout," earlier in this chapter.

Newspapers/Magazines The Commercial Appeal is Memphis's daily and Sunday newspaper. The arts-and-entertainment weekly is the *Memphis Flyer,* and the monthly city magazine is *Memphis Magazine.* Out-of-town newspapers are available at Davis-Kidd Booksellers and Borders.

Pharmacies There are about 60 **Walgreens Pharmacies** in the Memphis area (© **800/925-4733** for the Walgreens nearest you). Several have 24-hour prescription service, including the one at 1863 Union Ave. (© **901/272-1141** or 901/ 272-2006).

Police For police emergencies, phone © **911.**

Post Office The main post office is at 555 S. Third St., and there's a branch in East Memphis at 5821 Park Ave. in the White Station area. If you're downtown,

Peabody Place also has a branch. Hours are Monday to Friday 8:30am to 5:30pm and Saturday 10am to 2pm. For more information, dial ℂ **800/275-8777.**

Radio Memphis has more than 30 AM and FM radio stations. Some specialize in a particular style of music, including country, gospel, rhythm and blues, and jazz. WEVL at 89.9 FM plays diversified music such as alternative rock, rockabilly, blues, Cajun music, and jazz. National Public Radio (NPR) news and talk radio can be heard on 88.9 FM, and NPR classical programming can be heard at 91.1 FM.

Restrooms There are restrooms available to the public at hotels, restaurants, and shopping malls.

Safety Memphis is a large city with a serious crime problem, earning the dubious rank of America's violent crime capital in 2007. Take extra precaution with your wallet or purse when you're in a crush of people. At night, whenever possible, try to park your car in a garage, not on the street. When walking around town at night, stick to the busier streets, and hang with a crowd. Generally speaking, don't venture into deserted-looking areas alone at any time of day—either on foot or by car—and do not wander the streets of downtown or midtown alone after dark.

Taxes The state sales tax is 9.25%. An additional room tax of 6.7% on top of the state sales tax brings the total hotel-room tax to a whopping 15.95%.

Taxis See "Getting Around Memphis," above.

Television The six local television channels are 3 (CBS), 5 (NBC), 10 (PBS), 13 (FOX), 24 (ABC), and 30 (independent).

Time Zone Tennessee is in the central time zone—Central Standard Time (CST) or Central Daylight Time, depending on the time of year—making it 2 hours ahead of the West Coast and 1 hour behind the East Coast.

Transit Info Call ℂ **901/274-MATA** for the MATA bus system route and schedule information. Call ℂ **901/577-2640** for information on the Main Street Trolley.

Weather For weather information, phone ℂ **901/526-5261.**

14

Where to Stay in Memphis

Persistent attempts at urban renewal have reaped big rewards for downtown Memphis, which is enjoying a long-awaited transformation into a vibrant metropolitan area. Among downtown hotels, the ultra-chic new Westin on Beale Street is the luxury chain's first in Tennessee.

The city's better hotels used to be clustered in East Memphis, which is more than 20 miles by interstate highway from downtown. While these properties still attract business travelers as well as those with families wanting to avoid the drunken revelry that can sometimes consume the Beale Street area, downtown also has much to offer visitors of all budgets and backgrounds. If you book judiciously, you can avoid the rowdy after-hours crowds. Downtown Memphis also boasts an ever-increasing list of family-oriented attractions, making a stay here the best way to experience what Memphis is really all about.

The Midtown area is another option, and though less convenient to Beale Street, it is near many museums and restaurants. Elvis fans may want to stay near Graceland, but beyond the mansion, the area has little to offer. Besides, you can pick up The King's vibes no matter where you stay in Memphis. Like Waldo, he's everywhere.

Virtually all hotels now offer non-smoking rooms and others equipped for guests with disabilities. Many larger hotels are also adding special rooms for hearing-impaired travelers. When making a reservation, be sure to request the type of room you need.

If you'll be traveling with children, always check into policies regarding children. Some hotels let children under 12 stay free, while others set the cutoff age at 18. Still others charge you for the kids, but let them eat for free in the hotel's restaurant.

Almost all hotels offer special corporate and government rates. However, in this chapter I have listed only the official published rates (also known as rack rates). You may be able to get the corporate rates simply by asking; it's always worth a try. Most of the more expensive hotels have lower weekend rates, while inexpensive hotels tend to raise their rates slightly on the weekend.

If you get quoted a price that seems exorbitantly high, you might have accidentally stumbled upon a special holiday or event rate. Such rates are usually in effect for major Coliseum events and college football games. If this is the case, try scheduling your visit for a different date if possible. Barring this possibility, try calling around to hotels farther out of town, where rates aren't as likely to be affected by special events. In fact, at any time, the farther you get from major business districts, the less you're likely to spend on a room. If you don't mind driving 20 or 30 minutes, you can almost halve the amount you'll need to spend on a room.

For the purposes of this book, I have placed hotels in the following rate

Elvis Slept Here

You might not mistake this former housing project for an upscale hotel, but, then again, this is Memphis—where offbeat surprises seem to lurk around every corner.

Elvis Presley lived here at Lauderdale Courts with his parents, Vernon and Gladys, when he was still a wide-eyed teenager (September 1949 to January 1953). Spared from demolition, in recent years the site has been transformed into Uptown Square, 252 N. Lauderdale, a trendy apartment complex that has preserved its sole historic unit as "The Elvis Suite."

For $250 a night, tourists may rent this first-floor apartment that includes a 1950s-style kitchen and sleeping room for four people. Before you book, be aware that this is a non-smoking property without wheelchair access, and that there's a 2-night minimum and 6-night maximum per stay. For reservations, call (© 901/521-8219; www.lauderdalecourts.com).

---

categories: **very expensive,** more than $175 for a double room; **expensive,** $125 to $175; **moderate,** $75 to $125; and **inexpensive,** less than $75. Please keep in mind, however, that the rates listed below do not include taxes, which in Memphis add up to a whopping 15.95% (9.25% sales tax and 6.7% room tax).

1 Best Hotel Bets

- **Best Historic Hotel:** Even if **The Peabody Memphis,** 149 Union Ave. (© 800/PEABODY or 901/529-4000), weren't the *only* historic hotel in the city, it would likely still be the best. From the classic lobby to the excellent restaurants, and from the renovated rooms to the horse-drawn carriages waiting at the front door, everything here spells tradition and luxury. See p. 164.
- **Best for Families:** With its atrium lobby (complete with stream and resident ducks), indoor pool, and two-room suites with kitchenettes, the **Embassy Suites,** 1022 S. Shady Grove Rd. (© 800/EMBASSY or 901/684-1777), is a good bet if you've got kids with you. See p. 169.
- **Best Location:** In the heart of downtown, the **Holiday Inn Select Downtown,** 160 Union Ave. (© 888/HOLIDAY or 901/525-5491), offers an inviting lobby, a sushi restaurant, and a prime location near AutoZone Park and Beale Street. See p. 166.
- **Best View:** Ask for a west-side room on an upper floor of the **Marriott,** 250 N. Main St. (© 888/557-8740 or 901/527-7300), and you'll get sunsets with the Mississippi River and the Pyramid in the foreground. See p. 164.

2 Downtown

If you want to be where the action is, your first choice ought to be downtown. Besides Beale Street, this area is also where the majority of the city's major sporting events, concerts, and cultural performances take place. If you want to feel as though you've been to Memphis, you need to experience the city's exciting revitalization.

VERY EXPENSIVE

Madison Hotel 𝘈𝘈𝘈 *Moments*   A member of the prestigious Small Luxury Hotels of the World, this sleek new hotel occupies the site of a former bank building. The

Memphis Accommodations: Downtown & Midtown

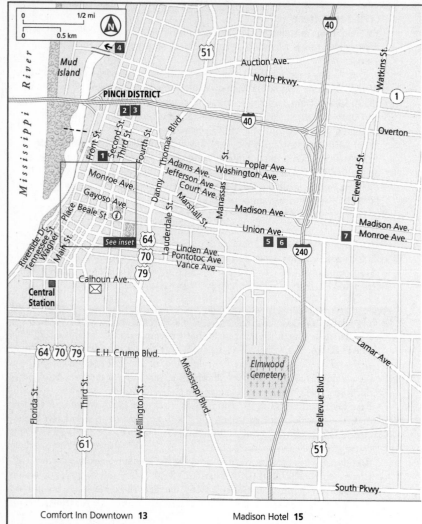

Comfort Inn Downtown **13**
Doubletree Memphis **19**
French Quarter Suites **8**
Hampton Inn and Suites Beale Street **11**
Holiday Inn Select Downtown **17**
Holiday Inn Select Medical
  Center Midtown **7**
Lauderdale Courts **3**

Madison Hotel **15**
Memphis Marriott Downtown **2**
Motel 6 **5**
Red Roof Inn **6**
Residence Inn **16**
River Inn of Harbor Town **4**
Sleep Inn Downtown at Court Square **1**
SpringHill Suites by Marriott **14**

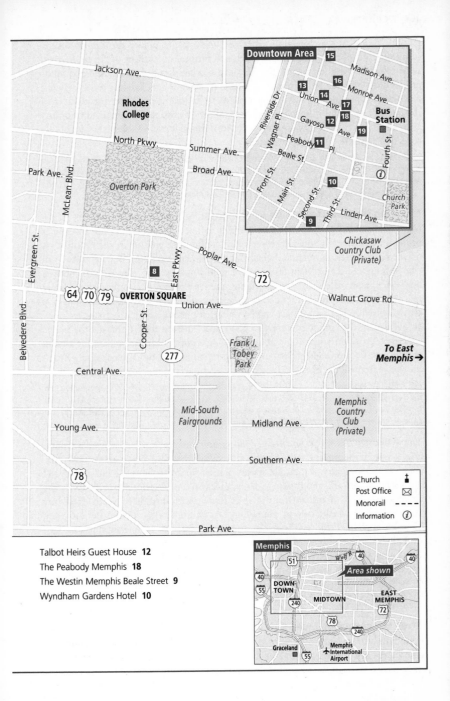

Talbot Heirs Guest House **12**
The Peabody Memphis **18**
The Westin Memphis Beale Street **9**
Wyndham Gardens Hotel **10**

graceful Beaux Arts architecture belies the bold, contemporary furnishings inside. From the chic lobby, with its grand piano and musical instrument motif, to the rich, solid colors in the guest rooms, the Madison is a contrast between classic and modern. Whirlpool baths or jet tubs are available in many rooms. Nightly turndown and twice-daily housekeeping service keep guests feeling pampered. Take the elevator to the outdoor rooftop for breathtaking views of the Mississippi River and surrounding downtown. Every Thursday evening from April through mid-October, the hotel hosts sunset parties here, featuring live jazz.

79 Madison Ave., Memphis, TN 38103. © **866/44-MEMPHIS** or 901/333-1200. Fax 901/333-1297. www.madison hotelmemphis.com. 110 units. $220–$260 double; $330 and up for suite. AE, DC, DISC, MC, V. Valet parking $15. **Amenities:** Restaurant/lounge; indoor pool; fitness center; concierge; 24-hr. room service; lobby library. *In room:* A/C, TV, dataport w/high-speed Internet access, minibar, coffeemaker, hair dryer, safe, CD-player alarm clock.

Memphis Marriott Downtown ⭐

Located at the north end of downtown, on the Main Street trolley line, the 19-floor Marriott connected to the convention center is primarily a convention hotel. Recently renovated from the ground up, the hotel is a bit off the beaten track, surrounded mostly by government buildings. But the trolley will take you up and down Main Street where there's more action. The wireless lobby is built on a grand scale with soaring ceilings, marble floors, and traditional furnishings that are a welcome contrast to the stark modernity of the lobby. My favorite rooms here are the corner rooms, which have angled walls that provide a bit more character. However, the standard king rooms are also good bets. The top three floors are the hotel's concierge levels and offer extra amenities. For views of the Mississippi, ask for a room on the 10th floor or higher. The hotel's main restaurant is a casual spot serving American and international fare. Breakfast and coffee are served in a small cafe.

250 N. Main St., Memphis, TN 38103. © **800/557-8740** or 901/527-7300. Fax 901/526-1561. www.marriott.com. 600 units. $209 and up double; $349–$545 suite. AE, DC, DISC, MC, V. Valet parking $18; self-parking $12. **Amenities:** Restaurant; lounge; large indoor pool; exercise area; hot tub; sauna; concierge; room service; valet; laundry service; Wi-Fi. *In room:* A/C, TV, dataport w/high-speed Internet access, coffeemaker, hair dryer, iron.

The Peabody Memphis ⭐ *Moments*

For years, The Peabody has enjoyed a reputation as one of the finest hotels in the South. While standard rooms aren't overly spacious or extraordinary, the public spaces dazzle. Marble columns, hand-carved and burnished woodwork, and ornate gilded plasterwork on the ceiling give the lobby the air of a palace. Its dominant feature is its Romanesque marble fountain. Here, the famous Peabody ducks, one of Memphis's biggest attractions, while away each day. Chez Philippe (p. 178), serving Asian- and French-inspired cuisine amid palatial surroundings, has long been among the best restaurants in Memphis.

149 Union Ave., Memphis, TN 38103. © **800/PEABODY** or 901/529-4000. Fax 901/529-3677. www.peabodymemphis. com. 464 units. $280–$295 double; $670 and up for suite. AE, DC, DISC, MC, V. Valet parking $21, self-parking $16. **Amenities:** 2 restaurants; 2 lounges; athletic facility with small pool; steam room; sauna; concierge; 24-hr. room service; massage; valet; laundry service; shoe-shine stand. *In room:* A/C, TV, 2 phone lines, dataport w/high-speed Internet access and Wi-Fi, hair dryer, iron.

River Inn of Harbor Town ⭐⭐

Opened in late 2007, this 28-room luxury boutique hotel sits discreetly within the upscale elegance of Harbor Town, a residential community on the ritzy island of Harbor Town. With a rooftop terrace offering unsurpassed views of the Memphis skyline as well as an undeveloped stretch along the lovely Mississippi River, the property is intimate and romantic. With fresh flowers, original artwork, and library-style sitting rooms throughout the condo-like hotel, the

The Peabody Ducks

It isn't often that you find live ducks in the lobby of a luxury hotel. However, ducks are a fixture at the **Peabody Memphis.** Each morning at 11am, the Peabody ducks, led by a duck-master, take the elevator down from their penthouse home, waddle down a red carpet, and hop into the hotel's Romanesque travertine-marble fountain. And each evening at 5pm they waddle back down the red carpet and take the elevator back up to the penthouse. During their entry and exit, the ducks waddle to John Philip Sousa tunes and attract large crowds of curious onlookers that press in on the fountain and red carpet from every side.

The Peabody ducks first took up residence in the lobby in the 1930s when Frank Schutt, the hotel's general manager, and friend Chip Barwick, after one too many swigs of Tennessee sippin' whiskey, put some of his live duck decoys in the hotel's fountain as a joke (such live decoys were legal at the time but have since been outlawed as unsportsmanlike). Guests at the time thought the ducks were a delightfully offbeat touch for such a staid and traditional establishment, and since then ducks have become a beloved fixture at The Peabody.

inn is sumptuously furnished with traditional, Old South-meets-European élan. Nightly turn-down includes the ubiquitous chocolate truffle on your pillow and a glass of port wine. The Inn's location within the safe confines of a planned community, as well as its proximity to manicured, riverside nature trails, makes it one of the few Memphis properties ideal for fitness-minded folks who relish early-morning or sunset walks.

50 Lt. Harbor Town Square, Memphis, TN 38103. ⓒ 877/222-1531 or 901/260-3333. Fax: 901/260-3291. www.riverinn memphis.com. 28 units. $245-$340 double; $375-$595 suites. Rates include gourmet breakfast. AE, DISC, MC, V. Free parking. **Amenities:** Business center; exercise room, 2 restaurants; 24-hour concierge. In-room: A/C, TV, dataport w/high-speed Internet access.

The Westin Memphis Beale Street 🟉🟉   Downtown's newest full-service luxury hotel is a stunner: The city's first Westin property is a sleek, contemporary property perched at the foot of famed Beale Street. Exquisitely appointed two-room corner suites overlook the NBA Grizzlies' FedEx Forum, just steps away. Entirely smoke-free and wired for Internet access throughout, the hotel is a rarity in that it accepts pets (dogs under 40 pounds). All standard rooms have work desks; flatscreen TVs; and radio-alarm clocks with iPod docking stations. Westin's signature "Heavenly Beds," with plush, pillow-top mattresses and 250-thread-count sheets, as well as thick bath robes and oversized showers with dual massaging shower heads nurture relaxation. The spacious lobby lounge and Daily Grill offer American cuisine in a chic yet casual setting, while Starbucks offers refreshment for the caffeine-impaired.

170 Lt. George W. Lee Avenue. ⓒ 800/WESTIN1 or 901/334-5900. westin.com/bealestreet. Fax 901/334-5901. 203 units. From $199 suites. AE, DISC, MC, V. Valet parking $21, self-parking $18. **Amenities:** Restaurant; lounge; concierge; 24-hr. room service; business center; fitness center; valet; laundry service; shoe-shine stand. *In-room:* A/C, cable TV with pay movies and videogames, Wi-Fi, mini-bar, iron, hair dryer, safe.

EXPENSIVE

Doubletree Memphis 🎁 Across the street from AutoZone Park baseball stadium, the all-wireless Doubletree is housed in a former Radisson property that features a T.G.I. Friday's restaurant. This hotel, which stays packed with tour groups and conventions, has a very busy and rather impersonal feel. However, the location is ideal if Beale Street and/or baseball are on your agenda. Regular rooms are large and have modern furnishings and standard-size bathrooms. If you're willing to spend a bit more money, the executive rooms are particularly attractive and a bit more luxurious.

185 Union Ave., Memphis, TN 38103. © **800/222-8733** or 901/528-1800. Fax 901/524-0759. www.doubletree.com. 280 units. $179–$299 double; $219–$309 suite. AE, DC, DISC, MC, V. Valet parking $10. **Amenities:** Restaurant; lounge; outdoor pool; small exercise room; hot tub; sauna. *In room:* A/C, TV w/pay movies, dataport w/high-speed Internet access and Wi-Fi, coffeemaker, hair dryer, iron.

Hampton Inn & Suites–Beale Street 🎁🎁 *(Value)* You can't get closer to spending the night on Beale Street unless you pass out on the pavement after a blues-soaked binge of bar-hopping. This award-winning property is not your typical chain hotel; in fact, it's touted by Hampton as their top hotel in the world. This stylish, curved building sits on a corner lot, jutting out into the heart of the action along Beale and Peabody Place. (Try to get a corner room with an iron balcony and watch the revelry like it's Mardi Gras.) The lobby is Wi-Fi accessible, and there's free Internet access available 24 hours a day in the hotel's business center. Rooms are tastefully decorated and public areas immaculate and well-maintained, and service is among the friendliest in town. Free local calls and a breakfast cafe that serves the best beignets north of Louisiana all combine to make this hotel an outstanding value.

175 Peabody Place, Memphis, TN 38103. © **901/260-4000.** Fax 901/260-4050. www.hampton-inn.com. 144 units. $185 double; $265 suite. Rates include continental breakfast. AE, DC, DISC, MC, V. Self-parking $15. **Amenities:** Restaurant; indoor pool; business center; exercise room. *In room:* A/C, TV w/pay movies, dataport w/high-speed Internet access, coffeemaker, iron.

Holiday Inn Select Downtown 🎁 Across the street from The Peabody, this downtown Holiday Inn is in the heart of the downtown action. The guest rooms, though not large, do have comfortable chairs and big windows. But be advised that some of those windows butt up against other concrete buildings. Rooms facing south afford the best views of the bustle along Union Avenue below. The entire property is wireless. Foodies may appreciate that the hotel is mere footsteps away from the city's best German (Erika's), Thai (Sawaddi), and barbecue (The Rendezvous) restaurants, not to mention across the corner from Huey's, Memphis's beloved burger-and-beer joint. The hotel also houses one of the freshest sushi bars in town (Sekisui; p. 183).

160 Union Ave., Memphis, TN 38103. © **888/HOLIDAY** or 901/525-5491. Fax 901/529-8950. www.hiselect.com. 192 units. $199–$209 double. AE, DC, DISC, MC, V. Parking $15. **Amenities:** Restaurant; lounge; modest outdoor pool on rooftop terrace; $7 per-day for use of off-site fitness center; limited room service. *In room:* A/C, TV w/pay movies, dataport w/high-speed Internet access, coffeemaker, hair dryer, iron.

Residence Inn by Marriott Memphis Downtown 🎁🎁 One of the newest hotels in downtown Memphis is located in one of its historic buildings, a 13-story Art Deco brick edifice built in the 1930s. The fully renovated high-rise hotel features 90 suites, ranging from studio rooms with queen beds and sofa beds, to 2-bedroom units with sitting rooms and full kitchens. This well-run, entirely nonsmoking property is your best bet if you're looking for an extended, home-like stay in the downtown area. Close to attractions, great restaurants, and the Main Street Trolley line, its location is ideal. Rooms have fully stocked kitchens and sitting rooms with pull-out sofas and fireplaces. Other perks include a complimentary social hour each weekday evening, and a complimentary breakfast with freshly made waffles. For a non-refundable cleaning fee ($100), you can even bring your pet.

110 Monroe Ave., Memphis, TN 38103. © 901/578-3700. Fax: 901/578-3999. www.marriott.com. 90 suites. $189-$259 doubles. Rates include cooked-to-order breakfast. AE, DISC, MC, V. Valet parking $15; off-site self-parking $5. **Amenities:** Business center; exercise room; limited room service; valet service; coin-operated laundry; safes at the front desk. *In-room:* A/C, TV, fully furnished kitchens; dual-line speaker telephones, dataport w/high-speed Internet access; hair dryer; iron.

SpringHill Suites by Marriott ★★ A good value for tourists who want a clean, comfortable suite at a reasonable price in a great location, this property is just a block from the Mississippi River. Step out the back door and hop on the trolley to reach Beale Street and other attractions. A cheerful, wireless lobby and adjacent breakfast room provide guests with a welcome greeting. Suites are spacious, tastefully decorated, and include well-lighted work spaces with multi-line speaker phones, kitchenettes, and soft couches. Rooms with south-facing windows have nice views of Court Square, a leafy park that dates back to before the turn of the last century. On the ground floor in front of the hotel, the small outdoor pool is gated and landscaped, though not very private.

21 N. Main St., Memphis, TN 38103. © 901/522-2100. Fax 901/522-2110. www.marriott.com. 102 units. $169 double. AE, DC, DISC, MC, V. Self parking $5. **Amenities:** Outdoor pool; business center; valet; self-service laundry. *In room:* A/C, cable/satellite TV w/pay movies, dataport w/high-speed Internet access and Wi-Fi, fridge, coffeemaker, hair dryer, iron, safe deposit boxes available at front desk.

Talbot Heirs Guesthouse ★ *(Finds* Trendy, contemporary styling is not something one often associates with the tradition-oriented South, which is what makes this upscale downtown B&B so unique. Each of the rooms is boldly decorated, in solid colors ranging from fire-engine red to peaceful periwinkle. Other rooms are done in rich, subtle earth tones and traditional furnishings. Most rooms have interesting modern lamps, and many have kilim rugs. The rooms vary in size from large to huge. Call ahead with your grocery list, and they'll have the fridge stocked for your arrival (for an added fee). Lots of interesting contemporary art further adds to the hip feel of this inn. Talbot Heirs is located right across the street from The Peabody Memphis hotel and only a few doors down from the trendy Automatic Slim's Tonga Club, which inspired this B&B's styling.

99 S. Second St., Memphis, TN 38103. © 800/955-3956 or 901/527-9772. Fax 901/527-3700. www.talbothouse. com. 8 units. $130–$275 double. Rates include continental breakfast. AE, DC, DISC, MC, V. Self-parking $10. **Amenities:** Concierge; massage; laundry service; dry cleaning. *In room:* A/C, cable TV, dataport w/high-speed Internet access, coffeemaker, hair dryer, iron, CD player.

MODERATE

Comfort Inn Downtown Memphis's only rooftop swimming pool is the best boast of this otherwise lackluster hotel that has a prime location on Front Street overlooking the Mississippi River. Despite updated exterior work and new signage, the hotel's rooms are a bit blander than others in its price range. Quite often, you'll see busloads of tour groups staying at the hotel. So if you're after a more intimate setting, you might want to look elsewhere first. Still the hotel is a viable option if other properties are booked.

100 N. Front St., Memphis, TN 38103. © 901/526-0583. Fax 901/525-7512. www.choicehotels.com. 71 units. $110–$140 doubles and suites. AE, DC, DISC, MC, V. Self-parking $5. **Amenities:** Outdoor pool. *In room:* A/C, TV, dataport w/high-speed Internet access, hair dryer.

Sleep Inn–Downtown at Court Square ☆ *Value*   You can't beat the location of this upscale motel, which fills up quickly during weekends when there is a lot happening downtown. Wedged between nostalgic Court Square and the banks of the Mississippi River, it's also on the Main Street trolley line. At only six stories, this motel is dwarfed by surrounding buildings. The modern design and economical rates, along with wireless access, ensure its appeal. Most rooms are large and comfortable, and business-class rooms come with fax machines, work desks, VCRs, and dual phone lines. The motel shares a parking lot with the adjacent SpringHill Suites.

40 N. Front St., Memphis, TN 38103. ℂ 800/424-6423 or 901/522-9700. Fax 901/522-9710. www.choicehotels.com. 124 units. $88–$129 double. Rates include continental breakfast. AE, DC, DISC, MC, V. Self-parking $5. **Amenities:** Small exercise room. *In room:* A/C, TV, Wi-Fi, coffeemaker, hair dryer, iron.

Wyndham Gardens Hotel ☆   The Wyndham offers an excellent location if your trip will take you to the nearby convention center or St. Jude Children's Research Hospital. However, if you want to be closer to the action of Beale Street, this property would not be the most convenient option. Renovated in the spring of 2008, this property offers a lush garden setting and library-like lobby with plantation shutters, marble floors, and Wi-Fi access. Rooms are modem-ready and equipped with easy chairs, TVs, and other modern amenities.

300 N. Second St., Memphis, TN 38103. ℂ **901/525-1800.** Fax 901/524-1859. www.wyndham.com. 230 units. $149 single or double. AE, DC, DISC, MC, V. Self-parking $10. **Amenities:** Restaurant; outdoor pool; exercise room; limited room service; dry cleaning. *In room:* A/C, TV w/pay movies, fax, dataport w/high-speed Internet access, coffeemaker, hair dryer, iron.

3 Midtown

Midtown is a reasonable alternative if you're looking for a quieter location that also offers cultural options but without the parking and traffic hassles that can sometimes snarl downtown. For locations of hotels in this section, see the "Memphis Accommodations: Downtown & Midtown" map on p. 162.

MODERATE

French Quarter Suites Hotel   Its perch in the heart of Overton Square used to be a big plus, but just as this fledgling midtown entertainment district has been upstaged by a newly revitalized downtown, so have the few hotels here. Though this building looks charming enough with its French Quarter–style courtyards and balconies, the guest rooms and public areas suggest that the hotel has not been as well maintained as others in town. On the plus side, all bathtubs have Jacuzzis.

2144 Madison Ave., Memphis, TN 38104. ℂ **800/843-0353** or 901/728-4000. Fax 901/278-1262. www.memphis frenchquarter.com. 103 units. $139–$159 double. AE, DC, DISC, MC, V. Free parking. **Amenities:** Outdoor pool; exercise room; limited room service; laundry service; complimentary airport shuttle. *In room:* A/C, TV w/pay movies, dataport/w high speed Internet access and Wi-Fi, wet bar, fridge, coffeemaker, hair dryer, iron.

INEXPENSIVE

In addition to the hotel listed below, national and regional chain motels in the area include the following (see also appendix C, "Useful Toll-Free Numbers & Websites," for toll-free telephone numbers): **Holiday Inn Select Medical Center/Midtown,** 1180 Union Ave. (ℂ **901/276-1175**), charging $89 double; **Red Roof Inn,** 42 S. Camilla St. (ℂ **901/526-1050**), charging $79 double; and **Motel 6,** 210 S. Pauline St. (ℂ **901/528-0650**), charging $54 double. Second floor and lobby have Wi-Fi.

4 East Memphis

If your visit to Memphis brings you to any of the suburban business parks in the perimeter of the city, East Memphis is a smart choice. It's centrally located between downtown hot spots and outlying suburbs, where companies such as Federal Express and International Paper have their corporate headquarters.

EXPENSIVE

Doubletree Hotel Memphis ★★   This East Memphis Hilton-owned hotel is a bit more convenient to midtown museums than other hotels in this area. However, the hotel's real appeal is that it is within walking distance of a couple of excellent restaurants and has a large indoor/outdoor pool. It's also only a very short drive to Corky's, one of the best barbecue joints in town. Built around a glass-walled atrium and lobby with wireless Internet, the eight-floor hotel has glass elevators so you can enjoy the views. Most rooms here are designed with the business traveler in mind and have two phones, radio/television speakers in the bathrooms, and large desks. Large, angled windows make the rooms seem a bit larger than standard hotel rooms.

5069 Sanderlin Ave., Memphis, TN 38117. ℂ 800/445-8667 or 901/767-6666. Fax 901/683-8563. www.doubletree. com. 276 units. $179–$279 double; $219–$259 suite. AE, DC, DISC, MC, V. Free parking. **Amenities:** Restaurant; lounge; indoor/outdoor pool; exercise room; room service; valet; laundry service. *In room:* A/C, TV w/pay movies, dataport w/high-speed Internet access and Wi-Fi, fridge, coffeemaker, hair dryer, iron.

Embassy Suites ★★ *Kids*   With its many tropical plants and an artificial stream, the lobby of this modern atrium hotel looks more like a botanical conservatory than a hotel lobby. A waterfall, little beach, and giant goldfish add to the effect, and, not to be upstaged by The Peabody, this hotel even has a few resident ducks floating in its stream. Wireless Internet access is available in public areas. All the guest rooms here are spacious two-room suites that have kitchenettes, dining tables, two televisions, two phones, and sofa beds. The layouts of the rooms are good for both families and business travelers. The complete, cooked-to-order breakfast is served in the atrium, where, in the evening, there's also a complimentary manager's reception with free drinks. The moderately priced Frank Grisanti's Italian Restaurant just off the atrium serves lunch and dinner and is one of the best Italian restaurants in the city (p. 188).

1022 S. Shady Grove Rd., Memphis, TN 38120. ℂ 800/EMBASSY or 901/684-1777. Fax 901/685-8185. www. embassysuites.com. 220 units. $139–$219 double. Rates include full breakfast. AE, DC, DISC, MC, V. Free parking. **Amenities:** Restaurant; lounge; indoor pool; exercise room; hot tub; sauna; business center; room service; coin-op laundry; valet; laundry service; free airport transportation. *In room:* A/C, TV w/pay movies and video games, dataport w/high-speed Internet access and Wi-Fi, fridge, coffeemaker, hair dryer, iron.

Hilton Memphis ★★   This gleaming, round high-rise dominates the skyline in an upscale East Memphis area that's also convenient to Germantown and Collierville as

---

⌒ *Fun Fact* **The *Other* Ducklings**

The Peabody's ducks may be the best-known fowl around town. But few visitors realize that another upscale property, the **Embassy Suites** in East Memphis, also boasts such birds frolicking amidst its atrium's fountains and foliage. They don't get the red-carpet treatment, however. "Our ducks are from the other side of the pond," quips an Embassy Suites employee.

(Kids) Family-Friendly Hotels

Embassy Suites (p. 169)   The indoor pool and gardenlike atrium lobby provide a place for the kids to play even on rainy or cold days, and the two-room suites give parents a private room of their own. Video games are another plus for the kids.

Homewood Suites (below)   With a pool and basketball court and grounds that resemble an upscale apartment complex, this East Memphis hotel is a good bet for families. Plus, the evening social hour includes enough food to serve as dinner (and thus save you quite a bit on your meal budget).

well as to downtown and midtown. After being acquired by the Hilton hotel group in 2003, this former Adams Mark completed a $12-million renovation in 2004. The open, airy lobby has an artsy, modern ambience. In addition to featuring all the latest amenities, including digital climate-control, rooms were expanded and redecorated in cream and pastel colors. The entire property offers free Wi-Fi. However, the property's popularity as a convention hotel can sometimes make the Hilton feel crowded.

939 Ridge Lake Blvd., Memphis, TN 38120. ☎ 800/774-1500 or 901/684-6664. Fax 901/762-7496. www.hilton.com. 412 units, including seven suites. $149–$219 double; $279–$679 suite. AE, DC, DISC, MC, V. Free parking. Located off Ridgeway Center Pkwy. at I-240 and Poplar Ave., exit 15 east. **Amenities:** Restaurant; lounge; outdoor pool; fitness center; hot tub; business center; room service; valet; laundry service; complimentary airport shuttle. *In room:* A/C, TV w/pay movies, Wi-Fi, coffeemaker, hair dryer, iron.

Homewood Suites & (Kids)   Homewood Suites offers spacious accommodations. The suites, which are arranged around a landscaped central courtyard with a swimming pool and basketball court, resemble an apartment complex rather than a hotel. The wireless lobby features pine furnishings and artwork. Early American styling sets the tone in the suites, many of which have wrought-iron beds. There are two televisions in every suite, as well as full kitchens and big bathrooms with plenty of counter space. Though there's no restaurant on the premises, you can pick up microwave meals in the hotel's convenience shop. There is also a complimentary social hour on weeknights that includes enough food to pass for dinner.

5811 Poplar Ave. (just off I-240), Memphis, TN 38119. ☎ 800/CALL-HOME or 901/763-0500. Fax 901/763-0132. www.homewood-suites.com. 140 units. $169–$209 double. Rates include cooked breakfast. AE, DC, DISC, MC, V. Free parking. **Amenities:** Outdoor pool; exercise room; passes to Gold's Gym; hot tub; valet; laundry service; complimentary shuttle to airport; basketball court; local shopping and restaurants. *In room:* A/C, TV, dataport w/high-speed Internet access, kitchen, coffeemaker, hair dryer, iron.

Memphis Marriott East   You'll find this hotel about midway between the airport and the Poplar Avenue exit. Catering primarily to corporate travelers, this property has a large courtyard garden near the lobby, with travertine and red marble floors. Though most of the rooms are a bit smaller than you might hope, the king rooms are well laid out and have large work desks with phones. Try for one of the upper floors to get a good view of the surrounding countryside. In the back of the lobby, there's an elegant piano bar. The dark-wood bar gives this lounge a classic air. Wi-Fi is available in the lobby and business center.

East Memphis Accommodations

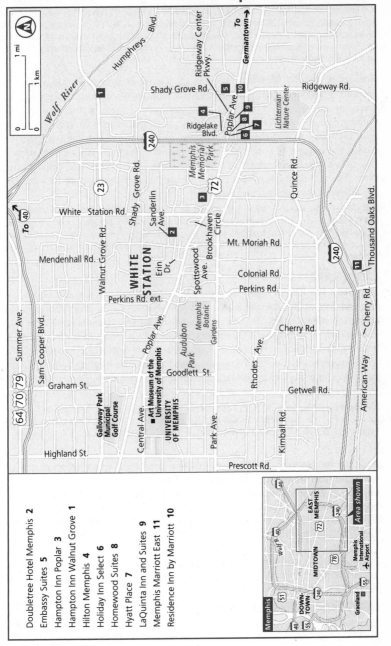

Doubletree Hotel Memphis **2**

Embassy Suites **5**

Hampton Inn Poplar **3**

Hampton Inn Walnut Grove **1**

Hilton Memphis **4**

Holiday Inn Select **6**

Homewood Suites **8**

Hyatt Place **7**

LaQuinta Inn and Suites **9**

Memphis Marriott East **11**

Residence Inn by Marriott **10**

2625 Thousand Oaks Blvd., Memphis, TN 38118. ⓒ **800/627-3587** or 901/362-6200. Fax 901/360-8836. www.marriott hotels.com/memtn. 320 units. $209 double; $300–$450 hospitality suite. AE, DC, DISC, MC, V. Free parking. **Amenities:** Restaurant; lounge; indoor and outdoor pool; exercise room; hot tub; sauna; concierge; business center; room service; valet; laundry service; complimentary airport shuttle. *In room:* A/C, TV w/pay movies, fax, dataport w/high-speed Internet access, coffeemaker, hair dryer, iron.

Residence Inn by Marriott ⚶

Though it's not as attractively designed as the nearby Homewood Suites, this extended-stay property offers many of the same conveniences and amenities, including a wireless lobby. It benefits from being within walking distance of several excellent restaurants. Some suites have rooms that open onto the lobby, while others have windows to the outside and tiny triangular balconies. You can choose a one-bedroom or two-bedroom suite, but whichever size suite you choose, you'll have plenty of space, including a full kitchen and perhaps a fireplace. The two-bedroom suites have loft sleeping areas. Be sure to ask for a room on the side away from the railroad tracks.

6141 Old Poplar Pike, Memphis, TN 38119. ⓒ **800/331-3131** or 901/685-9595. Fax 901/685-1636. www.marriott. com. 105 suites. $149–$209 suite. Rates include continental breakfast as well as light dinner 5:30–7pm Mon–Thurs. AE, DC, DISC, MC, V. Free parking. **Amenities:** Outdoor pool; valet; laundry service; complimentary social hour; sports court; grocery-shopping service. *In room:* A/C, TV w/pay movies, dataport w/high-speed Internet access, coffeemaker, hair dryer, iron.

MODERATE

Hampton Inn Poplar

This Hampton Inn, conveniently located inside the I-240 ring and close to several major museums (not to mention Corky's barbecue restaurant, across the street), offers the sort of dependable accommodations that have made Hampton Inns so popular. Rooms with king-size beds, easy chairs, and a desk are geared toward business travelers, while those with sofa beds make a good choice for leisure travelers and families. The outdoor pool, surrounded by attractively landscaped gardens, is far enough away from the street that it isn't too noisy. There's plenty of free parking, too.

5320 Poplar Ave., Memphis, TN 38119. ⓒ **800/HAMPTON** or 901/683-8500. Fax 901/763-4970. www.hamptoninn. com. 126 units. $119–$149 double. Rates include cooked breakfast. AE, DC, DISC, MC, V. Free parking. **Amenities:** Outdoor pool. *In room:* A/C, TV w/pay movies, dataport w/high-speed Internet access and Wi-Fi, coffeemaker, hair dryer, iron.

Holiday Inn Select

This modern 10-story hotel offers quick access to east-side restaurants and to the interstate, so it is easy to get downtown to Beale Street or to Graceland. Though the hotel caters primarily to corporate travelers, a sunny indoor pool area makes it appealing to vacationers as well. The entire hotel offers Wi-Fi access. Overall, the rooms are fresh and views from upper floors are pleasant. Corner king rooms are particularly spacious. Suites include a microwave and fridge.

5795 Poplar Ave., Memphis, TN 38119. ⓒ **800/HOLIDAY** or 901/682-7881. Fax 901/685-2407. www.hiselect.com/ mem-epoplar. 243 units. $109–$159 double; $250–$350 suite. AE, DC, DISC, MC, V. Free parking. **Amenities:** Indoor pool; exercise room; whirlpool; room service; valet; laundry service; complimentary airport shuttle. *In room:* A/C, cable TV, Wi-Fi, coffeemaker, hair dryer, iron.

INEXPENSIVE TO MODERATE

National and regional motel chains in the area include the following (see also Appendix C for toll-free telephone numbers): **Hyatt Place,** 1220 Primacy Pkwy. (ⓒ **901/ 680-9700**), charging $109 to $149 double; and **La Quinta Inn & Suites,** 1236 Primacy Pkwy. (ⓒ **901/374-0330**), charging $69–$99 double.

5 The Airport & Graceland Areas

Obviously, if you need to be near the airport, any of these properties will suit your needs. But truthfully, the airport area encompasses neighborhoods most locals would not feel safe driving in late at night. To get a sense of what Memphis is all about, you really should try to stay in or near downtown. Besides, with the plethora of tour buses and shuttle services available, access to Graceland is as easy from downtown as it is from the airport area.

MODERATE

Courtyard Memphis Airport ★★   This clean, well-maintained property, located a few miles from the main airport terminal, has earned a reputation as the airport area's top choice among corporate road warriors. Resembling a modern, well-landscaped office park, the hotel offers rooms (and 14 suites) well equipped for business travelers. There are large work desks, daily newspaper delivery, and dinner delivery service from local restaurants. The property underwent a complete renovation in 2006.

1780 Nonconnah Blvd., Memphis, TN 38132. © 901/396-3600. Fax 901/332-0706. www.marriott.com. 145 units. $109–$159 double. $174 suite. AE, DC, DISC, MC, V. Free parking. **Amenities:** Outdoor pool; exercise room; whirlpool. *In room:* A/C, TV w/pay movies, dataports w/high-speed Internet access, coffeemaker, iron, hair dryer, safe-deposit box available at front desk.

Elvis Presley's Heartbreak Hotel–Graceland ★★ *(Moments)*   If your visit to Memphis is a pilgrimage to Graceland, there should be no question as to where to stay. This Graceland-operated hotel has a gate right into the Graceland parking lot, with Elvis's home right across Elvis Presley Boulevard. In the lobby, you'll find two big portraits of The King and decor that would fit right in at the mansion. In the back courtyard, there's a smallish, heart-shaped outdoor pool. Indoors, four themed suites include the irresistibly named "*Burning Love* Suite." (Feel your temperature rising?) If you don't want to shell out big bucks for the entire suite, ask to split it and just rent a portion (or one room) of the suite. Many guests do this, I'm told. If this place has one drawback, it's that there's no in-room Internet access, although it's available in the lobby.

3677 Elvis Presley Blvd., Memphis, TN 38116. © **877/777-0606** or 901/332-1000. Fax 901/332-1636. www. elvis.com. 128 units. $110–$135 regular suite; $520 themed suite. AE, DC, DISC, MC, V. Free parking. **Amenities:** Heart-shaped outdoor pool. *In room:* A/C, TV w/24-hr. Elvis movies, coffeemaker, hair dryer, iron.

Holiday Inn Select Memphis Airport ★   Totally wired for Internet access, this is one of the most attractive airport-area hotels. Step through the doors of this large property and you enter a vast, cavernous lobby with a vaguely Mediterranean feel. Inside, there's an espresso bar and lounge. Suites include a fridge and microwave.

2240 Democrat Rd., Memphis, TN 38132. © **901/332-1130.** Fax 901/398-5206. www.hiselect.com. 374 units. $119 double; $369 suite. AE, DC, DISC, MC, V. Free parking. **Amenities:** Restaurant; outdoor pool; 2 tennis courts; exercise room; room service; complimentary airport shuttle. *In room:* A/C, TV w/pay movies, Wi-Fi, coffeemaker, hair dryer, iron.

Radisson Inn Memphis Airport ★ *(Finds)*   If you're in town on a quick business meeting or plan to arrive late at night, this hotel right on the grounds of the airport fits the bill. All the rooms are well soundproofed so you don't have to worry about losing sleep because of overhead jets. The rooms themselves are rather dark and are not very memorable, but many are set up for business travelers with a desk and comfortable chair. The hotel's restaurant is casual with a very traditional atmosphere and menu. The outdoor pool is set in a pleasant (though sometimes noisy) sunken garden area between two wings of the hotel. The property is Wi-Fi accessible throughout.

2411 Winchester Rd., Memphis, TN 38116. © **800/333-3333** or 901/332-2370. Fax 901/398-4085. www.radisson. com. 211 units. $119 double; $159 suite. AE, DC, DISC, MC, V. Free parking. **Amenities:** Restaurant; lounge; outdoor pool; 2 tennis courts; exercise room; room service; 24-hr. complimentary airport shuttle. *In room:* A/C, TV, dataport w/high-speed Internet access and Wi-Fi, coffeemaker, hair dryer, iron.

INEXPENSIVE

Aside from the hotels below, visitors may search for chain motels (see Appendix C for toll-free telephone numbers).

Clarion Hotel   Situated close to both the airport and Graceland, this may appeal to Elvis fans on a budget. Despite the Wi-Fi-accessible lobby, the entire hotel is rather dim and seems to have a faded-glory feel to it. The presence of both a bar and a night-club is an indication that people who stay here like to party. The guest rooms are ade-quate, though none too memorable. Some of the rooms have microwaves.

1471 E. Brooks Rd., Memphis, TN 38116. © **800/424-6423** or 901/332-3500. Fax 901/346-0017. www.choice hotel.com. 249 units. $149 double. Rates include continental breakfast. AE, DC, DISC, MC, V. Free parking. **Amenities:** Outdoor pool; room service; complimentary airport shuttle. *In room:* A/C, cable TV, dataport, fridge, coffeemaker, hair dryer, iron.

Days Inn at Graceland   With Graceland right across the street, it's no surprise that Elvis is king at this budget motel. Just look for the Elvis mural on the side of the build-ing and the neon guitar sign out front, and you'll have found this unusual Days Inn. In the lobby, and on the room TVs, are round-the-clock Elvis videos.

3839 Elvis Presley Blvd., Memphis, TN 38116. © **800/329-7466** or 901/346-5500. Fax 901/345-7452. www. daysinn.com. 61 units. $79–$89 double. Rates include continental breakfast. AE, DC, DISC, MC, V. Free parking. **Amenities:** Guitar-shaped outdoor pool. *In room:* A/C, TV, dataport w/high-speed Internet access.

Where to Dine in Memphis

For a city most often associated with pork barbecue and Elvis's famous fried peanut-butter-and-banana sandwiches, Memphis has a surprisingly diverse restaurant scene. From escargots to etouffée and fajitas to focaccia, there's all manner of ethnic and gourmet fare around town. You'll also find plenty of barbecued ribs, fried pickles, purple-hull peas, butter beans, meat loaf, and mashed potatoes. And you might be surprised by the wealth of trendy restaurants you'd expect to encounter in any major metropolitan area. Drawing on influences from around the country and around the world, these New American and New Southern restaurants serve dishes so complex and creative that they often take a paragraph to describe on a menu.

Gourmet and ethnic foods aside, what Memphis can claim as its very own is slow-smoked, hand-pulled pork shoulder barbecue, to which you can add the spicy sauces of your choosing—chili vinegar, hot sauce, whatever. If this doesn't appeal to you, then maybe Memphis's famous ribs will. These are cooked much the same way as the pork shoulder and come dry or

wet—that is, with the sauce added by you (dry) or cooked in (wet). See the "Barbecue" section at the end of this chapter.

Among the better chain restaurants to be found in Memphis are **Bonefish Grill,** 1250 N. Germantown Pkwy. (© 901/753-2220; www.bonefishgrill. com); **Carrabba's,** 5110 Poplar Ave. (© 901/685-9900; www.carrabbas.com); **P.F. Chang's China Bistro,** 1181 Ridgeway Rd. (© 901/818-3889; www. pfchangs.com); **Ruth's Chris Steakhouse,** 6120 Poplar at Shady Grove (© 901/761-0055; www.ruthschris.com); and **Texas de Brazil Churrascaria,** 150 Peabody Place (© 901/526-7600; www. texasdebrazil.com), featuring tableside, hand-carved meats.

For these listings, I have classified restaurants in the following categories (estimates do not include beer, wine, or tip): **very expensive** for meals costing more than $50; **expensive** if a complete dinner would cost $30 or more; **moderate,** where you can expect to pay between $15 and $30 for a complete dinner; and **inexpensive,** where a complete dinner can be had for less than $15.

1 Best Dining Bets

- **Best Spot for a Romantic Dinner:** If you feel like playing prince or princess for a night, there's no more romantic place to do so than amid the palatial surroundings of **Chez Philippe,** 149 Union Ave. (© 901/529-4188), at the opulent Peabody hotel. See p. 178.
- **Best Spot for a Celebration:** Amusing decor and food as creative as the atmosphere make **Automatic Slim's Tonga Club,** 83 S. Second St. (© 901/525-7948), a good spot for a casual celebration. See p. 182.

- **Best for Kids:** Like Nashville, downtown Memphis has a cavernous **Spaghetti Warehouse** restaurant that's been a longtime favorite for young children. They can dine in an old trolley car while deciding whether to order the burger or a plate of pasta and meatballs. Spaghetti Warehouse, 40 W. Huling. ⓒ **901/521-0907.** www.meatballs.com. See p. 185.

- **Best Nostalgic Diner:** Grab a booth at **The Arcade,** a last-of-its-kind downtown institution, if you want to feel as if you've gone back in time. Home-style breakfasts, burgers, and pizzas are best bets at this old-school eatery that's anchored this corner since 1919. The Arcade, 540 S. Main St. ⓒ **901/526-5757.** www.arcade restaurant.com. See p. 184.

- **Best Soul Food:** What Swett's Restaurant is to Nashville, the **Fourway** is to Memphis—a historic, minority-owned restaurant that makes the best sweet-potato pie, fried catfish, and black-eyed peas you're ever likely to encounter. Always busy, it's a spacious, family-friendly restaurant offering full service (as opposed to Swetts' cafeteria format). Fourway Restaurant, 998 Mississippi Blvd. ⓒ **901/507-1519.** See p. 192.

2 Restaurants by Cuisine

AMERICAN
The Arcade Restaurant 𝒢
  (Downtown, $, p. 184)
Café 1912 (Midtown, $$, p. 186)
D'Bo's Buffalo Wings 'N' Things 𝒢
  (South Memphis, $, p. 192)
Elfo's Restaurant 𝒢 (Midtown, $,
  p. 187)
EP Delta Kitchen and Bar (Down-
  town, $$, p. 183)
Grill 83 𝒢𝒢 (Downtown, $$$,
  p. 178)
Huey's 𝒢 (Downtown, $, p. 184)
Spaghetti Warehouse (Downtown, $,
  p. 185)
Stella 𝒢𝒢 (Downtown, $$$, p. 182)

BARBECUE
A&R Barbecue (South Memphis, $,
  p. 193)
Beale St. Bar-B-Que (Downtown, $,
  p. 193)
Blues City Café (Downtown, $$,
  p. 193)
Corky's 𝒢 (East Memphis, $, p. 190)
Cozy Corner (Midtown, $, p. 193)
Interstate Bar-B-Que 𝒢 (South of
  Downtown, $, p. 192)

Neely's B-B-Q (Downtown, East
  Memphis, $, p. 193)
Payne's (South of Downtown, $,
  p. 193)
Rendezvous 𝒢𝒢 (Downtown, $,
  p. 184)

CAJUN
Café 61 𝒢 (Downtown, $$, p. 182)
Owen Brennan's Restaurant 𝒢 (East
  Memphis, $$, p. 191)
Pearl's Oyster House (Downtown, $,
  p. 184)

CALIFORNIAN
Napa Café (East Memphis, $$$,
  p. 188)

CHINESE
Saigon Le 𝒢 (Midtown, $, p. 187)

CONTINENTAL
Encore 𝒢𝒢 (Downtown, $$$, p. 178)
Grill 83 𝒢𝒢 (Downtown, $$$,
  p. 178)
The Inn at Hunt Phelan 𝒢
  (Downtown, $$$, p. 178)
Paulette's 𝒢 (Midtown, $$, p. 186)

FRENCH

Chez Philippe ★★ (Downtown, $$$$, p. 178)

La Baguette ★ (East Memphis, $$, p. 194)

GERMAN

Erika's ★★ (Downtown, $, p. 184)

ITALIAN

Café Toscana (East Memphis, $$, p. 190)

Elfo's Restaurant ★ (Midtown, $, p. 187)

Frank Grisanti's Italian Restaurant ★ (East Memphis, $$$, p. 188)

Fratelli's (East Memphis, $, p. 193)

Spaghetti Warehouse (Downtown, $, p. 185)

Spindini ★★ (Downtown, $$$, p. 179)

JAPANESE

Do Sushi Bar and Lounge (Midtown, $, p. 187)

Sekisui of Japan ★★ (East Memphis, Midtown, Downtown, $$, p. 183)

MEDITERRANEAN

Casablanca Cafe ★★ (Midtown, $$, p. 186)

MEXICAN/SOUTHWESTERN

Salsa Cocina Mexicana ★★ (East Memphis, $, p. 191)

NEW AMERICAN

Automatic Slim's Tonga Club ★★ (Downtown, $$, p. 182)

Beauty Shop ★★★ (Midtown, $$$, p. 185)

Café Society ★ (Midtown, $$, p. 186)

Circa ★★ (Downtown, $$, p. 182)

Erling Jensen–The Restaurant ★★★ (East Memphis, $$$, p. 187)

Jarrett's ★★★ (East Memphis, $$, p. 190)

Napa Café (East Memphis, $$$, p. 188)

NEW SOUTHERN

Brushmark (Midtown, $$, p. 194)

Chez Philippe ★★ (Downtown, $$$, p. 178)

The Grove Grill ★ (East Memphis, $$, p. 190)

McEwen's on Monroe ★★ (Downtown, $$$, p. 179)

PACIFIC RIM

Tsunami ★★ (Midtown, $$$, p. 185)

SEAFOOD

Do Sushi Bar and Lounge (Midtown, $, p. 187)

Jarrett's ★★★ (East Memphis, $$, p. 190)

Tsunami ★★ (Midtown, $$$, p. 185)

SOUL FOOD

Ellen's Soul Food ★ (Midtown, $, p. 192)

SOUTHERN

Alcenia's ★ (Downtown, $, p. 183)

Blue Plate Café (East Memphis, $, p. 191)

Fourway Restaurant ★★★ (South Memphis, $, p. 192)

Gus's World Famous Fried Chicken ★ (Downtown, $, p. 184)

Patrick's ★ (East Memphis, $, p. 191)

SOUTHWESTERN

Salsa Cocina Mexicana ★★ (East Memphis, $, p. 191)

STEAK

Folk's Folly Prime Steak House ★★ (East Memphis, $$$, p. 188)

VIETNAMESE

Pho Saigon ★ (Midtown, $, p. 187)

Saigon Le ★ (Midtown, $, p. 187)

THAI

Sawaddii (Downtown, $$, p. 183)

3 Downtown

VERY EXPENSIVE

Chez Philippe 𝄞 ASIAN/FRENCH   Still the most opulent dining room in Memphis (though the Peabody's palatial flagship restaurant has lost a bit of its cache in recent years), Chez Philippe enthralls affluent gourmands who relish its Old South splendor. On the menu, Cuban-born, French-trained chef Reinaldo Alfonso exploits Asian influences in dishes such as seaweed salad with soba noodles, cucumbers, and daikon radishes in a sugar-cane-sesame vinaigrette; and wild salmon slathered in citrus-soy barbecue sauce with a crispy, sushi-rice cake and carrot-ginger puree. Other options include the unusual veal osso bucco dumplings as well as the comforting warm apple fritters with walnut-maple ice cream. Prices are the steepest in town, but expect to be pampered.

The Peabody Memphis hotel, 149 Union Ave. ℂ 901/529-4188. www.peabodymemphis.com. Reservations recommended. Main courses $65–$70. AE, DC, DISC, MC, V. Tues–Sat 6–10pm.

EXPENSIVE

Encore 𝄞𝄞 CONTINENTAL   Jose Gutierrez is one of the best-known chefs in Memphis. After manning the stoves at The Peabody's posh Chez Philippe for more than two decades, he opened Encore in late 2005. By design a casually upscale, affordably priced fine-dining restaurant, Encore succeeds on all counts. A soothing, Zen-like ambience pervades the sophisticated dining room, with dark woods and dramatic, back-lit curtained walls. Gutierrez, an award-winning chef born in Provence, France, shows relaxed versatility with the menu, offering such eclectic entrees as bouillabaisse; New York strip with *pommes frites*; and a roasted leg of lamb with "poor man's cheesy potatoes." A burger here will set you back $10, a bargain for ground-to-order sirloin topped with bacon bits on a scratch-made roll, with choice options as roasted red-pepper aioli, and blue, Gruyere, or cheddar cheese. Soups, salads, and starters are equally enticing: proscuitto-wrapped asparagus bundles are served with coriander vinaigrette, while chorizo sausage spices up the hearty French lentil soup. Crème brulee, sorbets, and other desserts are first-rate. Encore also has a full bar and well-chosen wine list.

150 Peabody Place, Suite 111. ℂ 901/528-1415. www.encore-memphis.com. Main courses $18–$25. AE, MC, V. Daily 5-10pm.

Grill 83 𝄞 AMERICAN/CONTINENTAL   Tucked inside the intimate boutique hotel The Madison is this chic, dimly lit, fine-dining restaurant and lounge. It is a dark, narrow room with vintage black-and-white photographs on the walls and well-dressed diners enjoying brandies and ports after multi-course gourmet meals. Open for breakfast and lunch, Grill 83 shines at dinner. Exquisitely prepared steaks (the signature is a 16-oz. Kansas City bone-in filet) and succulent seared sea bass are served with artful garnishes and such sides as grilled asparagus with lemon butter. Service is polished and professional.

The Madison Hotel, 83 Madison Ave. ℂ 901/333-1224. www.grill83.com. Reservations recommended. Main courses $23–$42. AE, DC, DISC, MC, V. Sun–Thurs 6:30am–10pm; Fri–Sat 6:30am–11pm.

The Inn at Hunt Phelan 𝄞 CREOLE/CONTINENTAL   What's so much fun about dining at the Inn at Hunt Phelan is how cozy and welcome you can feel in such a grand, storied place. The restaurant—made up of a collection of small dining rooms on the first floor of a restored 1828 antebellum mansion—is a welcome retreat just outside the hustle of downtown Memphis. Inside the mansion, now a lovely B&B, the restaurant caters to both inn guests and outside visitors. On a recent visit here, the salad of artichokes, wild boar pancetta, and olive vinaigrette was a delightful beginning. The morel mushrooms with a grit cake, fava beans, and okra was rich and a nice tip of the hat to Southern food tradition, but the lamb with cous cous entree proved that the chef is definitely not living in the past. An impressive dessert and wine list round out the menu—your waiter will be happy to make recommendations, should you not know where to begin. If you'd rather sit outside than inside, consider dining at the more laid-back Veranda Grill, which offers the entire menu from the restaurant in addition to more low-tech food, ranging from a BLT to a burger to a cheese plate. The Veranda Grill is located behind the inn in the back garden, an ideal spot on a comfortable Tennessee evening. If you're eating indoors, at least have a drink out back before moving inside. The friendly bartender will gladly prepare a unique, not to be forgotten (unless you have one too many, that is) cocktail for you.

The Inn at Hunt Phelan. 533 Beale St. © 901/525-8225. www.huntphelan.com. Reservations recommended. Main courses $27–$34 dinner. Sunday brunch $11–$24. AE, DC, MC, V. Tues–Sat 5:30pm–"until"; Sun brunch 11am–3pm. Veranda Grill Mon–Fri 5:30pm–1am; Fri–Sat 5:30pm–2am.

McEwen's on Monroe ★★ CONTEMPORARY SOUTHERN   The exposed brick walls, white table cloths, and well-spaced tables are your first clue that McEwen's is a classy, comfortable kind of place. It offers a relaxed yet sophisticated atmosphere with food to match. Located downtown on Monroe Avenue, McEwen's is a lunchtime favorite with the business crowd, but at night it caters to a wide swath of folks looking for delicious food in a genial setting. The crowd here can choose from a number of "Southern fusion" appetizers including sweet potato empanadas, barbeque duck confit enchiladas, and buttermilk fried oysters, and entrees such as pan-seared scallops with stone-ground cheddar grits or peppered seared beef tenderloin served with a lobster potato cake. Though this is no place to stick to your diet, they do have a few options on the lighter side. At lunchtime go for the soup and salad combo. After dark, try the watercress salad, with mandarin oranges, roasted red and yellow bell peppers, with a cojita cheese blood orange vinaigrette. Ask to see their sizeable wine list. For dessert, nothing will make you happier than McEwen's famous banana cream pie. The award-winning confection will make you swoon, Southern style.

122 Monroe Ave. © 901/527-7085. www.mcewensonmonroe.com. Main courses $7–$12 lunch; $20–$30 dinner. AE, DC, MC, V. Mon–Fri 11am–2pm; Mon–Thurs 5:30–10pm; Fri–Sat 5:30–11pm. Bar open later.

Spindini ★★ ITALIAN   Judd Grisanti comes from a long line of Italian chef/ restaurateurs who have earned well-deserved success and recognition in Memphis. Spindini is the newest venture from the Grisanti clan, and it is a sophisticated showstopper. Opened in 2007 in downtown's thriving South Main arts district, the long, narrow restaurant is flanked by a banquette with tightly spaced tables and a classy bar adorned with decorative glass sculptures. A wood-burning oven at the back of the restaurant emits a warm glow, as the kitchen churns out appetizers and entrees that have been cooked, or rather "kissed by the fire" there. Wood-fired steaks, seared fish, and fresh pasta dishes are excellent. The Tuscan Butter may be one of the best appetizers in town—an ice-cream-sized scoop of spreadable mascarpone and goat cheese drenched in a tangy tomato sauce and served with soft, slender slices of warm garlic bread. The only thing that keeps me from giving this restaurant three stars is its

Memphis Dining: Downtown & Midtown

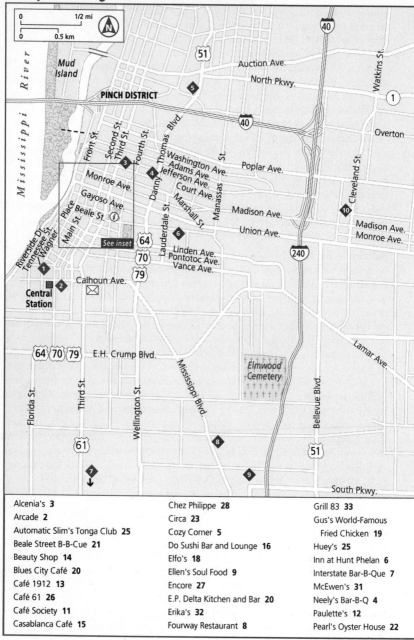

Alcenia's **3**
Arcade **2**
Automatic Slim's Tonga Club **25**
Beale Street B-B-Cue **21**
Beauty Shop **14**
Blues City Café **20**
Café 1912 **13**
Café 61 **26**
Café Society **11**
Casablanca Café **15**

Chez Philippe **28**
Circa **23**
Cozy Corner **5**
Do Sushi Bar and Lounge **16**
Elfo's **18**
Ellen's Soul Food **9**
Encore **27**
E.P. Delta Kitchen and Bar **20**
Erika's **32**
Fourway Restaurant **8**

Grill 83 **33**
Gus's World-Famous
   Fried Chicken **19**
Huey's **25**
Inn at Hunt Phelan **6**
Interstate Bar-B-Que **7**
McEwen's **31**
Neely's Bar-B-Q **4**
Paulette's **12**
Pearl's Oyster House **22**

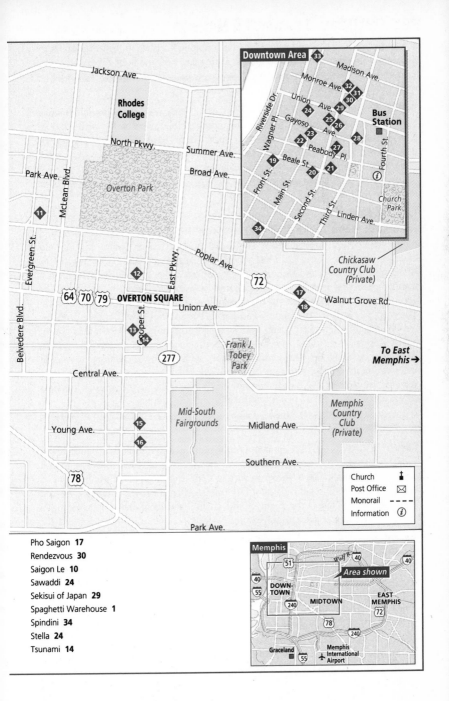

Jackson Ave.

Rhodes
College

North Pkwy.

Summer Ave.

Broad Ave.

Park Ave.

McLean Blvd.

Overton Park

Evergreen St.

Belvedere Blvd.

East Pkwy.

Poplar Ave.

Downtown Area 33

Madison Ave.

Monroe Ave. 32 31
30
Union Ave. 29
24
25 26
Gayoso Ave.
23
22
Peabody Pl. 27
Beale St. 28
19
20 21

Riverside Dr.
Wagner Pl.
Front St.
Main St.
Second St.
Third St.
Fourth St.

**Bus
Station**

ⓘ

Church
Park

34

Linden Ave.

Chickasaw
Country Club
(Private)

72

17
18

Walnut Grove Rd.

**To East
Memphis →**

64 70 79 **OVERTON SQUARE**

Union Ave.

Cooper St.

13
14

277

Central Ave.

15
16

Young Ave.

Frank J.
Tobey
Park

Mid-South
Fairgrounds

Midland Ave.

Memphis
Country
Club
(Private)

78

Southern Ave.

Park Ave.

Church	🛉
Post Office	✉
Monorail	– – –
Information	ⓘ

Pho Saigon **17**
Rendezvous **30**
Saigon Le **10**
Sawaddi **24**
Sekisui of Japan **29**
Spaghetti Warehouse **1**
Spindini **34**
Stella **24**
Tsunami **14**

Memphis

Wolf R.
40
51
40
40
55
DOWN-
TOWN
240
MIDTOWN
EAST
MEMPHIS
72
78
240
Graceland
Memphis
International
Airport
55
Area shown

service, which can be indifferent as the busy wait staff rushes to turn over tables to people wait-listed in the cramped lounge seating area near the front door.

383 S. Main St. ℂ 901/578-2767. www.spindini-memphis.com. Reservations recommended. Pizzas and main courses $13–$32. AE, DISC, DC, MC, V. Sun–Wed 5–10pm; Thurs–Sat 5-11pm.

Stella ✦ CONTEMPORARY AMERICAN Anchoring the historic Brodnax building downtown, Stella is that rare fine-dining establishment that's casual yet chic. The globally inspired Delta cuisine offers such stalwart entrees as strip steak, lobster, rack of lamb, and seared tuna or salmon. Unexpected finds include the savory crawfish cheesecake appetizer dusted with Creole spices.

39 S. Main St. ℂ 901/526-4950. www.stellamemphis.com. Main courses $27–$42 dinner. AE, DC, DISC, MC, V. Mon–Sat starting at 5:30pm.

MODERATE

Automatic Slim's Tonga Club ✦✦ NEW AMERICAN For relaxed artiness and superb food, try Automatic Slim's. The name "Automatic Slim" comes from an old blues song, and the Tonga Club was a local teen hangout popular in the early 1960s. Artists from New York and Memphis created the decor (they're credited on the menu), including zebra-print upholstered banquettes, slag-glass wall sconces, and colorfully upholstered bar stools. Be sure to try a cocktail with some of the fruit-soaked vodka. The food here is as creative as the atmosphere. The coconut-mango shrimp with citrus *pico de gallo* is a piquant starter. Salads are adventurous plates of fresh field greens, lightly vinegared and tossed with sun-dried cherries, goat cheese, and sunflower seeds. The tasty quesadillas are cheesy tortillas topped with cilantro and onions. If you can stand the heat, try the succulent Jamaican jerk chicken, served with black beans and rice. In summer, ask for the creamy tomato basil soup. It goes great with Slim's coyote chips, crisps of potato with horseradish dipping sauce.

83 S. Second St. ℂ 901/525-7948. Reservations recommended. Main courses $16–$25. AE, DC, MC, V. Mon–Fri 11am–2pm; Mon–Thurs 5–10pm; Fri–Sat 5–11pm.

Café 61 ✦ CAJUN This Cajun/American/Asian amalgam is run by the folks at On Teur, another favorite eatery in Midtown. Succulent sandwiches, salads, and fish dishes are specialties. The lively decor, with its floor-to-ceiling portraits of blues greats B.B. King and W. C. Handy, is pure Delta funk—a cross between Highway 61 and Route 66. But one bite of the creamy, Cajun crawfish macaroni-and-cheese, and you'll think you've died and gone to heaven.

85 S. Second St. ℂ 901/523-9351. Reservations recommended for parties of 6 or more. Main courses $10–$25. AE, DC, DISC, MC, V. Mon–Thurs 11am–11pm; Fri–Sat 11am–midnight. (Bar remains open later on weekends.)

Circa ✦✦ NEW SOUTHERN One of the newest fine-dining restaurants and upscale bars downtown, Circa has been a place to see and be seen since it opened in mid-2007. Young local restaurateur and French-trained chef-owner John Bragg has pulled out all the stops to create a sleek, cosmopolitan space dominated by wall-to-ceiling wine racks dividing rows of candle-lit tables. Polished service, including expert wine recommendations made from an extensive list, make meals here feel special. We enjoyed the crisp spinach salad with crab meat; seared five-spice-encrusted tuna with wasabi mashed potatoes; and a generous surf-and-turf combo that paired succulent lobster with juicy, lean steak. Braised lamb shanks, crispy duck breast, and pan-roasted grouper are among the menu's other entrees. Plan ahead if you want to order the bananas foster soufflé, which takes 30 minutes to prepare.

119 S. Main, Suite 100. © **901/522-1488**. www.circamemphis.com. Main courses $10–$26. AE, DISC, DC, MC, V. Tues–Sat 5–11pm; Sun–Mon 5–10pm.

EP Delta Kitchen and Bar AMERICAN   This cool-looking, high-profile restaurant on a prime location on Beale Street is somewhat of an oddity. It was built and opened with great fanfare in the late 1990s by the folks who run Graceland, as sort of a swanky, Elvis-ized version of a Hard Rock Café. Lisa Marie herself visited for its paparazzi-studded launch, but with mediocre food the eatery eventually folded. Fortunately in 2007, one of Memphis's most well-respected restaurateurs, chef Jimmy Ishii (of Sekisui fame, among other favorite dining establishments citywide) jumped in to take a stab at reviving the space. The new menu is a mishmash of culinary styles they've dubbed "Memphis and Mississippi River cuisine," with offerings ranging from meatloaf and Cajun/Creole gumbo to grilled pork chops and peanut butter cheesecake. There's a full bar, frequent live music, and unusual late-night noshes, like the $11 lobster "pronto pup."

126 Beale at Second © **901/527-1444**. www.epdeltakitchen.com. Main courses $15–$28. MC, V. Open daily for dinner.

Sawaddii THAI   Robust and spicy Thai specialties such as beef noodles, satays with spicy peanut dipping sauce, crab Rangoon, and coconut-milk-based soups are served at this new restaurant just a few blocks from The Peabody Memphis hotel. A tastefully appointed dining room combines deep orange and black accents to a nice effect. Service can be slow and the language barrier a problem, but these quibbles shouldn't deter adventurous diners.

121 Union Ave. © **901/529-1818**. Reservations accepted. Main courses $7–$18. AE, DISC, MC, V. Mon–Fri 11am–2:30pm; Sun–Thurs 5:30–9pm; Fri–Sat 5–10pm.

Sekisui of Japan ★★ JAPANESE   Unlike Japanese restaurants that almost go overboard on tranquility, Sekisui is a noisy and active place, especially on weekends. The sushi bar prepares platters of assorted fish, from appetizer tidbits to a huge sushi boat that includes octopus, conch, snapper, and flying-fish-roe sushi. Fiery wasabi, a splash of soy, and shredded ginger add zing. Tempura, teriyaki, and *yakizakana* dinners come with rice, a wonderful miso soup, and salad. Some locations offer a separate *robata* grill menu. Among the other Sekisui locations are those at 25 S. Belvedere St. (© **901/725-0005**), and in the suburban Humphreys Center shopping center, 50 Humphreys Blvd., at Walnut Grove Road (© **901/747-0001**).

Inside the Holiday Inn Select downtown at 160 Union Ave. © **901/523-0001**. www.sekisuiusa.com. Reservations recommended on weekends. Main courses $9–$26. AE, DC, DISC, MC, V. Mon–Fri 11:30am–2pm; Sun–Thurs 5–9pm; Fri–Sat 5–10pm.

INEXPENSIVE

Alcenia's ★ SOUTHERN   This down-to-earth breakfast/lunch hangout looks like the kind of place where Stella got her groove back. The decor is shabby chic, where orange walls and purple beaded curtains blend right in with the potted plants, African artwork, and tulle draped from the ceiling. Best known for its homemade preserves, Alcenia's serves up salmon croquettes, pancakes, and biscuits for breakfast. Sandwiches and Southern-style munchies are available at other hours. Call ahead to see if Alcenia's famous bread pudding is on the menu that day.

317 N. Main St. © **901/523-0200**. Main courses $7–$9. AE, DC, MC, V. Tues–Fri 11am–5pm; Sat 8am–1pm. (Occasionally open evenings for special events; call ahead.)

The Arcade Restaurant ✵ *Value* AMERICAN   Established in 1919, the Arcade stands as a reminder of the early part of the century when this was a busy neighborhood, bustling with people and commerce. Although this corner is not nearly as lively as it once was, the restaurant attracts loyal Memphians and out-of-towners who stop by for the home-style cooking and pizzas. Because the proprietors have an annoying habit of closing down when business is slow, you might want to call ahead if you're making the Arcade your destination.

540 S. Main St. ℂ 901/526-5757. www.arcaderestaurant.com. Breakfast $6–$8; lunch $6–$8; pizza $7–$20. DC, DISC, MC, V. Daily 7am–3pm.

Erika's ✵✵ *Finds* GERMAN   The city's only German restaurant is a cozy beer hall frequented more by locals than tourists. Perhaps this is because it gets upstaged or else overlooked in favor of The Rendezvous, the must-visit rib joint that shares the same building. However, if you'd rather forgo ribs in favor of a tangy sauerbraten with cooked red cabbage, give Erika's a try. Chef Erika's yeast rolls, served warm and fragrant from the oven, are huge mounds of sweet, yeasty bliss. Also excellent are the spaetzle, schnitzel, bratwurst, and fluffy dumplings.

52 S. Second St. ℂ 901/526-5522. Main courses $5–$11. AE, DISC, MC, V. Tues–Fri 11am–2pm; Fri–Sat 5:30–9:30pm.

Gus's World Famous Fried Chicken ✵ SOUTHERN   In a decidedly dingy juke-joint setting off the beaten path downtown sits this franchise of the legendary Gus's in Mason, Tennessee. Black and white, young and old, hip and square—they and every other demographic all converge here for spicy-battered chicken, beans, slaw, and pies. Service is friendly but slow, so don't go here if you're in a hurry. (If you'd like to take a road trip to the Real McCoy, the original Gus's is at 505 Hwy. 70 W., Mason, ℂ 901/294-2028. Call ahead for hours.)

310 S. Front St. ℂ 901/527-4877. Main courses $6–$9. AE, MC, V. Open daily 11am–9pm.

Huey's ✵ AMERICAN   Ask Memphians where to get the best burger in town, and you'll invariably be directed to Huey's. This good-times tavern also has one of the most extensive beer selections in town. The original Huey's, at 1927 Madison Ave. (ℂ 901/726-4372), in the Overton Square area, is still in business. In recent years, suburban locations have also sprouted up in East Memphis and beyond.

77 S. Second St. ℂ 901/527-2700. www.hueyburger.com. Reservations not accepted. Main courses $5–$10. AE, DISC, MC, V. Daily 11am–2am.

Pearl's Oyster House ✵ CAJUN   An old warehouse in downtown's South Main Street district has found renewed energy as a spacious, laid-back Gulf Coast–style seafood joint. Platters of plump oysters can be ordered raw or fried, or try the juicy pan-roasted mussels. Cajun gumbos and etoufee are rich, roux-based soups studded with chunks of Andouille sausage and fish. Fried-shrimp po'boys are encased in shredded lettuce inside chewy French baguettes. More substantial fare includes fresh catfish fried in butter, and the seasonal crawfish boil—a spicy-hot favorite with corn-on-the-cob and new potatoes.

299 S. Main St. ℂ 901/522-9070. www.pearlsoysterhouse.com. Main courses $10–$19. AE, DISC, DC, MC, V. Mon–Sat from 11am; closing times vary.

The Rendezvous Restaurant ✵✵ *Moments* BARBECUE   The Rendezvous has been a downtown Memphis institution since 1948, and it has a well-deserved reputation for serving the best ribs in town. You can see the food being prepared in an old open kitchen as you walk in, but more important, your sense of smell will immediately perk up as the fragrance of hickory-smoked pork wafts past. You'll also likely be intrigued by all manner of strange objects displayed in this huge but cozy cellar. And when the waiter comes to take your order, there's no messin' around; you're expected to know what you want when you come in—an order of ribs. Also be sure to ask if they still have any of the red beans and rice that are served nightly until the pot is empty. This Memphis landmark is tucked along General Washburn Alley, across from the Peabody Hotel. Upstairs, you'll find a large bar.

52 S. Second St. 🄫 **901/523-2746.** www.hogsfly.com. Main plates $6.50–$18. AE, DC, DISC, MC, V. Tues–Thurs 4:30–10:30pm; Fri 11:30am–11pm; Sat noon–11pm.

Spaghetti Warehouse *(Kids* AMERICAN/ITALIAN   Families and tourists on budgets seek out this sprawling, noisy old warehouse brimming with antiques and amusing collectibles. Food is middle-of-the-road. Simple American burgers are served alongside Italian staples such as lasagna and spaghetti. Though this longtime Memphis eatery may lack the buzz of newer restaurants, it certainly has staying power.

40 W. Huling. 🄫 **901/521-0907.** www.meatballs.com. Main plates $6–$16. AE, MC, V. Sun–Thurs 11am–10pm; Fri–Sat 11am–11pm.

4 Midtown

For locations of restaurants in this section, see the "Memphis Dining: Downtown & Midtown" map on p. 180.

EXPENSIVE

Beauty Shop 🟊🟊🟊 NEW AMERICAN   The first and most important thing you need to know is *not* that this hip eatery sits inside an old 1960s-style beauty shop, but that it's the brainchild of Karen Blockman Carrier, the creative force behind Memphis's coolest restaurant (Automatic Slim's). Yes, the atmosphere is kitschy and fun. You can, indeed, dine in refurbished hair-dryer chairs. But what keeps the place packed with all the beautiful people is the fantastic food: globally inspired salads (I loved the Thai Cobb), entrees such as the whole striped bass, or the best BLTA (bacon, lettuce, tomato, and avocado sandwich) you've ever tasted.

966 S. Cooper St. 🄫 **901/272-7111.** Reservations highly recommended. Main courses $18–$26. AE, MC, V. Mon–Fri 11am–3pm; brunch Sat 10am–2pm, Sun 10am–3pm; dinner Mon–Thurs 5–10pm, Fri–Sat 5–11pm.

Tsunami 🟊🟊 PACIFIC RIM/SEAFOOD   Consistently ranked by locals as one of their favorite restaurants in Memphis, Tsunami serves creative Pacific Rim cuisine. Tropical colors over cement floors and walls enliven the otherwise uninspired setting. But the food's the thing. Appetizers run the gamut from potsticker dumplings with chile-soy dipping sauce, to shrimp satay with Thai peanut sauce. Among chef/owner Ben Smith's other specialties are roasted sea bass with black Thai rice and soy beurre blanc, wasabi-crusted tuna, and duck breast with miso-shiitake risotto. Crème brûlée fans should not miss Smith's sublime Tahitian-vanilla version of this classic. A judicious list of Australian and French wines includes champagne and a handful of ports.

928 S. Cooper St. 🄫 **901/274-2556.** www.tsunamimemphis.com. Reservations recommended. Main courses $18–$28; small plates $7–$18. AE, MC, V. Mon–Fri 11am–2pm; Mon–Sat 5:30–10pm.

MODERATE

Café 1912 AMERICAN   At the edge of the Cooper-Young district in midtown, this casual bistro and bar is especially popular with neighborhood residents. Rickety wooden tables and straw-seat chairs line the painted cement floor in the main dining room, behind which is a separate bar area. (Ask for a table away from the front door, where it can become cold and drafty in chilly weather.) Daily specials include fresh fish and soups, or try the perennially popular beef tenderloin encrusted with smoked olive tapenade; potato puree and red-wine sauce. The best dessert here is the ample fruit and cheese plate, featuring generous wedges of soft, semi-soft, and hard cheese.

243 S. Cooper ⓒ 901/722-2700. Main courses $16–$20. AE, DISC, DC, MC, V. Mon–Thurs 5:30–9:30pm; Fri–Sat 5:30–10:30pm; Sun 5:30–9pm.

Café Society ⓕ NEW AMERICAN   Named after a Parisian cafe, this lively bistro has a vague country-inn feel about it and is a popular ladies' lunch spot and pre-theater restaurant. As in a French cafe, you'll find convivial conversations at the small bar and outdoor seating on the street where you can sit and people-watch. Start out with some French onion soup or honey-baked brie, followed up with the likes of salmon with a sesame- and poppyseed crust or braised lamb shank with a pear brandy and walnut glaze. Lunches are reasonably priced and offer a chance to sample some of the same fine food that is served at dinner. There are also monthly four-course wine and food tastings for which reservations are required.

212 N. Evergreen St. ⓒ 901/722-2177. Reservations recommended. Main courses $13–$27. AE, DC, MC, V. Mon–Fri 11:30am–2pm; Fri–Sun 5–10:30pm.

Casablanca Cafe ⓕⓕ MEDITERRANEAN   Craving a "Big Mac of the Middle East?" You can get the so-called falafel pita sandwich at this comfortably exotic eatery in the Cooper-Young neighborhood. The chef/owner imports all of his spices and ingredients such as olive oil from his native Middle East. A hard-working, congenial host, he mingles with customers and offers helpful suggestions for appetizers such as baba ganoush, pureed lentil soup, and silky hummus served with a basket of soft, warm pita bread. You can also indulge in generously stuffed gyros or Greek salads, including tabbouleh or crisp lettuce with olives and feta cheese. Entrees included grilled rack of lamb with mango sauce, and Holy Land shish kabob. Exotic Moroccan tagine dishes—seafood or lamb baked in clay pots—serve two people.

2156 Young Ave. ⓒ 901/722-2700. www.casablancamemphis.com. Main courses $13–$21; sandwiches $6–$8. AE, DISC, DC, MC, V. Mon–Thurs 5:30–9:30pm; Fri–Sat 5:30–10:30pm; Sun 5:30–9:30pm.

Paulette's ⓕ CONTINENTAL   Paulette's has long been one of Memphis's most beloved restaurants. Cozy as a French country inn, the space is filled with antiques and traditional European paintings. Specialties here include the Hungarian *gulyas* and *uborka salata* (cucumber salad in a sweet vinegar dressing). Not to be missed are the popovers with strawberry butter that accompany most entrees. Among the main courses, the beef filet is delicious, as are the chicken livers bourguignon, and Louisiana crab cakes. Though the dessert list is quite extensive, you should be sure that someone at your table orders the Kahlúa-mocha pie, made with a pecan-coconut crust.

2110 Madison Ave. ⓒ 901/726-5128. Reservations recommended. Main courses $9–$25. AE, DC, DISC, MC, V. Sun–Thurs 11am–9pm; Fri–Sat 11am–10:30pm.

INEXPENSIVE

Do Sushi Bar and Lounge JAPANESE/SEAFOOD Spare furnishings in this brick storefront overlooking the intersection of Cooper and Young streets in Midtown keep the focus on people-watching and tasting. Celebrated local restaurateur and caterer Karen Blockman Carrier is the force behind this sushi restaurant, called Do (pronounced "dough"), where the menu includes everything from sashimi rolls and seaweed salad to tempura, soba noodle, and grilled fish dishes. Clean, vibrant flavors and friendly, knowledgeable service are hallmarks here.

964 Cooper St. ✆ 901/272-0830. Main courses under $10. AE, DC, DISC, MC, V. Tues–Sat 5–11pm.

Elfo's Restaurant ✪ AMERICAN/ITALIAN In Memphis, the Grisanti family has become synonymous with Italian restaurants. That being said, Elfo's offers its lunch-only patrons a more eclectic menu than you might expect. Traditional favorites such as prosciutto-stuffed tortellini, and Elfo Pasta with garlicky shrimp and mushrooms remain in place but are augmented by American fare, including crab cakes, chicken salad, grilled salmon with asparagus, and cakes and cobblers. Like the other Grisanti restaurants, tablecloths and place settings are immaculate, service is cordial and efficient, and the food is always delicious.

3092 Poplar Ave. (inside Chickasaw Oaks). ✆ 901/888-0402. www.elfosrestaurant.com. Main courses $6–$16. AE, DC, DISC, MC, V. Mon–Sat 11am–2pm.

Pho Saigon ✪ *(Value)* VIETNAMESE Noodle dishes, spring and egg rolls, and piquant soups are served in plentiful portions at this clean, family-run restaurant off Poplar Avenue near Midtown. There's nothing fancy about Pho Saigon's interior, but basic chairs and tables and a few knickknacks are all that's necessary. The menu is extensive, the wait staff friendly and helpful with suggestions, and the food fresh and utterly addictive.

2946 Poplar Ave. ✆ 901/458-1644. Main courses $5–$8. MC, V. Daily 10am–9pm.

Saigon Le ✪ *(Finds)* VIETNAMESE/CHINESE A popular lunch spot, Saigon Le is in an urban neighborhood close to the medical center district and is popular with hospital workers. Friendly service and generous portions of Chinese and Vietnamese dishes are the standards here. The kung pao beef is spicy, and the vegetable egg foo yung is plump with vegetables. Saigon Le's Vietnamese specialties include flavorful noodle, meat, fish, and vegetable dishes such as charcoal-broiled pork, spring rolls with vermicelli, and clear noodle soup with barbecued pork, shrimp, and crabmeat. At just under $6, the lunch special may be the best bargain in town.

51 N. Cleveland St. ✆ 901/276-5326. Reservations not accepted. Main courses $6–$15. DC, DISC, MC, V. Mon–Sat 11am–9pm; closed Sun.

5 East Memphis

EXPENSIVE

Erling Jensen–The Restaurant ✪✪✪ NEW AMERICAN Chef Erling Jensen made a name for himself at the popular La Tourelle and has now ventured out on his own at this eponymous restaurant located in a converted suburban home just off Poplar Avenue near the Ridgeway Inn. Understated elegance and contemporary art set the tone for Jensen's innovative cuisine. Well grounded in the French kitchen, Jensen brings a somewhat traditional flavor to his menu. You might start a meal with crawfish mousse with penne pasta and Oregon truffles; a Parmesan, goat-cheese, and Vidalia-onion tart; or seared Sonoma foie gras with pears and sauternes. A diverse assortment of entrees makes decision-making difficult, but among the options you might encounter ostrich with a ginger demiglace; vanilla-bean and Brazil nut–crusted orange roughy (a firm-fleshed white fish); or rack of lamb with a pecan, mustard, garlic, and molasses crust. There is always a wide assortment of house-made sorbets and ice creams (chocolate-marzipan-chunk ice cream, mango sorbet) available for dessert, but, of course, there are also more artistic confections, such as warm chocolate tart with roasted bananas and honey-almond-crunch ice cream. The large staff is well trained to provide impeccable service.

1044 S. Yates St. (C) 901/763-3700. www.ejensen.com. Reservations highly recommended. Main courses $31–$46. AE, DC, MC, V. Daily 5–10pm.

Folk's Folly Prime Steak House 🎇🎇 STEAKS   Indeed, there are better-known chain steakhouses in Memphis, but there is none more beloved than this local institution. You'll find Folk's Folly just off Poplar Avenue—it's the corner building with the royal-blue awning. Just off the parking lot is a tiny butcher shop that's part of the restaurant; in the meat cases inside, you'll see the sort of top-quality meats they serve here (the likes of which you'll probably never see at your neighborhood market). Steaks are the specialty of the house, and steaks are what they do best. However, you can start your meal with anything from blackened catfish to seafood gumbo or even fried pickles. Among the prime cuts of beef are aged sirloins, filet mignons, and T-bones. Seafood offerings include Alaskan king crab legs, salmon filets, and jumbo Maine lobsters.

551 S. Mendenhall Rd. (C) 901/762-8200. www.folksfolly.com. Reservations recommended. Main courses $20–$45. AE, DC, MC, V. Mon–Thurs 5:30–10pm; Fri–Sat 5:30–11pm; Sun 5:30–9pm.

Frank Grisanti's Italian Restaurant 🎇 NORTHERN ITALIAN   Tucked into a corner of the lobby of the Embassy Suites Hotel, this classy little restaurant serves some of the most authentic Italian food in Memphis. The atmosphere evokes the Old South far more than it does the trattorias of Rome, and the clublike setting attracts a well-heeled clientele. If you prefer a more casual setting, ask for a table on the atrium patio. The seafood and veal dishes are among the strong points here, and there are plenty of these to choose from. The *bistecca toscano* and *scampi portofino* are two of the most popular dishes here. If pasta is what you're after, the Elfo Special is worth considering—plenty of big shrimp and lots of garlic. There is also an elegant little bar in case you happen to arrive early.

In the Embassy Suites Hotel, 1022 S. Shady Grove Rd. (C) 901/761-9462. www.frankgrisanti.com. Reservations recommended weekends. Main courses $32. AE, DC, DISC, MC, V. Mon–Thurs 11am–10pm; Fri–Sat 11am–10:30pm; Sun 5–10pm.

Napa Café CALIFORNIAN/NEW AMERICAN   In an upscale East Memphis shopping center near the Doubletree Hotel is this comfortable restaurant specializing in California cuisine. Favored entrees are the potato-encrusted halibut and the rack of lamb. As its name implies, Napa Café has an award-winning wine list. What's more, private dinners for parties of two or more are available in the restaurant's cozy wine cellar if you book them in advance.

5101 Sanderlin Dr. Suite 122. (C) 901/683-0441. www.napacafe.com. Reservations recommended. Main courses $16–$29. AE, DC, DISC, MC, V. Mon–Fri 11am–2pm; Mon–Thurs 5–9pm; Fri–Sat 5–10pm.

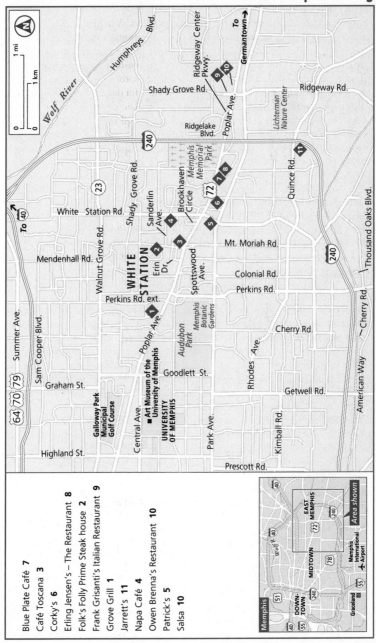

Blue Plate Café **7**

Café Toscana **3**

Corky's **6**

Erling Jensen's – The Restaurant **8**

Folk's Folly Prime Steak house **2**

Frank Grisanti's Italian Restaurant **9**

Grove Grill **1**

Jarrett's **11**

Napa Café **4**

Owen Brenna's Restaurant **10**

Patrick's **5**

Salsa **10**

MODERATE

Café Toscana ITALIAN   Dark-red walls and colorful still life paintings provide aesthetic oomph to this small but bustling Italian cafe in East Memphis. Perfectly grilled seafood entrees, meaty pasta dishes, and fresh green salads make this a pleasant after-work dinner-date spot. Enjoy another glass of wine, but skip the desserts, which are uninspired.

5007 Black Rd. (✆ **901/761-9522.** www.cafetoscanausa.com. Reservations recommended. Main courses $12–$22. AE, DISC, MC, V. Mon–Thurs 5–10pm; Fri–Sat 5–10:30pm.

Corky's ✿ *Kids* BARBECUE   Corky's is good-natured and boisterous, with rock-'n'-roll tunes piped both indoors and out. Aromatic barbecue permeates the air. An argument over which is the best barbecue restaurant in Memphis persists, but this one pretty much leads the pack when it comes to pulled pork shoulder barbecue, topped with tangy coleslaw. Photographs and letters from satisfied customers line the rough-paneled lobby, where you always have to wait for a table. Corky's even has a toll-free number (✆ **800/9-CORKYS**) to get their delicious ribs shipped "anywhere." There's also a drive-up window for immediate barbecue gratification. A downtown location at 175 Peabody Place (✆ **901/529-9191**) is right around the corner from Beale Street. The suburbs have a Corky's at Dexter Road in Cordova (✆ **901/737-1988**).

5259 Poplar Ave. (✆ **901/685-9744.** www.corkysbbq.com. Reservations not accepted. Main courses $4–$20. AE, DC, DISC, MC, V. Sun–Thurs 10:45am–9:30pm; Fri–Sat 10:45am–10pm.

The Grove Grill ✿ NEW SOUTHERN   Located in one of East Memphis's upscale shopping plazas, this big restaurant and oyster bar is a merger of contemporary and traditional decor and cuisine. The menu focuses primarily on seafood (and so does the art on the walls), with contemporary renditions of Southern favorites predominating. Three varieties of fresh oysters on the half shell are available. If you don't opt for the oysters, consider the crab and crawfish cakes with lemon-fennel remoulade or the oyster and artichoke soup. For an entree, the low-country shrimp and grits is a natural, or for a richer and less traditional dish, try the grilled pompano with crawfish beurre blanc. Entrees are served a la carte, so you'll need to pick a few dishes from the side-orders list, which reads like the veggie list in a traditional meat-and-three restaurant—warm blue-cheese slaw, grilled asparagus, and fried grit soufflé. The lunch menu is light on entrees other than sandwiches but does have plenty of interesting appetizers, soups, and salads.

Laurelwood Shopping Center, 4550 Poplar Ave. (✆ **901/818-9951.** www.thegrovegrill.com. Reservations recommended. Main courses $9–$30. AE, DC, DISC, MC, V. Daily 11am–2:30pm and 5:30–9pm.

Jarrett's ✿✿✿ *Finds* NEW AMERICAN/SEAFOOD   Jarrett's has the feel of a neighborhood restaurant but attracts people from all over the city. The setting may not sound auspicious—a nondescript East Memphis shopping plaza just before Quince Road crosses I-240—but the long and reasonably priced menu (fresh fish is a specialty) shows off the creativity of chef Richard Farmer, who is considered one of Memphis's finest. To start a meal, try the smoked trout ravioli with Arkansas caviar, the smoked quail spring rolls, or the prawns with macadamia-nut barbecue sauce. After such a bold opening, it is often difficult to maintain the creativity, but Jarrett's tries with such entrees as grilled yellowfin tuna with mango-jalapeño salsa, roasted pork tenderloin on onion-apple compote and applejack-sage demiglace, and filet of beef with mushroom and black-truffle Madeira sauce. The small, oak-lined bar is a popular after-work hangout, and in the summer, there is a garden patio dining area wedged between two buildings and shaded by pine trees.

Yorkshire Square shopping plaza, 5689 Quince Rd. © 901/763-2264. www.jarretts.com. Reservations accepted only for parties of 6 or more. Main courses $14–$33. AE, MC, V. Mon–Sat 5–10pm.

Owen Brennan's Restaurant ⊛ CAJUN   Located in one of East Memphis's most upscale shopping plazas and used as a set in the movie *The Firm*, Owen Brennan's has long been an East Memphis tradition, particularly for power lunches. The interior manages to conjure up the Big Easy with its Mardi Gras jesters and float decorations. Cuisine is flamboyant Cajun and Creole, from fluffy crab beignets to silky turtle soup. House specialties include the requisite blackened dishes, as well as hearty gumbos bursting with seafood. Desserts are so heavy they might make you woozy: The dense bread pudding is moistened with rum, and the caramelized Bananas Foster is drenched in it as well.

Regalia Shopping Center, 6150 Poplar Ave. © 901/761-0990. www.brennansmemphis.com. Reservations recommended. Main courses $11–$23. AE, DC, DISC, MC, V. Mon–Thurs 11am–9:30pm; Fri 11am–10:30pm; Sat 9:30am–10:30pm; Sun 10am–2pm.

INEXPENSIVE

Blue Plate Cafe ⊛ SOUTHERN   Hearty breakfasts brimming with fried sausage, bacon, ham and eggs at this yellow cottage help Memphis retain its ranking as one of the most overweight populations in the United States. Southern-style grits and buttermilk biscuits with gravy also do their part. Lunch and dinner are also served, featuring home-style meat-and-three choices in plentiful portions.

5469 Poplar Ave. © 901/761-9696. Main courses $5–$9. AE, DISC, DC, MC, V. Mon–Sat 6am–8:30pm; Sun 7am–2:30pm.

Patrick's Steaks and Spirits ⊛ *Kids* SOUTHERN   Over the past 2 years Patrick's has morphed from a reincarnation of the old Buntyn, a local meat-and-three diner since the 1930s, to a casual steakhouse and bar. But make no mistake: The daily plate lunches are what keep the loyal clientele coming back. Homemade yeast rolls and fat cornbread muffins are served warm from the oven. Whether you order the calf's liver smothered in onions, the Tuesdays-only fried chicken, or hefty homemade meatloaf, you can be sure the portions will be large. Entrees come with your choice of two vegetables from a long list that includes fried okra, turnip greens, purple-hull peas, and cheesy, baked macaroni shells.

Park Ave. at Mt. Moriah. © 901/682-2852. www.patricksmemphis.com. Main courses $8–$18. AE, DISC, MC, V. Daily 11am–10pm.

Salsa Cocina Mexicana ⊛⊛ MEXICAN/SOUTHWESTERN   Hands-down my favorite Mexican restaurant in Memphis, Salsa is a locally owned gem tucked into an upscale shopping center behind Ruth's Chris Steakhouse. Mexican standards are all delicious, as are the flavorful chicken in citrus-chipotle sauce, and a sirloin steak topped with grilled poblano peppers. You can even relish the side dishes including creamy refried beans and a robust salsa picante. Wash it all down with an icy margarita. Service is attentive—they really care that you enjoy your meal. Mexican music plays softly in the background. When vast platters of enchiladas, guacamole, and rice show up at your table, you'll know that you've come to the right place.

Regalia Shopping Center, 6150 Poplar Ave. © 901/683-6325. Reservations accepted only for parties of 6 or more. Main courses $5–$14. AE, DC, DISC, MC, V. Mon–Sat 11am–10pm.

6 South Memphis & Graceland Area

INEXPENSIVE

D'Bo's Buffalo Wings 'N' Things *✦* AMERICAN   Order a beer and a basket of wings and watch the game on TV, or call ahead and take home a couple hundred of these succulent chicken drummies and tips that are deep-fried and then slathered in mild, hot, or "suicidal" red sauces. Entrepreneur David Boyd and his wife started D'Bo's about a decade ago, selling wings out of a food trailer at area festivals. Their lip-smacking wings caught on like wildfire. Now there are D'Bo's locations throughout the city and beyond. If wings aren't your thing, the restaurant also serves great hamburgers and fries. D'Bo's has a nice location (there are others throughout the area) near the Reverend Al Green's church, Full Gospel Tabernacle, but unfortunately, this particular location isn't open on Sundays.

4407 Elvis Presley Blvd. ℂ 901/345-9464. www.dboswings.com. Main courses $5–$9. AE, DC, DISC, MC, V. Mon–Thurs 11am–10pm; Fri–Sat 11am–midnight.

Ellen's Soul Food *✦* *Finds* SOUL FOOD   From turnip greens and pigs' feet to peach pie and the most mouth-watering fried chicken you're ever likely to taste in your lifetime, go find this long-treasured local landmark before the tourists catch on. Ellen's may look like a hole in the wall, but once you step inside the nondescript room with its narrow lunch counter, you'll realize it's home.

601 S. Parkway E. ℂ 901/942-4888. Main courses $6–$8. Cash only. Tues–Sun noon–7pm.

Fourway Restaurant *✦✦✦* *Value* *Kids* SOUTHERN   If you're looking for the legendary Fourway Grill, this is it. The cherished South Memphis family restaurant serves the tastiest soul food in town. Eat dessert first. Try the velvety sweet potato pie. Then dig into some juicy fried green tomatoes, pork chops, catfish, or chicken and round it out with black-eyed peas and crumbly cornbread. If he's not too busy, ask the proprietor to reminisce about the old days of this historic black neighborhood, which locals hope is poised for a comeback.

998 Mississippi Blvd. ℂ 901/507-1519. Reservations recommended for large groups. Main courses $6–$9. MC, V. Tues–Sat 11am–7pm; Sun 11am–5pm.

Interstate Bar-B-Que *✦* BARBECUE   Corky's may be a bit flashier, but Interstate Bar-B-Que has the kind of grit and street cred that no suburban East Memphis eatery could muster. Located off Interstate 55 on South Third Street (a great stop-off if you're driving south from downtown to Graceland), Interstate is a former grocery store-turned barbecue joint. Insurance agent Jim Neely launched the biz in the 1970s in a then-dicey part of town. Though urban renewal efforts at seem to have eluded the still-blighted neighborhood, Interstate Bar-B-Que is a bright, welcoming spot. Long before *USA Today* proclaimed it the best place in America for a pork barbecue sandwich, locals and tourists already knew it. Along with pork and beef ribs and shredded barbecue, Interstate smokes a mean, spice-rubbed turkey breast. Chicken halves are slow-roasted in hickory-wood pits, to achieve a tender, moist flavor. Sides include sugary baked beans, coleslaw, potato salad, and barbecued spaghetti. For world-wide delivery, call ℂ 888/227-2793.

2265 S. Third St. ℂ 901/775-2304. www.jimneelysinterstatebarbecue.com. Sandwiches $4.85-$5.30; dinner platters $6.25-$8.75. Mon–Thurs 11am–10pm; Fri–Sat 11am–11pm; Sun 11am–5pm. MC, V.

7 Barbecue

Memphis claims to be the barbecue capital of the world, and with more than 100 barbecue restaurants and the annual Memphis in May World Championship Barbecue Cooking Contest, it's hard to argue the point. The standard barbecue here comes in two basic types—hand-pulled pork shoulder (pulled off the bone rather than cut off) and pork ribs. The latter can be served wet or dry (that is, with or without sauce). The best pulled pork shoulder in town is at **Corky's** (p. 190) and the best ribs are served at **The Rendezvous** (p. 184).

However, it isn't just pork shoulder and ribs that get barbecued here in Memphis. You can get barbecued spaghetti, barbecued pizza, and even barbecued bologna! Everyone in town seems to have his or her own favorite barbecue joint, and listed below are some of the ones that consistently get the best reviews.

The **Cozy Corner,** 745 N. Parkway (© 901/527-9158), is just what it sounds like and is located in midtown Memphis. **Neely's B-B-Q,** 670 Jefferson Ave. in downtown (© 901/521-9798), and 5700 Mt. Moriah Rd. in East Memphis (© 901/795-4177), does the usual, but also does barbecued spaghetti and barbecued bologna. The **Beale St. Bar-B-Que,** 205 Beale St. (© 901/526-6113), is a serviceable place to grab 'cue if you're doing the blues thing, but Beale Street's best ribs are at **Blues City Café,** 138 Beale St. (© 901/526-3637; www.bluescitycafe.com). They make mean tamales, too.

Down near Graceland, which is located in one of the city's poorer neighborhoods, there is an abundance of barbecue joints and bonafide dives worth the drive: Try **Payne's,** 1393 Elvis Presley Blvd. (© 901/942-7433); **Interstate Bar-B-Que Restaurant** (p. 192)**,** and **A&R Bar-B-Q,** 1802 Elvis Presley Blvd. (© 901/774-7444), the last of which draws raves for authentic barbecued sandwiches, ribs, and spaghetti.

8 Coffeehouses, Cafes & Pastry Shops

Sure, there's a Starbucks at practically every other intersection, but wouldn't you really rather patronize a coffee shop where you can soak up some local atmosphere? If so, your first stop should be downtown, to the **Center for Southern Folklore,** Pembroke Square (© 901/525-3655; www.southernfolklore.com). It's a one-of-a-kind cafe of culture where you can belt back a cappuccino while admiring local crafts, outsider art, and hear great music almost any time of the day. At the edge of the Cooper-Young neighborhood, you can quaff a cup o' joe and listen to live music or poetry at **Otherlands,** 641 S. Cooper St. (© 901/278-4994). Farther down the street, you'll find **Java Cabana,** 2170 Young Ave. (© 901/272-7210; www.javacabanacoffeehouse.com), a grungy little dive teeming with twentysomethings.

Up the street, **Precious Cargo Exchange,** 381 N. Main St. (© 901/578-8446), is a grittier, more soulful coffee shop that doubles as a funky corner bar and magnet for eccentrics.

For more substantial fare, such as meat-and-cheese sandwiches on grilled focaccia, head east toward **Fratelli's in the Garden,** 750 Cherry Rd. (© 901/685-1566, ext. 118; www.fratellisfinecatering.com). Relocated from downtown to the Memphis Botanic Garden, the market and deli offers tiramisu for dessert, and take-home gourmet pastas, olive oils, cheeses, and imported beers. If the coffee cravings hit while you're shopping in East Memphis, **High Point Coffee,** 4610 Poplar Ave. (© 901/761-6800) is convenient to Oak Court Mall and other upscale retail spots. Beware: Its drive-through is packed during morning rush hour.

The most bucolic view in town can be found inside the Memphis Brooks Museum of Art, where the **Brushmark Restaurant,** 1934 Poplar (© **901/544-6225;** www. brooksmuseum.org), overlooks the lush greenery of Overton Park. One of the café's signature dishes is the spicy African peanut soup, but the menu is being augmented with other enticing Southern specialties by renowned local chef Wally Joe, who took over in 2007. A special-occasion lunch spot, the bistro is open for lunch daily except Monday, when the museum is closed, and Thursday evening by reservation.

Exquisite quiche Lorraine, zesty tomato bisque, and chicken salad sandwiches on chewy loaves of freshly baked French bread are delectable choices at **La Baguette,** 3088 Poplar Ave. (© **901/458-0900**). Well-to-do ladies lunch regularly at this bistro inside tony Chickasaw Oaks shopping center adjacent to the new library. Best of all are the luscious pastries, including photo-worthy fruit tarts, croissants, and éclairs. Farther east, be on the lookout for Davis-Kidd Booksellers. Part coffee shop, part wine bar and cafe with indoor/outdoor seating, **Bronte Bistro,** 387 Perkins Rd. Extension (© **901/374-0881;** www.daviskidd.com), located inside the bookstore, is where the intelligentsia gather for delectable salads and sandwiches, conversation, and liquid refreshment.

Exploring Memphis

Just as in Nashville, music is the heart of Memphis, and many of the city's main attractions are related to Memphis's musical heritage. The blues first gained widespread recognition here on Beale Street, and rock 'n' roll was born at Sun Studio. W. C. Handy, the father of the blues, lived here for many years, and Elvis Presley made his Memphis home—Graceland—a household word. You'll find the history of the Memphis sound on exhibit at several museums around the city, including a couple devoted exclusively to music.

Downtown Memphis has experienced a long-awaited renaissance over the last few years, with such renovation projects as Memphis Central Station, a historic 1914 train depot. Also adding vitality is Peabody Place, one of the nation's largest mixed-use development and historic preservation projects. In addition to housing the funky Center for Southern Folklore (p. 234), it includes a 22-screen Cineplex and IMAX 3-D Theater.

There's more. The Gibson Guitar Plant, a 75,000-square-foot guitar manufacturing facility and showcase lounge, offers visitors the chance not only to hear these instruments performed but also to see them being made.

South of downtown, Soulsville USA: the Stax Museum of American Soul Music is a must-see attraction.

1 The Roots of Memphis Music: Graceland, Beale Street & More

If you're going to Memphis, you're most likely going to Graceland, but there are also several other museums and sites here tied to the history of rock and blues music. Although the blues was born down in the Mississippi Delta south of Memphis, it was on Beale Street that this soulful music first reached an urban audience. Today, after a period of abandonment, **Beale Street** is once again Memphis's busiest entertainment district. Visitors can hear blues, rock, jazz, country, and even Irish music on Beale Street. To learn more about the various musical styles that originated along the Mississippi River, visit the **Mississippi River Museum** on Mud Island (p. 204), where there are several rooms full of exhibits on New Orleans jazz, Memphis blues, rockabilly, and Elvis. All of these places are more fully described below.

In addition to being the birthplace of the blues and the city that launched Elvis and rock 'n' roll, Memphis played an important role in soul music during the 1960s. Isaac Hayes and Booker T and the MGs recorded here at **Stax Studio.** Other musicians who

---

Impressions
The seven wonders of the world I have seen, and many are the places I have been. Take my advice, folks, and see Beale Street first.
—W. C. Handy

Memphis Attractions: Downtown & Midtown

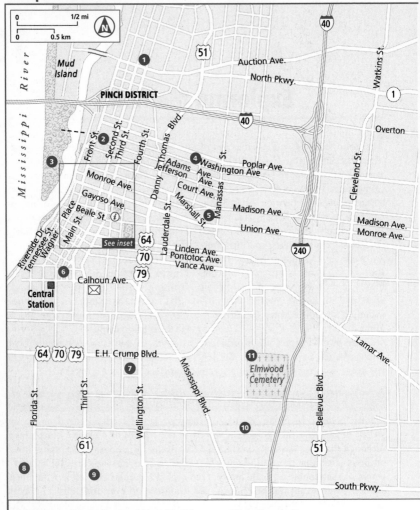

Art Museum of the University of Memphis **27**
Beale Street **17**
Belz Museum of Asian & Judaic Art **18**
Children's Museum of Memphis **23**
Church Park **22**
Cotton Museum of Memphis **16**
Graceland **9**
Historic Elmwood Cemetery **11**
Lichterman Nature Center **26**

Mason Temple **7**
Memphis Botanic Garden **24**
Memphis Brooks Museum of Art **12**
Memphis Fire Museum **2**
Memphis Rock 'n' Soul Museum **20**
Memphis River Boats **15**
Memphis Zoo and Aquarium **14**
Mud Island Mississippi River Museum **3**
National Civil Rights Museum **6**

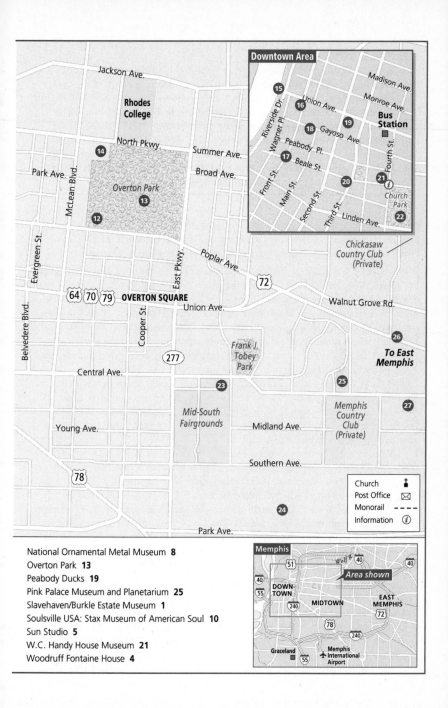

National Ornamental Metal Museum **8**
Overton Park **13**
Peabody Ducks **19**
Pink Palace Museum and Planetarium **25**
Slavehaven/Burkle Estate Museum **1**
Soulsville USA: Stax Museum of American Soul **10**
Sun Studio **5**
W.C. Handy House Museum **21**
Woodruff Fontaine House **4**

Ernest C. Withers

African-American Ernest C. Withers, 85, a respected photojournalist who documented Beale Street in the 1950s and most of the important events of the Civil Rights movement, died on Oct. 15, 2007. Known throughout the world for his black-and-white photographs of such martyrs as the Reverend Martin Luther King, Jr., Withers was one of Memphis' most beloved local figures. At his funeral, the Reverend Samuel Kyles emphasized Withers' significance in helping transform 20th-century attitudes: "It is said that a drop of water can knock holes in stone, not by violence but by oft-falling... (Withers' camera) knocked holes in the stones of ignorance—one click at a time."

---

launched their careers from Memphis include Muddy Waters, Albert King, Al Green, Otis Redding, Sam and Dave, Sam the Sham and the Pharaohs, and the Box Tops.

Below are the sites that music fans won't want to miss while in Memphis.

Beale Street 👁👁 *Moments*   To blues fans, Beale Street is the most important street in America. The musical form known as the blues—with roots that stretch back to the African musical heritage of slaves brought to the United States—was born here. W. C. Handy was performing on Beale Street when he penned "Memphis Blues," the first published blues song. Shortly after the Civil War, Beale Street became one of the most important streets in the South for African Americans. Many of the most famous musicians in the blues world got their starts here; besides Handy, other greats include B.B. King, Furry Lewis, Alberta Hunter, Rufus Thomas, and Isaac Hayes.

And the blues continues to thrive here. Today, though parts of downtown Memphis has been abandoned in favor of suburban sprawl, Beale Street continues to draw fans of blues and popular music, and nightclubs line the blocks between Second and Fourth streets. The Orpheum Theatre, once a vaudeville palace, is now the performance hall for Broadway road shows, and the New Daisy Theatre features performances by up-and-coming bands and once-famous performers. Historic markers up and down the street relate the area's colorful past, and two statues commemorate the city's two most important musicians: W. C. Handy and Elvis Presley. In addition to the many clubs featuring nightly live music (including B.B. King Blues Club and the Hard Rock Cafe), there's also a small often-overlooked museum, the W. C. Handy House—and the museum-like A. Schwab Dry Goods store. For an update of events, check out www.bealestreet.com. Allow a full afternoon to browse the shops and restaurants, or make a night of it if you're into barhopping and live music.

Belz Museum of Asian and Judaic Art   Founded in 1998 by world travelers and art lovers Jack and Marilyn Belz (he's the owner of The Peabody hotel empire), this unexpected downtown museum features pieces culled from the couple's extensive collection. Chinese art from the Qing and Tang dynasties include stunning silver boxes, imperial tomb figurines, ink-on-paper portraits, and intricate jade and ivory carvings. Alongside these treasures are European art objects, Russian lacquer boxes, as well as contemporary modern Jewish art.

119 S. Main St. ✆ **901/523-ARTS**. www.belzmuseum.org. $6 adults, $5 seniors, $4 students. Tues–Fri 10am–5:30pm; Sat–Sun noon–5pm.

Cotton Museum of Memphis   "Glorious and notorious." Both adjectives apply to the history of cotton, one of the most significant agricultural crops in the history of the Deep South. African slaves did the back-breaking labor of picking the cotton, while in downtown Memphis, wealthy merchants and brokers bought and sold the lucrative commodity that was loaded onto Mississippi River barges for shipment to the entire world. This interesting museum, on the site of the 1939 Memphis Cotton Exchange building, features exhibits that explore cotton's legacy and its importance to Memphis's growth.

65 Union Ave. (℃) 901/531-7826. www.cottonmuseumofmemphis.org. Admission $5 adults, $4.50 seniors, $4 students, $3 children 6–12.

Graceland 🏛🏛   It seems hard to believe, but Graceland, the former home of rock-'n'-roll-legend Elvis Presley and annually the destination of tens of thousands of love-struck pilgrims searching for the ghost of Elvis, is the second most visited home in America. Only the White House receives more visitors each year. A look around at the crowds waiting in various lines at this sprawling complex makes it clear that Elvis, through his many recordings, numerous movie roles, and countless concerts, appealed to a wide spectrum of people. Today, more than a quarter-century after Elvis's death, Graceland draws visitors of all ages from all over the world.

Purchased in the late 1950s for $100,000, Graceland today is Memphis's biggest attraction and resembles a small theme park or shopping mall in scope and design. There are his two personal jets, the Elvis Presley Automobile Museum, the Sincerely Elvis collection of Elvis's personal belongings, the *Walk a Mile in My Shoes* video, and, of course, guided tours of Graceland itself. If your time here is limited to only one thing, by all means, go for the mansion tour. It's the essence of the Big E. All the rest is just icing on Elvis's buttercream-frosted cake.

In late 2007 Graceland's owners announced plans for a massive expansion and renovation of the complex surrounding the mansion. As of this book's deadline, however, no start date had yet been announced. Until then, plan on being able to tour Elvis's office; his racquetball building; a small exhibit of personal belongings, memorabilia, and awards; a display of his many gold records; and finally, Elvis's grave (in the Meditation Garden). Then it's back across Elvis Presley Boulevard, where you can watch a film about The King and visit the other Graceland attractions. True fans will want to do it all.

The Elvis Presley Automobile Museum includes not only his famous 1955 pink Cadillac, a 1956 purple Cadillac convertible, and two Stutz Blackhawks from the early 1970s, but also motorcycles and other vehicles. Accompanying this collection are videos of Elvis's home movies and a fast-paced compilation of car-scene clips from dozens of Elvis movies, which are shown in a sort of drive-in-theater setting.

A re-creation of an airport terminal serves as the entrance to the *Lisa Marie* and *Hound Dog II* private jets. The former was once a regular Delta Air Lines passenger jet that was customized (at a cost of $800,000) after Elvis purchased it in 1975 for

---

(*Fun Fact*   **Elvis-in-Chief**

You probably already knew that former president Bill Clinton's U.S. Secret Service code name was "Elvis." Now The King and the Commander-in-Chief are further linked in history. Clinton's presidential library in Little Rock, Arkansas, features his personal collection of Elvis memorabilia. Most of the items are gifts given to the president during his two terms in the White House.

Elvis Trivia

- Elvis's first hit single was "Mystery Train." Recorded at Sun Studio, it made it to number one on the country charts in 1955.
- In 1956, Elvis became the second white person to have a number-one single on *Billboard*'s rhythm-and-blues chart. The song was "Don't Be Cruel." The B-side was "Hound Dog."
- Elvis's first million-selling single and gold record came in 1956, when he recorded "Heartbreak Hotel" as his first release for RCA.
- During his career, Elvis won three Grammy Awards, all of which were for gospel recordings. Two of these awards were for the same song—a studio version and a live version of "How Great Thou Art."
- Elvis made 31 films and sang in all but one of these. *Charro!*, a Western released in 1969, was the only movie in which he didn't break into song at some point.
- The soundtrack to Elvis's movie *GI Blues* was on the album chart for a total of 111 weeks, 10 of which were at number one. This was his first movie after returning from service in the army.
- Highway 51 South, which runs past the gates of Graceland, was renamed Elvis Presley Boulevard in 1971, while Elvis was still alive.
- Elvis's first network-television appearance came in January of 1956 when he appeared on *Stage Show*, which was hosted by Tommy and Jimmy Dorsey.
- On a night in 1975, Bruce Springsteen, hoping to meet Elvis, jumped the fence at Graceland and ran up to the house. Unfortunately, Elvis wasn't at home, and the guards escorted Springsteen off the property.
- The King holds the record for sold-out shows in Vegas: 837 performances at the Las Vegas Hilton over a 10-year period.
- In 2003, an Elvis CD featuring his 30 number-one hits was released and became an international success. To date, sales have reached triple platinum.
- Elvis has sold more than a billion records worldwide, according to some industry estimates. That's more than any other act in recorded history.

$250,000. The *Hound Dog II* is much smaller and was purchased after the *Lisa Marie* was acquired.

"Sincerely Elvis" is Graceland's most revealing exhibit. This is a collection of many of Elvis's personal belongings. Here you'll see everything from some of Elvis's personal record collection (including albums by Tom Jones and Ray Charles) to a pair of his sneakers. One exhibit displays gifts sent to Elvis by fans. Included are quilts, needlepoint, and even a plaque made from woven chewing gum wrappers.

The Graceland exhibits strive to reveal Elvis the man and Elvis the star. Some of the surprising facts passed on to visitors include these: Elvis was an avid reader and always traveled with lots of books; Elvis didn't like the taste of alcohol; among his favorite movies were *Blazing Saddles* and the films of Monty Python.

Throughout the year there are several special events at Graceland. Elvis's birthday (Jan 8, 1935) is celebrated each year with several days of festivities. However, mid-August's Elvis Week, commemorating his death on August 16, 1977, boasts the greatest Elvis celebrations both here at Graceland and throughout Memphis. Each year from Thanksgiving until January 8, Graceland is decorated with Elvis's original Christmas lights and lawn decorations.

Early risers should be aware that most mornings it is possible to visit Elvis's grave before Graceland officially opens. This special free walk-up period is daily from 7:30 to 8:30am. If you're buying a ticket for the whole shebang, allow at least 2 to 3 hours or more (depending upon your devotion to the King).

3734 Elvis Presley Blvd. ⓒ 800/238-2000 or 901/332-3322. www.elvis.com. Graceland Mansion Tour $27 adults; $24 seniors and students; $10 children 7–12. The Platinum Tour (includes admission to all Graceland attractions, including Elvis's Automobile Museum, tours of Elvis's custom jets [the *Lisa Marie* and *Hound Dog II*], and Sincerely Elvis film presentation) $32 adults; $29 seniors; $15 children 7–12. Graceland Elvis Entourage VIP Tour (includes the "Elvis After Dark" exhibit) $68 for all ages. Tour reservations can be made 24 hrs. in advance and are recommended if you have a tight schedule. Mar–Oct Mon–Sat 9am–5pm, Sun 10am–4pm; Nov–Feb 10am–4pm daily. (Dec–Feb mansion tour does not operate Tues). Closed Thanksgiving, Dec 25, and Jan 1. Take Bellevue South (which turns into Elvis Presley Blvd.) south a few miles of downtown, past Winchester Ave. Graceland is on the left.

Memphis Rock 'N' Soul Museum ⓕ

With rare recordings and videos, archival photographs and interactive multimedia displays, the past century of American popular music is presented in "Social Crossroads," the first exhibition ever presented by the Smithsonian Institution outside of Washington, D.C. From field hollers and gospel hymns to the turn-of-the-century blues of W. C. Handy, it's all here. Narrated tours on portable audio players allow visitors to customize their tours and musical selections. And with each new artist, from Otis Redding and Al Green to Earth, Wind & Fire, Memphis shines. Allow an hour.

191 Beale St. ⓒ 901/205-2533. www.memphisrocknsoul.org. Admission $10 adults, $7 children 5–17. Daily 10am–7pm (last tour starts at 6:15pm). Downtown at the new FedEx Forum arena, a half-block south of Beale and Third sts.

Soulsville USA: Stax Museum of American Soul Music ★★★ *Moments*

Groove on down to Soulsville USA, one of the city's best attractions, which celebrates Memphis soul music. Opened in spring 2003, the museum sits near the site of the original (sadly, long-ago demolished) Stax recording studio, which during the 1960s and 1970s cranked out world-famous hits by Otis Redding; Booker T and the MGs; The Bar-Kays; Al Green; Aretha Franklin; Earth, Wind & Fire; and others. Don't miss Isaac Hayes's (of *Shaft* and *South Park* fame) gold-plated, shag-carpeted *Superfly* Cadillac, which is on display. First-rate multimedia exhibitions, beginning with a thrilling video introduction in a darkened theater, take visitors back to a place and time when

---

Fun Fact The Men Who Would be King

2007 was the first year Graceland sanctioned an impersonators' competition, dubbed the Ultimate Elvis Tribute Artist Contest. Stakes were high as competitors tried to hip-shake and out-snarl each other: The winner received $5,000 cash, a $5,000 Graceland shopping spree, and both a recording session at Memphis's Sun Records (where Elvis got his big break in the 1950s) as well as a contract to perform on a cruise ship.

racism deeply divided the South. Stax, however, was an anomaly, a virtually colorblind collaborative where black and white musicians, staff, and studio executives worked together in a shared musical passion. At interactive kiosks, you'll get a chance to hear hundreds of songs and watch archival video. Stax ties to Elvis, The Beatles, and Elton John are mentioned. Elsewhere, Aerosmith, Elvis Costello, U2's Bono and scores of others offer heartfelt tributes to the lasting legacy of Stax (and Memphis's Sun) recording studios. Allow at least 90 minutes—or an entire afternoon, if you're a true soul sister—to tour the museum. And if the spirit moves, you can also cut loose on its psychedelic dance floor.

926 E. McLemore Ave. ℭ 901/946-2535. www.soulsvilleusa.com. Admission $10 adults, $9 seniors, $7 children ages 9–12, free for children 8 and under with paid adult or senior admission. Mar–Oct Mon–Sat 9am–4pm, Sun 1–4pm; Nov–Feb Mon–Sat 10am–4pm, Sun 1–4pm. Closed major holidays. Take Danny Thomas Blvd. south to Mississippi Blvd. Turn left onto Mississippi Blvd., then left on E. McLemore Ave.

Sun Studio ⧀⧀   If Elvis Aaron Presley hadn't come to Sun Studio in the early 1950s to record a song as a birthday present for his mother (so the story goes), musical history today might be very different. Owner and recording engineer Sam Phillips first recorded, in the early 1950s, such local artists as Elvis Presley, Jerry Lee Lewis, Roy Orbison, and Carl Perkins, who together created a sound that would shortly become known as rock 'n' roll. Over the years Phillips also helped start the recording careers of the blues greats B.B. King and Howlin' Wolf and country giant Johnny Cash. By night, Sun Studio is still an active recording studio and has been used by such artists as U2, Spin Doctors, The Tractors, and Bonnie Raitt. The place has great vibes, and for those who know their music history, touching Elvis's microphone will be a thrill beyond measure. However, if you aren't well-versed in this particular area of pop culture, a visit to this one-themed Sun Studio may leave you wondering what all the fuss is about. Allow an hour.

706 Union Ave. (at Marshall Ave.) ℭ 800/441-6249 or 901/521-0664. www.sunstudio.com. Admission $10 adults, free for children under 12 accompanied by parent. Daily 10am–6pm (studio tours conducted on the hour, 10:30am–5:30pm). Closed some holidays.

W. C. Handy House Museum *Finds*   A far cry from the opulence of Graceland, this tiny clapboard shotgun shack was once the Memphis home of the bluesman W. C. Handy—"the father of the blues"—and was where he was living when he wrote "Beale Street Blues" and "Memphis Blues." Although the house has only a small collection of Handy memorabilia and artifacts, there are numerous evocative old photos displayed, and the commentary provided by the museum guide is always highly informative. The tour lasts about 20 minutes.

352 Beale St. (at Fourth Ave.). ℭ 901/527-3427. Admission $3 adults, $2 children. Summer Tues–Sat 10am–5pm; winter Tues–Sat 11am–4pm.

Fun Fact Chef's Salad Days

Long before he garnered fame at Stax recording studio in Memphis, before the *Theme from Shaft* won him an Academy Award, and way before his gig as the voice of *South Park*'s beloved character Chef made him a household name for a whole new generation of fans . . . Isaac Hayes was a shoeshine boy on Beale Street.

Elvis Beyond the Gates of Graceland

You've come to Memphis on a pilgrimage and spent the entire day at Graceland. You've cried, you've laughed, you've bought a whole suitcase full of Elvis souvenirs, but still you want more of Elvis. No problem. Elvis is everywhere in Memphis.

If you're a hard-core Elvis fan and plan to visit his grave during the early-morning free visitation period at Graceland, you'll want to find a hotel as close to the mansion as possible. Directly across the street from Graceland are two properties that cater specifically to Elvis fans. Both the **Heartbreak Hotel–Graceland** and the **Days Inn at Graceland** offer round-the-clock, free, in-room Elvis videos. The former hotel actually has a pathway into the Graceland parking lot, while the latter motel has a guitar-shaped swimming pool.

Also, if you can, plan your visit for dates around Elvis's January 8 birthday festivities or during **Elvis Week,** which commemorates his death on August 16. During these festivities, you might catch an all-Elvis concert by the Memphis Symphony Orchestra, the *Taking Care of Business* Elvis-tribute ballet by Ballet Memphis, or the Elvis laser-light show at the Sharpe Planetarium in the **Pink Palace Museum.**

Any time of year, you can visit **Sun Studio,** the recording studio that discovered Elvis and where he made his first recordings. Though the studio isn't very large, its musical history is enough to give people goose bumps and bring tears to their eyes. A highlight of a visit here is a chance to actually touch the microphone that Elvis used to make his first recordings. The late Sam Phillips (who died in 2003), once brought his new musicians here to sign contracts, and this is where Elvis most certainly whiled away many hours. For a tongue-in-cheek tribute to Elvis, check out the coin-operated shrine to the King at the **Center for Southern Folklore** (p. 234) in Pembroke Square downtown. In Midtown, take a 20-minute tour that details Elvis Presley's connection with the historic Memphian Theater. Find out which movies Elvis used to watch here with his entourage, and hear stories about his visits. Tickets are $5; for reservations, call Playhouse on the Square at ✆ **901/725-0776.**

To visit the spots around town where Elvis once walked, book a tour with **American Dream Safari** (✆ **901/527-8870**), which tools guests around town in a 1955 Cadillac to see such Elvis haunts as Humes High School, Poplar Tunes, Sun Studio, and the housing project where he lived as a teenager.

2 Nonmusical Memphis Attractions

MUSEUMS

Art Museum of the University of Memphis   Memphis takes its name from the ancient capital of Egypt, and here in the Art Museum of the University of Memphis you can view artifacts from ancient Memphis. An outstanding collection of Egyptian art and artifacts makes this one of the most interesting museums in Memphis. Among the items on display is a loaf of bread dating from between 2134 B.C. and 1786 B.C. A hieroglyph-covered sarcophagus contains the mummy of Iret-Iruw, who died around

2,200 years ago. Numerous works of art and funerary objects show the high level of skill achieved by ancient Egyptian artists. In addition to the Egyptian exhibit, there is a small collection of West African masks and woodcarvings, and changing exhibitions in the main gallery. Allow 30 minutes to an hour. Tip: Your best bet for parking on campus is the Fogelman Executive Center garage, which costs about $1 an hour.

3750 Norriswood St., CFA Building, Room 142. (✆) **800/669-2678** or 901/678-2224. www.amum.org. Free admission. Mon–Sat 9am–5pm. Closed university holidays and for changing exhibitions. Turn south off of Central Ave. onto Deloach St. (between Patterson and Zach Curlin sts.) to Norriswood St.

Dixon Gallery & Gardens ⭐

The South's finest collection of French and American Impressionist and post-Impressionist artworks is the highlight of this exquisite museum, set on 17 wooded acres. The museum, art collection, and surrounding 17 acres of formal and informal gardens once belonged to Margaret and Hugo Dixon, who were avid art collectors. After the deaths of the Dixons, their estate opened to the public as an art museum and has since become one of Memphis's most important museums. The permanent collection includes works by Henri Matisse, Pierre Auguste Renoir, Edgar Degas, Paul Gauguin, Mary Cassatt, J. M. W. Turner, and John Constable. With strong local support, the museum frequently hosts temporary exhibits of international caliber. Twice a year, the Memphis Symphony Orchestra performs outdoor concerts in the Dixon's formal gardens. Allow an hour for the museum, and more time for the gardens.

4339 Park Ave. (✆) **901/761-5250**. www.dixon.org. Admission $7 adults, $5 seniors and students, $3 for children 7–17. Tues–Fri 10am–4pm; Sat 10am–5pm; Sun 1–5pm. Located adjacent to Audubon Park, off Park Ave. at Cherry Rd. (between Getwell Rd. and Perkins Rd.).

Memphis Brooks Museum of Art

First opened in 1916 as the Brooks Memorial Art Gallery, this is the oldest art museum in Tennessee; it contains one of the largest art collections of any museum in the mid-South. With more than 7,000 pieces in the permanent collection, the Brooks frequently rotates works on display. The museum's emphasis is on European and American art of the 18th through the 20th centuries, with a very respectable collection of Italian Renaissance and baroque paintings and sculptures as well. Some of the museum's more important works include pieces by Auguste Rodin, Pierre Auguste Renoir, Thomas Hart Benton, and Frank Lloyd Wright. Take a break from strolling through the museum with a stop in the Brushmark Restaurant. Allow an hour to 90 minutes.

Overton Park, 1934 Poplar Ave. (between N. McLean Blvd. and E. Parkway N.). (✆) **901/544-6200**. www.brooks museum.org. Admission $12 adults, $10 seniors, $6 students, free for children under 6. Tues–Wed and Fri 10am–4pm; Thurs 10am–8pm; Sat 10am–5pm; Sun 11:30am–5pm.

Mud Island River Park (Kids)

Mud Island is more than just a museum. The 52-acre park on Mud Island is home to several attractions, including the **River Walk** and the **Mississippi River Museum.** If you have seen any pre-1900 photos of the Memphis waterfront, you may have noticed that Mud Island is missing from the photos. This island first appeared in 1900 and became permanent in 1913. In 1916, the island joined with the mainland just north of the mouth of the Wolf River, but a diversion canal was dug through the island to maintain a free channel in the Wolf River.

To learn all about the river, you can follow a 5-block-long scale model of 900 miles of the Mississippi River. Called the **River Walk,** the model is complete with flowing water, street plans of cities and towns along the river, and informative panels that include information on the river and its history.

On Mud Island you can rent bicycles, kayaks, and paddleboats (the latter two are not for use on the Mississippi River itself, of course) by the hour or half day, allowing plenty of time for a leisurely exploration of the area. Evenings during the summer, the **Mud Island Amphitheater** hosts touring acts along the likes of Jimmy Buffett, Norah Jones, and Rob Thomas. Allow an hour, or make a day of it.

125 N. Front St. (at Adams Ave.). ⓒ 800/507-6507 or 901/576-7241. www.mudisland.com. Mississippi River Museum $8 adults, $6 seniors, $5 children 5–12; grounds only free. Summer daily 10am–8pm; spring and fall daily 10am–5pm; closed Mondays. Closed Nov–Mar. To reach Mud Island, take the monorail from Front St. at Adams Ave.

National Civil Rights Museum 🌟🌟🌟 *Moments*   Dr. Martin Luther King, Jr., came to Memphis in early April of 1968 in support of the city's striking garbage collectors. He checked into the Lorraine Motel as he always did when visiting Memphis. On April 4, he stepped out onto the balcony outside his room and was shot dead by James Earl Ray. The assassination of King struck a horrible blow to the American civil rights movement and incited riots in cities across the country. However, despite the murder of the movement's most important leader, African Americans continued to struggle for the equal rights that were guaranteed to them under the U.S. Constitution.

Saved from demolition, the Lorraine Motel was remodeled and today serves as the nation's memorial to the civil rights movement. In evocative displays, the museum chronicles the struggle of African Americans from the time of slavery to the present. Multimedia presentations and life-size, walk-through tableaux include historic exhibits: a Montgomery, Alabama, public bus like the one on which Rosa Parks was riding when she refused to move to the back of the bus; a Greensboro, North Carolina, lunch counter; and the burned shell of a freedom-ride Greyhound bus. Allow 2 to 3 hours.

450 Mulberry St. (at Huling Ave.). ⓒ 901/521-9699. www.civilrightsmuseum.org. Admission $12 adults, $10 seniors and students, $8.50 children 4–17, free for children under 4. Daily 9am–5pm; closed Tuesday.

National Ornamental Metal Museum 🌟 *Finds*   Set on parklike grounds on a bluff overlooking the Mississippi, this small museum is dedicated to ornamental metalworking in all its forms. There are sculptures displayed around the museum's gardens, a working blacksmith shop, and examples of ornamental wrought-iron grillwork such as that seen on balconies in New Orleans. Sculptural metal pieces and jewelry are also prominently featured both in the museum's permanent collection and in temporary exhibits. Be sure to take a look at the ornate museum gates. They were created by 160 metalsmiths from 17 countries and feature a fascinating array of imaginative rosettes. Just across the street is a community park that includes an ancient Native American mound. Allow 1 hour or more.

374 Metal Museum Dr. ⓒ 877/881-2326 or 901/774-6380. www.metalmuseum.org. Admission $5 adults, $4 seniors, $3 students and children 5–18, free for children under 5. Tues–Sat 10am–5pm; Sun noon–5pm. Closed 1 week between exhibit changes and the week between Christmas and New Year's. Take Crump Blvd. or I-55 toward the Memphis-Arkansas Bridge and get off at exit 12-C (Metal Museum Dr.), which is the last exit in Tennessee; the museum is 2 blocks south.

Pink Palace Museum 🌟 *Kids*   "The Pink Palace" was the name locals gave to the ostentatious pink-marble mansion that grocery store magnate Clarence Saunders built shortly after World War I. It was Saunders who had revolutionized grocery shopping with the opening of the first Piggly Wiggly self-service market in 1916. Unfortunately, Saunders went bankrupt before he ever finished his "Pink Palace," and the building was acquired by the city of Memphis for use as a museum of cultural and natural history.

Among the exhibits here is a full-scale reproduction of the maze of aisles that con-stituted an original Piggly Wiggly. Other walk-through exhibits include a pre–Piggly Wiggly general store and an old-fashioned pharmacy with a soda fountain. Memphis is a major medical center; accordingly, this museum has an extensive medical-history exhibit. On the lighter side, kids enjoy such exhibits as a life-size mechanical tricer-atops, a real mastodon skeleton, and a hand-carved miniature circus that goes into ani-mated action. In the planetarium, there are frequently changing astronomy programs as well as rock-'n'-roll laser shows (the annual August Elvis laser show is the most popu-lar). There is also an IMAX movie theater here. Allow 1 to 2 hours.

3050 Central Ave. (between Hollywood and Highland). ✆ 901/320-6320, or 901/763-IMAX for IMAX schedule. www.memphismuseums.org. Museum $7.25 adults, $6.75 seniors, $5.75 children 3–12, free for children under 3. IMAX $8 adults, $7.25 seniors, $6.25 children 3–12. Combination tickets available. Call for IMAX showtimes. Museum hours Mon–Sat 9am–5pm; Sun noon–5pm.

HISTORIC BUILDINGS

Slavehaven Underground Railroad Museum/Burkle Estate *(Finds*   Secret tun-nels and trap doors evoke a period before the Civil War when this house was a stop on the underground railroad used by runaway slaves in their quest for freedom. The house is filled with 19th-century furnishings and has displays of artifacts from slavery days. Takes about an hour to get through the house.

826 N. Second Ave. (between Chelsea and Bicknell aves.). ✆ 901/527-3427. Admission $6 adults, $4 students. Sum-mer Mon–Sat 10am–4pm; winter Wed–Sat 10am–4pm.

Woodruff-Fontaine House   Located in a downtown neighborhood known as Vic-torian Village, the Woodruff-Fontaine House displays an equally elaborate Victorian aesthetic, in this case influenced by French architectural styles. Built in 1870, the fully restored 16-room home houses period furnishings. Mannequins throughout the house display the fashions of the late 19th century. Allow 30 minutes.

Victorian Village, 680 Adams Ave. ✆ 901/526-1469. Admission $10 adults, $8 seniors, $6 students. Wed–Sun noon–3:30pm. Guided tours every 30 min. Between Neely and New Orleans sts. next to Mallory-Neely House.

OTHER MEMPHIS ATTRACTIONS

Chucalissa Archaeological Museum *(Kids*   The Chucalissa Archaeological Museum is built on the site of a Mississippian-period (A.D. 900–1600) Native Ameri-can village. Dioramas and displays of artifacts discovered in the area provide a cultural history of Mississippi River Valley Native Americans. The reconstructed village includes several family dwellings, a shaman's hut, and a chief's temple atop a mound in the center of the village compound. The chance to walk through a real archaeolo-gist's trench and to explore a Native American village thrills most children. Allow 1 to 2 hours.

1987 Indian Village Dr. ✆ 901/785-3160. www.chucalissa.org. Admission $5 adults, $3 seniors and children 4–11, free for children under 4. Tues–Sat 9am–5pm; Sun 1–5pm. South of Memphis off U.S. 61 and adjacent to the T. O. Fuller State Park.

Memphis Zoo & Aquarium *(★★ (Kids*   A pair of adorable panda bears from China are the top draw these days at this increasingly appreciated tourist attraction. Mem-phis's Egyptian heritage is once again called upon in the imposing and unusual entranceway. Built to resemble an ancient Egyptian temple, the zoo's entry is covered with traditional and contemporary hieroglyphics. A recently completed $30-million renovation has added a 5-acre primate habitat, an exhibit of nocturnal animals, and

Pyramid or White Elephant?

On North Riverside Drive at the base of the Hernando-Desoto Bridge to Arkansas you'll see this 32-story, stainless-steel landmark. Built in the early 1990s in honor of Memphis's Egyptian namesake, the long-vacant former concert arena and sports venue is reportedly being eyed as a potential new location for retail giant Bass Pro Shops.

an extensive big-cat area with habitats that are among the best zoo exhibits in the country. The new Northwest Passage exhibit features polar bears, seals, and sea lions. In addition to the regular admission, there is a nominal fee to see the pandas in the China exhibit. Allow 2 hours or more.

Overton Park, 2000 Prentiss Place. ℂ 901/276-WILD. www.memphiszoo.org. Admission $13 adults, $12 seniors, $8 children 2–11. Admission free to Tennessee residents Tues 2pm to close. Parking $3 during summer season. Mar 1 to last Sat in Oct daily 9am–6pm; last Sun in Oct to Feb daily 9am–5pm. Located inside Overton Park off of Poplar Ave. (2000 block) between N. McLean Blvd. and E. Parkway N.

PARKS & GARDENS

In downtown Memphis, between Main Street and Second Avenue and between Madison and Jefferson avenues, you'll find **Court Square,** the oldest park in Memphis. With its classically designed central fountain, restored gazebo, and stately old shade trees, this park was long a favored gathering spot of Memphians. Numerous historic plaques around the park relate the many important events that have taken place in Court Square. (Hint: Don't sit here and expect to enjoy a snack or picnic lunch—you'll be accosted by dive-bombing pigeons and aggressive, overweight squirrels.)

A block to the west, you'll find **Jefferson Davis Park,** which overlooks Mud Island and Riverside Drive. Several Civil War cannons face out toward the river from this small park. Below Jefferson Davis Park, along Riverside Drive, you'll find **Tom Lee Park,** which stretches for 1½ miles south along the bank of the Mississippi and is named after a local African-American hero who died saving 32 people when a steamer sank in the Mississippi in 1925—even though he, himself, could not swim. This park is a favorite of joggers and is the site of various festivals, including the big Memphis in May celebration. A parallel park called **Riverbluff Walkway** is the newest development atop the bluff on the east side of Riverside Drive. And just north of The Pyramid in Harbor Town, an exclusive, 950-home planned community neighborhood (similar to Seaside and Celebration FL), lies **Greenbelt Park.** Its tree-shaded trails and pristine picnic area offers the city's most picturesque, unspoiled views of the Mississippi River.

Located in Midtown and bounded by Poplar Avenue, East Parkway North, North Parkway, and North McLean Boulevard, **Overton Park** is one of Memphis's largest parks and includes not only the Memphis Zoo and Aquarium, but the Memphis Brooks Museum of Art, the Memphis College of Art, and the Overton Park Municipal Golf Course, as well as tennis courts, hiking and biking trails, and an open-air theater. The park's large, old shade trees make this a cool place to spend an afternoon in the summer, and the surrounding residential neighborhoods are some of the wealthiest in the city.

Historic Elmwood Cemetery   Victims of war, disease, and natural causes are buried in this historic garden cemetery on the outskirts of downtown Memphis. Dating back to 1852, the majestic, 80-acre sanctuary is brimming with elaborate marble sculptures, simple headstones, and towering shade trees. Take a guided tour or stroll the grounds alone to get a sense of the city's rich history. Descendants such as 1920s bandleader Jimmie Lunceford, Civil War historian and author Shelby Foote, and African-American Civil Rights photographer Ernest Withers are laid to rest here. Most haunting, however, is "No Man's Land," public lots marking the gravesites of 1,500 victims of the 1878 yellow fever epidemic. Maps are available in the Victorian Garden Cottage that serves as the Visitors Center.

824 South Dudley St. ℂ 901/774-3212. www.elmwoodcemetery.org. Free admission (donations accepted). Grounds open daily 8am–4:30pm; office closed Saturday at noon and Sunday.

Lichterman Nature Center   Often overlooked by tourists, this well-maintained, wooded nature preserve in the heart of East Memphis is one of Memphis' most family-friendly attractions. Open year-round, the center offers hiking trails, scientific demonstrations, and other hands-on activities on 65 acres and within its museum-like Backyard Wildlife Center. With a grassy meadow and lake as well as woods, there are plenty of educational opportunities for learning about various wildlife habitats. Lichterman is part of the Memphis Museum System, which also includes the Pink Palace and other sites.

5992 Quince Rd. ℂ 901/767-7322. www.memphismuseums.org. $6 adults, $5.50 seniors, $4.50 children (ages 3–12). Tues–Thurs 9am–4pm; Fri–Sat 9am–5pm.

Memphis Botanic Garden ⚘   With 20 formal gardens covering 96 acres, this rather large botanical garden requires a bit of time to visit properly. You'll find something in bloom at almost any time of year, and even in winter the Japanese garden offers a tranquil setting for a quiet stroll. In April and May, the Ketchum Memorial Iris Garden, one of the largest in the country, is in bloom, and during May, June, and September the Municipal Rose Garden is alive with color. A special Sensory Garden is designed for people with disabilities and has plantings that stimulate all five senses. A Children's Garden for toddlers and youngsters with special needs is also in the works. The 4-acre garden, which will include a water feature, is expected to open by fall 2009. Allow at least an hour.

Audubon Park, 750 Cherry Rd. ℂ 901/576-4100. www.memphisbotanicgarden.com. Admission $5 adults, $4 seniors and students, $3 children. Mar–Oct Mon–Sat 9am–6pm, Sun 11am–6pm; Nov–Feb Mon–Sat 9am–4:30pm, Sun 11am–4:30pm. Located across from Audubon Park Golf Course on Cherry Rd., between Southern and Park aves.

3 African-American Heritage in Memphis

For many people, the city of Memphis is synonymous with one of the most significant, and saddest, events in recent American history—the assassination of Dr. Martin Luther King, Jr. The Lorraine Motel, where King was staying when he was shot, has in the years since the assassination become the **National Civil Rights Museum** (p. 205).

Long before the civil rights movement brought King to Memphis, the city had already become one of the most important cities in the South for blacks. After the Civil War and the abolition of slavery, Memphis became a magnet for African Americans, who came here seeking economic opportunities. **Beale Street** (p. 198) was where they headed to start their search. Beale Street's most famous citizen was W. C. Handy, the father of the blues, who first put down on paper the blues born in the cotton fields of the Mississippi Delta. **W. C. Handy Park,** with its statue of the famous blues musician, is about halfway down Beale Street, and Handy's small house, now the

(Fun Fact **Native Singing Son**

Grammy-winning pop star Justin Timberlake's latest venture is a record label named for his home state: Tennman Records. The former Mouseketeer and 'N Sync teen idol is from the north-Memphis suburb of Millington.

W. C. Handy House Museum (p. 202), is also now on Beale Street. At the **Memphis Rock 'N' Soul Museum** (p. 201), just a block off Beale Street, you can learn more about Handy and other famous African-American blues musicians who found a place for their music. Best of all is the **Soulsville USA: Stax Museum of American Soul Music** (p. 201), which has been drawing rave reviews since it opened a few years ago in a resurgent South Memphis neighborhood. Another museum with exhibits on famous black musicians is the **Pink Palace Museum and Planetarium** (p. 205).

Church Park, on the corner of Beale and Fourth streets (and once the site of a large auditorium), was established by Robert R. Church, a former slave and Memphis businessman who became the city's first black millionaire. The park was a gathering place for African Americans in the early 1900s, when restrictive Jim Crow laws segregated city parks.

Gospel music was part of the inspiration for the blues that W. C. Handy wrote, and that music came from the churches of the black community. The tradition of rousing musical accompaniment in church continues at many of the city's churches, but none is more famous than the **Full Gospel Tabernacle,** 787 Hale Rd. (© 901/396-9192), which is where one-time soul-music star Al Green now takes to the pulpit as a minister. Sunday service is at 11am. **Mason Temple Church of God in Christ,** 930 Mason St. (© 901/947-9300), is the international headquarters of the Church of God in Christ and was where Dr. Martin Luther King, Jr., gave his "I've been to the mountaintop" speech shortly before his death.

If you'd like a guide to lead you through the most important sites in Memphis's African-American heritage, contact **Heritage Tours** (© 901/527-3427; www.heritagetoursmemphis.com), which offers both a 1-hour Beale Street Walking Tour ($5) and 3- to 4-hour Memphis Black Heritage Tours ($25 adults, $15–$20 youths). Heritage Tours also operates both the W. C. Handy House Museum and the Slavehaven/Burkle Estate Museum.

Heritage Tours also visits another worthwhile out-of-town attraction, the **Alex Haley House Museum** (© 731/738-2240). If you prefer to go on your own, it's a pleasant day trip by car to reach the small town of Henning, about 45 miles north of downtown Memphis on U.S. 51. The home is now a museum containing memorabilia and old portraits of the Haley family. Nearby is the family burial site, where Haley (author of *Roots: The Saga of an American Family*) and many of his ancestors, including Chicken George, are buried. The museum is open Tuesday to Saturday 10am to 5pm and Sunday 1 to 5pm. Admission is $5 for adults and $3 for students.

4 Especially for Kids

Many of Memphis's main attractions will appeal to children as well as to adults, but there are also places that are specifically geared toward kids. In addition to the attractions listed below, see also the Pink Palace Museum and Planetarium (p. 205), the Memphis Zoo and Aquarium (p. 206), the Chucalissa Archaeological Museum

(p. 206), the Mud Island/Mississippi River Museum (p. 204), and the Peabody Ducks (p. 165).

ATTRACTIONS FOR KIDS

Children's Museum of Memphis ⊛   Located adjacent to the Liberty Bowl Memorial Stadium, the children's museum offers fun, hands-on activities that can be enjoyed by children and adults alike. A real fire engine invites climbing, while the museum's kid-sized city lets little ones act like grown-ups: They can go shopping for groceries, stop by the bank to cash a check, or climb up through a 22-foot-tall skyscraper. Special traveling exhibitions are often booked at the museum, so call ahead to find out what special programs are being offered during your stay. Allow 2 to 3 hours.

2525 Central Ave. ℭ 901/458-2678. www.cmom.com. Admission $7 adults, $6 seniors and children 1–12. Tues–Sat 9am–5pm; Sun noon–5pm. Closed some holidays. Between Airways and Hollywood.

Golf and Games Family Park   Located on the east side of town just off I-40 at exit 12A, this miniature golf and games complex claims to be the largest of its kind in the world; whether or not that claim is true, your kids will find plenty to do. There are more than 50 holes of miniature golf, a driving range, baseball batting cages, a go-kart track, swimming pool, video game room, and picnic tables. A laser-tag arena is also an option. Allow 2 to 3 hours.

> ⟮ **Fun Fact** **Fields of Greens**
>
> In 1966, a soybean field was reborn as the world's largest golf-and-games family park, Memphis Golf and Games.

5484 Summer Ave. (at Pleasant View Rd.). ℭ 901/386-2992. www.golfandgamesmemphis.com. All-day wristband $25. Sun–Thurs 8am–11pm; Fri–Sat 8am–1am. (Closes 1 hr. earlier during school year).

Memphis Fire Museum   Billed as the only fire museum in the country that combines history along with an interactive fire-safety educational program, this often-overlooked kids' attraction has lots to offer, and safety lessons to teach. Highlights include a talking horse and a simulation that allows visitors to feel like they are standing inside of a burning house. Though far from being a 'thrill-ride' experience, parents should keep in mind that the scene, which includes a sofa bursting into flames and a rise in temperature as the fire engulfs the house, may be too intense for easily frightened youngsters.

118 Adams St. ℭ 901/320-5650. www.firemuseum.com. $6 adults, $5 children 3–12. Mon–Sat 9am–5pm.

WALKING TOUR   **DOWNTOWN MEMPHIS**

Start:	**The Peabody Memphis hotel, on the corner of Union Avenue and Second Street.**
Finish:	**Carter Seed Store, at the corner of Front Street and Union Avenue.**
Time:	**Approximately 2 hours, not including time spent at museums, shopping, meals, and other stops. It's best to plan on spending the whole day doing this walking tour.**
Best Times:	**Spring and fall, when the weather isn't so muggy, and Friday and Saturday, when The Rendezvous is open for lunch.**
Worst Times:	**Summer days, when the weather is just too muggy for doing this much walking. Be mindful of safety, and don't attempt this walking tour after dark.**

Walking Tour: Downtown Memphis

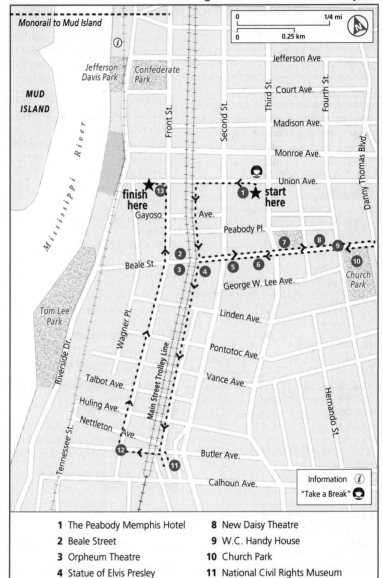

1 The Peabody Memphis Hotel
2 Beale Street
3 Orpheum Theatre
4 Statue of Elvis Presley
5 B.B. King's Blues Club
6 A. Schwab's Dry Goods Store
7 W.C. Handy Park

8 New Daisy Theatre
9 W.C. Handy House
10 Church Park
11 National Civil Rights Museum
12 Cotton Row
13 Carter Seed Store

Start your tour of Memphis's main historic districts at the posh:

❶ Peabody Memphis hotel

This is the home of the famous Peabody ducks, which spend their days contentedly floating on the water of a marble fountain in the hotel's lobby. The ducks make their grand, red-carpet entrance each morning at 11am (and the crowds of onlookers begin assembling before 10:30am).

TAKE A BREAK

By the time the crowds thin out and you've had a chance to ogle The Peabody's elegant lobby, you may already be thinking about lunch. If it's a Friday or Saturday, you can fortify yourself at **The Rendezvous**, 52 S. Second St., one of Memphis's favorite barbecue spots.

From The Peabody, walk 1 block west to Main Street, which is a pedestrian mall down which runs an old-fashioned trolley. Turn left, and in 2 blocks you'll come to:

---

❷ Beale Street

Which is where W. C. Handy made the blues the first original American music when he committed "Memphis Blues" to paper. Today, this street of restored buildings is Memphis's main evening-entertainment district.

On the corner of Main and Beale, you can't miss the:

❸ Orpheum Theatre

Originally built as a vaudeville theater in 1928, the Orpheum features a classic theater marquee and beautiful interior decor. Today, it's Memphis's main performing-arts center.

Across Main Street from the theater stands a:

❹ Statue of Elvis Presley

A visit to this statue is a must for Elvis fans. Bring your camera.

Continuing east on Beale Street to the corner of Second Street will bring you to:

❺ B.B. King Blues Club & Grill

Named for the Beale Street Blues Boy himself, this is the most popular club on the street, and though B.B. King only plays here twice a year, there is still great live blues here almost every night.

A few doors down the street, you'll come to the:

❻ A. Schwab Dry Goods Store

This store has been in business at this location since 1876, and once inside, you may think that nothing has changed since the day the store opened. You'll find an amazing array of the odd and the unusual.

At Beale and Third streets, you can take a breather in:

❼ W. C. Handy Park

There always seems to be some live music in this park, also the site of a statue of Handy.

A block south along Beale Street from this park you'll find the:

❽ New Daisy Theatre

This is a popular venue for contemporary music, including rock, blues, and folk.

A few doors down from the New Daisy, you'll find the restored:

❾ W. C. Handy House

Though it wasn't always on this site, this house was where Handy lived when making a name for himself on Beale Street.

Diagonally across the intersection is:

❿ Church Park

Robert Church, a former slave who became the city's first African-American millionaire, gave the African-American citizens of Memphis this park in 1899.

Now head back up Beale Street and take a left on Main. This is the street down which the trolley runs, so if you're feeling tired, you can hop on the trolley and take it south a few blocks. If you walk, turn left on Butler Street, and if you ride, walk east on Calhoun Street. In a very short block, you'll come to the:

⓫ National Civil Rights Museum

Once the Lorraine Motel, it was here that Dr. Martin Luther King, Jr., was assassinated on April 4, 1968. The motel has been converted into a museum documenting the struggle for civil rights.

After visiting this museum, head west on Butler Street and turn right on Front Street. You will now be walking through:

⓬ Cotton Row and Cotton Museum

In the days before and after the Civil War, and continuing into the early part of the 20th century, this area was the heart of the Southern cotton industry. Most of America's cotton was once shipped through the docks 2 blocks away. This area of warehouses and old storefronts is now a designated historic district, and many of the buildings have been renovated.

Just before you reach the corner of Front and Union streets, watch for the:

⓭ Carter Seed Store

It's on the west side of the street and is sort of a small version of A. Schwab. The emphasis here is on agricultural supplies and seeds. The candy counter is straight out of the 19th century.

5 Organized Tours

RIVER TOURS

Although the economic heart of Memphis has moved to the eastern suburbs, this is still a Mississippi River town; no visit to Memphis would be complete without spending a bit of time on Ole Man River. **Memphis Riverboats,** 45 S. Riverside Dr. (© **800/221-6197** or 901/527-5694; www.memphisriverboats.net) operates several paddle-wheelers, all of which leave from a dock on "the cobblestones" at the foot of Monroe Avenue in downtown Memphis. From March through November, there are 1½-hour sightseeing cruises, and in the summer, there are sunset dinner cruises and party cruises. The barbecue-buffet dinner cruises include live music.

The 1½-hour sightseeing cruise costs $18 for adults; $16 for seniors, military, and students; $10 for children 4 to 17 (free for children under 4). The evening dinner cruise costs $45 for adults, $43 for seniors and military, and $30 for children.

CITY TOURS

You'll find half a dozen or more horse-drawn carriages lined up in front of The Peabody Memphis hotel most evenings, operated by **Carriage Tours of Memphis** (© **888/267-9100** or 901/527-7542; www.carriagetoursofmemphis.com). Gentle equine giants with names like Chester, Marley, Doc, and Jane proudly clop along city streets while human tour guides—accompanied by big, friendly dogs, sometimes wearing funny hats—regale passengers with Memphis trivia. Tours are offered year-round (see-through plastic canopies keep you relatively dry during rainy weather); and rates vary.

If you're just in town for a short time, or if you prefer to let someone else do the planning and navigating, L and A City Sightseeing Tours (© **901/370-6666;** www.l-a-sightseeingtours.com), will pick you up at your hotel and shuttle you around the city and make sure you don't miss any important sights. Two 3-hour tours are offered, including the Memphis city tour ($26 adults, $18 children) and the Graceland tour ($40 adults, $30 children). A combination tour with both Graceland and the city of Memphis lasts 8 hours. Prices are $60 for adults, $31 for children.

Blues City Tours of Memphis, 325 Union Ave. (© **901/522-9229;** www.memphisite.com/bluescity), offers tours similar to the Gray Line tours. There is a half-day city tour that takes you past all the city's most important attractions, and there are also Graceland tours, Beale Street night-on-the-town tours, and casino tours to

---

Fun Fact **Funny Faithful?**

First Congregational Church (1000 S. Cooper; ℂ 901/278-6786; www.firstcongo. com) is widely regarded as an all-inclusive, welcoming church with a progressive view on social issues—and a sense of humor. Better known to locals as "First Congo," it attracts new worshippers with irreverent ads, including one that mentions its unicyclists and art-house theater connections among its Top 10 Reasons to Visit. In traffic-choked Memphis, where road-rage is rampant, No. 8 on that list holds special appeal: "So much parking you won't even *care* if the person next to you takes two spaces."

Mississippi. The city tour costs $20 for adults and $10 for children; the Elvis Graceland Tour, $30 for adults and $19 for children; after-dark dinner tour, $60 for adults and $50 for children (includes an evening on Beale Street with 2 clubs, 2 shows, 2 drinks, 2 meals with a choice of barbecue, chicken, or catfish and any cover charges). They also offer tours to the Tunica, MS casinos—a smart bet if you plan to drink alcohol while you're there.

For a thoroughly unique tour of Memphis, book a tour with **American Dream Safari** (ℂ **901/527-8870;** www.americandreamsafari.com). This is your chance to be chauffeured around town in a '55 Cadillac, with stops at such key Elvis sites as Humes High School (where he went to school) and Poplar Tunes (where he used to buy records). Other popular itineraries include a Sunday morning gospel tour and brunch, or the irreverently named (given Memphis's high crime rate) "Drive-By-Shooting" photographers' tour. Really, though, what American Dream Safari offers would be better described as authentic experiences than mere tours. Prices vary, from the Jukejoint Full of Blues for $75 per person (which includes admission to three Delta-area clubs), to $225 per person for an 8-hour pilgrimage along historic Highway 61. It includes blues-museum admission and lunch in Clarksdale, MS.

6 Outdoor Activities

GOLF   Memphis's public golf courses include the **Stoneridge Golf Course,** 3049 Davies Plantation Rd. (ℂ 901/382-1886); as well as those operated by the Memphis Parks Commission. They include facilities at **Audubon Park,** 4160 Park Ave. (ℂ 901/683-6941); the **Davy Crockett Park Municipal Golf Course,** 4380 Range Line Rd. (ℂ 901/368-3374); **Fox Meadows Park,** 3064 Clark Rd. (ℂ 901/362-0232); **Galloway Park,** 3815 Walnut Grove Rd. (ℂ 901/685-7805); and **Overton Park,** 2080 Poplar Ave. (ℂ 901/725-9905).

TENNIS   The Memphis Parks Commission operates seven public tennis courts all over the city. The most convenient to downtown and midtown is **Leftwich,** 4145 Southern Ave. (ℂ **901/685-7907**).

7 Spectator Sports

AUTO RACING   At the multi-track **Memphis Motorsports Park,** 5500 Victory Lane, Millington (ℂ **866/407-7333** or 901/358-7223; www.memphismotorsports park.com), there is everything from drag racing to NASCAR series action. The season runs from early spring to autumn. Call for ticket and schedule information.

BASEBALL The **Memphis Redbirds Baseball Club,** 175 Toyota Plaza, Suite 300 (© 901/721-6050; www.memphisredbirds.com), a Triple-A affiliate of the St. Louis Cardinals, plays at AutoZone Park, located 2 blocks east of The Peabody Memphis hotel on Union Avenue.

BASKETBALL The **Memphis Grizzlies** (© 901/205-1234; www.nba.com/grizzlies) are the city's first NBA team, having relocated from Vancouver, British Columbia, in 2001. Since 2004, they have played at their new downtown arena, the FedEx Forum.

The **University of Memphis Tigers** (© 888/867-UOFM or 901/678-2331; www.gotigersgo.com) regularly pack in crowds of 20,000 or more people when they play the FedEx Forum. The Tigers often put up a good showing against nationally ranked NCAA teams, which makes for some exciting basketball. Call for ticket and schedule information.

FOOTBALL The **Liberty Bowl Football Classic** (© 901/729-4344) is the biggest football event of the year in Memphis and pits two of the country's top college teams in a December postseason game. As with other postseason college bowl games, the Liberty Bowl is extremely popular and tickets go fast. This game is held at the **Liberty Bowl Memorial Stadium** (www.libertybowl.org) on the Mid-South Fairgrounds at the corner of East Parkway South and Central Avenue.

GOLF TOURNAMENTS The **Standford St. Jude Golf Classic** (© 901/748-0534), a PGA charity tournament, is held each year in late spring at the Tournament Players Club at Southwind.

GREYHOUND RACING Across the river in Arkansas, greyhounds race at the **Southland Greyhound Park,** 1550 N. Ingram Blvd., West Memphis, Arkansas (© 800/467-6182 or 870/735-3670). Matinee post time is at 1pm; evening races start at 7:30pm.

HORSE SHOWS Horse shows are popular in Memphis, and the biggest of the year is the **Germantown Charity Horse Show** (© 901/754-0009; www.gchs.org), held each June at the Germantown Horse Show Arena, which is just off Poplar Pike at Melanie Smith Lane in Germantown.

TENNIS The **Regions Morgan Keegan Championships** (© 901/765-4401 or 901/685-ACES), a part of the ATP Tour, is held each year in February at the Racquet Club of Memphis. Call for ticket and schedule information.

8 Side Trips from Memphis

Because of its location in the far southwestern corner of Tennessee, Memphis doesn't have the wealth of convenient day-trip options that Nashville has. For example, you could head west into Arkansas if you're interested in seeing Bill Clinton's presidential library in Little Rock, or drive north if the flat expanse of rural Missouri's bootheel holds any appeal (probably not). Look east, and you're at least a three-hour drive to Nashville. Due to the distances involved, all of these options are perhaps better suited to overnight trips than simple daylong escapes. But here's the good news: Head south from downtown Memphis, and you're only a few miles from the Mississippi Delta—the mother lode for blues-loving pilgrims who travel here from all over the world.

CLARKSDALE

An unmistakable vibe pervades the languid Mississippi Delta town of Clarksdale, about an hour's drive south of Memphis, Tennessee. It's by turns eerie and endearing, a flat landscape where fertile fields, endless railroad tracks, and run-down shacks are giving way to pockets of progress—an upscale restaurant, a strip mall full of dollar stores and fast-food drive-throughs, a museum celebrating the blues music that took root here in the early 20th century and changed the course of popular music.

Clarksdale also happens to be Tennessee Williams country. The cherished American playwright, author of such masterworks as *A Streetcar Named Desire* and *The Glass Menagerie,* grew up here. Young Tom, who later adopted the name 'Tennessee,' lived in the parsonage of St. George's Episcopal Church, where his grandfather was pastor. Self-guided walking tours of the historic neighborhood are available.

If you don't plan to return to Memphis the same day, this is a good place to begin a driving tour of legendary **Highway 61 (U.S. 61),** the two-lane road that took blues legends such as Muddy Waters, Robert Johnson, and B.B. King north from the impoverished cotton plantations of the south to the cities of Memphis and Chicago to the north. The long drive south will take you through the proverbial dusty Delta towns, and cities such as Greenville, Vicksburg and, finally, where Mississippi meets Louisiana in the southwest part of the state, historic Natchez.

ESSENTIALS

GETTING THERE   By Car   The major route into Clarksdale is **Highway 61** from Memphis to the north.

VISITOR INFORMATION   Contact the **Clarksdale/Coahoma County Chamber of Commerce,** 1540 Desoto Ave., Clarksdale, MS 39614 (© **800/626-3764** or 662/627-7337; www.clarksdaletourism.com).

WHAT TO SEE & DO

As you ease into town, your first stop should be at **The Crossroads,** at the intersection of highways 49 and 61. The site is legendary as the place where bluesman Robert Johnson is said to have sold his soul to the devil in exchange for the guitar prowess that has made him one of the most revered musicians of the past century. A guitar statue marks the spot.

From here, your next stop should be the **Delta Blues Museum,** 1 Blues Alley (© **662/627-6820;** www.deltabluesmuseum.org). Housed in a renovated train depot built in 1918, it includes a treasure-trove of old blues memorabilia, including the log cabin where Muddy Waters grew up, on a cotton plantation not far from here. There are displays, musical instruments, and costumes of some of the Mississippi-born greats, such as Albert King, James Cotton, and Son House. Admission is $7 adults, $5 children 6 to 12; it is open daily except Sunday. Bessie Smith fans can do a drive-by tour of the **Riverside Hotel,** 615 Sunflower Ave. (© **662/624-9163**), the former blacks-only hospital where the great blues singer died after a car crash in 1937. Blues legends Sonny Boy Williamson II, Ike Turner, Robert Nighthawk, and even politician Robert F. Kennedy once stayed here. Today it still operates as a motel, but most visitors see it only from their windshields.

While downtown, don't miss **Cathead Delta Blues & Folk Art,** 252 Delta Ave. (© **662/624-5992;** www.cathead.biz). The store sells new blues CDs, DVDs, and books as well as eye-catching—and affordable—folk and outsider art. The hepcat-cool

hot spot also serves as a clearinghouse for what's going on around town. Check Cathead's chalkboard that tells of weekly music events and updates. The store also occasionally has book signings and special events. You'll likely find the owner chatting up tourists who've made the pilgrimage here for some serious blues sightseeing.

WHERE TO STAY & DINE

There's a pitiful lack of decent hotels in Clarksdale. Your best bet is to grab one of the inexpensive to moderately priced chain properties along State Street. Clean and modern with comfortable rooms and discounted rates is the Best Western, 710 S. State St. (© **662/627-9292**).

Hands-down the best restaurant in town is **Madidi,** 164 Delta Ave. (© **662/627-7770;** www.madidires.com), the upscale eatery and bar opened in 2001 by actor Morgan Freeman, who grew up in the area and is still seen around town from time to time. (He is also a partner in **Ground Zero Blues Club,** reminiscent of an old juke-joint, in downtown.) Other popular venues are **Abe's Bar-B-Que,** 616 State St. (© **662/624-9947**); and **Sarah's Kitchen,** 203 Sunflower Ave. (© **662/627-3239**), which serves Southern cooking 3 days a week—lunch and dinner Thursdays through Saturdays only.

Shacking Up

In the lodging category of too-creepy for anyone but the most die-hard blues fan, there's the one-of-a-kind **Shack Up Inn,** 001 Commissary Circle (© 662/624-8329; www.shackupinn.com), on old Highway 49 south of Clarksdale. Billed as Mississippi's oldest B&B (and that stands for Bed and Beer), the property is on the site of a weedy rural cotton gin littered with rusting antique farming implements, old road signs, and crumbling sharecropper shacks that have been modernized enough to accommodate easy-to-please travelers in search of a good time and a place to crash—and great music at the on-premises Commissary club. In 2004, the inn opened up 10 new 'gin bins,' private rooms within the gin warehouse that's now a makeshift 'inn.' Rates, which range from $55 to $85 per room, include a Moon Pie on your pillow. Sweet dreams. . . .

OXFORD

Home to the University of Mississippi, "Ole Miss," Oxford is a quaint small town where daily life revolves around its 150-year-old Court Square. A popular weekend destination for out-of-towners and visiting alumni, Oxford offers an enticing array of great art galleries, bookstores, restaurants, and historic homes. Although it's proximity to Memphis (about 70 miles away) makes it a doable day-trip, Oxford's offbeat charms might entice you to stay a day or two.

ESSENTIALS

GETTING THERE   By Car   The major route into Oxford is **I-55** from both the north (Memphis) and south (Jackson). It's about a 90-minute drive.

VISITOR INFORMATION   Contact the **Oxford Tourism Council,** 107 Courthouse Square, Suite 1, Oxford, MS 38655 (© **800/758-9177** or 662/234-4680; www. touroxfordms.com).

EXPLORING THE AREA

Oxford's favorite son is Nobel Prize–winning author William Faulkner, whose residence from 1930 until his death in 1963 was his beloved home, **Rowan Oak,** Old Taylor Road (© 662/234-3284). A tour of the grounds, with its graceful magnolias and old farm buildings, is a trip back in time. Inside, literary enthusiasts can still marvel at the author's old manual typewriter, and read his handwritten outline for *A Fable,* which is scrawled on the wall of his study. It's closed Mondays and major holidays.

The most popular pastime in Oxford is simply strolling **The Square,** where travelers might spot former local residents such as John Grisham. **Square Books,** 160 Courthouse Square (© **662/236-2262;** www.squarebooks.com), in business since 1870, is regarded as one of the best independent bookstores in the country. Down the street is its bargain-priced annex, **Off Square Books,** 129 Courthouse Square (© **662/236-2828**). Thousands of discounted and remaindered books cram shelves and bins. It's also the site of Square Books' author signings and readings, as well as *Thacker Mountain Radio,* Oxford's original music and literature radio show. Best-selling authors such as Robert Olen Butler, Elmore Leonard, and Ray Blount, Jr., have read their works on the live show. Musical guests have run the gamut from Elvis Costello and Marty Stuart to the Del McCoury band and the North Mississippi Allstars. The show is recorded live from 5:30–6:30pm Thursdays.

Next door, **Southside Gallery,** 150 Courthouse Square (© **662/234-9090**), is an always-interesting place that showcases everything from photography, painting, and sculpture to outsider art by the likes of Howard Finster.

WHERE TO STAY & DINE

Because of its proximity to Memphis, Oxford is a popular day-trip destination for many travelers. Perhaps as a result, there are only a handful of hotels and motels, most of them chains on the outskirts of town that cater to the parents of college kids and other travelers to the university.

Among the cleanest and most modern choices are the **Comfort Inn,** 1808 Jackson Ave. S. (© **662/234-6000**), which has a small outdoor pool ($80 plus tax); the larger **Days Inn,** 1101 Frontage Rd. (© **662/234-9500;** $70 plus tax); and **Holiday Inn Express and Suites,** 112 Heritage Rd. (© **800/465-4329** or 662/236-2500). Rates run about $99 double.

Call ahead and book early if you want to reserve a room at one of the city's bed-and-breakfast properties, which are often booked during weekends when Ole Miss has home football games or other major events. You won't see it advertised much because the place is always full, but try to book a stay at **Puddin' Place,** 1008 University Ave. (© **662/234-1250**), a spotless, cheerfully decorated 1892 house that has two large suites with private bathrooms. The owner is in the process of adding a private cottage in the tree-shaded back yard. Gourmet breakfasts are included in the room rates, which usually run $115 double (during Ole Miss football season it's $350 for the 2-night minimum weekend stay, and the hotel sells out these weekends months in advance).

For guests who don't mind rather simple furnishings and a lack of pizzazz, try the **Oliver-Britt House Inn,** 512 Van Buren Ave. (© **662/234-8043**). The white-columned, redbrick structure has a welcoming front porch packed with potted plants and flowers. There are five guest rooms, all with private bathroom but no phone. Rates run $105 to $150 double; continental breakfast is available weekdays, and a full breakfast is served on weekends.

City Grocery, 152 Courthouse Square (© **662/232-8080;** www.citygroceryoxford. com), is one of the best restaurants in Mississippi. New Orleans–born chef John Currence finesses spicy cheese grits topped with plump shrimp, mushrooms, and smoked bacon, while offering an array of tempting gourmet salads, soups, and Cajun delicacies. Main courses cost $20 to $25. Reservations are recommended.

Bottletree Bakery, 923 Van Buren Ave. (© **662/236-5000**), is a must if you crave caffeine and the aroma of warm muffins being pulled from the oven. The cheery nook serves pastries and freshly baked breads as well as fine coffees, sandwiches, and salads. Oxford's favorite dive bar is **Proud Larry's,** 211 S. Lamar Blvd. (© **662/236-0050**), where live music and drink specials augment a simple menu of burgers, pasta, salads, and hand-tossed pizzas.

17

Shopping in Memphis

In the last few years, downtown has come a long way in attracting new retail tenants. Gradually, the number of vacant, boarded-up buildings is diminishing. With the recent opening of new shopping/entertainment complexes such as Pembroke Square and Peabody Place, there are now dozens of options for strolling and/or spending. In addition, there are still a few tourist-friendly Beale Street stalwarts that are great for sniffing out the perfect Memphis souvenir. Out in the trendy neighborhoods in midtown Memphis, you still find a few other stores that merit visiting. For the most part, however, Memphis shopping means shopping malls—and most of those are out in East Memphis and beyond, a region of sprawling, new, and mostly quite affluent suburbs.

1 The Shopping Scene

As in Nashville and other cities of the New South, the shopping scene in Memphis is spread out. If you want to go shopping in this city, you'll need to arm yourself with a good map, get in the car, and start driving. Most people head to the shopping malls and plazas (there are dozens) in East Memphis to find quality merchandise. However, in recent years some interesting and trendy shops have started to pop up in Peabody Place and in the South Main Historic District of downtown.

Shopping malls and department stores are generally open Monday to Saturday 10am to 9pm and Sunday noon to 6pm. Many smaller mom-and-pop stores located outside malls and shopping centers are closed on Sundays. Call ahead to check store hours.

2 Shopping A to Z

ANTIQUES

Memphis's main antiques district is at the intersection of Central Avenue and South Cooper Street. High-quality shops offering furniture and decorative arts, both rare and budget-priced antiques, as well as jewelry and gifts abound. Most businesses are open Monday to Saturday. For more information, visit www.memphisantiquedistrict.com.

Flashback With 1950s furniture becoming more collectible with each passing year, it should come as no surprise that Memphis, the birthplace of rock 'n' roll in the early 1950s, has a great vintage furniture store. In addition to 1950s furnishings and vintage clothing, this store sells stuff from the '20s, '30s, and '40s, including a large selection of European Art Deco furniture. 2304 Central Ave. ℭ 901/272-2304. www.flashback memphis.com.

Headley Menzies Interior Design The prices here reflect the clientele's means, and sumptuous antiques from Europe and England predominate. However, there are also throw pillows made from antique fabrics, French pâté urns, and other more affordable pieces. 766 S. White Station Rd. ⓒ 901/761-3161. www.headleymenzies.com.

Market Central Antiques and Gardens   More than 100 bays exhibit an eclectic array of vintage furnishings and other antiques at this huge warehouse in Midtown. Local artwork is also for sale. 2215 Central Ave. ⓒ 901/278-0888. www.marketcentral memphis.com.

Palladio International Antique Market   Fine European furnishings, Persian rugs, and decorative art, including works by Memphis artists, are displayed in elegant surroundings. An onsite cafe makes a pleasant place to enjoy a cup of tea with pastries or a sandwich. 2169 Central Ave. ⓒ 901/276-3808. www.palladioantiques.com.

Toad Hall Antiques   Furniture, primitives, lamps, and mirrors comprise the eclectic merchandise selection at this Cooper Young landmark. Look for the smiling, relaxed frog painted on the outside of the brick building. Inside, browse for French and English as well as American decorative objects, jewelry, and other affordably priced gifts. 2129 Central Ave. ⓒ 901/726-0755. www.toadhallmemphis.com.

ART

David Lusk Gallery   In the most sophisticated, upscale art gallery in town, gallery owner David Lusk showcases the South's finest contemporary artists. A wide variety of media is represented, including glass and photography. Lively receptions, educational events, and charitable efforts make this one of the most active galleries in the city. Laurelwood Center, 4540 Poplar Ave. ⓒ 901/767-3800. www.davidluskgallery.com.

Jay Etkin Gallery   Artist and gallery owner Jay Etkin, a native New Yorker, has for nearly 20 years been one of Memphis's most outspoken and active advocates for local contemporary artists. His inviting downtown loft studio in the South Main Historic District is a must for anyone in search of affordable, often delightfully offbeat, works of art. 409 S. Main St. ⓒ 901/543-0035. www.jayetkingallery.com.

Joysmith Studio ⓚⓚ *Finds*   Brenda Joysmith, a longtime San Francisco–area artist who trained at the Art Institute of Chicago, had earned an international reputation before she returned to her native Memphis a few years ago. Best known for her pastel portraits of African-American women and children, Joysmith's works are featured in many national museums, in corporate collections, in books, and on the sets of popular television shows, such as *Cosby*. Maya Angelou and Oprah Winfrey are among her celebrity fans. There's a retail shop in her studio selling affordable prints and other merchandise. 46 Huling Ave. ⓒ 901/543-0505. www.joysmith.com.

Lisa Kurts Gallery   Longtime gallery owner Lisa Kurts represents regional and national artists in a range of media, most often paintings and two-dimensional works. Look for her space next to an interior decorator's office just north of Poplar Avenue in East Memphis. 766 S. White Station Rd. ⓒ 901/683-6200. www.lisakurts.com.

BOOKS

Bookstar   Housed in the converted Plaza Theatre, a big shopping plaza movie theater, this is the city's biggest discount bookstore. Many selections are marked down 20% to 30%, including the latest *New York Times* hardcover and paperback bestsellers. The store also sells gift items and has a coffee shop. 3402 Poplar Ave. ⓒ 901/323-9332.

Memphis Shopping: Downtown & Midtown

A Schwab's Dry Goods **19**
Bella Notte **13**
Burke's Book Store **13**
Champion's Pharmacy and Herb Store **6**
Chickasaw Oaks Village **15**
Flashback **10**
Gibson Guitar Memphis **3**
Goner Records **13**
Jay Etkin Gallery **16**

Joysmith Studio **4**
Kittie Kyle Collection **15**
Love Me Tender **18**
Market Central Antiques **12**
Memphis Drum Shop **9**
Memphis Farmer's Market **5**
Memphis Flea Market **14**
Memphis Music **17**
Miss Cordelia's Grocery **1**

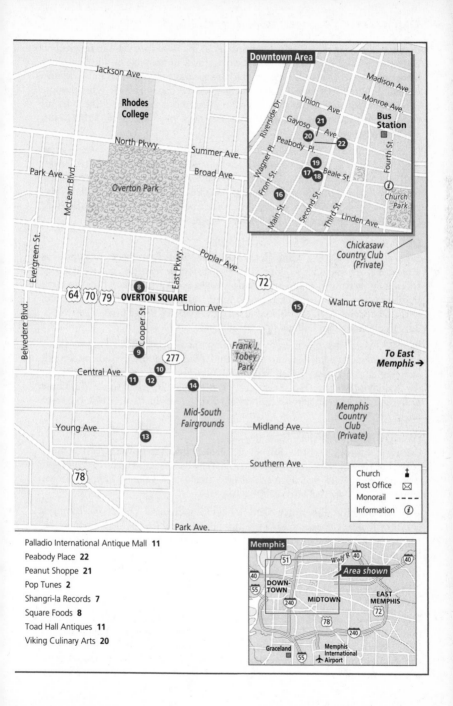

Palladio International Antique Mall **11**

Peabody Place **22**

Peanut Shoppe **21**

Pop Tunes **2**

Shangri-la Records **7**

Square Foods **8**

Toad Hall Antiques **11**

Viking Culinary Arts **20**

Burke's Book Store *★* *Finds*   After decades in the same location, the region's best and most beloved independent bookstore relocated to new digs in the flourishing Cooper-Young neighborhood nearby. Burke's specializes in used, old, and collectible books. However, they have a good selection of new books as well. When favorite Memphis son John Grisham pens a new bestseller, this is usually where he holds his first book signing before embarking on national tours. 936 S. Cooper ℂ **901/278-7484.** www.burkesbooks.com.

Davis-Kidd Booksellers *★★* *Kids*   Located in the prestigious Laurelwood Center shopping plaza, this large bookstore is a perennial favorite of Memphis readers. Books, CDs, periodicals, a cozy cafe, and a delightful assortment of unique gift items make for some of the most pleasurable browsing in the East Memphis area. A children's play area will keep the little ones occupied with fun and educational pursuits. Laurelwood Center, 387 Perkins Rd. Extended. ℂ **901/683-9801.** www.daviskidd.com.

DEPARTMENT STORES

Dillard's   Dillard's is a Little Rock, Arkansas–based department store that has expanded across the country. This is their biggest store in Tennessee, and it has a wide selection of moderately priced merchandise. Good prices and plenty of choices make this store a favorite of Memphis shoppers. You'll find other Dillard's department stores in the **Oak Court Mall** (ℂ 901/685-0382), the **Hickory Ridge Mall** (ℂ 901/360-0077), and **Wolfchase Galleria** (ℂ 901/383-1029).

Macy's   Macy's department stores are the most upscale in Memphis. The Oak Court Mall location is probably the most convenient for visitors to the city. Other stores can be found in the **Hickory Ridge Mall,** 6001 Winchester Rd. (ℂ 901/369-1271); in the **Southland Mall,** 1300 E. Shelby Dr. (ℂ 901/348-1267); and in the **Wolfchase Galleria,** 2760 N. Germantown Parkway (ℂ 901/937-2600). Oak Court Mall, 4545 Poplar Ave. ℂ **901/766-4199.**

DISCOUNT SHOPPING

Lakeland Factory Outlet   Savings at stores such as Vanity Fair, Danskin, Bass, Nike, Van Heusen, Corning-Revere, and Old Time Pottery range up to 75% off regular retail prices. You'll find the mall just off I-40 about 30 minutes from downtown Memphis. 3536 Canada Rd., Lakeland. ℂ **901/386-3180.**

Williams-Sonoma Clearance Outlet   Williams-Sonoma, one of the country's largest mail-order companies, has a big distribution center here in the Memphis area, and this store is where they sell their discontinued lines and overstocks. If you're lucky, you just might find something that you wanted but couldn't afford when you saw it in the catalog. 4708 Spottswood Ave. ℂ **901/763-1500.** www.williamssonoma.com.

FASHIONS
MEN'S

James Davis   You'll find Giorgio Armani here for both men and women. In addition to tailored and casual clothing, sportswear, outerwear, and shoe brands such as Bruno Magli and Cole Haan, they carry women's apparel, accessories, and lingerie, as well as glamorous evening gowns. Laurelwood Center, 400 Grove Park Rd. ℂ **901/767-4640.** www.jamesdavisstore.com.

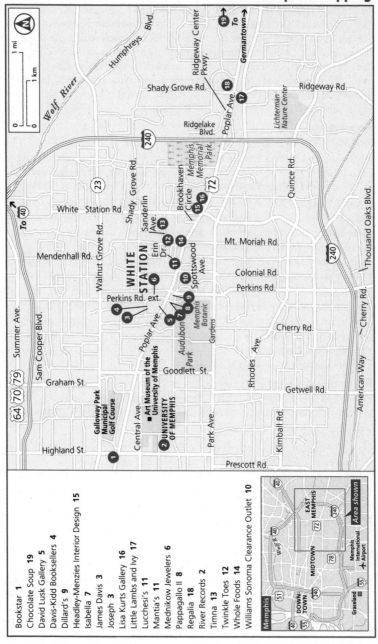

East Memphis Shopping

Bookstar **1**
Chocolate Soup **19**
David Lusk Gallery **5**
Davis-Kidd Booksellers **4**
Dillard's **9**
Headley-Menzies Interior Design **15**
Isabella **7**
James Davis **3**
Joseph **3**
Lisa Kurts Gallery **16**
Little Lambs and Ivy **17**
Lucchesi's **11**
Mantia's **11**
Mednikow Jewelers **6**
Pappagallo II **8**
Regalia **18**
River Records **2**
Timna **13**
Twinkle Toes **12**
Whole Foods **14**
Williams Sonoma Clearance Outlet **10**

225

Love Me Tender of Memphis ⚐   Window shop at this Beale Street boutique and you'll think Elvis never left the building. Fifties' era table-lamps, a console television set, and other vintage décor set the stage for what's on sale inside: the brand-name Memphis Flash Clothes are pricey but stylish. There are Elvis-inspired pink pastel long-sleeved shirts, nubby wool jackets, snug trousers, and suede loafers. Fans can also paw over souvenirs such as Elvis key chains, calendars, recordings, and cigarette lighters. At $3, the Elvis Hawaiian (coconut-flavored) lip balm promises improved kiss-ability. 126 Beale St. ℭ **901/527-2722. www.eplmt.com.**

WOMEN'S

Isabella   This chic women's boutique carries designers not usually found in other Memphis stores, such as Anlo, Rachel Pally, Trina Turk, and Ella Moss. If you're craving a stylish new pair of jeans, this is the place to scour. You might even find a belt or other invaluable accessory. Laurelwood Collection, 4615 Poplar Ave. ℭ **901/683-3538.**

Joseph   *Harper's Bazaar* named this high-fashion, East Memphis favorite as one of the top 95 specialty stores in America. With everything from cosmetics and shoes to coats by such noted designers as Zac Posen and Norma Kamali, it's easy to see why. 418 S. Grove Park. ℭ **901/767-1609. www.josephstores.com.**

Kittie Kyle Kollection   You'll find this great little shop in the Chickasaw Oaks Plaza. The boutique represents small designers from around the country, with an emphasis not on current fashion trends, but personal and functional style. There's also a wide selection of jewelry and accessories. 3092 Poplar Ave. ℭ **901/452-2323.**

Muse   One of the first boutiques to take off in the newly energized South Main Historic district a few years ago was Muse. Still going strong, this trendy shop boasts of its focus on artistic clothing for women and fashion-conscious men alike. 517 S. Main St. ℭ **901/526-8737. www.memphismuse.com.**

Pappagallo II   If you're a fan of the Pappagallo fashions and shoes, you won't want to miss this store at the corner of Poplar Avenue and Perkins Road. There's a second store at 2109 West St. in Germantown. Laurelwood Collection. 4615 Poplar Ave. ℭ **901/761-4430.**

CHILDREN'S

Chocolate Soup   This store is practically crammed with clothes that are colorful and easy to care for. Designs that grow with the child and hand-sewn appliqués make the clothing here unique. There are also plenty of brightly colored toys and assorted things to keep kids entertained. Germantown Village Square, Poplar Avenue and Germantown Parkway. ℭ **901/754-7157.**

Little Lambs and Ivy   This beloved local children's store has a name as cuddly as its clothing, which includes everything from velour separates to sweaters and fancy party dresses. Among the brand names carried are Lilly Pulitzer, Kissy-Kissy, and Rabbit Moon. 1227 Ridgeway Rd., Suite 315. ℭ **901/767-5262. www.mylittlelambsandivy.com.**

Twinkle Toes Children's Shoes   Why shop department or discount stores when you can indulge your little tykes with customized service at this East Memphis boutique? From Ecco, Lacoste, and Oilily to New Balance, this kid-friendly retailer carries merchandise for infants through children's size 7. 5040 Sanderlin Ave. ℭ **901/766-2900.**

FOOD, GIFTS & SOUVENIRS

A. Schwab Dry Goods Store ★★★ *Kids* *Moments*   This store is as much a Memphis institution and attraction as it is a place to shop. With its battered wood floors and tables covered with everything from plumbing supplies to religious paraphernalia, A. Schwab is a step back in time to the days of general stores. The offerings here are fascinating, even if you aren't in the market for a pair of size-74 men's overalls. You can still check out the 44 kinds of suspenders, the wall of voodoo love potions and powders, and the kiosk full of Elvis souvenirs. What else will you find at Schwab's? Bongo drums and crystal balls; shoeshine kits and corncob pipes; long thermal underwear and cotton petticoats; voodoo potions and praying hands and plastic back-scratchers. Don't miss this place! Open Monday through Saturday 9am to 5pm. 163 Beale St. ℭ 901/523-9782.

Bella Notte ℱ *(Finds)* Luscious soaps, handmade cards, and thoughtful gifts are gorgeously displayed in this too-easily overlooked boutique in the heart of historic Cooper-Young. Don't be put off by the protective bars on the windows. It's a quirky, independently owned little shop worth a look. 2172 Young Ave. ℭ 901/726-4131.

Champion's Pharmacy and Herb Store This one-of-a-kind retailer and medicine-wagon museum is also an old-school drug store and pharmacy that still sells an eye-popping array of herbal remedies and nostalgic patent medicines (Packer's Pine Tar Soap, Lydia E. Pinkham Tonic, Red Clover Salve, Old Red Barn Ointment). 2369 Elvis Presley Blvd. (2¼ miles north of Graceland). ℭ 901/948-6622. www.theherbalman.com.

The Peanut Shoppe *(Kids)* In business since 1951, this tiny but mightily aromatic shop is easily spotted: Look for the larger-than-life Mr. Peanut character tapping with his cane on the front window of the shop. Inside, you'll inhale the warm, toasty scent of all kinds of nuts—freshly roasted on the premises and still displayed in nostalgic glass counters and then weighed on old-fashioned scales. For fans of the monacled big guy, there's also lots of Mr. Peanut memorabilia on display. 24 S. Main St. ℭ 901/525-1115. www.memphispeanutshoppe.com.

Viking Culinary Arts ℱ Everything and the kitchen sink await inside this spacious retail store and demonstration area for Greenwood, MS–based Viking ranges and appliances. Recently relocated from downtown to this East Memphis shopping center, the store offers top-of-the-line cookware and gadgets galore, making it a great place to shop for the cooking enthusiast on your gift list. 1215 Ridgeway Blvd. ℭ 901/578-5822. www.vikinghomechef.com.

JEWELRY

Mednikow Open since 1891, this is one of the largest and most highly respected jewelry stores in Memphis, offering exquisite diamond jewelry, Rolex and Cartier timepieces, Mikimoto pearls, David Yurman designs, and other beautiful baubles. 474 Perkins Rd. Extended. ℭ 901/767-2100. www.mednikow.com.

Timna Adjacent to the East Memphis Doubletree, Timna features hand-woven fashions and hand-painted silks by nationally acclaimed artists. A broad selection of contemporary jewelry includes both fanciful pieces made of metals and stones to more hard-edged industrial designs, with prices ranging from $40 to several hundred dollars. 5101 Sanderlin Centre. ℭ 901/683-9369.

MALLS/SHOPPING CENTERS

Chickasaw Oaks Village ℱ This indoor shopping center is built to resemble an 18th-century village street and houses salons, specialty shops such as Perry Nicole Fine Art, and upscale ladies' clothing boutiques such as Ella. 3092 Poplar Ave. ℭ 901/794-6022. www.chickasawoaksvillage.com.

Laurelwood   Tucked in behind a Sears store in an older shopping center, this newer shopping plaza houses several upscale clothing stores, Davis-Kidd Booksellers, restaurants, and Memphis's best travel agency (Regency Travel). Poplar Avenue and Perkins Road Extended. ℂ 901/682-8436. www.laurelwoodmemphis.com.

Oak Court Mall   With both a Macy's and a Dillard's and 80 specialty shops, this mall surrounds a pretty little park full of sculptures, and the parking lot is full of big, old shade trees. The attention to preserving a parklike setting makes this place stand out from most malls. 4465 Poplar Ave. at Perkins Road. ℂ 901/682-8928. www.oakcourtmall.com.

Peabody Place   This massive downtown development includes familiar retail chains as well as a 22-screen movie theater, clothing boutiques, gift shops, whimsical courtyard sculptures, and an ice cream parlor. 150 Peabody Place. ℂ 901/271-PLAY. www.peabodyplace.com.

The Regalia   Swank shops specializing in everything from fine linen to lingerie are featured at this upscale shopping center next door to the Embassy Suites Hotel and just off I-240. Cokesbury has a nice bookstore here. Clothing stores include Oak Hall for men's and women's apparel, and A Pea in the Pod for chic maternity wear. Salsa and Owen Brennan's, two excellent, locally owned restaurants, also have been longtime anchor tenants. Poplar Avenue and Ridgeway Road. ℂ 901/767-0100.

The Shops of Saddle Creek   Located out in the heart of Germantown, Memphis's most affluent bedroom community, this shopping center is home to such familiar national chain stores as Sharper Image, Banana Republic, Crabtree & Evelyn, Ann Taylor, GapKids, and similarly fashionable lesser-known stores. 5855 River Bend Rd. ℂ 901/761-2571. www.shopsofsaddlecreek.com.

Wolfchase Galleria ⊛   The suburbs' biggest and best mall is this mammoth (more than 1-million-sq.-ft.) retail center in the northeastern metro area that includes Dillard's and Macy's, plus scores of restaurants and specialty shops. From Pottery Barn finds and Godiva chocolates to Looney Tunes toys at the Warner Brothers store, this always-crowded mall also has a children's carousel and a multiplex cinema with stadium seating. 2760 N. Germantown Pkwy. ℂ 901/381-2769. www.wolfchasegalleria.com.

MARKETS

Luchessi's   Pastas such as fettucine and tortellini, along with homemade sauces, hearty breads, and take-and-bake pizzas are made fresh daily at this East Memphis market. Green garden salads as well as creamy prepared salads (potato, pasta, chicken, etc.) are available by the pound, along with gorgonzola, balsamic, and other dressings. Sandwiches, panini, and ready-to-heat take-home entrees such as eggplant lasagna and ravioli with meat sauce also tempt hungry shoppers. 540 S. Mendenhall (at Sanderlin). ℂ 901/766-9922. www.luchessis.com.

Mantia's ⊛   East Memphis is where you'll find this international foods market and deli. Cheeses from throughout the world are a specialty. It's also a great place to pick up some picnic fare before heading to one of Memphis's many parks. 4856 Poplar Ave. ℂ 901/762-8560. www.mantias.com.

Memphis Farmer's Market   Each Saturday morning at the train station downtown, farmers from throughout the region bring their produce to sell at this open-air market. Look for red-ripe Tennessee tomatoes; turnip, mustard, and collard greens; and other Southern crops. The market is seasonal, open May through the end of October. 545 S. Main St. ℂ 901/575-0580. www.memphisfarmersmarket.com.

Memphis Flea Market *Kids*   Held on the third weekend of every month, this huge flea market has more than 2,000 spaces. Goods on sale here run the gamut from discount jeans and perfumes to antiques and other collectibles. 955 Early Maxwell Blvd., Mid-South Fairgrounds. ✆ **901/276-3532**. www.memphisfleamarket.com.

Miss Cordelia's Grocery   Picnic goodies such as deli sandwiches, bakery-style cookies and cakes, and fresh fruits are available at this small local grocery store and market in Harbor Town, just north of The Pyramid. Bottled juices, teas, and even pre-packaged sushi kits (chopsticks and wasabi included) from local restaurant Sekisui make it easy to grab a meal to enjoy at nearby Greenbelt Park on the Mississippi River. 737 Harbor Bend Rd. ✆ **901/526-4772**. www.misscordelias.com.

Square Foods   This locally owned complete health-food store offers groceries, produce, frozen and bulk foods, as well as vitamins and herbs. The deli specializes in vegetarian fare, though fish is sometimes an option, too. 937 S. Cooper. ✆ **901/728-4371**. www.squarefoods.com.

Whole Foods *☆*   Formerly Wild Oats, this immaculate East Memphis store converted to a Whole Foods Market in early 2008. Along with the chain's usual mix of organic produce, bins of bulk beans, rice and grains, and health-conscious canned, frozen, and packaged foods, there are deli-style counters offering fresh salads, meats, cheeses, sandwiches, and sweet treats. 5022 Poplar Ave. ✆ **901/685-2293**. www.wholefoods.com.

MUSIC

Goner Records   Take a stroll in the Cooper-Young neighborhood, and you'll stumble across this cool, home-grown record shop. Punk, funk, rock, rhythm-and-blues, and everything in between, co-exist here. Flip through bins of vinyl LPs, 78 records, and CDs. Goner also sells turntables and doubles as a fledgling indie record company. 2152 Young Ave. ✆ **901/725-0095**. www.goner-records.com.

Memphis Music   Recordings by blues greats such as Leadbelly and many others are a specialty of this otherwise touristy music shop that also sells Memphis souvenirs and T-shirts with images of famous blues and jazz musicians. 149 Beale St. ✆ **901/526-5047**. www.memphismusicstore.com.

Pop Tunes   Although its current clientele is more attune to artists such as hip-hop homeboys Three 6 Mafia, this scuffed-up shop wedged next to a row of bail bonds businesses (and the razor-wired downtown jail) has been around since 1946, when a neighborhood kid named Elvis used to hang here. 308 Poplar Rd. ✆ **901/525-6348**.

River Records   The city's premier collector's record shop for four decades, River Records also sells baseball cards, comic books, CDs, and posters. Located in the University of Memphis area, River also stocks a few Elvis Presley records and memorabilia. 822 S. Highland St. ✆ **901/324-1757**.

Shangri-La Records *☆☆* *Finds*   With Memphis's best selection of new and used rockabilly, as well as soul, R&B, reggae, and rock, Shangri-La is a bonafide goldmine for bargain browsers with offbeat musical appetites. It's all stuffed inside this nondescript old house in midtown. Shangri-La also offers offbeat, behind-the-scenes tours of Memphis. 1916 Madison Ave. ✆ **901/274-1916**. www.shangri.com.

MUSICAL INSTRUMENTS

Gibson Beale Street Showcase   Not only can you watch Gibson guitars being manufactured, and hear them performed, you may also purchase a variety of Gibson and Epiphone stringed instruments and other merchandise. Public tour times vary, so call ahead and make a reservation before you head out. 145 Lt. George W. Lee Ave. (C) 800/444-2766 or 901/544-7998. www.gibsonmemphis.com.

Memphis Drum Shop   Now entering its third decade in business, this reliable midtown retailer sells new, used, vintage, and custom drums, cymbals, parts, and accessories. Percussion instruments are also repaired, and can even be rented, at this fun shop. 878 S. Cooper St. (C) 901/276-2328. www.memphisdrumshop.com.

SHOES & BOOTS

In addition to the following shoe and boot stores, you'll find an excellent selection of shoes at the **Dillard's** department store in the Mall of Memphis shopping mall.

DSW Shoe Warehouse   With savings of 20% to 50% off standard retail prices and an excellent selection of major-label shoes, this store is open 7 days a week. Germantown Village Square, Germantown Parkway at Poplar Avenue. (C) 901/755-2204. www.dswshoe.com.

Oak Hall   Men with exquisite taste and deep pockets have turned to this exclusive clothier for nearly 150 years. The store sells men's and women's clothing as well as top-of-the-line shoes by Mark Mason, Gravati, Ermengildo Zegna, and Canali. 6150 Poplar. (C) 901/761-3580. www.oakhall.com.

Rack Room Shoes   Conveniently situated in the same mall as DSW Shoe Warehouse, this store offers good discounts on Timberland, Rockport, Nike, Reebok, and Bass shoes, among other lines. Germantown Village Square, 7690 Poplar Ave. at Germantown Parkway. (C) 901/754-2565. www.rackroomhoes.com.

18

Memphis After Dark

For a century, Memphis has nurtured one of the liveliest club scenes in the South, and the heart and soul of that nightlife has always been Beale Street. Whether your interest is blues, rock, opera, ballet, or Broadway musicals, you'll probably find entertainment to your liking on this lively street. However, there is more to Memphis nightlife than just Beale Street. In downtown Memphis, historic South Main Street has emerged as a fledgling arts community, with galleries, boutiques, and a growing number of buzz-worthy restaurants. You'll also find several theater companies performing in midtown near Overton Square, which has several popular bars, restaurants, and a few clubs. Nightlife is livelier in the gay-friendly Cooper-Young Neighborhood, at the intersection of Cooper Street and Young Avenue. Delis, boutiques, and a dozen or so excellent restaurants keep the young crowds coming.

Other places to check for live music are the respective rooftops of The Peabody Memphis hotel and the Madison Hotel. Each summer, the hotels sponsor sunset cocktail parties that are extremely popular.

To find out about what's happening in the entertainment scene while you're in town, pick up a copy of the *Memphis Flyer,* Memphis's free arts-and-entertainment weekly, which comes out on Thursday. You'll find it in convenience, grocery, and music stores; some restaurants; and nightclubs. You could also pick up the Friday edition of the *Commercial Appeal,* Memphis's morning daily newspaper. The "Playbook" section of the paper has very thorough events listings.

For tickets to sporting events and performances at the FedEx Forum, Mud Island Amphitheater, and Mid-South Coliseum, your best bet is to contact **Ticketmaster** (© 901/525-1515), which accepts credit card payments for phone orders. Alternatively, you can stop by a Ticketmaster sales counter and pay cash for tickets. There are Ticketmaster counters at Cat's Compact Discs stores around the city.

The **Memphis hotline** (© 901/75-ELVIS) offers information on current music, entertainment, arts, and sports 24 hours a day.

1 Beale Street & Downtown

Beale Street is the epicenter of Memphis's nightclub scene. This street, where the blues gained widespread recognition, is now the site of scores of nightclubs, bars, restaurants, and souvenir shops. Relatively tame and family-friendly by day, the neon district gets quite rowdy after dark, when barricades allow for pedestrians only. While blues purists looking for authenticity may be disappointed at the predominance of local cover bands that reign here, others, including curious conventioneers and hard-drinking partyers, seem eager enough to accept the Branson-esque tourist product

Memphis After Dark

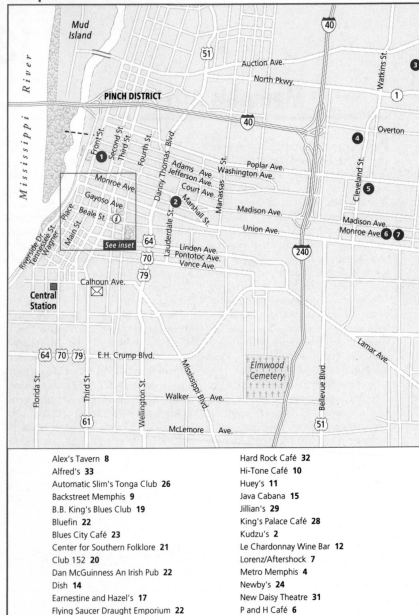

Alex's Tavern **8**	Hard Rock Café **32**
Alfred's **33**	Hi-Tone Café **10**
Automatic Slim's Tonga Club **26**	Huey's **11**
Backstreet Memphis **9**	Java Cabana **15**
B.B. King's Blues Club **19**	Jillian's **29**
Bluefin **22**	King's Palace Café **28**
Blues City Café **23**	Kudzu's **2**
Center for Southern Folklore **21**	Le Chardonnay Wine Bar **12**
Club 152 **20**	Lorenz/Aftershock **7**
Dan McGuinness An Irish Pub **22**	Metro Memphis **4**
Dish **14**	Newby's **24**
Earnestine and Hazel's **17**	New Daisy Theatre **31**
Flying Saucer Draught Emporium **22**	P and H Café **6**
Gibson Lounge **34**	Pat O'Brien's Memphis **30**

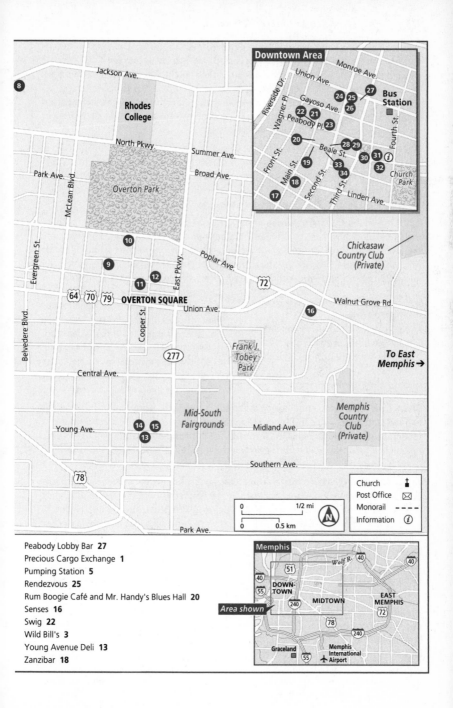

Peabody Lobby Bar **27**
Precious Cargo Exchange **1**
Pumping Station **5**
Rendezvous **25**
Rum Boogie Café and Mr. Handy's Blues Hall **20**
Senses **16**
Swig **22**
Wild Bill's **3**
Young Avenue Deli **13**
Zanzibar **18**

into which Beale Street has gradually devolved over the years. For links to various clubs and other businesses along Beale, click on **www.bealestreet.com**.

Clustered around Beale Street are many other notable restaurants and bars with lively after-hours activity. Some, like Earnestine and Hazel's, are tired-looking, time-worn stalwarts that boast more bar credibility than some of the swank new martini bars, such as Swig. Nevertheless, there's something for just about all entertainment appetites within the span of a few short blocks.

Alfred's ⊛   This spacious club on the corner of Third and Beale has 1950s rock 'n' roll most weekends, with a variety of bands currently packing the house. With its corner location and upstairs, outdoor patio, Alfred's also makes a great vantage point for people-watching and late-night drinking and eating. The kitchen's open until 3am. 197 Beale St. ⓒ **901/525-3711**. www.alfreds-on-beale.com. Cover $5–$10.

B.B. King Blues Club ⊛⊛ (Moments)   Yes, the club's 80-something namesake "King of the Blues" does play here occasionally, though not on a regular basis. However, any night of the week you can catch blazing blues played by one of the best house bands in town. Because of the name, this club attracts famous musicians who have been known to get up and jam with whomever is on stage that night. Ruby Wilson is among the regulars well worth checking out. Upstairs, a new third-floor restaurant opened in the fall of 2007. It's Itta Bena, named for B.B.'s Mississippi hometown. 147 Beale St. ⓒ **800/443-0972** or 901/524-5464; www.bbkingsclub.com. Cover– $7–$10 (usually $50–$170 for B.B.'s increasingly infrequent, but always sold-out, concerts).

> **Impressions**
>
> Beale Street is the life to me. We that play the blues, we're proud of it. It's somethin' religious.
>
> —B.B. King

Blues City Café ⊛   This club across the street from B.B. King Blues Club takes up two old storefronts, with live blues wailing in one room (called the Band Box) and a restaurant serving steaks, tamales, and barbecue in the other. If you're looking to tank up on good food before a night of crawling the clubs along Beale Street, this is the best place to do it. 138–140 Beale St. ⓒ **901/526-3637**. www.bluescitycafe.com. Cover $4–$5.

Center for Southern Folklore ⊛⊛⊛ (Finds)   After bouncing between various locations on or around Beale Street for the past 10 years, this offbeat treasure that's part coffeehouse/part folk-art flea market has landed in Pembroke Square, one of downtown's prime addresses. Warm and welcoming, it's a laid-back space where you can get a meal or some munchies, sip a latte or a beer, surf the Internet, or buy anything from books, CDs, and postcards to handmade quilts, outsider-art creations, and even cornhusk dolls and corncob pipes. Best of all, you can hear the Delta's most authentic roots musicians performing at almost any time of day. Better yet, it's a nonsmoking venue. 119 S. Main St. ⓒ **901/525-3655**. www.southernfolklore.com. No cover.

Earnestine & Hazel's ⊛ (Finds)   Although it's actually 4 blocks south of Beale Street, this downtown dive, which was once a sundry store that fronted for an upstairs brothel, has become one of Memphis's hottest nightspots. In 2004 it was the greasy backdrop for the Jack White/Loretta Lynn video *Portland, Oregon*. On Friday and Saturday nights, there's a piano bar early; and then later in the night, the best jukebox in Memphis keeps things on a slow simmer. Things don't really get cookin' here until after midnight. 531 S. Main St. ⓒ **901/523-9754**. No cover.

Hard Rock Cafe   As you'd expect, this Hard Rock location is packed with rock and blues memorabilia. Look for gold musical notes on the brick sidewalk out front that celebrate famous Memphis musicians through the years. Live music is offered only occasionally, and it's usually staged in conjunction with local charity benefits. Incidentally, the Hard Rock Cafe was founded by Isaac Tigrett, a philanthropist-entrepreneur and former Memphis resident. 315 Beale St. ✆ **901/529-0007. www.hardrock.com.** Cover usually around $5 after 9pm.

Jillian's   In Peabody Place, you'll find the Memphis location of this popular chain of themed entertainment complexes. From bowling and billiards to bars, video cafes, game rooms, and dancing, there is enough variety to keep the attention-deficit-disorder masses from boredom. 150 Peabody Place. ✆ **901/543-8800. www.jillians.com.** Fees vary by activity.

King's Palace Café ✪   With its battered wood floor, this bar has the most authentic, old-time feel of any club on Beale Street. Though this is primarily a restaurant serving decent Cajun food, including a knockout gumbo, there's frequent live jazz and blues. 162 Beale St. ✆ **901/521-1851. www.kingspalacecafe.com.** No cover.

The New Daisy Theatre   The stage at the New Daisy has long been the place to see regional and national rock bands, but these days the theater books a surprisingly wide variety of entertainment, from boxing matches to the touring alternative-rock bands. Bob Dylan filmed a video here from his Grammy-winning *Time Out of Mind* CD (fitting, because Memphis musicians were featured on that work). More recent acts to have played the venue include hometown heroes Justin Timberlake and the North Mississippi Allstars. 330 Beale St. ✆ **901/525-8981. www.newdaisy.com.** Ticket prices vary according to event.

Pat O'Brien's Memphis   Hoist a Hurricane (a potent cocktail) at this replica of the famed New Orleans nightspot that opened on Beale a few years ago. It's been quite a hit with the Mardi Gras set. This vast, brick drinking hall with the green awnings boasts a big, boozy beer hall, a posh piano bar, as well as a multilevel outdoor patio, complete with a fountain—and decent views of the Memphis skyline hovering a few blocks away. 310 Beale St. ✆ **901/529-0900. www.patobriens.com/memphis.html.** Cover varies.

Rum Boogie Cafe & Mr. Handy's Blues Hall   Dozens of autographed guitars, including ones signed by Carl Perkins, Stevie Ray Vaughan, Joe Walsh, George Thorogood, and other rock and blues guitar wizards, hang from the ceiling at the Rum Boogie. There's live music nightly, with guest artists alternating with the house band, which plays everything from blues to country. 182 Beale St. ✆ **901/528-0150. www.rumboogie.com.** Cover $3–$5 after 9pm.

> **Impressions**
> *I'd rather be here than any place I know.*
> —W. C. Handy, referring to Beale Street

2 The Rest of the Club & Music Scene

JAZZ, ROCK, REGGAE & R&B

Gibson Lounge   A block away from Beale Street is the Gibson Guitar Factory, where they make the stringed instruments in this oasis for serious music lovers. The cool little club offers an eclectic line-up of talent including unknown up-and-coming singer-songwriters, rock bands, and jazz artists as well as established stars seeking an intimate venue where their music—not just the drink specials—get top billing. 539 S. 145 Lt. George W. Lee Ave. *©* **901/544-7998**. www.gibsonmemphis.com. Cover varies.

Newby's   Located close to the University of Memphis, this cavernous club is a popular college hangout with two stages—one large, one small. There's live rock, mostly by local and regional acts, most nights of the week. Funk and alternative rock have been pretty popular here of late. 539 S. Highland St. *©* **901/452-8408**. www.newbysmemphis.com. Cover $5–$10.

Precious Cargo Exchange   From reggae and hip-hop to DJ mixers and open-mic nights, this globally-minded bar and coffeehouse offers a refreshing diversity of entertainment. A little off the beaten path—at the increasingly uneventful north end of Main Street—the weathered purple building has plenty of atmosphere, too, with funky folk art behind the bar and colorful lighting fixtures dangling from the walls. 381 N. Main. *©* **901/578-8446**. Cover $5–$10.

> **Impressions**
>
> *People ask me what I miss about Memphis. And I said "Everything."*
> —Elvis Presley

Wild Bill's 🎕🎕🎕   Beer sells by the quart, but you'll have to bring your own hard liquor to this gritty urban juke joint that's also as many light-years away from the glitz of Beale Street as you can get. Locals and rhythm-and-blues-loving tourists pack the nondescript room and sit in hard-back chairs at long tables before the band stars cranking out soul and blues classics. The music is hypnotizing, and sweaty patrons—young and old, black and white—drink and dance with abandon. If you want an authentic Memphis music experience, check it out. Fri–Sat 9pm–2am. 1580 Vollintine Ave. *©* **901/726-5473**. Cover $5–$10.

Zanzibar   This Africa-inspired cafe in downtown's South Main arts district features occasional live jazz and other genres of music on weekends. Call ahead to make sure it's open, as hours vary. 412 S. Main St. *©* **901/543-9646**. No cover.

FOLK

Java Cabana   Located just down from the corner of Cooper and Young streets, this 1950s retro coffeehouse has occasional poetry readings and live acoustic music, singer-songwriters, and jazz on different nights of the week. Although you can't get alcohol here, you can indulge in all manner of coffees—and enjoy a smoke-free environment. 2170 Young St. *©* **901/272-7210**. No cover.

3 The Bar & Pub Scene

BARS
DOWNTOWN

Automatic Slim's Tonga Club 🎕🎕   With a funky urban decor, fabulous menu, and live music on Friday nights, Automatic Slim's Tonga Club attracts the artsy and upscale twenty-, thirty- and fortysomething crowd. Yummy martinis made with fruit-soaked vodka are a bar specialty. 83 S. Second St. *©* **901/525-7948**.

Bluefin 🎕   This ultra-hip sushi lounge lures young professionals, who mingle to sip champagne and cocktails on cushy seating under a cobalt glow that permeates the posh lounge. Open for lunch, dinner, and late-night noshing, the menu specialty is mainly devoted to fresh sushi of every stripe and color. 135 S. Main St. ℭ **901/528-1010.** www.bluefinmemphis.com.

The Peabody Lobby Bar ☆ There's no more elegant place in Memphis for a drink, but be sure you drop in well after the crowds who've gathered to watch the Peabody ducks do their daily march have dispersed, usually shortly after 5pm. Piano music is featured in the evenings. If you're a middle-aged or older traveler with refined tastes and an appreciation of historic, Old South charm, you'll feel right at home relaxing here with a cocktail or a glass of wine. The Peabody Memphis, 149 Union Ave. ℭ **901/529-4000.** www.peabodymemphis.com.

The Rendezvous Restaurant Although best known for its barbecued ribs and waiters with attitude, The Rendezvous also has a big beer hall upstairs from the restaurant. It's a noisy, convivial spot, and a convenient place to start a night on the town or kill some time while you wait for a table in the restaurant. 52 S. Second St. ℭ **901/523-2746.** www.hogsfly.com.

Swig Martini Bar ☆ This tony downtown lounge boasts nearly 40 different martinis, including chocolate, fresh-fruit, and candy flavors. The Jolly Rancher even comes with a lollipop. A magnet for attractive singles, the nightspot has one of the city's best sushi bars—as well as one of its few cigar bars. Plush seating combined with a mellow, sophisticated ambience create a cosmopolitan vibe. 100 Peabody Place. ℭ **901/522-8515.** www.swigmartini.com.

MIDTOWN

Alex's Tavern Bikers, working professionals, barflies, and nearby Rhodes College students all feel at home at this laid-back bar. You won't find many tourists here, but if you want to hang with the locals, play a little shuffleboard, and groove to the jukebox, stop in for a cheeseburger and an ice-cold beer. 1445 Jackson Ave. ℭ **901/278-9086.**

Dish Anchoring the Cooper-Young district, arguably the trendiest corner in Memphis, is Dish. A sleek tapas bar, it specializes in late-night dining. The lively bar attracts the young and the fashionable, who gather to sip a variety of flavored martinis and other spirits while lounging on floor-pillows or dancing to DJ-driven tunes. 948 S. Cooper St. ℭ **901/276-0002.** www.dishmemphis.com.

Hi Tone Café ☆☆ Cutting-edge acts along the lines of the Disco Biscuits headline frequent late-night gigs at this ultra-hip hangout located across the street from the Memphis College of Art in Overton Park. Elvis Costello liked it so much he and The Imposters filmed a live concert there for their DVD release, *Club Date: Live in Memphis.* 1913 Poplar Ave. ℭ **901/278-8663.** www.hitonememphis.com.

Huey's This funky old dive is a midtown Memphis institution, known as the home of the best burgers in town. However, it's also a great place to sip a beer. But be warned: Spitting cocktail toothpicks at the ceiling is a favorite pastime of patrons. Sounds silly, but it's fun. Graffiti on the walls is also encouraged. 1927 Madison Ave. ℭ **901/726-4372.** www.hueyburger.com.

Kudzu's Named for the creeping wild vines that smother Southern landscapes in Chia-Pet-like green shag carpeting, Kudzu's is a long-time local bar favorite with an unmistakable, deep-green paint job. Wildly popular for its trivia quiz nights, the place has a friendly, Irish-pub sort of vibe. Pints of Guinness, along with other beers, are available, as is wine. The grub is pretty good too; Kudzu's has excellent burgers, along with salads, sandwiches, and tamales. 603 Monroe Ave. ℭ **901/525-4924.**

Gambling on the Mississippi

Move over Las Vegas and Atlantic City. Gamblers craving glitzy surroundings to go with their games of chance have a new option at the north end of the Mississippi Delta. Just south of Memphis, across the Mississippi state line, casinos are sprouting like cotton plants in the spring. In fact, these casinos are being built in the middle of the delta's cotton fields, rapidly replacing the region's white gold as the biggest business this neck of the delta has seen since cotton was king.

Back in the heyday of paddle-wheelers on the Mississippi, showboats and gamblers cruised the river, entertaining the masses and providing games of chance for those who felt lucky. In recent years, those days have returned to the Mississippi River as riverboats and floating casinos have opened in states bordering Tennessee. You still won't find any blackjack tables in God-fearing Tennessee, but you don't have to drive very far for a bit of Vegas-style action.

The nearest casinos are about 20 miles from downtown Memphis near the town of Robinsonville, Mississippi, while others are about 35 miles south of Memphis near Tunica, Mississippi. From Memphis, take either Tenn. 61 or I-55 south. If you take the interstate, get off at either the Miss. 304 exit or the Miss. 4 exit, and head west to the river, watching for signs as you drive.

Twelve miles south of the Mississippi state line, off U.S. 61 near the town of Robinsonville, you'll find **Goldstrike Casino,** 1010 Casino Center Dr. (© **888-24K-PLAY** or 866-245-7511), and **Sheraton Casino,** 1107 Casino Center Dr. (© **800/391-3777** or 662/363-4900). Continuing south on U.S. 61 and then west on Miss. 304, you come to **Sam's Town Hotel and Gambling Hall,** 1477 Casino Strip Blvd. (© **800/456-0711** or 662/363-0711); **Fitzgerald's Casino,** 711 Lucky Lane (© **800/766-LUCK** or 662/363-5825); **Hollywood Casino,** 1150 Commerce Landing (© **800/871-0711** or 662/357-7700); and **Harrah's,** 1100 Casino Strip Blvd. (© **800/HARRAHS** or 662/363-7777). Continuing south on U.S. 61 to Tunica and then heading west on either Mhoon Landing Road or Miss. 4, you'll come to **Bally's Saloon and Gambling Hall,** 1450 Bally's Blvd. (© **800/38-BALLY**).

Besides the casinos, the area also offers outlet mall shopping, golf, spas, and other activities. For more information, go to **www.tunicamiss.com.**

Le Chardonnay Wine Bar   Located in Overton Square, this is Memphis's original wine bar. With a dark, wine-cellar feel, Le Chardonnay tends to attract casual young executive types, as well as people headed to the Playhouse on the Square, which is right across the parking lot. As expected, it has a great wine list. 2100 Overton Square Lane (at Cooper and Madison sts.). © **901/725-1375.**

P&H Café   Both a dilapidated looking dive as well as a beloved neighborhood landmark, the P&H ("Poor and Hungry") is a smoke-choked bar that has been a favored hangout for drinking, smoking, and shooting pool since 1961. Beer flows freely, washing down such cheap eats as spaghetti and meat sauce, stuffed burgers, and chicken-fried steak (about $7 each). 1532 Madison Ave. © **901/726-0906.** www.pandhcafe.com.

Young Avenue Deli Not so much a delicatessen as it is a cool hangout for young adults who like to eat and drink, this laid-back spot also features occasional live music. There's an impressive list of beers by the bottle and draft, and munchies such as Greek salads, chili-cheese fries, and a build-your-own quesadilla station. 2119 Young Ave. (✆ 901/278-0034. www.youngavenuedeli.com. Cover $5–$20, depending on bands playing.

EAST MEMPHIS

Belmont Grill A great neighborhood bar, Belmont is a popular watering hole for locals who like to stop by after work to unwind. As plain as a rundown roadhouse, it's unpretentious and casual. The eatery some might call a "greasy spoon" also happens to serve terrific pub grub. Try the cheeseburgers or go for the catfish po' boys. 4970 Poplar Ave. (✆ 901/767-0305. No cover.

Fox and Hound Pub and Grille Perhaps the most gregarious sports bar in town, this preppie watering hole is within walking distance of the East Memphis Doubletree Hotel. It's a favorite choice for fans who want to catch a game on a big-screen while kicking back with buddies over beer and half-time billiards. Corporate road-warrior business travelers will also feel at home here. 5101 Sanderlin. (✆ 901/763-2013. www.fhrg.com.

BREWPUBS

Boscos Squared Live jazz sizzles on Sundays at this popular Overton Square brew pub, known for its Famous Flaming Stone Beer. Locally owned, Boscos also boasts a terrific restaurant menu with great wood-fired-oven pizzas. An outdoor patio is perfect for large parties. If you're a cheap date (or you just like saving money), you'll appreciate that parking is free and much less hassle-free than at the downtown and Beale Street brewpubs. Plus, the food is better. 2120 Madison Ave. (✆ 901/432-2222. No cover.

Dan McGuinness: An Irish Pub With a full bar, an array of draught beers including Guinness Stout, Newcastle Brown Ale, and Bud Light, as well as premium import beers (Heineken, Corona, and so on), drink and general merriment come first at this desperate-to-be-Dublin-esque pub downtown. A short menu offers sausages, soups, and sandwiches for munching on between pints. A large, covered patio allows drinkers to toast the passing throngs on South Main Street. 150 Peabody Place, Suite 115. (✆ 901/ 527-8500. www.danmcguinnesspub.com.

Flying Saucer Draught Emporium When Beale Street becomes too crowded, the locals make tracks to this beer lovers' paradise right around the corner. Frequent music and a lively pub atmosphere with diversions such as trivia contests keep the blues at bay and patrons satisfied—and coming back for more. 130 Peabody Place. (✆ 901/523-8536. www.beerknurd.com.

DANCE CLUBS

Club 152 ⟨ Beale Street's best dance club is a favorite with energetic young straight adults who bump and grind the night away on three floors. DJs crank up techno, house, and alternative dance music for revelers who don't usually stop until the early morning hours. 152 Beale St. (✆ 901/544-7011. www.bealestreet.com. Cover fees vary.

Senses A nondescript warehouse in a blighted part of midtown by day, this sizzling dance club comes alive late at night. A strict dress code (no jeans) helps maintain the upscale vibe, as gorgeous male and female twentysomethings weave between Senses' six different clubs, sipping fancy cocktails and bumping and grinding into the wee hours. 2866 Poplar. (✆ 901/454-4081. www.sensesmemphis.com. Cover $5–$10.

GAY BARS

Backstreet Memphis   Like Memphis's other few gay bars, karaoke, and cabaret drag shows keep things lively, but it's dancing that draw many young, energetic party-goers to this midtown nightspot. 2018 Court Ave. ✆ **901/276-5522.** www.backstreet memphis.com.

Lorenz/Aftershock   Weekend drag shows promise a randy good time at this neighborhood Midtown bar. Next door at Aftershock, DJs keep the gay crowd dancing until the early morning hours. 1528 Madison Ave. ✆ **901/274-8272.**

Metro Memphis   A hot dance club that also offers weekly karaoke and drag shows, this popular gay bar is one where lesbians and straight partygoers can feel equally at home. 1349 Autumn St. ✆ **901/274-8010.** www.metromemphis.com.

Pumping Station   Darts, billiards, and explicit videos are after-hours pursuits at this discrete midtown haunt. There's also a crudely constructed treehouse on the patio out back. A strictly gay male bar, it's know for catering to a slightly more mature crowd. 1382 Poplar. ✆ **901/272-7600.** www.pumpingstationmemphis.com.

4 The Performing Arts

With Beale Street forming the heart of the city's nightclub scene, it seems appropriate that Memphis's main performance hall, the Orpheum Theatre, would be located here also. A night out at the theater can also include a visit to a blues club after the show.

CLASSICAL MUSIC, OPERA & BALLET

Although blues and rock 'n' roll dominate the Memphis music scene, the city also manages to support a symphony, an opera, and a ballet. The symphony performs, and big-name performers and lecturers often appear, at the new 2,100-seat **Cannon Center for the Performing Arts,** 255 N. Main St. (✆ **800/726-0915;** www.thecannon center.com), adjacent to the downtown center. Another of the city's premier performing-arts venues is the **Orpheum Theatre,** 203 S. Main St. (✆ **901/525-3000;** www. orpheum-memphis.com), which was built in 1928 as a vaudeville hall. The ornate, gilded plasterwork on the walls and ceiling give this theater the elegance of a classic opera house and make this the most spectacular performance hall in the city.

In addition to performing at the Cannon Center, the orchestra also occasionally performs at other venues, including the suburban Germantown Performing Arts Center and outdoor concerts at the lovely Dixon Gallery and Gardens. The extremely popular **Sunset Symphony,** an outdoor extravaganza held on the banks of Tom Lee Park overlooking the Mississippi River each year as part of the Memphis in May International Festival, is always a highlight of the symphony season and one of the city's definitive Memphis experiences. The **Memphis Symphony** (✆ **901/324-3627;** www.memphis symphony.org) box office is at 3100 Walnut Grove Rd. (tickets $12–$76).

Opera Memphis (✆ **901/257-3100;** www.operamemphis.org) also performs at both the Orpheum and Cannon Center, annually staging three or four operas (tickets $20–$70). The company, which for more than 50 years has been staging the best of classical opera and innovative new works for appreciative Memphis audiences, also has built a reputation for its extensive educational outreach program.

Ballet Memphis (✆ **901/737-7322;** www.balletmemphis.org), widely regarded as the city's crown jewel of performing arts groups, performs at both the Orpheum and Cannon Center (tickets $20–$70). For sentimentalists, the highlight of each season is the annual holiday performance of *The Nutcracker,* but exciting world premieres and contemporary dance works also rate high priority on the company's mission.

THEATER

Memphis has a relatively well-developed theater scene with numerous opportunities to attend live stage productions around the city. **Theatre Memphis,** 630 Perkins Rd. Extended (© **901/682-8323;** www.theatrememphis.org), is a commendable community theater that's been around for more than 75 years. Located on the edge of Audubon Park, it has garnered regional and national awards for excellence. There are two stages here—a 435-seat main theater that does standards, and a 100-seat, blackbox theater known as Next Stage, where less mainstream productions are staged. Adult ticket prices range from $23–$28.

Staging productions of a higher artistic caliber are two sister theaters in Midtown: **Circuit Playhouse,** 1705 Poplar Ave. (© **901/726-4656**), and **Playhouse on the Square,** 51 S. Cooper St. (© **901/726-4656;** www.playhouseonthesquare.org) are the only professional theaters in Memphis, and between them they stage about 25 productions each year. Off-Broadway plays are the rule at the Circuit Playhouse (with the occasional premiere), while at Playhouse on the Square, Broadway-worthy dramas, comedies, and musicals dominate. Recent seaons' offerings have spanned the gamut from *Pirates of Penzance* to *Doubt* (tickets $15–$30).

Impressions

Memphis ain't a bad town, for them that like city life.

—*Light in August,* by William Faulkner

OTHER VENUES

Since its opening in 2004, the 18,400-seat **FedEx Forum,** 191 Beale St. (© **901/205-1234;** www.fedexforum.com), though primarily the venue for the NBA Memphis Grizzlies team, has booked big-name rock acts such as Elton John and The Rolling Stones.

From late spring through early fall, Memphians frequently head outdoors for their concerts, and the **Mud Island Amphitheater,** 125 N. Front St. (© **800/507-6507** or 901/576-7241; www.mudisland.com), is where they head most often. With the downtown Memphis skyline for a backdrop, the 5,000-seat Mud Island Amphitheater is the city's main outdoor stage. The concert season includes many national acts with the emphasis on rock and country music concerts, such as recent headliners Norah Jones and Willie Nelson. Though the monorail usually runs only during the summer months, outside of summer it runs here on concert evenings.

Appendix A:
Nashville in Depth

Though Nashville's fortunes aren't exclusively those of the country music industry, the city is inextricably linked to its music. These days country music is enjoying greater popularity than ever before (it's now a $2-billion-a-year industry), bringing newfound importance to this city. On any given night of the week in The District, you can hear live music in two dozen clubs and bars—and not all of the music is country music. There are blues bars, jazz clubs, alternative-rock clubs, even Irish pubs showcasing Celtic music.

Nashville also has its share of shopping malls, theme restaurants, stadiums, and arenas, but it is music that drives this city. Nashville should be able to attract not only fans of country music but just about anyone who enjoys a night on the town. With all the new developments taking place around Nashville, it is obvious that Nashville is a city ascendant, rising both as a city of the New South and as Music City.

1 A Look at the Past

Long before the first Europeans set foot in middle Tennessee, Native Americans populated this region of rolling hills, dense forests, and plentiful grasslands. Large herds of deer and buffalo made the region an excellent hunting ground. However, by the late 18th century, when the first settlers arrived, continuing warfare over access to the area's rich hunting grounds had forced the various battling tribes to move away. Though there were no native villages in the immediate area, this did not eliminate conflicts between Native Americans and settlers.

FRONTIER DAYS The first Europeans to arrive in middle Tennessee were French fur trappers and trader Charles Charleville, who established a trading post at a salt lick, and another Frenchman named Timothy Demonbreun, who made his home in a cave on a bluff above the Cumberland River. By the middle part of the century, the area that is now Nashville came to be known as French Lick because of the salt lick.

Throughout the middle part of the century, the only other whites to explore the area were so-called long hunters. These hunters got their name from the extended hunting trips, often months long, that they would make over the Appalachian Mountains. They would bring back stacks of buckskins, which at the time sold for $1. Thus, a dollar came to be called a "buck." Among the most famous of the long hunters was Daniel Boone, who may have passed through French Lick in the 1760s.

The Indian Treaty of Lochaber in 1770 and the Transylvania Purchase in 1775 opened up much of the land west of the Appalachians to settlers. Several settlements had already sprung up on Cherokee land in the Appalachians, and these settlements had formed the Watauga Association, a sort of self-government. However, it was not until the late 1770s that the first settlers began to arrive in middle Tennessee. In 1778, James Robertson, a member of the Watauga

Association, brought a scouting party to the area in his search for a place to found a new settlement.

The bluffs above the Cumberland River appealed to Robertson, and the following year he returned with a party of settlers. This first group, comprised of men only, had traveled through Kentucky and arrived at French Lick on Christmas Eve 1779. The women and children, under the leadership of John Donelson, followed by flatboat, traveling 1,000 miles by river to reach the new settlement and arriving in April 1780. This new settlement of nearly 300 people was named Fort Nashborough after North Carolinian General Francis Nash. As soon as both parties were assembled at Fort Nashborough, the settlers drew up a charter of government called the Cumberland Compact. This was the first form of government in middle Tennessee.

Fort Nashborough was founded while the Revolutionary War was raging, and these first settlers very soon found themselves battling Cherokee, Choctaw, and Chickasaw Indians—whose attacks were incited by the British. The worst confrontation was the Battle of the Bluffs, which took place in April 1781, when settlers were attacked by a band of Cherokees.

By 1784, the situation had grown quieter, and in that year the settlement changed its name from Nashborough to Nashville. Twelve years later, in 1796, Tennessee became the 16th state in the Union. Nashville at that time was still a tiny settlement in a vast wilderness, but in less than 20 years, the nation would know of Nashville through the heroic exploits of one of its citizens.

In 1814, at the close of the War of 1812, Andrew Jackson, a Nashville lawyer, led a contingent of Tennessee militiamen in the Battle of New Orleans. The British were soundly defeated and Jackson became a hero. A political career soon followed, and in 1829, Jackson was elected the seventh president of the United States.

In the early part of the 19th century, the state government bounced back and forth between eastern and middle Tennessee, and was twice seated in Knoxville, once in Murfreesboro, and had once before been located in Nashville before finally staying put on the Cumberland. By 1845, work had begun on constructing a capitol building, which would not be completed until 1859.

THE CIVIL WAR & RECONSTRUCTION

By 1860, when the first rumblings of secession began to be heard

Dateline

- **9000 B.C.** Paleo-Indians inhabit area that is now Nashville.
- **A.D. 1000–1400** Mississippian-period Indians develop advanced society characterized by mound-building and farming.
- **1710** French fur trader Charles Charleville establishes a trading post in the area.

- **1765** A group of long hunters camp at Mansker's Lick, north of present-day Nashville.
- **1772** Wautauga Association becomes first form of government west of the Appalachians.
- **1775** Transylvania Purchase stimulates settlement in middle Tennessee.
- **1778** James Robertson scouts the area and decides to found a settlement.

- **1779** Robertson's first party of settlers arrives on Christmas Eve.
- **1780** Second of Robertson's parties of settlers, led by Colonel John Donelson, arrives by boat in April; in May, settlement of Nashborough founded.
- **1781** Battle of the Bluffs fought with Cherokee Indians.

continues

Fun Fact

Nashville's One Cent Savings Bank (now known as Citizens Savings Bank & Trust) was the nation's first bank owned and operated by African Americans.

across the South, Nashville was a very prosperous city, made wealthy by its importance as a river port. Tennessee reluctantly sided with the Confederacy and became the last state to secede from the Union. This decision sealed Nashville's fate. The city's significance as a shipping port was not lost on either the Union or the Confederate army, both of which coveted the city as a means of controlling important river and railroad transportation routes. In February 1862, the Union army occupied Nashville, razing many homes in the process. Thus, Nashville became the first state capital to fall to the Union troops.

Throughout the Civil War, the Confederates repeatedly attempted to reclaim Nashville, but to no avail. In December 1864, the Confederate army made its last stab at retaking Nashville, but during the Battle of Nashville they were roundly rebuffed.

Though the Civil War left Nashville severely damaged and in dire economic straits, the city quickly rebounded. Within a few years, the city had reclaimed its important shipping and trading position and also developed a solid manufacturing base. The post–Civil War years of the late 19th century brought a newfound prosperity to Nashville. These healthy economic times left the city with a legacy of grand classical-style buildings, which can still be seen around the downtown area.

Fisk University, one of the nation's first African-American universities, was founded in 1866. Vanderbilt University was founded in 1873, and in 1876, Meharry Medical College, the country's foremost African-American medical school, was founded. With this proliferation of schools of higher learning, Nashville came to be known as the "Athens of the South."

THE 20TH CENTURY   At the turn of the century, Nashville was firmly established as one of the South's most important cities. This newfound significance had culminated 3 years earlier with the ambitious Tennessee Centennial Exposition of 1897, which left as its legacy to the city Nashville's single most endearing structure—a full-size reconstruction of

- **1784** The small settlement's name changed from Nashborough to Nashville.
- **1796** Tennessee becomes the 16th state.
- **1814** Andrew Jackson, a Nashville resident, leads the Tennessee militia in the Battle of New Orleans and gains national stature.
- **1840** Belle Meade plantation home built.

- **1843** State capital moved from Murfreesboro to Nashville.
- **1850** Nashville is site of convention held by nine Southern states that jointly assert the right to secede.
- **1862** Nashville becomes first state capital in the South to fall to Union troops.
- **1864** Battle of Nashville, last major battle initiated by the Confederate army.

- **1866** Fisk University, one of the nation's first African-American universities, founded.
- **1873** Vanderbilt University founded.
- **1897** The Parthenon built as part of the Nashville Centennial Exposition.
- **1920** Nashville becomes center of nation's attention as Tennessee becomes 36th state to give women the vote, thus ratifying the

the Parthenon. Though Nashville's Parthenon was meant to last only the duration of the exposition, it proved so popular that the city left it in place. Over the years, the building deteriorated until it was no longer safe to visit. At that point, the city was considering demolishing this last vestige of the Centennial Exposition, but public outcry brought about the reconstruction, with more permanent materials, of the Parthenon.

About the same time the Parthenon was built, trains began using the new Union Station, a Roman-Gothic train station. The station's grand waiting hall was roofed by a stained-glass ceiling, and, with its gilded plasterwork and bas-reliefs, was a symbol of the waning glory days of railroading in America. Today, Union Station has been restored and is one of Nashville's two historic hotels.

In 1920, Tennessee played a prominent role in the passing of the 19th Amendment to the U.S. Constitution, which gave women the right to vote in national elections. As the 36th state to ratify the 19th Amendment, the Tennessee vote became the most crucial battle in the fight for women's suffrage. Surprisingly, both the pro-suffrage and the anti-suffrage organizations were headquartered in the Beaux Arts–style Hermitage Hotel. In 1994, this hotel was completely renovated; now known as the Westin Hermitage, it is the city's premier historic hotel.

The 20th century also brought the emergence of country music as a popular musical style. The first recordings of country music came from Tennessee, and though it took a quarter of a century for "hillbilly" music to catch on, by 1945 Nashville found itself at the center of the country music industry. The city embraced this new industry and has not looked back since.

2 The Nashville Sound: From Hillbilly Ballads to Big Business

Country music is everywhere in Nashville. You can hardly walk down a street here without hearing the strains of a country melody. In bars, in restaurants, in hotel lobbies, on trolleys, in the airport, and on the street corners, country musicians sing out in hopes that they, too, might be discovered and become the next big name. Nashville's reputation as Music City attracts thousands of hopeful musicians and songwriters every year, and though very few of them make it to the big time, they provide the music fan with myriad opportunities to hear the

19th amendment to the U.S. Constitution.

- **1925** WSM-AM radio station broadcasts first *Grand Ole Opry* program.
- **1943** *Grand Ole Opry* moves to Ryman Auditorium in downtown Nashville.
- **1944** Nashville's first recording studio begins operation at WSM-AM radio.
- **1950s** Numerous national record companies open

offices and recording studios in Nashville.

- **Late 1950s to early 1960s** Record company competition and pressure from rock 'n' roll change the sound of country music, giving it a higher production value that comes to be known as the "Nashville sound."
- **1972** Opryland USA theme park opens in Nashville.

- **1974** *Grand Ole Opry* moves to a new theater at the Opryland USA theme park.
- **1993** Ryman Auditorium closes for a renovation that will make the *Grand Ole Opry*'s most famous home an active theater once again.
- **1994** With the opening of the Wildhorse Saloon and the Hard Rock Cafe and the reopening of the Ryman Auditorium, Nashville

continues

occasional great, undiscovered performer. Keep your ears tuned to the music that's the pulse of Nashville and one day you just might be able to say, "I heard her when she was a no-name playing at a dive bar in Nashville years ago."

As early as 1871, a Nashville musical group, the Fisk University Jubilee Singers, had traveled to Europe to sing African-American spirituals. By 1902, the city had its first music publisher, the Benson Company, and today, Nashville is still an important center for gospel music. Despite the fact that this musical tradition has long been overshadowed by country music, there are still numerous gospel-music festivals throughout the year in Nashville.

The history of Nashville in the 20th century is, for the most part and for most people, the history of country music. Though traditional fiddle music, often played at dances, had been a part of the Tennessee scene from the arrival of the very first settlers, it was not until the early 20th century that people outside the hills and mountains began to pay attention to this "hillbilly" music.

In 1925, radio station WSM-AM went on the air and began broadcasting a show called *The WSM Barn Dance,* which featured live performances of country music. Two years later, it renamed the show the *Grand Ole Opry,* a program that has been on the air ever since and is the longest-running radio show in the country. The same year that the *Grand Ole Opry* began, Victor Records sent a recording engineer to Tennessee to record the traditional country music of the South. These recordings helped expose this music to a much wider audience than it had ever enjoyed before, and interest in country music began to grow throughout the South and across the nation.

In 1942, Nashville's first country music publishing house opened, followed by the first recording studio in 1945. By the 1960s, there were more than 100 music publishers in Nashville and dozens of recording studios. The 1950s and early 1960s saw a rapid rise in the popularity of country music, and all the major record companies eventually opened offices here. Leading the industry at this time were brothers Owen and Harold Bradley, who opened the city's first recording studio not affiliated with the *Grand Ole Opry.* CBS and RCA soon followed suit. Many of the industry's biggest and most familiar names first recorded in Nashville at this time, including Patsy Cline, Hank Williams, Brenda Lee, Dottie West, Floyd Cramer, Porter Wagoner, Dolly Parton, Loretta Lynn, George Jones, Tammy Wynette, Elvis Presley, The

becomes one of the liveliest cities in the South.

- **1996** Nashville Arena opens in downtown Nashville.
- **1997** Bicentennial Capitol Mall State Park opens north of state capitol building.
- **1999** NFL Tennessee Titans move into new Coliseum and NHL Nashville Predators into Gaylord Entertainment Center (now Sommet Center) downtown.

- **2000** Titans take a trip to the Super Bowl as AFC champs. Opry Mills, a 1.2-million-square-foot entertainment and shopping complex, rises from the ashes of the demolished Opryland amusement park.
- **2001** Two new world-class venues open downtown: the Frist Center for the Visual Arts and the Country Music Hall of Fame.

- **2005** Centennial Park, a 132-acre green oasis and home to the Parthenon in Nashville's West End, becomes one of the first parks in the U.S. to get wireless Internet access.
- **2006** Nashville celebrates its bicentennial.

Everly Brothers, Perry Como, and Connie Francis.

During this period, country music evolved from its hillbilly music origins. With growing competition from rock 'n' roll, record producers developed a cleaner, more urban sound for country music. Production values went up and the music took on a new sound, the "Nashville sound."

In 1972, the country music–oriented Opryland USA theme park (now supplanted by a shopping mall) opened on the east side of Nashville. In 1974, the *Grand Ole Opry* moved from the Ryman Auditorium, its home of more than 30 years, to the new Grand Ole Opry House just outside the gates of Opryland.

In more recent years, country music has once again learned to adapt itself to maintain its listenership. Rock and pop influences have crept into the music, opening a rift between traditionalists (who favor the old Nashville sound) and fans of the new country music, which for the most part is faster and louder than the music of old. However, in Nashville, every type of country music, from Cajun to contemporary, bluegrass to cowboy, honky-tonk to Western swing, is heard with regularity. Turn on your car radio anywhere in America and run quickly through the AM and FM dials: You'll likely pick up a handful of country music stations playing music that got its start in Nashville.

Appendix B:
Memphis in Depth

Memphis is a city with an identity problem. Though conservative and traditional, it has spawned several of the most important musical forms of the 20th century (blues, rock 'n' roll, and soul). And although it has been unable to cash in on this musical heritage (in the profitable way Nashville has with country), Memphis is still the mecca of American music. Memphis started out as an important Mississippi River port, but urban sprawl has carried the city's business centers ever farther east—so much so that the Big Muddy has become less a reason for being than simply a way of distinguishing Tennessee from Arkansas. With a population of a million people in the metropolitan area, Memphis is reinventing itself.

Memphis is primarily known for being the city where Graceland is located, but how long can the Elvis craze sustain itself? A city needs diversity and an identity of its own. To that end, in the past few years Memphis has made considerable progress. One of the greatest hurdles to overcome has been the legacy of racial tension that came to a head with the assassination here of Martin Luther King, Jr., and the rioting that ensued. Racial tensions are still frequently named as the city's foremost civic problem, even though the casual observer or visitor may not see any signs of these difficulties. Racial tensions combined with post–World War II white flight to the suburbs of East Memphis left downtown a mere shell of a city, but today, this is changing.

These days, downtown is the most vibrant area in the metropolitan Memphis area. A new baseball stadium, the renovation of Beale Street (known as the home of the blues), and a spate of newly constructed museums, hotels, restaurants, and shops are breathing fresh life into downtown Memphis. This has succeeded not only in keeping office workers after-hours to enjoy the live music in the street's many nightclubs, but luring residents in the outlying suburban areas to flock downtown as well—a concept that was unheard of 10 years ago.

For the time being, though, Elvis is still king in Memphis. A quarter-century after the entertainer's death, Graceland remains the number-one tourist attraction in the city. Throughout the year, there are Elvis celebrations, which leave no doubt that this is still a city, and a nation, obsessed with Elvis Presley. Less popular but equally worth visiting are such attractions as Sun Studio, where Elvis made his first recording, the Rock 'n' Soul Museum, and the Memphis Music Hall of Fame, which has displays on Elvis and many other local musicians who made major contributions to rock, soul, and blues music.

1 A Look at the Past

Located at the far western end of Tennessee, Memphis sits on a bluff overlooking the Mississippi River. Directly across the river lies Arkansas, and only a few miles to the south is Mississippi. The area, which was long known as the "fourth Chickasaw bluff," was chosen as a strategic site by Native Americans as well as French, Spanish, and finally American explorers and soldiers. The most important reason for choosing this site for the city was that the top of the bluff was above the high-water mark of the Mississippi and, thus, was safe from floods.

Habitation of the bluffs of the Mississippi dates from nearly 15,000 years ago, but it was between A.D. 900 and 1600, during the Mississippian period, that the native peoples of this region reached a cultural zenith. During this 700-year period, people congregated in large, permanent villages. Sun worship, a distinctive style of artistic expression, and mound building were the main characteristics of this culture. The mounds, which today are the most readily evident reminders of this native heritage, were built as foundations for temples and can still be seen in places such as the Chucalissa Archaeological Museum. However, by the time the first Europeans arrived in the area, the mound builders had disappeared and been replaced by the Chickasaw Indians.

As early as 1541, Spanish explorer Hernando de Soto stood atop a 100-foot bluff and looked down on the mighty Mississippi River. More than 100 years later, in 1682, French explorer Sieur de La Salle claimed the entire Mississippi River valley for his country. However, it would be more than 50 years before the French would build a permanent outpost in this region.

In 1739, the French built Fort Assumption on the fourth Chickasaw bluff. From this spot, they hoped to control the Chickasaw tribes, who had befriended the English. By the end of the 18th century, the Louisiana Territory had passed into the hands of the Spanish, who erected Fort San Fernando on the bluff over the Mississippi. Within 2 years the Spanish had decamped to the far side of the river and the U.S. flag flew above Fort Adams, which had been built on the ruins of Fort San Fernando.

A treaty negotiated with the Chickasaw Nation in 1818 ceded all of western Tennessee to the United States, and within the year, John Overton, General James Winchester, and Andrew Jackson (who would later become president of the United States) founded Memphis as a speculative land investment. The town was named for the capital of ancient Egypt, a reference to the Mississippi being the American Nile. However, it would take the better part of the century before the city began to live up to its grand name.

GROWTH OF A RIVER PORT The town of Memphis was officially incorporated in 1826, and for the next 2 decades grew slowly. In 1845, the establishment of a naval yard in Memphis gave the town

Dateline

- **1541** Hernando de Soto views Mississippi River from fourth Chickasaw bluff, site of today's Memphis.
- **1682** La Salle claims Mississippi Valley for France.
- **1739** French governor of Louisiana orders a fort built on fourth Chickasaw bluff.
- **1795** Manuel Gayoso, in order to expand Spanish lands in North America,

erects Fort San Fernando on Mississippi River.
- **1797** Americans build Fort Adams on ruins of Fort San Fernando, and the Spanish flee to the far side of the river.
- **1818** Chickasaw Nation cedes western Tennessee to the United States.
- **1819** Town of Memphis founded.
- **1826** Memphis is incorporated.

- **1840s** Cheap land makes for boom times in Memphis.
- **1857** Memphis and Charleston Railroad completed, linking the Atlantic and the Mississippi.
- **1862** Memphis falls to Union troops but becomes an important smuggling center.
- **1870s** Several yellow-fever epidemics leave the city almost abandoned.

continues

a new importance. Twelve years later, the Memphis and Charleston Railroad linked Memphis to Charleston, South Carolina, on the Atlantic coast. With the Mississippi Delta region beginning just south of Memphis, the city played an important role as the main shipping port for cotton grown in the delta. This role as river port, during the heyday of river transportation in the mid-19th century, gave Memphis a link and kinship with other river cities to the north. With its importance to the cotton trade of the Deep South and its river connections to the Mississippi port cities of the Midwest, Memphis developed some of the characteristics of both regions, creating a city not wholly of the South or the Midwest, but rather, a city in between.

In the years before the outbreak of the Civil War, the people of Memphis were very much in favor of secession, but it was only a few short months after the outbreak of the war that Memphis fell to Union troops. Both the Union and the Confederacy had seen the importance of Memphis as a supply base, and yet the Confederates had been unable to defend their city—on June 6, 1862, steel-nosed ram boats easily overcame the Confederate fleet guarding Memphis. The city quickly became a major smuggling center as merchants sold to both the North and the South.

Within 2 years of the war's end, tragedy struck Memphis. Cholera and yellow fever epidemics swept through the city, killing hundreds of residents. This was only the first, and the mildest, of such epidemics to plague Memphis over the next 11 years. In 1872 and 1878, yellow-fever epidemics killed thousands of people and caused nearly half the city's population to flee. In the wake of these devastating outbreaks of the mosquito-borne disease, the city was left bankrupt and nearly abandoned.

However, some people remained in Memphis and had faith that the city would one day regain its former importance. One of those individuals was Robert Church, a former slave, who bought real estate from people who were fleeing the yellow-fever plague. He later became the South's first African-American millionaire. In 1899, on a piece of land near the corner of Beale and Fourth streets, Church established a park and auditorium where African Americans could gather in public.

CIVIL RIGHTS MOVEMENT   In the years following the Civil War, freed slaves from around the South flocked to Memphis in search of jobs. Other African-American professionals, educated in the North, also came to Memphis to establish

- **1879** Memphis declares bankruptcy and its charter is revoked.
- **1880s** Memphis rebounds.
- **1890s** Memphis becomes largest hardwood market in the world, attracting African Americans seeking to share in city's boom times.
- **1892** First bridge across Mississippi south of St. Louis opens in Memphis.
- **1893** Memphis regains its city charter.

- **1899** Church Park and Auditorium, the city's first park and entertainment center for African Americans, are built.
- **1909** W. C. Handy, a Beale Street bandleader, becomes the father of the blues when he writes first blues song for mayoral candidate E. H. "Boss" Crump.
- **1916** Nation's first self-service grocery store opens in Memphis.

- **1925** Peabody hotel built. Tom Lee rescues 23 people from sinking steamboat.
- **1928** Orpheum Theatre opens.
- **1940** B.B. King plays for first time on Beale Street, at an amateur music contest.
- **1952** Jackie Brenston's "Rocket 88," considered the first rock-'n'-roll recording, is released by Memphis's Sun Studio.

new businesses. The center for this growing community was Beale Street. With all manner of businesses, from lawyers' and doctors' offices to bars and houses of prostitution, Beale Street was a lively community. The music that played in the juke joints and honky-tonks began to take on a new sound that derived from the spirituals, field calls, and work songs of the Mississippi Delta cotton fields. By the first decade of the 20th century, this music had acquired a name—the blues.

The music that expressed itself as the blues was the expression of more than a century of struggle and suffering by African Americans. By the middle of the 20th century, that long suffering had been given another voice—the civil rights movement. One by one, school segregation and other discriminatory laws and practices of the South were challenged. Equal treatment and equal rights with whites was the goal of the civil rights movement, and the movement's greatest champion and spokesman was Dr. Martin Luther King, Jr., whose assassination in Memphis threw the city into the national limelight in April 1968.

In the early months of 1968, the sanitation workers of Memphis, most of whom were African Americans, went out on strike. In early April, Dr. King came to Memphis to lead a march by the striking workers; he stayed at the Lorraine Motel, just south of downtown. On April 4, the day the march was to be held, Dr. King stepped out onto the balcony of the motel and was gunned down by an assassin's bullet. Dr. King's murder did not, as perhaps had been hoped, end the civil rights movement. Today, the Lorraine Motel has become the National Civil Rights Museum. The museum preserves the room where Dr. King was staying the day he was assassinated and includes many evocative exhibits on the history of the civil rights movement. The museum recently received a major renovation and expansion.

By the time of Dr. King's murder, downtown Memphis was a classic example of urban decay. The city's more affluent citizens had moved to the suburbs in the post–World War II years, and the inner city had quickly become an area of abandoned buildings and empty storefronts. However, beginning in the 1970s, a growing desire to restore life to downtown Memphis saw renovation projects undertaken. By the 1980s, the renewal process was well under way, and the 1990s saw a continuation of this slow but steady revitalization of downtown.

- **1955** Elvis Presley records his first hit record at Sun Studio.
- **1958** Stax Records, a leader in the soul-music industry of the 1960s, founded.
- **1968** Dr. Martin Luther King, Jr., assassinated at Lorraine Motel.
- **1977** Elvis Presley dies at Graceland, his home on the south side of Memphis.
- **1983** Renovated Beale Street reopens as tourist attraction and nightlife district.

- **1991** National Civil Rights Museum opens in former Lorraine Motel. Pyramid completed.
- **1992** Memphis elects its first African-American mayor.
- **1993** Two movies based on John Grisham novels, *The Firm* and *The Client,* are filmed in Memphis.
- **1998** Memphis booms with $1.4 billion in expansion and renovation projects.

- **2000** Memphis Redbirds baseball team play their first season in new, $68.5-million AutoZone Park downtown.
- **2001** Grizzlies move to Memphis, becoming city's first, long-awaited NBA team.
- **2002** Groundbreaking begins on FedEx Forum downtown.
- **2003** Sun Studio founder Sam Phillips dies.
- **2003** Soulsville USA: Stax Museum of American Soul

continues

2 The Cradle of American Music

The blues, rock 'n' roll, and soul are sounds that defined Memphis music, and together these styles have made a name for Memphis all over the world. Never mind that the blues is no longer as popular as it once was, that Memphis long ago had its title of rock-'n'-roll capital usurped (by Cleveland, home of the Rock and Roll Hall of Fame), and that soul music evolved into other styles. Memphis continues to be important to music lovers as the city from which these sounds first emanated.

The blues, the first truly American musical style, developed from work songs and spirituals common in the Mississippi Delta in the late 19th and early 20th centuries. But the roots of the blues go back even farther, to traditional musical styles of Africa. During the 19th century, these musical traditions (brought to America by slaves) went through an interpretation and translation in the cotton fields and churches—the only places where African Americans could gather at that time. By the 1890s, freed slaves had brought their music of hard work and hard times into the nightclubs of Memphis.

BEALE STREET   It was here, on Beale Street, that black musicians began to fuse together the various aspects of the traditional music of the Mississippi Delta. In 1909, one of these musicians, a young bandleader named William Christopher Handy, was commissioned to write a campaign song for E. H. "Boss" Crump, who was running for mayor of Memphis. Crump won the election, and "Boss Crump's Blues" became a local hit. W. C. Handy later published his tune under the title "Memphis Blues." With the publication of this song, Handy started a musical revolution that continues to this day. The blues, which developed at about the same time that jazz was first being played down in New Orleans, would later give rise to both rock 'n' roll and soul music.

Beale Street became a center for musicians, who flocked to the area to learn the blues and showcase their own musical styles. Over the next 4 decades, Beale Street produced many of the country's most famous blues musicians. Among these was a young man named Riley King, who first won praise during an amateur music contest. In the 1940s, King became known as the Beale Street "Blues Boy," the initials of which he incorporated into his stage name when he began calling himself B.B. King. Today, B.B. King Blues Club is Beale Street's

Music opens in South Memphis.
- 2004 FedEx Forum basketball arena and concert venue opens at foot of Beale Street.
- 2005 Films including *Hustle & Flow, Forty Shades of Blue,* and *Walk the Line* were shot in Memphis.
- 2006 Craig Brewer's *Black Snake Moan* is shot in Memphis.

- 2007 Ground-breaking begins on Ground Zero Blues Club, a Clarksdale, MS–based juke-joint and restaurant partly owned by Oscar-winning actor Morgan Freeman.

most popular nightclub. Several times a year, King performs at the club, and the rest of the year blues bands keep up the Beale Street tradition. Other musicians to develop their style and their first followings on Beale Street include Furry Lewis, Muddy Waters, Albert King, Bobby "Blue" Bland, Alberta Hunter, and Memphis Minnie McCoy.

By the time B.B. King got his start on Beale Street, the area was beginning to lose its importance. The Great Depression shut down a lot of businesses on the street, and many never reopened. By the 1960s, there was talk of bulldozing the entire area to make way for an urban-renewal project. However, in the 1970s, an interest in restoring old Beale Street developed. Beginning in 1980, the city of Memphis, together with business investors, began renovating the old buildings between Second and Fourth streets. New clubs and restaurants opened, and Beale Street once again became Memphis's main entertainment district. Today true blues music is harder to find, however, as cover bands playing well-known Sun and Stax hits for tourists dominate the street.

HERE COMES THE KING   From the earliest days of Beale Street's musical popularity, whites visited the street's primarily black clubs. However, it wasn't until the late 1940s and early 1950s that a few adventurous white musicians began incorporating into their own music the earthy sounds and lyrics they heard on Beale Street. One of these musicians was a young man named Elvis Presley.

In the early 1950s, Sun Studio owner Sam Phillips began to record such Beale Street blues legends as B.B. King, Howlin' Wolf, Muddy Waters, and Little Milton, but his consumer market was limited to the African-American population. Phillips was searching for a way to take the blues to a mainstream (read:

white) audience, and a new sound was what he needed. That new sound showed up at his door in 1954 in the form of a young delivery-truck driver named Elvis Presley, who, according to legend, had dropped in at Sun Studio to record a song as a birthday present for his mother. Phillips had already produced what many music scholars regard as the first rock-'n'-roll record when, in 1952, he recorded Jackie Brenston's "Rocket 88."

Two years later, when Elvis showed up at Sun Studio, Phillips knew that he had found what he was looking for. Within a few months of Elvis's visit to Sun Studio, three other musicians—Carl Perkins, Jerry Lee Lewis, and Johnny Cash—showed up independently of one another. Each brought his own interpretation of the crossover sound between the blues and country (or "hillbilly") music. The sounds these four musicians crafted soon became known as rockabilly music, the foundation of rock 'n' roll. Roy Orbison would also get his start here at Sun Studio.

ROCK 'N' ROLL 'N' SOUL, TOO   In the early 1960s, Memphis once again entered the popular-music limelight when Stax/Volt Records gave the country its first soul music. Otis Redding, Isaac Hayes, Booker T and the MGs, and Carla Thomas were among the musicians who got their start at this Memphis recording studio.

Some 10 years after Sun Studio made musical history, British bands such as The Beatles and The Rolling Stones latched onto the blues and rockabilly music and began exporting their take on this American music back across the Atlantic. With the music usurped by the British invasion, the importance of Memphis was quickly forgotten. Today, Memphis is no longer the musical innovator it once was, though in late 2003 city planners began strategizing on a bold new initiative to promote Memphis as the independent record label capital of the industry. Until that comes to pass, however, there's still an abundance of good music to be heard in its clubs. Musicians both young and old are keeping alive the music that put the city on the map.

3 Two Memphis Traditions: Pork Barbecue & the Meat-and-Three

Memphis's barbecue smoke is inescapable. It billows from chimneys all across the city, and though it is present all year long, it makes its biggest impact in those months when people have their car windows open. Drivers experience an inexplicable, almost Pavlovian response. They begin to salivate, their eyes glaze over, and they follow the smoke to its source—a down-home barbecue joint.

In a region obsessed with pork barbecue, Memphis lays claim to the title of being the pork-barbecue capital of the world. Non-Southerners may need a short barbecue primer. Southern pork barbecue is, for the most part, just exactly what its name says it is—pork that has been barbecued over a wood fire. There are several variations on barbecue, and most barbecue places offer the full gamut. My personal favorite is hand-pulled shoulder, which is a barbecued shoulder of pork from which meat is pulled by hand after it's cooked. What you end up with on your plate is a pile of shredded pork to which you can add your favorite hot sauces.

Barbecued ribs are a particular Memphis specialty; these come either dry-cooked or wet-cooked. If you order your ribs dry-cooked, they come coated with a powdered spice mix and it's up to you to apply the sauce, but if you order it wet-cooked, the ribs will have been cooked in a sauce. Barbecue is traditionally served with a side of coleslaw (or mustard slaw) and perhaps baked beans or potato salad. In a pulled-pork-shoulder sandwich, the coleslaw goes in the sandwich as a lettuce replacement. Corky's is the undisputed king of Memphis barbecue, while The Rendezvous is famed for its dry-cooked ribs.

The city's other traditional fare is good old-fashioned American food—here, as in Nashville, known as "meat-and-three," a term that refers to the three side vegetables that you get with whatever type of meat you happen to order. While this is very simple food, in the best "meat-and-three" restaurants, your vegetables are likely to be fresh (and there's always a wide variety of choices). Perhaps because of the Southern affinity for traditions, Memphians both young and old flock to "meat-and-three" restaurants for meals just like Mom used to fix.

Appendix C:
Useful Toll-Free Numbers & Websites

AIRLINES

Air Canada
☎ 888/247-2262
www.aircanada.ca

Air New Zealand
☎ 800/262-1234 or
    800/262-2468 in the U.S.
☎ 800/663-5494 in Canada
☎ 0800/737-767 in New Zealand
www.airnewzealand.com

Alaska Airlines
☎ 800/426-0333
www.alaskaair.com

American Airlines
☎ 800/433-7300
www.aa.com

American Trans Air
☎ 800/225-2995
www.ata.com

America West Airlines
☎ 800/235-9292
www.americawest.com

British Airways
☎ 800/247-9297
☎ 0870/850-9850 in Britain
www.britishairways.com

Continental Airlines
☎ 800/525-0280
www.continental.com

Delta Air Lines
☎ 800/221-1212
www.delta.com

Midwest Express
☎ 800/452-2022
www.midwestexpress.com

Northwest Airlines
☎ 800/225-2525
www.nwa.com

Qantas
☎ 800/227-4500
☎ 612/9691-3636 in Australia
www.qantas.com

Southwest Airlines
☎ 800/435-9792
www.southwest.com

United Airlines
☎ 800/241-6522
www.united.com

US Airways
☎ 800/428-4322
www.usairways.com

Virgin Atlantic Airways
☎ 800/862-8621 in continental U.S.
☎ 0293/747-747 in Britain
www.virgin-atlantic.com

CAR-RENTAL AGENCIES

Advantage
☎ 800/777-5500
www.advantagerentacar.com

Alamo
☎ 800/327-9633
www.alamo.com

Avis
© 800/331-1212 in continental U.S.
© 800/TRY-AVIS in Canada
www.avis.com

Budget
© 800/527-0700
www.budget.com

Dollar
© 800/800-4000
www.dollar.com

Enterprise
© 800/325-8007
www.enterprise.com

Hertz
© 800/654-3131
www.hertz.com

National
© 800/CAR-RENT
www.nationalcar.com

Payless
© 800/PAYLESS
www.paylesscarrental.com

Rent-A-Wreck
© 800/535-1391
www.rentawreck.com

Thrifty
© 800/367-2277
www.thrifty.com

MAJOR HOTEL & MOTEL CHAINS

Baymont Inns & Suites
© 800/301-0200
www.baymontinns.com

Best Western International
© 800/528-1234
www.bestwestern.com

Clarion Hotels
© 800/CLARION
www.hotelchoice.com

Comfort Inns
© 800/228-5150
www.hotelchoice.com

Courtyard by Marriott
© 800/321-2211
www.courtyard.com or
www.marriott.com

Days Inn
© 800/325-2525
www.daysinn.com

Doubletree Hotels
© 800/222-TREE
www.doubletree.com

Econo Lodges
© 800/55-ECONO
www.hotelchoice.com

Fairfield Inn by Marriott
© 800/228-2800
www.marriott.com

Hampton Inn
© 800/HAMPTON
www.hampton-inn.com

Hilton Hotels
© 800/HILTONS
www.hilton.com

Holiday Inn
© 800/HOLIDAY
www.basshotels.com

Howard Johnson
© 800/654-2000
www.hojo.com

Hyatt Hotels & Resorts
© 800/228-9000
www.hyatt.com

ITT Sheraton
© 800/325-3535
www.starwood.com

Knights Inn
© 800/843-5644
www.knightsinn.com

La Quinta Motor Inns
© 800/531-5900
www.laquinta.com

Marriott Hotels
© 800/228-9290
www.marriott.com

Microtel Inn & Suites
© 888/771-7171
www.microtelinn.com

Motel 6
© 800/4-MOTEL6
www.motel6.com

Quality Inns
© 800/228-5151
www.hotelchoice.com

Radisson Hotels International
© 800/333-3333
www.radisson.com

Ramada Inns
© 800/2-RAMADA
www.ramada.com

Red Carpet Inns
© 800/251-1962
www.reservahost.com

Red Lion Hotels & Inns
© 800/547-8010
www.hilton.com

Red Roof Inns
© 800/843-7663
www.redroof.com

Residence Inn by Marriott
© 800/331-3131
www.marriott.com

Rodeway Inns
© 800/228-2000
www.hotelchoice.com

Sleep Inn
© 800/753-3746
www.sleepinn.com

Super 8 Motels
© 800/800-8000
www.super8.com

Travelodge
© 800/255-3050
www.travelodge.com

Vagabond Inns
© 800/522-1555
www.vagabondinn.com

Wyndham Hotels and Resorts
© 800/822-4200 in continental U.S. and
    Canada
www.wyndham.com

Index

See also Accommodations and Restaurant indexes, below.

The new way to
get AROUND town.

Make the most of your stay. Go Day by Day!

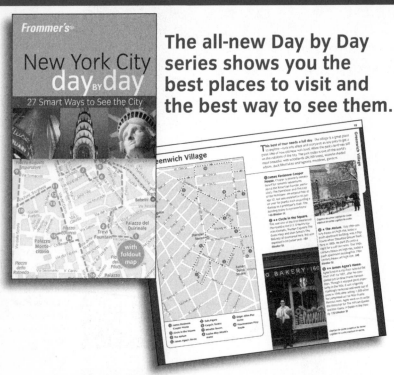

The all-new Day by Day series shows you the best places to visit and the best way to see them.

- Full-color throughout, with hundreds of photos and maps
- Packed with 1–to–3–day itineraries, neighborhood walks, and thematic tours
- Museums, literary haunts, offbeat places, and more
- Star-rated hotel and restaurant listings
- Sturdy foldout map in reclosable plastic wallet
- Foldout front covers with at-a-glance maps and info

The best trips start here. **Frommer's®**

A Branded Imprint of ⊕WILEY
Now you know.

A Guide for Every Type of Traveler

Frommer's Complete Guides

For those who value complete coverage, candid advice, and lots of choices in all price ranges.

Pauline Frommer's Guides

For those who want to experience a culture, meet locals, and save money along the way.

MTV Guides

For hip, youthful travelers who want a fresh perspective on today's hottest cities and destinations.

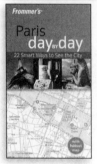

Day by Day Guides

For leisure or business travelers who want to organize their time to get the most out of a trip.

Frommer's With Kids Guides

For families traveling with children ages 2 to 14 seeking kid-friendly hotels, restaurants, and activities.

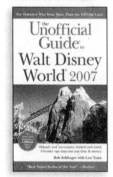

Unofficial Guides

For honeymooners, families, business travelers, and others who value no-nonsense, *Consumer Reports*–style advice.

For Dummies Travel Guides

For curious, independent travelers looking for a fun and easy way to plan a trip.

Visit Frommers.com

WILEY
Now you know.

Wiley, the Wiley logo, For Dummies, and the Unofficial Guide are registered trademarks of John Wiley & Sons, Inc. and/or its affiliates. Frommer's is a registered trademark of Arthur Frommer, used under exclusive license. MTV is a registered trademark of Viacom International, Inc.

FROMMER'S® COMPLETE TRAVEL GUIDES

Alaska
Amalfi Coast
American Southwest
Amsterdam
Argentina
Arizona
Atlanta
Australia
Austria
Bahamas
Barcelona
Beijing
Belgium, Holland & Luxembourg
Belize
Bermuda
Boston
Brazil
British Columbia & the Canadian
　Rockies
Brussels & Bruges
Budapest & the Best of Hungary
Buenos Aires
Calgary
California
Canada
Cancún, Cozumel & the Yucatán
Cape Cod, Nantucket & Martha's
　Vineyard
Caribbean
Caribbean Ports of Call
Carolinas & Georgia
Chicago
Chile & Easter Island
China
Colorado
Costa Rica
Croatia
Cuba
Denmark
Denver, Boulder & Colorado Springs
Eastern Europe
Ecuador & the Galapagos Islands
Edinburgh & Glasgow
England
Europe
Europe by Rail

Florence, Tuscany & Umbria
Florida
France
Germany
Greece
Greek Islands
Guatemala
Hawaii
Hong Kong
Honolulu, Waikiki & Oahu
India
Ireland
Israel
Italy
Jamaica
Japan
Kauai
Las Vegas
London
Los Angeles
Los Cabos & Baja
Madrid
Maine Coast
Maryland & Delaware
Maui
Mexico
Montana & Wyoming
Montréal & Québec City
Morocco
Moscow & St. Petersburg
Munich & the Bavarian Alps
Nashville & Memphis
New England
Newfoundland & Labrador
New Mexico
New Orleans
New York City
New York State
New Zealand
Northern Italy
Norway
Nova Scotia, New Brunswick &
　Prince Edward Island
Oregon
Paris
Peru

Philadelphia & the Amish Country
Portugal
Prague & the Best of the Czech
　Republic
Provence & the Riviera
Puerto Rico
Rome
San Antonio & Austin
San Diego
San Francisco
Santa Fe, Taos & Albuquerque
Scandinavia
Scotland
Seattle
Seville, Granada & the Best of
　Andalusia
Shanghai
Sicily
Singapore & Malaysia
South Africa
South America
South Florida
South Korea
South Pacific
Southeast Asia
Spain
Sweden
Switzerland
Tahiti & French Polynesia
Texas
Thailand
Tokyo
Toronto
Turkey
USA
Utah
Vancouver & Victoria
Vermont, New Hampshire & Maine
Vienna & the Danube Valley
Vietnam
Virgin Islands
Virginia
Walt Disney World® & Orlando
Washington, D.C.
Washington State

FROMMER'S® DAY BY DAY GUIDES

Amsterdam
Barcelona
Beijing
Boston
Cancun & the Yucatan
Chicago
Florence & Tuscany

Hong Kong
Honolulu & Oahu
London
Maui
Montréal
Napa & Sonoma
New York City

Paris
Provence & the Riviera
Rome
San Francisco
Venice
Washington D.C.

PAULINE FROMMER'S GUIDES: SEE MORE. SPEND LESS.

Alaska
Hawaii
Italy

Las Vegas
London
New York City

Paris
Walt Disney World®
Washington D.C.

FROMMER'S® PORTABLE GUIDES

Acapulco, Ixtapa & Zihuatanejo
Amsterdam
Aruba, Bonaire & Curacao
Australia's Great Barrier Reef
Bahamas
Big Island of Hawaii
Boston
California Wine Country
Cancún
Cayman Islands
Charleston
Chicago
Dominican Republic

Florence
Las Vegas
Las Vegas for Non-Gamblers
London
Maui
Nantucket & Martha's Vineyard
New Orleans
New York City
Paris
Portland
Puerto Rico
Puerto Vallarta, Manzanillo &
    Guadalajara

Rio de Janeiro
San Diego
San Francisco
Savannah
St. Martin, Sint Maarten, Anguila &
    St. Bart's
Turks & Caicos
Vancouver
Venice
Virgin Islands
Washington, D.C.
Whistler

FROMMER'S® CRUISE GUIDES

Alaska Cruises & Ports of Call

Cruises & Ports of Call

European Cruises & Ports of Call

FROMMER'S® NATIONAL PARK GUIDES

Algonquin Provincial Park
Banff & Jasper
Grand Canyon

National Parks of the American West
Rocky Mountain
Yellowstone & Grand Teton

Yosemite and Sequoia & Kings
    Canyon
Zion & Bryce Canyon

FROMMER'S® WITH KIDS GUIDES

Chicago
Hawaii
Las Vegas
London

National Parks
New York City
San Francisco

Toronto
Walt Disney World® & Orlando
Washington, D.C.

FROMMER'S® PHRASEFINDER DICTIONARY GUIDES

Chinese
French

German
Italian

Japanese
Spanish

SUZY GERSHMAN'S BORN TO SHOP GUIDES

France
Hong Kong, Shanghai & Beijing
Italy

London
New York
Paris

San Francisco
Where to Buy the Best of Everything.

FROMMER'S® BEST-LOVED DRIVING TOURS

Britain
California
France
Germany

Ireland
Italy
New England
Northern Italy

Scotland
Spain
Tuscany & Umbria

THE UNOFFICIAL GUIDES®

Adventure Travel in Alaska
Beyond Disney
California with Kids
Central Italy
Chicago
Cruises
Disneyland®
England
Hawaii

Ireland
Las Vegas
London
Maui
Mexico's Best Beach Resorts
Mini Mickey
New Orleans
New York City
Paris

San Francisco
South Florida including Miami &
    the Keys
Walt Disney World®
Walt Disney World® for
    Grown-ups
Walt Disney World® with Kids
Washington, D.C.

SPECIAL-INTEREST TITLES

Athens Past & Present
Best Places to Raise Your Family
Cities Ranked & Rated
500 Places to Take Your Kids Before They Grow Up
Frommer's Best Day Trips from London
Frommer's Best RV & Tent Campgrounds in the U.S.A.

Frommer's Exploring America by RV
Frommer's NYC Free & Dirt Cheap
Frommer's Road Atlas Europe
Frommer's Road Atlas Ireland
Retirement Places Rated